# A Guide to Game Theory

**PEARSON**
**Education**

We work with leading authors to develop the
strongest educational materials in game theory,
bringing cutting-edge thinking and best learning
practice to a global market.

Under a range of well-known imprints, including
Financial Times Prentice Hall, we craft high quality
print and electronic publications which help readers to
understand and apply their content, whether studying
or at work.

To find out more about the complete range of our
publishing, please visit us on the World Wide Web at:
www.pearsoned.co.uk

# A Guide to Game Theory

## Fiona Carmichael

**FT** Prentice Hall
FINANCIAL TIMES

*An imprint of* **Pearson Education**
Harlow, England • London • New York • Boston • San Francisco • Toronto • Sydney • Singapore • Hong Kong
Tokyo • Seoul • Taipei • New Delhi • Cape Town • Madrid • Mexico City • Amsterdam • Munich • Paris • Milan

**Pearson Education Limited**
Edinburgh Gate
Harlow
Essex CM20 2JE
England

*and Associated Companies throughout the world*

*Visit us on the World Wide Web at:*
www.pearsoned.co.uk

**First published 2005**

© Pearson Education Limited 2005

ISBN 0 273 68496 5

**British Library Cataloguing-in-Publication Data**
A catalogue record for this book is available from the British Library.

**Library of Congress Cataloging-in-Publication Data**
A catalog record for this book is available from the Library of Congress.

10 9 8 7 6 5 4 3 2 1
08 07 06 05 04

Typeset in 9/12pt Stone Serif by 30.
Printed and bound in Great Britain by Henry Ling Ltd, at the Dorset Press, Dorchester, Dorset.

*The publisher's policy is to use paper manufactured from sustainable forests.*

To Jessie and Rosie

# CONTENTS

# PREFACE

This book gives an introductory overview of game theory. It has been written for people who have little or no prior knowledge of the theory and want to learn a lot without getting bogged down in either thousands of examples or mathematical quicksand. Game theory is a technique that can be used to analyse strategic problems in diverse settings. Its application is not limited to a single discipline such as economics or business studies and this book reflects this interdisciplinary potential. A wide range of examples and applications are used including decision problems confronted by firms, employers, unions, footballers, partygoers, politicians, governments, non-governmental organisations and communities. Students on different social and natural sciences programmes where game theory is part of the curriculum should therefore find this book useful. It will be particularly helpful for students who sometimes feel daunted by mathematical language and expositions. I have written it with them in mind and have kept the maths to a minimum to prevent it from becoming overbearing.

Mathematical language can act as a barrier that stops theories like game theory, that have their origins in mathematics, from being applied elsewhere. This book aims to break down these barriers and the exposition relies heavily on a logical approach aided by tables and diagrams. Often this is all that is needed to convey the essential aspects of the scenario under investigation. However, this won't always be the case and sometimes, in order to get closer to the real world, it is helpful to use mathematical language in order to give precision to what might otherwise be very long and possibly rambling explanations.

In the first four chapters of this book you will learn about many of the important ideas in game theory: concepts like zero-sum games, the prisoners' dilemma, Nash equilibrium, credible threats and more. In the subsequent chapters the analysis is built up in a step-by-step way in order to incorporate more of the interesting features of the world we live in, such as risk, information asymmetries, signals, long-term relationships, learning and negotiation. Naturally, the insights generated by the theory are likely to be more useful the greater the degree of reality incorporated into the analysis. The trade-off is that the more closely the analysis mirrors the real world the more intricate it becomes. To help you thread your way through these intricacies a small number of examples are followed through and analysed in detail. An alternative approach might be to build on the material in the earlier chapters by applying it in some specific but relatively narrowly-defined circumstances. This alternative would bypass many of the potential uses of game theory and, I think, do you and the theory a disservice.

As you read through the chapters in this book you will find that there are plenty of opportunities for you to put into practice the game theory you learn by working through puzzles, or more formally in the language of the classroom, exercises and problems. The exercises are embedded in the text of the chapters and there are additional problems and discussion questions at the end of the chapters. Working through problems is a really good way of testing your understanding and you may find that learning game theory is a bit like learning to swim or ride a bike in that it is something that you can only really understand by doing.

The plan of this book is as follows. In Chapter 1, some of the basic ideas and concepts underlying game theory are outlined and some examples are given of the kinds of scenario where game theory can be applied usefully. The objectives of using game theory in these circumstances are also discussed. In Chapter 2 simultaneous- or hidden-move games are analysed and the dominant strategy and Nash equilibrium concepts are defined. Some limitations of these solution concepts are also discussed.

The subject of Chapter 3 is the prisoners' dilemma, a famous hidden-move game. In Chapter 3 you will see how the prisoners' dilemma can be generalised and set in a variety of contexts. You will see that some important questions are raised by the prisoners' dilemma in relation to decision theory in general and ideas of rationality in particular. Examples of prisoners' dilemmas in the social, business and political spheres of life are explored. Some related policy questions in connection with public and open access goods and the free rider effect are analysed in depth using examples.

Dynamic games are analysed in Chapter 4 and you will learn how sequential decision making can be modelled using game theory and extensive forms. Examples are used to demonstrate why the idea of a Nash equilibrium on its own may not be enough to solve dynamic games. Backward induction is used to show that only a refinement of the Nash equilibrium concept, called a sub-game perfect Nash equilibrium, rules out non-credible threats. Games involving threats to prosecute trespassers and fight entry are used to explore the idea of commitment. The centipede game is also analysed and some questions are raised about the scope of the backward induction method.

All the games analysed in Chapters 1 to 4 involve an element of risk for the participants as they won't usually know what the other participants are going to do. This kind of information problem is central to the analysis of games. In Chapters 5 to 7 the analysis is extended to allow for even more of the risks and uncertainties that abound in the world we live in. In Chapter 5 you will see how hidden and chance moves are incorporated into game theory and decision theory more generally. Expected values and expected utilities are compared. Attitudes to risk are discussed and examples are used to explain the significance of risk aversion and risk neutrality. The experimental evidence relating to expected utility theory is considered in detail and the implications of that evidence for the predictive powers and normative claims of the theory are discussed.

In Chapter 6 the Nash equilibrium concept is extended to incorporate randomising or mixed strategies. Randomisation won't always appeal to individual players but can make sense in terms of a group or population of players. This possibility is explored in the context of evolutionary game theory. Some familiar examples such as chicken, coordination with assurance in the stag hunt game and the prisoners' dilemma are used to examine some of the key insights of evolutionary game theory. The concept of an evolutionary stable equilibrium is explained and used to explore ideas relating to natural selection and the evolution of social conventions.

In Chapter 7 the analysis of the previous chapters is extended by allowing for asymmetric information in one-shot games. Examples, some from previous chapters (such as the entry deterrence game and the battle of the sexes) and some that are new like the beer and quiche game, are developed to explain how incomplete information about players' identities changes the outcome of games. Bayes' rule and the idea of a Bayesian equilibrium are introduced. The role of signalling in dynamic games with asymmetric information is explored.

In Chapter 8 more realism is incorporated by allowing for the possibility that people play some games more than once. Backward induction is used to solve the finitely repeated prisoners' dilemma and the entry deterrence game. A paradox of backward induction is resolved by allowing for uncertainty about either the timing of the last repetition of the game, players' pay-offs or their state of mind. The prisoners' dilemma and the entry deterrence game are developed to allow for these kinds of uncertainties. In Chapter 9, the methodology used to analyse dynamic games in Chapter 4 is applied to strategic bargaining problems. In addition you will see some cooperative game theory. Nash's bargaining solution and the alternating-offers model are both outlined and bargaining solutions are derived for a number of examples. The related experimental evidence is also considered.

I hope that you enjoy working through the game theory in this book and that you find the games in it both interesting and challenging.

Lecturers can additionally download an Instructor's Manual and PowerPoint slides from http://www.booksites.net/carmichael.

# ACKNOWLEDGEMENTS

This book would not have been possible without the help of a number of people. They include Gerry Tanner who was constantly available for all kinds of advice. I also need to thank Dominic Tanner for his artwork. Claire Hulme pre-read most of the chapters. Sue Charles and Judith Mehta read the chapters that Claire didn't. I am grateful to all three of them for their comments. I also need to thank the reviewers who, at the outset of this project, made many useful suggestions. All the students on the Strategy and Risk module at the University of Salford who test drove the chapters deserve credit. A number of them, Carol, David, John and Mario in particular, noticed mistakes that I had missed. Unfortunately, the mistakes that remain are down to me. Lastly I need to thank two non-humans, Jessie and Rosie, who make the occasional appearance.

# PUBLISHER'S ACKNOWLEDGEMENTS

We would like to express our gratitude to the following academics, as well as additional anonymous reviewers, who provided invaluable feedback on this book in the early stages of its development.

Mark Broom, University of Sussex
Jonathan Cave, University of Warwick
Roger Hartley, Keele University

# 1

# GAME THEORY TOOLBOX

## Concepts and techniques

- Strategic interdependence
- Players
- Strategies
- Pay-offs
- Utility
- Equilibrium
- Simultaneous-move games, static games
- Strategic form, pay-off matrix
- Sequential-move games, dynamic games
- Extensive form, game tree
- Repeated games
- Constant-sum and zero-sum games
- Cooperative games.

After working through this chapter you will be able to:

- Describe a strategic situation as a game
- Explain the difference between simultaneous moves and sequential moves in games

- Show how a simultaneous-move game can be represented in a pay-off matrix

- Illustrate a sequential-move game in a game tree

- Explain what is meant by a zero-sum game

- Outline the difference between one-shot and repeated games

- Outline the difference between a cooperative and a non-cooperative game

- Distinguish between different categories of information in a game.

# Introduction

This chapter sets out a framework for understanding and applying game theory. It provides you with the tools that will enable you to use game theory to analyse a range of different problems. The general approach of game theory is outlined in the first part of the chapter; what it is and how and when it can be used. You will also see some examples of situations that could be usefully analysed as games. Some of the everyday language used by game theorists is explained and the type of outcome predicted by game theory is characterised. Two main categories of games are simultaneous-move games and sequential-move or dynamic games. These are both described in this chapter. You will see how pay-off matrices are used to capture the salient features of simultaneous-move games and how extensive forms or game trees are used to illustrate dynamic games. Games can be played only once or repeated, they can be co-operative or non-cooperative. Sometimes the participants in a game have shared interests and sometimes they don't. These distinctions are all explained. In some games the participants will have the same information and in others they won't. The amount of information in a game can affect its outcome and this possibility is discussed in the last section of this chapter. In the subsequent chapters of this book, the terminology that you are introduced to in this chapter and the different approaches that are outlined, will be developed so that you use game theory to interpret, explain and make predictions about the likely outcomes of decision problems that can be analysed as games.

## 1.1   The idea of game theory

The first important text in game theory was *Theory of Games and Economic Behaviour* by the mathematicians John von Neumann and Oskar Morgenstern published in 1944.[1] Game theory has evolved considerably since the publication of von Neuman and Morgenstern's book and its reach has extended far beyond the confines of mathematics. This is due in a large part to contributions in the 1950s from John Nash (1950, 1951). However, it was in the 1970s that game theory as a way of analysing strategic situations began to be applied in all sorts of diverse areas including economics, politics, international relations, business and biology. A number of important publications precipitated this breakthrough, however, and Thomas Schelling's book *The Strategy of Conflict* (1960) still stands out from a social science perspective.

Hutton (1996: 249) describes game theory as 'an intellectual framework for examining what various parties to a decision should do given their possession of inadequate information and different objectives'. This definition describes what game theory can be used for rather than what it is. It also implicitly characterises the distinctive features of a situation that make it amenable to analysis using game theory. These features are that the actions of the parties concerned impact on each other but exactly how this might happen is unknown. Interdependence and information are therefore critical aspects of the definition of game theory.

Game theory is a technique used to analyse situations where for two or more individuals (or institutions) the outcome of an action by one of them depends not only on the particular action taken by that individual but also on the actions taken by the other (or others). In these circumstances the plans or strategies of the individuals concerned will be dependent on expectations about what the others are doing. Thus individuals in these kinds of situations are not making decisions in isolation, instead their decision making is interdependently related. This is called *strategic interdependence* and such situations are commonly known as *games of strategy*, or simply games, while the participants in such games are referred to as *players*. In strategic games the actions of one individual or group impact on others and, crucially, the individuals involved are aware of this.

Because players in a game are conscious that the outcomes of their actions are affected by and affect others they need to take into account the possible actions of these other individuals when they themselves make decisions. However, when individuals have limited information about other individuals' planned actions (their *strategies*), they have to make conjectures about what they think they will do. These kinds of thought processes constitute strategic thinking and when this kind of thinking is involved game theory can help us to understand what is going on and make predictions about likely outcomes.[2]

> ## Games and who plays them
>
> - Strategic game: a scenario or situation where for two or more individuals their choice of action or behaviour has an impact on the other (or others).
>
> - Strategic interdependence: individuals' decisions, their choices about actions, impact on each other and therefore their decision making is interdependently related.
>
> - Player: a participant in a strategic game.
>
> - Strategy: a player's plan of action for the game.

Strategic thinking characterises many human interactions. Here are some examples:

(a) Two firms with large market shares in a particular industry making decisions with respect to price and output.

(b) Leaders of two countries contemplating a war with each other.

(c) The decision by a firm to enter a new market where there is a risk that the existing or incumbent firms will try to fight entry.

(d) Economic policy makers in a country contemplating whether to impose a tariff on imports.

(e) Leaders of two opposing factions in a civil war who are attempting to negotiate a peace treaty.

(f) Players taking/facing a penalty in association football.

(g) A tennis player deciding where to place a serve.

(h) Managers involved in the sale and purchase of players on the transfer market in association football.

(i) A criminal deciding whether to confess or not to a crime that he has committed with an accomplice who is also being questioned by the police.

(j) The decision by a team captain to declare in cricket.

(k) Family members arguing over the division of work within the household.

In all of the above situations the participants or players are involved in a strategic game. The outcome of their planned actions depends on the actions of others players and therefore their plans may be thwarted in that they do not achieve their desired outcome. For example, in scenario (a) the players are firms with large market shares. Markets where a small number of large firms control a large share of the market are called oligopolies. An example of an oligopoly is the automobile industry which is dominated by a small number of large multi-national companies all of whom are household names (the top five in terms of sales are General Motors, Ford, Daimler Chrysler, Toyota and Volkswagen). Because the firms in an oligopoly are large relative to the size of the industry as a whole, the actions of the firms are independent. For instance, if one firm lowers its price the others are likely to lose custom to the price cutter, or if one firm raises its output by any significant amount the market price will probably fall.[3] In both instances, the profits of the other firms will be lower because of the action of the first firm.

## Exercise 1.1

In examples (b) to (k) above can you identify the players and explain why and how their actions are interdependent?

There are no wrong or necessarily right answers to Exercise 1.1 but just by thinking about examples like these you will be thinking about strategic situations. This means you will already be starting to think strategically.

Strategic thinking involves thinking about your interactions with others who are doing similar thinking at the same time and about the same situation. Making plans in a strategic situation requires thinking carefully before you act, taking into account what you think the people you are interacting with are also thinking about and planning. Because this kind of thinking is complex we need some sharp analytical tools in order to explain behaviour and predict outcomes in strategic situations – this is what game theory is for.[4]

## 1.2 Describing strategic games

In order to be able to apply game theory a first step is to define the boundaries of the strategic game under consideration. Games are defined in terms of their rules. The rules of a game incorporate information about the players' identity and their knowledge of the game, their possible moves or actions and their *pay-offs*. The rules of a game describe in detail how one player's behaviour impacts on other players' pay-offs. A player can be an individual, a couple, a family, a firm, a pressure group, the government, an intelligent animal – in fact any kind of thinking entity that is generally assumed to act rationally and is involved in a strategic game with one or more other players.[5]

Players' pay-offs may be measured in terms of units of money or time, chocolate, beer or anything that might be relevant to the situation. However, it is often useful to generalise by writing pay-offs in terms of units of satisfaction or utility. Utility is an abstract, subjective concept and its use is widespread in economics. My utility from, say, a bar of chocolate is likely to be different from yours and anyway the two will not be directly comparable, but if we both prefer chocolate to pizza we will both derive more utility from the former. When a strategic situation is modelled as a game and the pay-offs are measured in terms of units of utility (sometimes called utils) then these will need to be assigned to the pay-offs in a way that makes sense from the player's perspectives. What usually matters most is the ranking between different alternatives. Thus if a bar of chocolate makes you happier than a pizza the number of utility units assigned to the former should be higher. The actual number of units assigned will not always be important. Sometimes it is simpler not to assign numbers to pay-offs at all. Instead we can assign letters or symbols to pay-offs and then stipulate their rankings. For example, instead of assigning a pay-off of, say, ten to a bar of chocolate and three to a pizza, we could simply assign the letter A to the chocolate and the letter B to the pizza and specify that A is greater than B (i.e. A > B). This can be quite a useful simplification when we want to make general observations about the structure of a game.[6] However, in some circumstances the actual value of the pay-offs is important and then we need to be a bit more precise (*see* Chapter 5).

Rational individuals are assumed to prefer more utility to less and therefore in a strategic game a pay-off that represents more utility will be preferred to one that represents less. Note that while this will always be true about levels of satisfaction or pleasure it will not always be the case when we are talking about quantities of material goods like chocolate – it is possible to eat too much chocolate. Players in a game are assumed to act rationally if they make plans or choose actions with the aim of securing their highest possible pay-off (i.e. they choose strategies to maximise pay-offs). This implies that they are self-interested and pursue aims. However, because of the interdependence that characterises strategic games, a player's best plan of action for the game, their preferred strategy, will depend on what they think the other players are likely to do.

The theoretical outcome of a game is expressed in terms of the strategy combinations that are most likely to achieve the players' goals given the information available to them. Game theorists focus on combinations of the players' strategies that can be characterised as *equilibrium* strategies. If the players choose their equilibrium strategies they are doing the best they can given the other players' choices. In these circumstances there is no incentive for any player to change their plan of action. The equilibrium of a game describes the strategies that rational players are predicted to choose when they interact. Predicting the strategies that the players in a game are likely to choose implies we are also predicting their pay-offs.

Games are often characterised by the way or order in which the players move. Games in which players move at the same time or their moves are hidden are called *simultaneous-move* or *static* games. Games in which the players move in some kind of predetermined order are call *sequential-move* or *dynamic* games. These two types of games are discussed in the following sections.

## Pay-offs, equilibrium and rationality

- Pay-off: measures how well the player does in a possible outcome of a game. Pay-offs are measured in terms of either material rewards such as money or in terms of the utility that a player derives from a particular outcome of a game.

- Utility: a subjective measure of a player's satisfaction, pleasure or the value they derive from a particular outcome of a game.

- Equilibrium strategy: a 'best' strategy for a player in that it gives the player his or her highest pay-off given the strategy choices of all the players.

- Equilibrium in a game: a combination of players' strategies that are a best response to each other.

- Rational play: players choose strategies with the aim of maximising their pay-offs.

## 1.3 Simultaneous-move games

In these kinds of games players make moves at the same time or, what amounts to the same thing, their moves are unseen by the other players. In either case, the players need to formulate their strategies on the basis of what they think the other players will do. We are going to look at three examples: hide-and-seek; a pub managers' game; and a penalty-taking game. The first of these is a hidden-move game and the second and third are simultaneous-move games. Both types of games are analysed using the pay-off matrix or the strategic form of a game. In the first and third games the interests of the players are diametrically opposed; if one wins the other effectively loses. Games like this are games of pure conflict. Often the pay-offs of the players in games of pure conflict add to a constant sum. When they do the game is a constant-sum game. Both Hide-and-seek and the penalty-taking game are constant-sum games. If the constant sum is zero the game is a zero-sum game. Most games are not games of pure conflict. There is usually some scope for mutual gain through coordination or assurance. In such games there will be mutually beneficial or mutually harmful outcomes so that there are shared objectives. Games like this are sometimes called mixed-motive games. The pub managers' game is a mixed-motive game.

## 1.3.1 Hide-and-seek

Hide-and-seek is played by two players called Robina and Tim. Robina chooses between only two available strategies: either hiding in the house or hiding in the garden. Tim chooses whether to look for her in the house or the garden. He only has 10 minutes to find Robina. If he looks where she is hiding (either the house or the garden) he finds her within the allotted time otherwise he does not. If Tim finds Robina in the time allotted he wins €50, otherwise Robina wins the €50.

Matrix 1.1 shows how the game looks from Robina's perspective. The figures in the cells of the matrix are her pay-offs in euros. In the first cell of Matrix 1.1, on the top row of the first column, the zero shows that if Robina hides in the house and Tim looks in the house she loses. In the second cell, reading across the matrix, the 50 indicates that if she hides in the house and Tim looks in the garden she wins €50. On the bottom row of the matrix the 50 in the first column indicates that if Robina hides in the garden and Tim looks in the house she wins the €50 but the zero in the second column shows that if she hides in the garden and Tim looks in the garden she loses.

**Matrix 1.1**  Robina's pay-offs in hide-and-seek

|  |  | Tim | |
| --- | --- | --- | --- |
|  |  | look in house | look in garden |
| Robina | hide in house | 0 | 50 |
|  | hide in garden | 50 | 0 |

Matrix 1.2 shows how the game looks from Tim's perspective. In Matrix 1.2 the pay-offs in the cells show that if Robina hides in the house and Tim looks in the house he finds her and wins the €50, but if he looks in the garden when she hides in the house he loses. Similarly, if Robina hides in the garden and Tim looks in the house he loses but if he looks in the garden when she hides in the garden he finds her and wins the €50.

**Matrix 1.2**  Tim's pay-offs in hide-and-seek

|  |  | Tim | |
| --- | --- | --- | --- |
|  |  | look in house | look in garden |
| Robina | hide in house | 50 | 0 |
|  | hide in garden | 0 | 50 |

To analyse the game we need to show both players' pay-offs in the same matrix.[7] This is done in Matrix 1.3 which is the strategic form or pay-off matrix of hide-and-seek. It shows all the possible pay-offs of the players that result from all their possible strategy combinations. It is a convention that in each cell the pay-off of the player whose actions are designated by the rows of the matrix are written first. The pay-offs of the player whose actions are denoted in the columns are written second. So in this pay-off matrix Robina's pay-offs are written first and her pay-offs and strategies are highlighted in blue. For example, the pay-offs in the cell in the top row of the first column are 0 to Robina and 50 to Tim. This shows that if Robina hides in the house and Tim looks in the house, Tim wins the €50 and Robina's pay-off is zero. The cell in the bottom row of the first column shows that if Robina hides in the garden and Tim looks in the house, Robina wins the €50 and Tim's pay-off is zero.

**Matrix 1.3**  The pay-off matrix for hide-and-seek

|  |  | Tim | |
| --- | --- | --- | --- |
|  |  | **look in house** | **look in garden** |
| **Robina** | hide in house | 0, 50 | 50, 0 |
|  | hide in garden | 50, 0 | 0, 50 |

## 1.3.2  Pub managers' game

In the pub managers' game the players are two managers of different village pubs, the King's Head and the Queen's Head. Both managers are simultaneously considering introducing a special offer to their customers by cutting the price of their premium beer. Each chooses between making the special offer or not. If one of them makes the offer but the other doesn't the manager who makes the offer will capture some customers from the other and some extra passing trade. But if they both make the offer neither captures customers from the other although they both stand to gain from passing trade. Any increase in customers generates higher revenue for the pub. If neither pub makes the discounted offer the revenue of the Queen's Head is €7 000 in a week and the revenue to the Kings Head is €8 000. The pay-off matrix for this game is shown in Matrix 1.4 below which shows the pay-offs as numbers representing revenue per week in thousands of euros.

**Matrix 1.4** Pay-off matrix for the Pub managers' game

| | | King's Head | |
|---|---|---|---|
| | | **special offer** | **no offer** |
| **Queen's Head** | **special offer** | 10, 14 | 18, 6 |
| | **no offer** | 4, 20 | 7, 8 |

Following the convention already noted in section 1.3.1, the pay-offs of the player whose actions are designated by the rows are written first. So in this game the pay-offs of the manager of the Queen's Head are written first and his strategies and pay-offs are highlighted in blue. The matrix shows that if the Queen's Head manager makes the special offer his pay-off is 10 (i.e. €10 000) if the King's Head manager also makes the offer, and 18 if he doesn't. Similarly if the King's Head manager makes the offer his pay-off is 14 if the Queen's Head manager also makes the offer, and 20 if he doesn't.

## Exercise 1.2

In the pub managers' game what are the pay-offs of the managers if neither of them makes the offer? What is the pay-off of the Queen's Head manager if he doesn't make the offer but the manager of the King's Head does? What is the pay-off of the King's Head manager if he doesn't make the offer but the manager of the Queen's Head does?

## Exercise 1.3

What do you think will be the outcome of the pub managers' game. What do you think the managers will do?

Give some thought to Exercise 1.3. Although we haven't actually looked at how to solve games yet, the pub managers' game has an equilibrium that you can probably work out just by using a little common sense. In Chapter 2 you will see how to solve games like this in a systematic way. You will then be able to check whether your intuition was correct.

In hide-and-seek and the pub managers' game the pay-offs represent monetary sums and it was convenient to do this. But this won't always be possible as the next game shows.

## 1.3.3 Penalty taking

In the penalty-taking game the two players are the striker taking the penalty and the goalkeeper. Let's assume that it is the last minute of the game and the score is one all. If the striker scores his team will win the game and if the goalkeeper saves the penalty his team will secure an honourable draw. If the striker scores he will be covered in glory and if the goalkeeper saves the penalty it will be he who is covered in glory. This time the pay-offs cannot really be measured in terms of money – being covered in glory is not really quantifiable in this way. Instead the pay-offs are best represented in terms of levels of subjective satisfaction or utility.

We can assume that if the striker misses, his satisfaction level is zero and if he scores, the goalkeeper's satisfaction level is zero. This is clearly a simplification. You might prefer to assign a negative score in these circumstances or even different low scores. You can do this but bear in mind that these scores are subjective representations and therefore the players' pay-offs are not directly comparable, even if we wanted to make this kind of comparison, which we don't. If the striker scores, his satisfaction level will be sky-high and similarly, the goalkeeper will feel sky-high if he saves the penalty. How do we record these sky-high satisfaction levels? Well here, what really matters is the ranking of the players' pay-offs so we could arbitrarily assign them a value of anything between 1 and some incredibly high figure like 100 billion. But smaller numbers are easier to handle so here I will use a pay-off of 10 to represent sky-high utility. You may prefer to add a few noughts and you should feel free to do that. You might also prefer to allocate different scores between the players for sky-high utility – perhaps you think the striker will feel happier if he scores than the goalkeeper will if he saves the penalty. But remember the scores are not directly comparable so this would really be an unnecessary complication.

In order to construct the pay-off matrix that corresponds to these pay-offs we need to make some additional assumptions. First of all we can assume that the striker always kicks the ball on target so he either scores or the goalkeeper makes a save. Second we can simplify the players' strategies by assuming that the striker can only kick to his right, his left or straight ahead, these are his strategy choices. Similarly the goalkeeper can only move to the striker's left, his right or he can stand his ground in the centre of the goal. If the goalkeeper's action mirrors the striker's he saves the penalty otherwise the striker scores. With these pay-offs and simplifying assumptions the pay-off matrix for this penalty-taking game looks like the one in Matrix 1.5 (I have highlighted the strategies and pay-offs of the striker).

**Matrix 1.5** Taking a penalty 1

**goalkeeper**

|  |  | left | centre | right |
|---|---|---|---|---|
| **striker** | **left** | 0, 10 | 10, 0 | 10, 0 |
|  | **centre** | 10, 0 | 0, 10 | 10, 0 |
|  | **right** | 10, 0 | 10, 0 | 0, 10 |

Notice that in the cells of Matrix 1.5 the pay-offs always add to the constant sum 10 since if one player's pay-off is 10 the other's is zero. Therefore the interests of the players, like those of Robina and Tim in hide-and-seek, are diametrically opposed (in hide-and-seek the equivalent constant sum is 50). In both these games there is only one winner and the other player is a loser. Games like penalty-taking and hide-and-seek are called *constant-sum games*. If the constant sum in question is zero then the game is a zero-sum game. But any constant-sum game can be represented as a *zero-sum game* by subtracting half the constant sum from every pay-off. To see this subtract 5 from all the pay-offs in Matrix 1.5 or 25 from all the pay-offs in Matrix 1.3. All constant or zero-sum games are games of pure conflict and their outcomes are sometimes difficult to predict (you will see why in Chapter 2, Section 2.4.3). However, games of pure conflict won't always be constant-sum games although they can usually be represented in this way.[8]

> ## Constant-sum and zero-sum games
>
> - Games in which the sum of the players' pay-offs is a constant. If the constant sum is zero the game is a zero-sum game. Constant-sum games are games of pure conflict; one player's gain is the other's loss.

In the penalty-taking game left, centre and right are the *pure strategies* of the striker and the goalkeeper. If the striker decides that he is going to kick the ball to the left this would imply that he had chosen one of his pure strategies. Alternatively he might prefer to randomise between his pure strategies by, for instance, mentally throwing a dice before he runs up to kick the ball (or actually throwing a dice before running onto the pitch). He could kick to the left if the dice showed a 1 or a 2, to the right if it showed a 3 or a 4 and to the centre of the goal otherwise. If he did this the probability of him choosing any one of his three pure strategies would be $\frac{1}{3}$. We could write this as ( $\frac{1}{3}$ left; $\frac{1}{3}$, centre; $\frac{1}{3}$, right). Strategies that mix up a player's pure strategies in this way are called *mixed strategies*. Mixed strategies like these can be useful in games of pure conflict like penalty taking, where one player doesn't want the other to be able to predict their move. Mixed strategies are explained in more detail in Chapter 6.

> ## Mixed strategy
>
> - A mix of pure strategies determined by a randomisation procedure.

In each of the games we have looked at so far we have used numbers to represent the players' pay-offs. If the ranking of the pay-offs is all that matters (as opposed to their absolute values) it is sometimes more convenient to write the players' pay-offs as letters. Using letters means that actual numbers do not have to be assigned to pay-offs and this can be useful if you want to generalise the results of one piece of analysis to other similar but not identical games. This will be something that we will want to do in many of the chapters of this book (*see* for example Chapter 3, Section 2). In the penalty game we could generalise the pay-offs in this way by substituting the letter W for the number 10 on the assumption that W is greater than zero (W > 0). Although the resulting game in Matrix 1.5.1 looks a bit different from the one in Matrix 1.5, in all important respects it is the same since W > 0 (as noted beneath the matrix). The striker still prefers outcomes in which his chosen strategy is not matched by the goalkeeper and the opposite is true for the goalkeeper.

**Matrix 1.5.1**  Taking a penalty 1 with non-numerical pay-offs

<table>
<tr><th></th><th></th><th colspan="3">goalkeeper</th></tr>
<tr><th></th><th></th><th>left</th><th>centre</th><th>right</th></tr>
<tr><th rowspan="3">striker</th><td>left</td><td>0, W</td><td>W, 0</td><td>W, 0</td></tr>
<tr><td>centre</td><td>W, 0</td><td>0, W</td><td>W, 0</td></tr>
<tr><td>right</td><td>W, 0</td><td>W, 0</td><td>0, W</td></tr>
</table>

W > 0

## 1.4  Sequential-move or dynamic games

In sequential-move games players make moves in some sort of order. This means one player moves first and the other player or players see the first player's move and can respond to it. Some illustrative examples are:

(i)    A firm considering entry into a monopolised industry where the incumbent may start a price war if it does enter.

(ii)   Chess.

(iii)  A series of offers and counter offers made by a potential buyer and seller of a house.

(iv)   A large firm, Apex, considering whether to launch an expensive advertising campaign which may be matched by its main rival, Convex.[9]

(v)    The leader of one country planning to invade another country.

(vi)   A film star who is deciding whether or not to sue a newspaper.

(vii)  A landowner who puts up a sign threatening to sue trespassers.

In each of these examples one of the players moves first and another sees the first player's move before deciding how to respond. This means that the order of moves is important and the analysis of this type of game has to take this into account. It is not always easy to do this using pay-off matrices and therefore sequential games are usually analysed using game trees or extensive forms like the one in Figure 1.1.

Figure 1.1 is drawn to represent the example in (iv). In this version of that game the two firms, Apex and Convex, choose between launching an advertising game or not. Apex moves first but the success of Apex's campaign depends on what Convex does. A, $C_1$ and $C_2$ represent the decision points in the game. Apex's choices are represented by the two branches that are drawn coming from the decision point or node labelled A. As Apex moves first this point is the first decision point in the game, the first point at which any player makes a move. At this point Apex chooses between launch or not launch. Whatever Apex decides Convex sees Apex's move and can respond. If Apex launches its campaign the game moves to $C_1$ where Convex decides whether to launch its

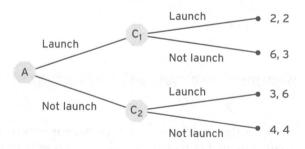

**Figure 1.1** The extensive form or game tree of Apex and Convex's advertising game

campaign or not knowing full well that Apex has launched its campaign. At $C_1$ Convex can respond aggressively by launching its own campaign or respond passively by doing nothing. If Apex decides not to launch the campaign then the game moves to $C_2$ where Convex decides whether to launch its own expensive advertising campaign or not.

The pay-offs represent the firm's profits in thousands of euros and they are written on the far right of the diagram at the endpoints or terminal nodes of the game tree, with Apex's pay-offs written first. It is a convention that the pay-offs are written in the same order as the players' moves, i.e. the pay-off of the player who moves first, in this case Apex, is written first. The pay-offs will always be written next to the terminal nodes of the appropriate branches of the game tree that mark the end of the game. In this game Apex's pay-off depends not only on its own initial move but also on Convex's response. Convex's pay-off similarly depends on Apex's initial move as well as its own move at either $C_1$ or $C_2$. If Convex responds aggressively to Apex's move, whatever it is, by launching its own campaign Apex's profits will be lower than if Convex had not launched its campaign. But if Apex does launch its campaign and Convex responds aggressively Convex's profits are also lower as Convex's action throws both firms into a damaging advertising war. However, if Apex doesn't launch its campaign Convex benefits most by launching its campaign. This is shown by the players' pay-offs at the ends of branches of the game tree. To see this look at the player's pay-offs. When Apex decides on launching the campaign, if Convex responds by launching its own campaign, Apex's pay-off is 2 and so is Convex's. But if Convex doesn't launch its own campaign both firms are better off – Apex's pay-off is 6 and Convex's is 3.

## Exercise 1.4

What is Apex's pay-off if it doesn't launch the campaign but Convex does? What is Convex's pay-off in these circumstances?

## Exercise 1.5

What is Apex's pay-off if it doesn't launch the campaign and Convex doesn't either? What is Convex's pay-off in these circumstances?

> ### Exercise 1.6
>
> Do you think Apex will launch its campaign? (Hint: What do you think Convex will do if Apex launches its campaign?)

The answer to Exercise 1.6 is not obvious but it is worth having a think about. In Chapter 4 we will use extensive forms like the one in Figure 1.1 to resolve sequential-move games like this game. You will be then be able to check whether your intuition was correct.

## 1.5 Repetition

Games that are only played once by the same players are called one-shot, single-stage or unrepeated games. Games that are played by the same players more than once are known as repeated, multi-stage or n-stage games where n is greater than one. The strategies of the players in repeated games need to set out the moves they plan to make at each repetition or stage of the game. These kinds of strategies are called meta-strategies.

The penalty game is a game that is likely to be played by the same players more than once; the same players in teams tend to take the penalties. Suppose the penalty game in Matrix 1.5 was played six times by the same two players. The striker's meta-strategy for this repeated game could be to kick to the left in the first two repetitions then to the centre of the goal then twice to the right and then to the centre again. We would write this as (left, left, centre, right, right, centre). Alternatively he could choose a mixed strategy by randomising between left, right and centre every time he went to kick the ball. If his mixed strategy prescribed that he played each of his pure strategies with a probability of one-third then over the course of the repeated game we would expect to see him kicking to the left, right and centre a third of the time each. Repeated games are analysed in Chapter 8 and in some of the repeated games we are going to look at the players play mixed strategies.

## 1.6 Cooperative and non-cooperative games

Whether a game is cooperative or not is a technical point. Essentially a game is cooperative if the players are allowed to communicate and any agreements they make about how to play the game as defined by their strategy choices are enforceable. Most of the games we will look at in this book are non-cooperative even though in some of them players choose between cooperating with each other or not (for example in the prisoners' dilemma games in Chapter 3). But being able to choose to cooperate does not make a game cooperative in the technical sense as such a choice is not necessarily binding. Being able to enforce agreements makes the analysis of cooperative games very different from that of non-cooperative games. Because agreements can be enforced the players have an incentive to agree on mutually beneficial outcomes. This leads cooperative game theory to focus on strategies that are implemented in the players' joint or collective interests. This is not the case in non-cooperative game theory where it is assumed that player's act only in their own self-interest. Some bargaining games are cooperative in this technical sense and these as well as non-cooperative bargaining games are analysed in Chapter 9.

## 1.7 N-player games

N is the number of players in the game. If a game has two players then it is a 2-player game. But if there are more than two players then the game is an N-player game where N is greater than 2. Most of the games we will look at in this book are 2-player games. The greater the number of players involved in a game the more complex it is likely to be.

## 1.8 Information

The equilibrium strategies of the players will depend on what kind of information players have about each other. In some games players will be very well informed about each other but this will not be true in all games. The information structure of a game can be characterised in a number of ways (see, for example, Montet and Serra, 2003: 4–6). The categories used in this book are perfect information, incomplete information and asymmetric information. If information is perfect then each player knows where they are in the game and who they are playing. If information is incomplete then a pseudo-player called 'nature' or 'chance' moves in a random way that is not clearly observed by all or some of the players. If not all the players observe the chance move then the information is also asymmetric. When information is asymmetric not all players have the same information. Instead some player has private information

In all the games in Chapters 2–4 the players have perfect information. This is unlikely in real life and if game theory is to be really useful it needs to incorporate imperfect information. You will see how to do this in Chapters 5, 6 and 7.

In the games analysed in these chapters one or more of the players is less than perfectly informed.

When information is not perfect there is uncertainty in one or more of the players' minds about where they are in a game or who they are playing. For the players this implies an extra element of risk. In risky situations the outcome is uncertain and this uncertainty is characterised by a probability distribution. In strategic games risk is incorporated in terms of the initial or prior beliefs of the players. In some situations the players may also be able to update their beliefs as and when they receive information (*see* Chapter 7). Risk is not unique to strategic games. It is also a feature of many situations where an individual's choice of action is not strategically related to that of anyone else. In these cases risk is non-strategic. You will see how to model non-strategic risk in Chapter 5.

Whether the situation is strategic or not, where risk is involved decision makers need to incorporate the relevant probabilities into their decision making. They do this by forming expectations about likely outcomes and rational decision makers are assumed to choose in order to maximise their expected pay-off. This is an average of all the possible pay-offs corresponding to a given choice. It is calculated by multiplying (or weighting) each pay-off by the probability that it will occur. If the pay-offs are written as units of money or even chocolate then this calculation generates an expected value in terms of either money or chocolate. If the pay-offs are written in terms of utility values then the calculation generates an expected utility. These two alternatives are discussed further in Chapter 5 but for the moment it may be helpful to note that expected utility is potentially the more useful measure as it can incorporate people's different attitudes to risk.

## Summary

In this chapter you have learned about some of the basic ideas and concepts that are central to game theoretic analysis. Games and game theory were defined in terms of strategic interdependence and some game theoretic terminology was explained. You have seen that games can be divided into two main groups according to whether they involve simultaneous or sequential moves. Simultaneous-move games are represented using pay-off matrices or strategic forms. Sequential-move or dynamic games are usually represented by extensive forms or game trees. Simultaneous-move and sequential games can be played only once or they can be repeated. In the next two chapters you will learn how to model and predict outcomes in single-stage simultaneous-move games. Sequential-move games are analysed in Chapter 4. In Chapters 5 and 6 single-stage games with incomplete information are analysed. Repeated games are the subject of Chapter 8. Strategic games can be either non-cooperative or cooperative. Most of the games you will see in this book are non-cooperative. Cooperative games are considered in Chapter 9.

## Answers to exercises

### 1.1

There are no explicitly right or wrong answers in this exercise. By way of an example an answer for (e) might go as follows: in the civil war the players are the two opposing factions. At least one of the factions needs to compromise in order for an agreement to be reached. If only one party compromises (or compromises more than the other) they lose out in the agreement but if neither compromises there will be no agreement and the war will continue (to the disadvantage of both). Interestingly scientists at the Santa Fe Institute in New Mexico have devised a game that models a scenario a bit like this to calculate how the probability of each party's decision to fight in a civil conflict or to compromise changes as the terms of the proposed agreement change (Dispatch report, *Guardian*, 18 November 2003).

### 1.2

If neither manager makes an offer the manager of the Queen's Head gets 7 and the manager of the King's Head gets 8. If the Queen's Head manager doesn't make the offer but the manager of the King's Head does the manager of the Queen's Head gets 4. If the King's Head manager doesn't make the offer but the manager of the Queen's Head does the manager of the King's Head gets 6.

### 1.3

Both managers are better off making the offer whatever the other manager does so there is no reason to expect them not to make the offer. The most likely outcome seems to be that both managers will make the offer. This is actually the dominant strategy equilibrium of the game as you will see in Chapter 2.

### 1.4

In these circumstances Apex's pay-off will be 3 and Convex's pay-off will be 6.

### 1.5

In these circumstances Apex's pay-off will be 4 and Convex's pay-off will be 4.

### 1.6

If Apex launches it gets either 6 if Convex doesn't launch or 2 if Convex does. As Convex gets 3 by not launching if Apex also launches but 2 otherwise it should not launch if Apex also launches. Apex is assumed to know this. If Apex doesn't launch it gets at most 4. So if Apex believes that if it launches Convex will not launch Apex should launch. Don't worry if this chain of logic is not altogether clear as sequential games like this will be examined in detail in Chapter 4.

## Problems

1 Think of one or two examples of real-life situations that could be represented as games and describe them using game theoretic terminology such as player, pay-offs and strategies.

2 In the examples you have thought of, do the players move simultaneously or sequentially and are their moves hidden or seen?

## Questions for discussion

1 What is meant by strategic interdependence?

2 How can player's pay-offs in games be represented?

## Notes

1 Philip Mirowski (2003) in *Machine Dreams: Economics becomes a cyborg science* devotes a whole chapter to John von Neumann. It is an interesting read.

2 Schelling (1960: 150) defines a strategic game in terms of dependence of one person's choice of action on what he expects another to do and a strategic move as an action by one person that influences another person's choice by affecting their expectations of how the first person will behave.

3 Except for some very expensive luxury items and some necessities, the relationship between consumer demand and price is assumed to be negative, i.e. if price rises demand falls and vice versa. Thus to encourage more sales in an industry market prices need to fall (assuming that no other important factors, for instance advertising or consumer tastes, change).

4 Binmore (1990) distinguishes three additional purposes of game theoretic models: description, investigation and prescription.

5 The thinking and rationality assumptions are not always applicable in evolutionary games (*see* Chapter 6).

6 If you want to know more about utility most introductory economics and all intermediate microeconomic textbooks have a chapter explaining how the concept is used to analyse various types of human behaviour (*see*, for example, Dawson, 2001, Chapter 4 in Himmelweit et al., 2001).

7 Or bimatrix as there is more than one pay-off in each cell.

8 Since in zero-sum games the pay-off of one player is just the negative of the other's, pay-off matrices for zero-sum games often only show the pay-offs of one of the players.

9 An oligopoly market dominated by only two large firms is called a duopoly.

# 2

# MOVING TOGETHER

## Concepts and techniques

- Simultaneous moves
- Dominant strategies and dominated strategies
- Dominant-strategy equilibrium
- Iterated-dominance equilibrium
- Nash equilibrium
- Pareto efficiency
- Assurance games.

After working through this chapter you will be able to:

- Analyse games in which the players move simultaneously or their moves are hidden
- Explain what is implied by a dominant strategy
- Determine the dominant-strategy equilibrium of a game if one exists
- Find the iterated-dominance equilibrium of a game if it has one
- Explain what is implied by the concept of a Nash equilibrium
- Determine whether a game has a Nash equilibrium
- Demonstrate that a dominant-strategy equilibrium is also a Nash equilibrium
- Show that some games have more than one Nash equilibrium and some games have none.

## Introduction

In this chapter you are going to learn how to analyse games in which the players choose their strategies and make their moves at the same time or their moves are hidden from each other. Games of this kind can be analysed in the same way. They are called simultaneous-move, static- or hidden-move games. You saw some examples of these kinds of games in Section 1.3 of Chapter 1. In the penalty-taking game and the pub managers' game the players moved simultaneously. In hide-and-seek Robina's move was, literally, hidden. Another example of a hidden move game is voting in an election where voters' choices are made in secret. In general elections, which can last several days, voters are kept deliberately uninformed about how others are voting by laws that prohibit the results of exit polls being revealed until polling is closed. In some countries polls are also prohibited for a few days leading up to an election. In games like this where the players' moves are hidden from each other and in games where the players move simultaneously a player's choice cannot be made contingent on another player's actions. Players therefore need to reason through the game from their own and the other players' perspectives in order to make a rational choice.

An underlying assumption of game theoretic models that enables players to carry out these kinds of thought processes is that they possess common knowledge that the other players are rational. This means that each player aims to choose a strategy that will secure their highest possible pay-off in the full knowledge that all the other players are trying to do exactly the same thing. The players will only be satisfied with their strategy choices if they are mutually consistent. By this I mean that no player could have improved their pay-off by choosing a different strategy given the strategy choices of the other players. If the strategy choices of the players are mutually consistent in this way then none of the players has an incentive to make a unilateral change. In these circumstances the strategies of the players constitute an equilibrium. However, the precise nature of the equilibrium will depend on the game in question. The main equilibrium concepts used to resolve simultaneous-move games are those of a dominant-strategy equilibrium, an iterated-dominance strategy equilibrium and a Nash equilibrium. We are going to consider each of these in turn.

## 2.1 Dominant-strategy equilibrium

In a dominant-strategy equilibrium every player in the game chooses their dominant strategy. A dominant strategy is a strategy that is a best response to *all* the possible strategy choices of all the other players. A game will only have a dominant-strategy equilibrium if all the players have a dominant strategy. To understand what this means we are going to look at a number of examples in detail. The first of these is the pub managers' game that you saw in Chapter 1, Section 1.3.2.

## 2.1.1 PUB MANAGERS' GAME

The players in this game are the two managers of different village pubs, the King's Head and the Queen's Head. They are simultaneously considering making a special offer to their customers. The strategic form of the pub managers' game is reproduced here as Matrix 2.1. As before, the pay-offs represent revenue per week in thousands of euros and to help you with the analysis that follows the strategy choices and the pay-offs of the Queen's Head manager are highlighted in colour.

**Matrix 2.1**  The pub managers' game

|  |  | King's Head | |
| --- | --- | --- | --- |
|  |  | **special offer** | **no offer** |
| **Queen's Head** | special offer | 10, 14 | 18, 6 |
|  | no offer | 4, 20 | 7, 8 |

In the pub managers' game there are four possible strategy combinations corresponding to four possible sets of pay-offs :

1  The Queen's Head does not make the special offer and neither does the King's Head: neither pub gains custom. The pay-off to the Queen's Head is 7 and the pay-off to the King's Head is 8.

2  The Queen's Head makes the special offer and so does the King's Head: both pubs gain customers. The pay-offs are 10 to the Queen's Head and 14 to the King's Head.

3  The Queen's Head makes the offer but the King's Head does not: the Queen's Head gains custom and the King's Head loses custom. The pay-offs are 18 to the Queen's Head and 6 to the King's Head.

4  The Queen's Head does not make the special offer but the King's Head does: the Queen's Head loses custom but the King's Head gains custom. The pay-offs are 4 to the Queen's Head and 20 to the King's Head respectively.

To see if the game has a dominant-strategy equilibrium we need to check whether both players have a dominant strategy. In this game they do. First let's consider the game from the perspective of the manager of the Queen's Head. If the Queen's Head manager makes the special offer his pay-off is either 10 or 18. It is 10 if the manager of the King's Head also makes the offer and 18 if he doesn't. If the manager of the Queen's Head doesn't make the offer then his pay-off is either 4 or 7. It is 4 if the manager of the King's Head also makes the offer. This is less than the 10 he would have got if he had introduced the offer. If he doesn't make the offer and neither does the manager of the King's Head then his pay-off is 7 which is also less than the 18 he would have got if he had introduced the offer in these circumstances.

This reasoning shows that the manager of the Queen's Head is better off if he makes the special offer whatever the manager of the King's Head does. Thus making the offer is a dominant strategy for him; it is a best response to whatever the manager of the King's Head decides to do. Take another look at Matrix 2.1. Each of the Queen's Head's pay-offs in the top row is higher than the corresponding pay-off in the same column of the bottom row (10 is greater than 4 and 18 is greater than 7). This shows that making the special offer is a dominant strategy of the manager of the Queen's Head.

Similar reasoning can be applied to the strategy choices of the manager of the King's Head to show that introducing the offer is also a dominant strategy for him. Visually this is clear in the matrix because each of the King's Head's pay-offs in the first column on the left is higher than the corresponding pay-off in the same row of the second column on the right (14 is greater than 6 and 20 is greater than 8). Since making the offer is a dominant-strategy for both pub managers the dominant strategy equilibrium of this game is for both managers to make the special offer. This equilibrium is written as {special offer, special offer}. When the equilibrium is written in this way it is conventional to write the equilibrium strategy of the player whose strategies are denoted in the rows of the pay-off matrix first. However in this game the equilibrium strategies of the players are the same and the order in which their strategies are written is not really an issue but this will not always be the case. At this point it would be a good idea to check your answer to Exercise 1.3. Was your intuition correct? Can you explain how you rationalised the answer you gave (whatever it was)?

The idea of a dominant-strategy equilibrium is an important one. In a dominant-strategy equilibrium all the players pick their dominant strategies, their best responses to all the available strategies of all the other players. If a player has a dominant strategy and he wants to maximise his pay-off then there is no reason to believe that he will choose anything else. Thus if a game has a dominant-strategy equilibrium we can be fairly bullish about predicting this as the likely outcome as long as the players are rational and the game captures all the salient aspects of the situation under examination. Unfortunately, games with dominant strategy equilibria may not be that common in real life although you are going to see a few more that do.

> ## Dominant strategies
>
> - Strongly dominant strategy: in a two-player game the pay-offs to a player from choosing a strongly dominant strategy are higher than those from choosing any other strategy in response to any strategy the other player chooses.
>
> - Weakly dominant strategy: in a two-player game the pay-offs to a player from choosing a weakly dominant strategy are (i) at least as high as those from choosing any other strategy in response to any strategy the other player chooses and (ii) higher than those from choosing any other strategy in response to at least one strategy of the other player.

## 2.1.2  Labour market legislation

In this game represented in Matrix 2.2 the governments of two neighbouring countries, Jesmania and Rosatia, are considering imposing new labour market legislation, e.g. legislation relating to health and safety, paternity rights or minimum wages. Polls have predicted that the new legislation will be a net vote winner for the government. This is true even though some votes are expected to be lost because firms have threatened to lay off workers due to the higher labour costs associated with complying with the legislation. The net gain in votes is expected to be much higher if the neighbouring country imposes similar legislation. But if the neighbouring country does not impose legislation their labour will be cheaper and some firms from the first country are expected to relocate to the second. This means more jobs will be lost in the country that introduces the legislation and the net gain in votes will be much smaller. The pay-offs in Matrix 2.2 are expected gains in millions of votes. As in the pub managers' game, the strategy choices and the pay-offs of the player whose strategies are given in the rows of the matrix, the Government of Jesmania, are highlighted.

**Matrix 2.2**  Legislation game

|  |  | government of Rosatia | |
|---|---|---|---|
|  |  | legislate | don't legislate |
| government of Jesmania | legislate | 5, 5 | 1, 0 |
|  | don't legislate | 0, 1 | 0, 0 |

In the legislation game the dominant strategy of both governments is to introduce the legislation. If Jesmania introduces the legislation and Rosatia does not then the expected number of votes gained by the government of Jesmania is only 1 million. But if Rosatia also introduces the legislation the government of Jesmania stands to gain 5 million extra votes. However, if the government of Jesmania doesn't introduce the legislation its votes do not increase at all; doing nothing achieves nothing. Thus to legislate is a dominant strategy for Jesmania, as it is for Rosatia, and the dominant-strategy equilibrium of this game is {legislate, legislate}.

You can see this in the matrix by comparing the pay-offs of the Jesmanian government on the top row with those on the bottom row. Each of the Jesmanian government's pay-offs on the top row is higher than the corresponding pay-off in the same column on the bottom row (5 is greater than 0 and 1 is greater than 0). Similarly each of the Rosatian government's pay-offs in the first column on the left are higher than the corresponding pay-off in the second column on the right.

However, if more firms were to relocate than expected as a result of only one country imposing the legislation then the actual net gain from legislation could be negative. In these circumstances legislation would not be a dominant strategy for either government. It is this kind of possibility, an aspect of globalisation, that can prevent governments introducing what many voters believe to be sensible legislation.

---

### Dominant-strategy equilibrium

- Strong dominant-strategy equilibrium: a combination of strongly dominant strategies; in a two-player game a pair of strategies that for each player are strictly best responses to all of the strategies of the other player.

- Weak dominant-strategy equilibrium: combination of dominant strategies where some or all of the strategies are only weakly dominant.

---

## 2.1.3 Port access

Before turning to the derivation of iterated-dominance equilibria we are going to look at one more example of a game with a dominant-strategy equilibrium. The port-access game is a simplified version of an example in Gates and Humes (1997: Chapter 2). The game represents a series of interactions in 1985 between the USA and New Zealand in connection with an ANZUS (Australia, New Zealand, United States) alliance exercise. In the simplified port-access game described here one country, the USA, requires port access for its naval vessels in the other country, New Zealand. However, New Zealand has declared itself a nuclear-free zone and may refuse to allow access unless the USA gives a guarantee that they are not carrying any nuclear weapons. Alternatively it can simply allow access to American ships without question. For security reasons the USA is unable to give any guarantees about their vessels' weaponry. In response to New Zealand's nuclear-free stance it can simply acquiesce by putting into harbour somewhere else or retaliate by declaring the alliance between the two countries void. The latter is assumed to be a costly alternative for both countries but more so for the USA.

The strategic form for the port-access game is shown in Matrix 2.3. As only the ranking of the pay-offs to the players is important and it is difficult to conceive of meaningful numerical equivalents for the utilities of the two governments, the pay-offs are delineated as letters. The pay-offs of the USA are A, B, C and D where $A > B > C > D$. New Zealand's pay-offs are a, b, c and d where $a > b > c > d$.

**Matrix 2.3**  Port access

**New Zealand**

|  | allow access | refuse access |
|---|:---:|:---:|
| **maintain alliance** | A, b | C, a |
| **void alliance** | B, d | D, c |

**USA** (row label, applies to the left of the two strategy rows)

For the USA: $A > B > C > D$
For New Zealand: $a > b > c > d$

New Zealand's highest pay-off, a, is earned when it maintains the confidence of its electorate by refusing access to American vessels but the USA maintains the alliance. The worst possible outcome for New Zealand (leading to a pay-off of d) arises if it allows access to USA vessels, losing the trust of its electorate, but the USA still voids the alliance. For the New Zealand government it is better to refuse access to USA vessels whatever the USA does since $a > b$ and $c > d$. Refusing access is therefore a dominant strategy for New Zealand.

The USA's highest pay-off, A, is earned when New Zealand allows access and the USA maintains the alliance. The worst outcome for the USA (leading to a pay-off of D) arises if New Zealand refuses access and it retaliates by voiding the alliance. The alliance is important to the USA and therefore it is always better to maintain the alliance whatever New Zealand does.

Because $A > B$ and $C > D$ maintaining the alliance is a dominant strategy for the USA. To be more precise it is a strictly dominant strategy. If either of these inequalities were equalities then maintaining the alliance would only have been a weakly dominant strategy for the USA. As $a > b$ and $c > d$ refusing entry is similarly a strictly dominant strategy for New Zealand (if either inequality were an equality then refusing entry would be a weakly dominant strategy). If both players choose their dominant strategies they will have no incentive to deviate from them. The dominant-strategy equilibrium of this game is therefore {maintain the alliance, refuse access}.

When the real-life version of this game was played out New Zealand refused entry but the USA retaliated by withdrawing from military relations with New Zealand. Why then was the dominant-strategy equilibrium not played out? Well, assuming the governments of the USA and New Zealand acted rationally the answer to this question must be that the port-access game described here does not fully capture all the salient features of the game that was actually played out. This is a valid criticism. First of all in the real-life version of this game the players did not move simultaneously – New Zealand moved first. In many, if not most strategic games the order of moves matters and as we shall see in Chapter 4, when sequential moves are incorporated the equilibrium of a game can change. Second, the pay-offs of the USA do not take into account how its other military relationships might be damaged by acquiescence. Doing so could change the pay-offs considerably even to the extent that maintaining the alliance is no longer a dominant strategy for the USA. Lastly, the port-access game may only have been one stage of a repeated game being played out by the USA with its allies. Modelling a game as a repeated game allows reputation effects to be incorporated and these can also change the predicted outcome as we shall see in Chapter 8. These kinds of considerations should alert you to some of the dangers implicit in game theoretic modelling. By necessity game theory simplifies and abstracts from the real world in order to develop hypotheses about how the real world works. But if important elements are left out in the modelling process little of consequence may be learned. It is therefore of considerable importance, when constructing game theoretic models, to try to capture as many of the salient features of the game's real-life counterpart as possible.

## Exercise 2.1

The players in the foreign investment game represented in Matrix 2.4 are two large firms, Art and Bart, that monopolise a domestic market. The firms are independently deciding whether to invest in new outlets abroad or not. The new investments cost money but open up new foreign markets thereby generating higher profits. If only one firm invests abroad it claims all the available foreign markets. If both of the firms invest in new outlets the foreign markets are shared. Each firm has to decide whether to make the foreign investments or not without knowing the other firm's choice. The pay-offs in Matrix 2.4 reflect the utilities of the firms' directors from the profits the firms make on the assumption that higher profits generate more utility. What is the dominant strategy equilibrium of this game? (Hint: ask yourself what is the preferred strategy of Art, the one that is a best response to whatever firm Bart chooses. Then ask yourself the same question about Bart. If it helps you can highlight the pay-offs of one of the players as I did in the pub managers' game and the legislation game.)

**Matrix 2.4** Foreign investment game

|  |  | Firm Bart | |
|---|---|---|---|
|  |  | invest | do not invest |
| Firm Art | invest | 5,  5 | 9,  3 |
|  | do not invest | 3,  9 | 3,  3 |

## Exercise 2.2

What is the dominant-strategy equilibrium of the friends game in Matrix 2.5? In this game Ms Row and Mr Column choose between accepting invitations to either a party or an event at a club. Mr Column and Ms Row are friends and their enjoyment from the activity they choose is greater if the other is there as well. However, both players also have a strong preference for going to the party whether the other goes there or not. The pay-offs indicate the players' utility from the four alternative outcomes.

**Matrix 2.5** Friends

|  |  | Mr Column | |
|---|---|---|---|
|  |  | party | club |
| Ms Row | party | 6, 5 | 3, 1 |
|  | club | 1, 3 | 2, 2 |

## 2.2 Iterated-dominance equilibrium

Many games do not have a dominant-strategy equilibrium. In this case we can look for an iterated-dominance equilibrium. A two-person game that doesn't have a dominant-strategy equilibrium may have an iterated-dominance equilibrium if one of the players has either a strongly or weakly dominant strategy. A strongly dominant strategy is one where the pay-off to the player from choosing that strategy is better than that from any other strategy in response to any strategy the other player picks. A weakly dominant strategy is one where the pay-off to the player from choosing that strategy is at least as good as any other strategy and better than some in response to whatever strategy the other player picks (*see* Section 2.3.1 for a more formal definition). If a player in a game has a dominant strategy all their other strategies are dominated strategies.

If one of the players in a two-player game has a dominant strategy then even if the other player doesn't the game may still have an iterated-dominance equilibrium. An additional requirement when the player with the dominant strategy has a choice of only two strategies is that the other player has a best response to the dominant strategy of the first player. More generally in a two-person game an iterated-dominance equilibrium is a strategy combination where for at least one player their equilibrium strategy (i) is as good any other strategy and better than some in response to all the non-dominated strategies of the other player and (ii) is a best response to the equilibrium strategy of the other player. For the other player, their equilibrium strategy is a best response to the equilibrium strategy of the first player. This sounds complicated but these ideas will become clearer as we look at some examples. First we will look at games with a strong iterated-dominance equilibrium and then at games with only a weak iterated-dominance equilibrium.

## 2.2.1 Friends or enemies?

The game in Matrix 2.6 is a variation on the friends game in Exercise 2.2 but this version of the game doesn't have a dominant-strategy equilibrium. In this game although Mr Column still has a preference for the party and still wants to be with Ms Row, she doesn't want to be with him at all, quite the opposite. In this game Mr Column is Ms Row's stalker. He wants to be with her but she doesn't want to be anywhere near him. However, Mr Column's preference for the party still makes going to the party a dominant strategy for him. But Ms Column doesn't have a dominant strategy she just wants to avoid Mr Column by choosing the opposite of whatever he chooses. Because Ms Row doesn't have a dominant strategy the game doesn't have a dominant-strategy equilibrium. But it does have a strong iterated-dominance equilibrium.

**Matrix 2.6** Friends or enemies 1

|  |  | Mr Column | |
|---|---|:---:|:---:|
|  |  | party | club |
| Ms Row | party | 1, 3 | 2, 0 |
|  | club | 2, 2 | 1, 1 |

To find the strong iterated-dominance equilibrium of a game, if one exists, all that you need to do is delete strongly dominated strategies from the strategic form of the game until only a single pair of strategies remain. In the friends or enemies 1 game club is a dominated strategy for Mr Column because his pay-off from choosing party is always higher than his pay-off from choosing club. If Ms Row chooses party and Mr Column chooses party his pay-off is 3 but if he chooses club his pay-off is 0. Similarly, if Ms Row chooses club Mr Column's pay-off from choosing party is 2 but if he chooses club his pay-off is only 1. Consequently he always gets less by choosing club which means that club is a strongly dominated strategy for Mr Column (party is a strongly dominant strategy) so if he is rational he will never choose club. Why would he when he can always do better by going to the party? Since Mr Column will never choose club we can delete the column corresponding to his choice of club. This produces Matrix 2.6.1.

**Matrix 2.6.1** Deleting Mr Column's dominated strategy of club

|  |  | Mr Column |
| --- | --- | --- |
|  |  | party |
| Ms Row | party | 1, 3 |
|  | club | 2, 2 |

In the game in Matrix 2.6.1 club is a dominant strategy for Ms Row (she gets 2 by going to the club and only 1 by going to the party) so we can also delete the row corresponding to her option of party. This leaves only one strategy for each player; club for Ms Row and party for Mr Column. This pair of strategies is the strong iterated-dominance equilibrium of the game. We found it by deleting the players' strongly dominated strategies, initially club for Mr Column and then party for Ms Row. This left only one pair of strategies: club for Ms Row and party for Mr Column, implying that the strong iterated-dominance equilibrium of the game is for Ms Row to go to the club and Mr Column to go to the party. This is written as {club, party} because, as noted above, it is conventional to write the equilibrium strategy of the player whose strategies are delineated by rows, Ms Row in this case, first.

## Iterated-dominance equilibrium

- An equilibrium found by deleting strongly or weakly dominated strategies until only one pair of strategies remains.

## 2.2.2 Political ambition

Matrix 2.7 represents a game called political ambition.[1] In this game the players are an incumbent member of parliament (the MP) who has a safe seat and a local councillor who is considering challenging the MP by standing for election herself. The incumbent MP is deciding between leaving office (resigning his parliamentary seat, perhaps to spend more time with his family) and standing for re-election. The MP enjoys his job and will only resign if an effective challenge can be mounted against him. The pay-offs represent the players' utilities from the alternative outcomes. In this particular version of political ambition the incumbent MP is very popular with his constituents and is electorally invulnerable; in the pay-off matrix this is represented by his higher pay-offs (in the first column on the left of the matrix) from standing whatever the challenger does. Resign is consequently a strongly dominated strategy for the MP and we can delete the right-hand column from the matrix. But the challenger's case is hopeless if the MP stands for re-election (this is represented by the challenger's pay-off of –15 in the cell on the bottom row of the first, the left-hand column). Deleting challenge for the challenger leaves only one pair of strategies remaining: no challenge and stand. This strategy pair constitutes the strong iterated-dominance equilibrium of the game which we can write as {no challenge, stand}.

**Matrix 2.7** Political ambition

|  |  | incumbent MP | |
|---|---|---|---|
|  |  | stand | resign |
| challenger | no challenge | 5, 10 | 0, 1 |
|  | challenge | -15, 9 | 15, 1 |

### Exercise 2.3

What would the pay-offs in political ambition look like if the incumbent MP was electorally vulnerable to a challenge? Can you construct a pay-off matrix that illustrates this possibility? Does the game you have constructed have an iterated-dominance equilibrium or dominant-strategy equilibrium?

## 2.2.3 Friends or enemies again

The game represented in Matrix 2.8 is called friends or enemies 2. In this version of the friends or enemies game both players receive an invite to a wedding on the same day as the party and the club event. Going to the wedding is a new option for the players and Mr Column prefers to go to the wedding if Ms Row also goes to the wedding. Consequently neither player has a dominant strategy. But will Ms Row ever want to go to the wedding? This seems unlikely as her pay-offs make going to the wedding a strongly dominated strategy. If Mr Column goes to the party she prefers the club, if he goes to the club she prefers the party and if he goes to the wedding she doesn't care where she goes as long as it isn't the wedding. She therefore has no reason to go the wedding and we can rule out wedding for Ms Row by deleting the bottom row of the matrix. Mr Column will never choose wedding in response to either party or club so we can rule out going to the wedding for him too. This leaves us with the original friends or enemies game represented in Matrix 2.6. You have already seen that the iterated-dominance equilibrium of that game was {club, party hence the iterated-dominance equilibrium of friends or enemies 2 must also be {club, party}.

**Matrix 2.8**  Friends or enemies 2

**Mr Column**

|  | party | club | wedding |
|---|---|---|---|
| **party** | 1, 3 | 2, 0 | 1, 1 |
| **club** | 2, 2 | 1, 1 | 1,0 |
| **wedding** | 1, 3 | 1, 4 | 0,5 |

(row label: **Ms Row**)

## 2.2.4  Friends or enemies 3

The game in Matrix 2.9 is another version of the friends or enemies game. It doesn't have a strong iterated-dominance equilibrium but it does have a weak iterated-dominance equilibrium. In this version of the game Ms Row still does not want to meet Mr Column and Mr Column is still stalking Ms Row. However, Mr Column's preference for the party is not as strong as it was. His pay-offs are such that if Ms Row goes to the party he also prefers to go the party but if she goes to the club he is indifferent between going to the club or the party. But by going to the club he risks ending up with nothing and since he can always do as well or better by going to the party why would he go to the club? There is no reason why he should and this is what makes club a weakly dominated strategy for Mr Column. We can therefore delete the column on the right corresponding to his choice of club. This makes club a dominant strategy for Ms Row and we can delete the top row of what's left of Matrix 2.9. As the only remaining strategy pair this makes {club, party} the iterated-dominance equilibrium of the game. But now it is only a weak iterated-dominance equilibrium as club is only weakly dominated by party for Mr Column.

**Matrix 2.9**  Friends or enemies 3

|  |  | Mr Column | |
|---|---|:---:|:---:|
|  |  | **party** | **club** |
| **Ms Row** | **party** | 1, 3 | 2, 0 |
|  | **club** | 2, 2 | 1, 2 |

## 2.2.5 Battle of the Bismarck Sea

The game represented in Matrix 2.10 is another game with a weak iterated-dominance equilibrium. It is a classic example referred to in many game theory texts. The players are the Japanese Navy and the USAF (the US Air Force). The Japanese Navy are transporting troops across the Bismarck Sea and the USAF wants to bomb them. The Japanese Navy are choosing between two routes, a northern or a southern route. The USAF has to decide where to send their planes to look for the Japanese Navy. If the USAF initially send their planes along the wrong route they can send them back out on the other route but the opportunity for bombing will be reduced and less damage will be inflicted on the Japanese Navy. The northern route is shorter than the southern route and therefore the Japanese Navy is more vulnerable to attack along the latter (they can be bombed for longer).

The pay-offs in this game indicate that north is a weakly dominant strategy for the Japanese Navy; because the southern route is longer, choosing south is as, or more costly than, choosing north, even if the USAF initially chooses north. Eliminating south for the Japanese Navy leaves north as a dominant strategy for the USAF and the strategy combination {north, north} as the weak iterated-dominance equilibrium of this game. In the real-life version of this game played out in the South Pacific in March 1943 this was the actual outcome.[2] Note that the battle of the Bismarck Sea is also a zero-sum game: the USAF's gain is the Japanese Navy's loss.

**Matrix 2.10**  Battle of the Bismarck Sea

|  |  | Japanese Navy | |
|---|---|:---:|:---:|
|  |  | **north** | **south** |
| **USAF** | **north** | 2, -2 | 2, -2 |
|  | **south** | 1, -1 | 3, -3 |

## 2.2.6 Weak iterations

Not every game that doesn't have a dominant-strategy equilibrium has an iterated-dominance equilibrium and more worryingly some games may have more than one weak iterated-dominance equilibrium. This possibility suggests that the concept of a weak iterated-dominance equilibrium may not be quite as useful as its name suggests. If there is more than one iterated-dominance equilibrium in a game how can any of them encapsulate the idea of dominance in a meaningful way?

To see what is implied in this kind of situation take a look at the abstract game represented in Matrix 2.11. In the weak iterations game the players choose between three alternative strategies and there are two weak iterated-dominance equilibria: {middle, centre} and {down, left}.

**Matrix 2.11**  Weak iterations

|   |   | Player B | | |
|---|---|---|---|---|
|   |   | **left** | **centre** | **right** |
|   | **up** | 3, 6 | 2, 6 | 1, 7 |
| **Player A** | **middle** | 2, 1 | 2, 7 | 2, 5 |
|   | **down** | 3, 7 | 1, 5 | 2, 6 |

To find the first iterated-dominance equilibrium in weak iterations, {middle, centre} you can delete down as this is a weakly dominated strategy for A. This makes left a strongly dominated strategy for B. Deleting left makes up a weakly dominated strategy for A. Deleting A's strategy of up leaves centre as a dominant strategy for B making {middle, centre} the iterated-dominance equilibrium. Alternatively, delete middle which is also weakly dominated for A, then centre, now strongly dominated for B. This leaves down as weakly dominant for A and deleting up leaves left as a dominant strategy for B making {down, left} the iterated-dominance equilibrium of the game. The problem here is a theoretical one, that there is more than one weakly dominated strategy and the order of deletion matters. This is something to be aware of when using the method of deleting weakly dominated strategies to find the equilibrium of a game. Evidence from experiments[3] also suggests that there are some descriptive limitations of the iterative method. For example, Beard and Beil (1994) tested the willingness of players to choose their iterated dominance strategies. In their experiments the players whose iterated-dominance strategies were not dominant strategies did not systematically choose the former. However, the majority of players with weakly dominant strategies did select them. These results have been replicated in other similar experiments and in experiments involving more iterations. The problem appears to be that while subjects in experiments are able to perform a number of steps of iterated reasoning for themselves they are less willing to believe that other players are able to do the same (*see* Camerer, 2003: 200–9 for a summary of these experimental results). Nevertheless this method can still be a useful and intuitively plausible way of resolving games like battle of the Bismarck Sea.

## 2.3  Nash equilibrium

In a Nash equilibrium the players in a game choose strategies that are best responses to each other. However, no player's Nash-equilibrium strategy, or more simply their Nash strategy, is necessarily a best response to any of the other strategies of the other players. Nevertheless, if all the players in a game are playing their Nash strategies none of the players has an incentive to do anything else. In every dominant strategy and iterated-dominance equilibrium the players' strategies are also best responses to each other. Therefore every dominant strategy and iterated-dominance equilibrium must also be a Nash equilibrium. But not every Nash equilibrium is also a dominant strategy equilibrium or even an iterated-dominance equilibrium.[4] Consequently there are games that have no dominant strategy or iterated-dominance equilibrium but do have a Nash equilibrium. However, some games have no equilibrium at all in pure strategies, as you will see.[5]

---

### Nash equilibrium

- A combination of players' strategies that are best responses to each other.

---

To help you to understand the concept of a Nash equilibrium we are going to look at a number of examples. The first of these is called computer wars 1. This game is represented in pay-off Matrix 2.12. The players in computer wars 1 are two computer companies that are simultaneously planning newspaper advertising campaigns. They plan their campaigns in secret and run them simultaneously. A promotional offer is an integral part of any campaign they run. Both companies choose between offering a lower price, a free printer or an extended guarantee. The pay-offs in Matrix 2.12 represent expected profits. The pay-offs show that whatever Chip offers, it is in Pin's best interests to make a different offer unless Chip offers the extended guarantee, in which case Pin should match Chip's offer. Chip always wants to match Tell's offer.

**Matrix 2.12** Computer wars 1

**Chip Inc**

| | | lower price | free printer | extended guarantee |
|---|---|---|---|---|
| **Pin Ltd** | **lower price** | 0, 4 | 4, 0 | 5, 3 |
| | **free printer** | 4, 0 | 0, 4 | 5, 3 |
| | **extended guarantee** | 3, 5 | 3, 5 | 6,6 |

To find the Nash equilibrium of computer wars 1 we need to identify each player's best response to each of the other's strategies. We could start by identifying Pin's best responses to each of Chip's three possible strategies. Then we could identify Chip's best responses to each of Pin's three possible strategies. If any two of the strategies we identify are best responses to each other then we will have found a strategy combination that constitutes a Nash equilibrium. This sounds complicated but once the best responses of each player are found it is straightforward to identify a Nash equilibrium if one exists. The trick then is to identify both players' best response strategies. The way we will do this here is by underlining the pay-offs corresponding to each player's best response to each of the strategies of the other. We can call these pay-offs their 'best response' pay-offs. If we follow this procedure for each player then any cell where both pay-offs are underlined will identify a Nash equilibrium. By the way, underlining isn't a requirement. You can identify the pay-offs corresponding to a player's optimal strategies in any way you choose e.g. by a * or a circle – indeed whatever takes your fancy. But underlining works just as well as anything else.[6]

To see how the underlining method works let's start by considering Pin's position. If Chip chooses lower price then Pin's best response is to offer a free printer; by choosing free printer his pay-off is 4 whereas he only gets 3 by choosing an extended guarantee and 0 by choosing to lower price. So in Matrix 2.12.1 I have underlined Pin's pay-off of 4 in the first cell of the middle row. If Chip chooses free printer then Pin's best response is to lower price so I have underlined his pay-off of 4 in the first row of the second column. If Chip chooses to offer an extended guarantee then Pin's best response is to also offer an extended guarantee and so I have underlined Pin's pay-off of 6 in the last row of the third column; he gets a pay-off of 6 by matching Chip and only 5 otherwise.

**Matrix 2.12.1** Pin's best responses to Chip

Chip Inc

|  |  | lower price | free printer | extended guarantee |
|---|---|---|---|---|
| **Pin Ltd** | **lower price** | 0, 4 | <u>4</u>, 0 | 5, 3 |
|  | **free printer** | <u>4</u>, 0 | 0, 4 | 5, 3 |
|  | **extended guarantee** | 3, 5 | 3, 5 | <u>6</u>,6 |

Following the same procedure for Chip leads to the pattern of underlining in Matrix 2.12.2. If Pin chooses lower price then Chip's best response is also to lower price and so I have underlined Chip's pay-off of 4 in the first cell of the top row. If Pin offers a free printer then Chip's best response is to also offer a free printer and so I have underlined Chip's pay-off of 4 in the middle row of the second column. If Pin offers the extended guarantee then Chip's best response is again to match Pin's offer as by doing this Chip's pay-off is 6 which is higher than the pay-off of 3 that results if he chooses either of the alternatives.

**Matrix 2.12.2** Chip's best responses to Pin

Chip Inc

|  |  | lower price | free printer | extended guarantee |
|---|---|---|---|---|
| **Pin Ltd** | **lower price** | 0, <u>4</u> | 4, 0 | 5, 3 |
|  | **free printer** | 4, 0 | 0, <u>4</u> | 5, 3 |
|  | **extended guarantee** | 3, 5 | 3, 5 | 6,<u>6</u> |

In Matrix 2.12.3 both players' best response pay-offs are underlined. The only cell with two underlinings is the third cell of the bottom row which is highlighted. The pay-off pair (6, 6) is the outcome if both players choose the extended guarantee. The double underlining means that choosing the extended guarantee is Pin's best response if Chip chooses the extended guarantee and choosing the extended guarantee is also a best response for Chip if Pin chooses the extended guarantee. Thus each player's strategy is a best response to the other's implying that {extended guarantee, extended guarantee} is the Nash equilibrium of computer wars 1.

**Matrix 2.12.3**  Pin and Chip's best responses to each other

Chip Inc

|  | | lower price | free printer | extended guarantee |
|---|---|---|---|---|
| **Pin Ltd** | **lower price** | 0, <u>4</u> | <u>4</u>, 0 | 5, 3 |
| | **free printer** | <u>4</u>, 0 | 0, <u>4</u> | 5, 3 |
| | **extended guarantee** | 3, 5 | 3, 5 | <u>6,6</u> |

To see that every dominant strategy equilibrium is also a Nash equilibrium we can look at the game in Matrix 2.13. Do you recognise this game? It is the same as the pub managers' game you saw represented in Matrix 2.1. You have already seen that the dominant-strategy equilibrium of this game is {special offer, special offer}. In Matrix 2.13 both managers' best response pay-offs are underlined. For the manager of the Queen's Head special offer is a best response to both special offer and no offers. I have therefore underlined the Queen's Head's pay-offs of 10 and 18 in the top row of the matrix. Special offer is also a best response for the manager of the King's Head to either special offer or no offer by the Queen's Head. I have therefore underlined the King's Head manager's pay-offs of 14 and 20 in the first column of the matrix. The two underlinings in the first cell of the top row show that special offer is a best response to special offer and that {special offer, special offer} is a Nash equilibrium as well as a dominant-strategy equilibrium.

**Matrix 2.13**  Pub managers game

King's Head

|  | | special offer | no offer |
|---|---|---|---|
| **Queen's Head** | **special offer** | <u>10</u>, <u>14</u> | <u>18</u>, 6 |
| | **no offer** | 4, <u>20</u> | 7, 8 |

To see that an iterated-dominance equilibrium is also a Nash equilibrium let's have another look at friends or enemies 3 that you first saw represented in Matrix 2.9. You have already seen that the weak iterated-dominance equilibrium of this game is {club, party}. The strategic form for friends or enemies 3 is redrawn as Matrix 2.14 with the players' best response pay-offs underlined. Mr Column's best response to Ms Row's choice of party is party but Mr Column is indifferent between party and club when Ms Row goes to the club. This means that both strategies are equally as good in response to Ms Row's choice of club and therefore it is appropriate to underline both of the corresponding pay-offs. For Ms Row club is a best response to party but party is a best response to club. As club is a best response to party for Ms Row and party is a best response to club for Mr Column {club, party} is a Nash equilibrium as well as an iterated-dominance equilibrium.

**Matrix 2.14**  Friends or enemies 3

|  |  | Mr Column | |
| --- | --- | :---: | :---: |
|  |  | **party** | **club** |
| **Ms Row** | **party** | 1, <u>3</u> | <u>2</u>, 0 |
|  | **club** | <u>2</u>, <u>2</u> | 1, <u>2</u> |

Because every dominant-strategy equilibrium and iterated-dominance equilibrium is also a Nash equilibrium it may be simpler, when looking for the equilibrium of the game, to start by looking for the Nash equilibrium. After identifying a Nash equilibrium it is relatively straightforward to check whether the Nash equilibrium is also a dominant strategy equilibrium or an iterated-dominance equilibrium. Look again at the Pub managers game where the Nash equilibrium is also a dominant-strategy equilibrium. The underlinings in pay-off Matrix 2.13 corresponding to the Queen's Head's best response pay-offs are all in the same (the top) row. Similarly, the underlinings identifying the King's Head's best response pay-offs are all in the same (the first) column. This shows in a visual way that each player has a dominant strategy and that the Nash equilibrium is also a dominant-strategy equilibrium. In friends or enemies 3 in Matrix 2.14 the situation is a bit different. Two of the three underlinings identifying Mr Column's best response pay-offs are in the same column (the first) but each of the underlinings identifying Ms Row's best response pay-offs are in different rows. This shows that Mr Column but not Ms Row has a weakly dominant strategy and therefore the Nash equilibrium in this case is also a weak iterated-dominance equilibrium.

## Exercise 2.4

In the version of computer wars in Matrix 2.15 Chip and Pin can only choose between lower price and free printer. Pin has secured a large consignment of cut price printers and free printer is now a dominant strategy for Pin but Chip still doesn't have a dominant strategy. What is the Nash equilibrium of computer wars 2? Is the Nash equilibrium also an iterated-dominance equilibrium and if so is it strong or weak?

**Matrix 2.15**  Computer wars 2

Chip Inc

| | lower price | free printer |
|---|---|---|
| Pin Ltd  lower price | 1, 6 | 2, 0 |
| free printer | 6, 2 | 4, 4 |

## Exercise 2.5

In computer wars 3 Chip can offer the third option of an extended guarantee but neither player has a dominant strategy. What is the Nash equilibrium of computer wars 3? Is the Nash equilibrium also an iterated-dominance equilibrium? If so is the iterated-dominance equilibrium strong or weak?

**Matrix 2.16**  Computer wars 3

Chip Inc

| | | lower price | free printer | extended guarantee |
|---|---|---|---|---|
| Pin Ltd | lower price | 1, 0 | 1, 2 | 0, 1 |
| | free printer | 0, 3 | 0, 1 | 2, 0 |

## 2.3.1  Some formal definitions

To give a formal definition of a dominant strategy for player A in a two-person game played with player B it is convenient to define the following:

(i)   $P(A_i, B_i)$ is player A's pay-off from choosing strategy $A_i$ when player B chooses strategy $B_i$.

(ii)  $P(A_{-i}, B_i)$ is player A's pay-off from choosing some strategy other than $A_i$ when player B chooses strategy $B_i$.

(iii) $P(A_i, B_{-i})$ is player A's pay-off from choosing $A_i$ when player B chooses some strategy other than $B_i$.

With the above definitions $A_i$ is a strictly dominant strategy for player A if for all the possible alternative strategies $A_{-i}$ and $B_{-i}$:

$$P(A_i, B_i) > P(A_{-i}, B_i) \text{ and } P(A_i, B_{-i}) > P(A_{-i}, B_{-i}) \qquad \text{condition (2.1)}$$

Condition (2.1) implies that all the $A_{-i}$ are dominated strategies. If either of the strict inequalities are equalities then $A_i$ is only a weakly dominant strategy.

A dominant-strategy equilibrium is a combination of strategies where every strategy of every player is a dominant strategy. Thus if we define the following in relation to player B's strategies:

(iv)   $P(B_i, A_i)$ is player B's pay-off from choosing strategy $B_i$ when player A chooses strategy $A_i$.

(v)   $P(B_{-i}, A_i)$ is player B's pay-off from choosing some strategy other than $B_i$ when player A chooses strategy $A_i$.

(vi)   $P(B_i, A_{-i})$ is player B's pay-off from choosing $B_i$ when player A chooses some strategy other than $A_i$.

Then $B_i$ is a strictly dominant strategy for B if for all the possible alternatives $B_{-i}$ and $A_{-i}$:

$$P(B_i, A_i) > P(B_{-i}, A_i) \text{ and } P(B_i, A_{-i}) > P(B_{-i}, A_{-i}) \qquad \text{condition (2.2)}$$

and if both conditions (2.1) and (2.2) are satisfied then $\{A_i, B_i\}$ is a strong dominant strategy equilibrium. If either of the inequalities in conditions (2.1) and (2.2) are equalities then $\{A_i, B_i\}$ is only a weak dominant strategy equilibrium.

Using definitions (i)–(ii) and (iv)–(v) above $A_i$ and $B_i$ will constitute a Nash equilibrium if:

$$P(A_i, B_i) > P(A_{-i}, B_i) \text{ and } P(B_i, A_i) > P(B_{-i}, A_i) \qquad \text{condition (2.3)}$$

If either of the inequalities in condition (2.3) is an equality then the Nash equilibrium is weak, otherwise it is strong.

Note that definitions (iii) and (vi) are not needed to define a Nash equilibrium. Now compare conditions (2.1) and (2.2) with condition (2.3). The first inequality in condition (2.3) is the same as the first inequality in condition (2.1) and the second inequality in condition (2.3) is the same as the first inequality in condition (2.2). Hence if conditions (2.1) and (2.2) are satisfied so is condition (2.3). This means that condition (2.3) is a necessary but not a sufficient condition for $A_i$ and $B_i$ to constitute a dominant-strategy equilibrium and therefore every dominant-strategy equilibrium must also be a Nash equilibrium. Condition (2.3) is also a necessary condition for $A_i$ and $B_i$ to constitute an iterated-dominance equilibrium if for at least one of the players the relevant inequality also holds with respect to all of the other player's non-dominated strategies.

① 2.4 **Some classic games**

A number of well-defined two-person simultaneous-move games have been used to generate general inferences about a range of strategic situations. These games have been around for many years and are widely used as illustrative examples. They include games of assurance, battle of the sexes, chicken and the war of attrition. They generally have multiple or problematic Nash equilibria. Some examples are analysed here. The whole of the next chapter is devoted to the prisoners' dilemma, probably the most famous strategic game of all.

### 2.4.1 Ranked coordination: coordination with assurance[7]

In coordination games the players have an incentive to coordinate their strategies in order to secure mutually beneficial outcomes or avoid mutually harmful ones. This will be more difficult in games with more than one Nash equilibrium. Have a look at the matching moves game represented in Matrix 2.17. The players in this game are managers of two firms who want to coordinate their price strategies. Their pay-offs represent their profits. There are two Nash equilibria in this game – can you identify them?

**Matrix 2.17** Matching moves

|  | | Firm Y | |
| --- | --- | :---: | :---: |
|  | | raise price | lower price |
| **Firm X** | **raise price** | 5, 5 | 1, 2 |
|  | **lower price** | 2, 1 | 3, 3 |

In matching moves the Nash equilibria are {raise price, raise price} and {lower price, lower price}. Do you think one of them is more likely to be the outcome of this game than the other? Well, in the {raise price, raise price} equilibrium both firms' pay-offs are higher than in the {lower price, lower price} equilibrium. Therefore both players prefer the former and for this reason it seems intuitively more likely to be the outcome of the game. The problem with the {lower price, lower price} equilibrium is that both players can benefit by switching to the {raise price, raise price} outcome. An outcome where at least one of the players can benefit if one or both does something else, without worsening the position of the other is called a Pareto inefficient outcome. {lower price, lower price} is a Pareto inefficient outcome as both players can benefit by changing their strategy to raise price. The {raise price, raise price} equilibrium on the other hand is

Pareto efficient as neither player could benefit by switching strategies without lowering the pay-off of the other. Since both players are advantaged by switching their strategies from lower price to raise price the {raise price, raise price} equilibrium is said to Pareto dominate the {lower price, lower price} alternative.

The firms' shared interests in securing the higher ranked Nash equilibrium {raise price, raise price} provides them with an element of assurance when they are choosing their strategies. Because {raise price, raise price} is advantageous to both of them it appears to be the more compelling of the two Nash equilibria. It may be that it acts as a kind of focal point for the players in that it stands out or has prominence and therefore they are able to coordinate their choices around it.[8]

However, in games with multiple equilibria Pareto domination won't automatically guarantee coordination. Consider the matching moves game in Matrix 2.17.1 where the pay-offs of Firm Y are a little different from those in Matrix 2.17. In the game in Matrix 2.17.1 the raise price strategy is risky for the manager of Firm Y. If he chooses raise price and for some reason Firm X does not, Firm Y's pay-off is –100. This is a lot less than he gets if he chooses lower price and Firm X chooses raise price. This added risk for Firm Y makes the Pareto dominant Nash equilibrium {raise price, raise price} seem less likely.

**Matrix 2.17.1** Matching moves with added risk for Firm Y.

|  |  | Firm Y | |
|---|---|---|---|
|  |  | raise price | lower price |
| Firm X | raise price | 5, 5 | 1, 2 |
|  | lower price | 2, -100 | 3, 3 |

- Pareto efficiency: an outcome is Pareto efficient if it is not possible to improve the pay-off of one player without lowering the pay-off of another.

- Pareto domination: outcome 1 Pareto dominates or is Pareto superior to outcome 2 if the pay-offs of one or more players is higher and none are lower in outcome 1.

- Pareto inefficiency: an outcome is Pareto inefficient if it is Pareto dominated by another outcome.

## 2.4.2 Weak ranking

In the game represented in Matrix 2.18 the two players are Mr English and Mr French who are driving their horse-drawn carriages towards each other along a track in Victorian England. Mr English has a preference for driving on the left and Mr French has a preference for driving on the right. Because they are in England where more of the people share Mr English's preferences, Mr English feels more strongly about driving on the left than Mr French does about driving on the right. There are two Nash equilibria in this game – can you identify them?

**Matrix 2.18**  Which side of the track?

|              |       | Mr French |       |
|--------------|-------|-----------|-------|
|              |       | right     | left  |
| **Mr English** | right | 2, 3    | 0, 0  |
|              | left  | 1, 1      | 3, 3  |

The two Nash equilibria in Which side of the track? are {left, left} and {right, right}. However, there is less assurance than in matching moves as {left, left} only weakly Pareto dominates {right, right}; Mr English prefers {left, left} but Mr French is indifferent between {left, left} and {right, right}. In this game Mr English's preference for {left, left} provides some assurance for Mr French that Mr English will choose left. This should perhaps encourage him to choose left himself. Mr English knows this and therefore {left, left} still seems the likely outcome even though it only weakly Pareto dominates {right, right}.

However, some further doubts about the strength of Pareto domination as a selection criteria are raised by the related experimental evidence.[9] Van Huyck, Battalio and Beil (1990) conducted a series of coordination games with Pareto ranked multiple equilibria. They found that subjects were unlikely to make initial choices that corresponded to the Pareto dominant equilibrium although in some cases players did converge to it after a number of repetitions. This was more likely when fewer players were involved. Cooper, DeJong, Forsythe and Ross (1990) ran experiments where respondents played two player games with a choice of three strategies. Each game had two Pareto ordered Nash equilibria. They found that Pareto dominance was not automatically a selection criteria. Subjects were also less likely to select strategies consistent with the Pareto dominant equilibrium when these strategies were associated with the kind of risk experienced by Firm Y in Matrix 2.17.1. An interpretation of these results suggested by Cooper et al. is that individuals may be uncertain as to the rationality of the other player in the game. In other experiments Cooper, DeJong, Forsythe and Ross (1989) found that subjects were much more likely to select the Pareto dominant equilibrium when one-way pre-play communication was allowed.[10]

## 2.4.3 Coordination without assurance

In coordination games without assurance there are multiple Nash equilibria but none of them Pareto dominates. In the Battle of the sexes[11] game represented in Matrix 2.19 the players want to meet up either at the party or the pub but John has a preference for the pub and Janet has a preference for the party.[12] The worst possible outcome for both of them is that Janet goes to the pub and John goes to the party. But Janet prefers to go to the pub if John is there than to go to the party if he is not and John would rather go to the party if Janet is there than go to the pub without her. You should be able to confirm that the two Nash equilibria are {pub, pub} and {party, party}. The problem for Janet and John is that John prefers the first equilibrium and Janet the second so how can they coordinate on either? There is no obvious answer to this question and in experiments involving battle of the sexes games coordination failure is common (*see* Camerer, 2003: Chapter 7). One way may be for one of the players to move first by pre-committing to their preferred venue. For example Jane could pre-commit to the party by buying a present for the host of the party. Alternatively John could pre-commit to the pub by joining the pub darts team. Moving first in this game also gives a player a first-mover advantage. For example, if the party didn't start till 9 pm John could get a head start on Jane by going down to the pub at 8 pm (*see* Chapter 5, Section 5.1 where a version of this game is considered in which John moves first).

**Matrix 2.19** Battle of the sexes

|  |  | Janet | |
|---|---|---|---|
|  |  | **pub** | **party** |
| **John** | **pub** | 3, 2 | 1, 1 |
|  | **party** | –1, –2 | 2, 3 |

Battle of the sexes has applications that go beyond gender relations. For example two food manufacturers may prefer to standardise the ingredients of their product in the interests of promoting consumer confidence, but they may have different preferences over which ingredients to use. Alternatively two neighbouring governments may both wish to adopt minimum wage legislation but they are likely to have different preferences about the level at which to set the minimum (the legislation game in Matrix 2.2 simplifies this problem by assuming that the governments can either introduce the legislation or not – they don't have discretion about how much legislation to introduce).

Chicken is another coordination game without assurance. There are multiple Nash equilibria but each player prefers a different equilibrium outcome. One of the non-equilibrium outcomes is truly a disaster for both of them but unlike Battle of the sexes the other is preferred by both players to their least preferred Nash equilibrium outcome. In the chicken game in Matrix 2.20, the two players are a couple of ageing boxers who are trying to maintain a media profile by challenging the other to a fight. Neither of them actually wants to fight but by backing down they lose credibility with their fans. If neither of them backs down the fight will go ahead. The two Nash equilibria are {challenge, back down} and {back down, challenge} but Smith prefers the first of these, in which Jones chooses back down and Jones prefers the second. {challenge, challenge} is a disaster for both of them and they both want to avoid this outcome. The other non-equilibrium outcome {back down, back down} is preferred by both Jones and Smith to their least preferred Nash equilibrium.

**Matrix 2.20**  Chicken 1 (war of attrition)

**Jones**

|  |  | back down | challenge |
|---|---|---|---|
| **Smith** | back down | 2, 2 | 0, 5 |
|  | challenge | 5, 0 | -20, -20 |

In chicken games it is not clear how the players will coordinate their strategies. One possibility considered in Chapter 6 is that the players choose their strategies according to some predetermined probability distribution such as fight with probability $\frac{1}{4}$ and back down with probability $\frac{3}{4}$. If players in a game choose their strategies in this way they are using mixed or randomisation strategies. Mixed strategies may have more appeal for players in games that are played over time or repeated. In a one-off game of Chicken 1, if both players choose challenge the –20 pay-off for each player is irretrievable. But in a repeated version of the game, in which both players are randomising between back down and challenge, a –20 pay-off could be recouped by a series of 5s or 2s. A game of chicken played over time is a war of attrition. If chicken 1 is played as a war of attrition then both players start with challenge which gives them a negative pay-off over time and the game continues until one of them chooses back down. The player who maintains the challenge for longest wins the war.

Chicken, especially when played as a war of attrition, has many applications.[13] It is possible to conceive of arms races as games of chicken and in 2003 the BBC and the British Government were accused of playing a game of chicken during the Hutton Inquiry because neither side was prepared to shift its position and admit making an error (*Guardian*, 19 August 2003: 4–5).[14]

## 2.4.4  Games of pure conflict

You have already seen two games of pure conflict in Chapter 1 (hide-and-seek and the penalty-taking game). Games of pure conflict are games where there is no scope for coordination because there are no mutually beneficial outcomes: there can only be one winner. Many games of pure conflict are constant-sum games. Consider the game represented in Matrix 2.21. This version of the friends or enemies game is a constant-sum game where the constant-sum is zero. It is a game of pure conflict because Ms Row doesn't care whether she goes to the party or the club, she just wants to avoid Mr Column. Mr Column on the other hand wants to see Ms Column so much that he too doesn't care whether he goes to the party or the club, he just wants to go where she goes. Does friends or enemies 4 have a Nash equilibrium?

**Matrix 2.21**  Friends or enemies 4

|  |  | Mr Column | |
| --- | --- | --- | --- |
|  |  | **party** | **club** |
| **Ms Row** | **party** | −1, 1 | 1, −1 |
|  | **club** | 1, −1 | −1, 1 |

Matrix 2.21.1 shows the best responses of Ms Row and Mr Column underlined. There is no cell in which both players' pay-offs are underlined and therefore no Nash equilibrium. There is no Nash equilibrium because there are no strategy pairs where the strategies are best responses to each other. For example, if both players choose party then Ms Row will want to switch to club and if she switches to club then Mr Column will want to switch from party. But if he does Ms Row will want to switch back to party. Every possible strategy combination is like this. One of the players will always want to deviate. Consequently there is no Nash equilibrium in friends or enemies 4, or to be more precise no Nash equilibrium in pure strategies.

**Matrix 2.21.1**  Friends or enemies 4: both player's best responses

|  |  | Mr Column | |
| --- | --- | --- | --- |
|  |  | **party** | **club** |
| **Ms Row** | **party** | −1, <u>1</u> | <u>1</u>, −1 |
|  | **club** | <u>1</u>, −1 | −1, <u>1</u> |

Similar reasoning applies in many but not all games of pure conflict. The battle of the Bismarck Sea is an exception. It is a game of pure conflict but there is a Nash equilibrium because one of the players has a (weakly) dominant strategy. In games with no Nash equilibrium in pure strategies it is difficult to predict what will happen. This problem is compounded in constant-sum games because unlike battle of the sexes or chicken there is a first-mover disadvantage. In Friends or enemies 4 if Ms Row moves first by going to the party Mr Column will surely follow which will be to Ms Row's disadvantage. Mr Column is in the same position. If he moves first Ms Row will just as surely avoid him which will be to his disadvantage. When there is a first-mover disadvantage the secret of success is to make your moves unpredictable. One way to do this is to act unsystematically by choosing between strategies in a random way. If a player does this they are choosing a mixed rather than a pure strategy. It turns out that all simultaneous-move two-player games, including constant-sum games, have a Nash equilibrium in mixed strategies (Glicksberg, 1952). Therefore it is a theoretical possibility for the players in a game with no Nash equilibrium in pure strategies to coordinate on a Nash equilibrium in mixed strategies. This possibility is discussed in detail in Chapter 6.

## Exercise 2.6

Taking a penalty 2 is a variation of taking a penalty 1, the game you saw in Chapter 1. In this version of the game the striker gains more satisfaction if he scores by kicking the ball into the corners of the goal. Does taking a penalty 2 have a Nash equilibrium (in pure strategies)? If not can you explain why? Does either player in this game have a first-over advantage?

**Matrix 2.22**  Taking a penalty 2

|          |        | goalkeeper |        |        |
|----------|--------|------------|--------|--------|
|          |        | **left**   | **middle** | **right** |
|          | **left**   | 0, 1   | 2, 0   | 2, 0   |
| **striker** | **middle** | 1, 0   | 0, 1   | 1, 0   |
|          | **right**  | 2, 0   | 2, 0   | 0, 1   |

## Summary

In this chapter a number of simultaneous- or hidden-move games were analysed in detail. You have seen that the analysis of these kinds of games focuses on strategies that are best responses to each other and therefore constitute an equilibrium. Three equilibrium concepts for static games were defined; dominant-strategy equilibrium, iterated-dominance equilibrium and Nash equilibrium (in pure strategies). You have learned how to derive each of these in two-person simultaneous-move games.

In a Nash equilibrium the players' strategies are best responses to each other. In a dominant-strategy equilibrium the players' strategies are best responses to all of the other players' strategies. In an iterated-dominance equilibrium the players' strategies are best responses not only to each other but also, for at least one of the players, to some of the other strategies of the other player. Because the conditions that need to be satisfied for a Nash equilibrium are necessary but not sufficient conditions for a dominant strategy and iterated-dominance equilibrium, every dominant-strategy and iterated-dominance equilibrium is also a Nash equilibrium. But not every Nash equilibrium is also a dominant-strategy or an iterated-dominance equilibrium. It may therefore be simpler when searching for the theoretical outcome of a game to start by looking for a Nash equilibrium and then, if one is found, check whether it is either a dominant-strategy or iterated-dominance equilibrium. If Nash equilibrium strategies are also dominant strategies then we can be more confident about predicting the Nash equilibrium as the outcome of the game.

A straightforward way of finding a Nash equilibrium is to underline or otherwise identify in the game's pay-off matrix each player's 'best response' pay-offs. These are the pay-offs that correspond to their best responses to each of the other players' strategies. After following this procedure you can look for cells in the pay-off matrix where both players' pay-offs are identified as best response pay-offs. The strategies corresponding to these pay-offs will be best responses to each other and will constitute a Nash equilibrium.

In Section 2.4 some classic games including chicken and battle of the sexes were analysed. You saw that some simultaneous two-player games have more than one Nash equilibrium and others have none. In games with assurance there are multiple equilibria but one of the Nash equilibria seems more plausible by virtue of Pareto dominance. However, in games like chicken it is difficult to predict how the players will coordinate their strategy choices. In games of pure conflict there may be no Nash equilibrium in pure strategies and one possibility is that players will try to create doubt in their opponent's mind by choosing mixed strategies.

The Nash equilibrium is an important concept that is used extensively in game theory. It does, however, have some limitations. First of all, as you have already seen, some games have multiple Nash equilibria and some have no Nash equilibria in pure strategies. Secondly, as you will see in the following chapters, the problem of multiple Nash equilibria gets worse as games become more complicated. This has led game theorists to refine the concept of a Nash equilibrium when moves are sequential and information is not perfect. Sequential move games are analysed in Chapter 4. In these games refinement of Nash equilibrium leads to the idea of a subgame perfect Nash equilibrium. In games with imperfect information the process of refinement leads to the concept of a Bayesian Nash equilibrium (*see* Chapter 7). Last but not least a long line of academics have raised objections to the underlying assumptions of Nash equilibrium such as rationality and common knowledge.[15]

## Answers to exercises

### 2.1

Whatever Bart does Art is always better off choosing invest; Art gets at most 3 by not investing and either 9 or 5 by investing. Whatever Art does Bart is also better off choosing invest. Consequently the dominant-strategy equilibrium is {invest, invest}

### 2.2

The dominant-strategy equilibrium is {party, party}. Both players prefer to go to the party whatever the other player does.

### 2.3

A wide range of correct answers is possible. Pay-off Matrix 2.7.1 shows one possibility. In Matrix 2.7.1 the pay-offs make no challenge a strongly dominated strategy for the challenger and the strong iterated-dominance equilibrium is {challenge, resign}.

**Matrix 2.7.1** Political ambition with a weak incumbent MP

|  |  | incumbent MP | |
| --- | --- | --- | --- |
|  |  | **stand** | **resign** |
| **challenger** | **no challenge** | 5, 10 | 0, 1 |
|  | **challenge** | 10, –15 | 15, 1 |

**2.4**

The Nash equilibrium of computer wars 2 can be found in three steps:

Step 1: Underline or otherwise indicate the pay-offs corresponding to Pin's best responses to each of Chip's strategies as shown in Matrix 2.15.1.

**Matrix 2.15.1**  Pin's best responses

|  |  | Chip Inc | |
| --- | --- | --- | --- |
|  |  | lower price | free printer |
| **Pin Ltd** | **lower price** | 1, 6 | 2, 0 |
|  | **free printer** | 6, 2 | 4, 4 |

Step 2: Underline the pay-offs corresponding to Chip's best responses to each of Pin's two strategies as shown in Matrix 2.15.2.

**Matrix 2.15.2**  Chip's best responses

|  |  | Chip Inc | |
| --- | --- | --- | --- |
|  |  | lower price | free printer |
| **Pin Ltd** | **lower price** | 1, 6 | 2, 0 |
|  | **free printer** | 6, 2 | 4, 4 |

Step 3: Combine the two matrices and check to see if a cell in the pay-off matrix has two underlinings as shown in Matrix 2.15.3.

**Matrix 2.15.3**  Both firms' best responses

|  |  | Chip Inc | |
| --- | --- | --- | --- |
|  |  | lower price | free printer |
| **Pin Ltd** | **lower price** | 1, 6 | 2, 0 |
|  | **free printer** | 6, 2 | 4, 4 |

There are two underlinings in the (highlighted) cell in the bottom row of the second column. This implies that offering the free printer is a best response by both players if the other also offers a free printer. {free printer, free printer} is therefore the Nash equilibrium of the game. This strategy combination is also a strong iterated-dominance equilibrium found by deleting Dime's strongly dominated strategy of lower price.

## 2.5

Pay-off Matrix 2.16.1 shows the best responses of both players underlined. The Nash equilibrium is {lower price, free printer}. This strategy combination is also a strong iterated-dominance equilibrium found by deleting Chip's strongly dominated strategy extended guarantee which makes free printer strongly dominated for Pin. Deleting Pin's strategy of free printer makes lower price strongly dominated for Tell.

**Matrix 2.16.1**

|  |  | Chip Inc | | |
|---|---|---|---|---|
|  |  | lower price | free printer | extended guarantee |
| Pin Ltd | lower price | 1, 0 | 1, 2 | 0, 1 |
|  | free printer | 0, 3 | 0, 1 | 2, 0 |

## 2.6

There is no Nash equilibrium in pure strategies in taking a penalty 2. Even though the pay-offs do not sum to a constant the game is still one of pure conflict and neither player has a dominant strategy; if the striker scores the goalkeeper effectively loses and vice versa. Neither player has a first-mover advantage, there is a first-mover disadvantage.

## Problems

1 Identify the Nash equilibria of the up-down, left-right game represented in Matrix 2.23. Is there more than one Nash equilibrium? If so are all the Nash equilibria also iterated-dominance equilibria? Are the iterated-dominance equilibria that exist strong or weak?

**Matrix 2.23** The up-down, left-right game

|  |  | player B | | | |
|---|---|---|---|---|---|
|  |  | left left | left right | right left | right right |
| player A | up | 2, 0 | 2, 0 | 3, 3 | 3, 3 |
|  | down | 4, 2 | 1, 1 | 1, 1 | 4, 2 |

2 Identify the Nash equilibria in the chicken game in Matrix 2.24. What kind of situation do you think is being modelled in chicken 2?

**Matrix 2.24** Chicken 2

|  |  | Rosie | |
|---|---|---|---|
|  |  | **stay** | **swerve** |
| **Jessie** | **stay** | -10, -10 | 2, -1 |
|  | **swerve** | -1, 2 | 1, 1 |

3 In the stag hunt game in Matrix 2.25 each player chooses between hunting a stag (which will only be successful if both players join in) and shooting a hare (which doesn't require the help of anyone else). There are two Nash equilibria in this game – which do you think is more likely?

**Matrix 2.25** Stag hunt

|  |  | player 2 | |
|---|---|---|---|
|  |  | **stag** | **hare** |
| **player 1** | **stag** | 5, 5 | 0, 1 |
|  | **hare** | 1, 0 | 1, 1 |

## Questions for discussion

1 Explain what is implied by a Nash equilibrium (in pure strategies) in a simultaneous-move game.

2 Why is every dominant-strategy equilibrium also a Nash equilibrium?

3 In what kinds of circumstances might the Nash equilibrium concept be of limited use in predicting the outcome of a game?

4 How do you think that games of pure conflict like penalty taking are resolved in practice?

## Answers to problems

1 There are 3 Nash equilibria as shown in Matrix 2.23.1. They are: {down, left left}, {up, right left} and {down, right right}. The last of these is a weak iterated-dominance equilibrium found initially by deleting B's strongly dominated strategy left right. And then left left and right left.

**Matrix 2.23.1** The up-down, left-right game

| A | left left | left right | right left | right right |
|---|---|---|---|---|
| | | | **B** | |
| up | 2, 0 | **2**, 0 | **3, 3** | 3, **3** |
| down | **4, 2** | 1, 1 | 1, 1 | **4, 2** |

2 In chicken 2, the two Nash equilibria are {stay, swerve} and {swerve, stay} but Jessie prefers the first of these and Rosie prefers the second. {stay, stay} is a disaster for both players and both players prefer {swerve, swerve} to the other's preferred Nash equilibrium.

This version of chicken represents a classic case in which the two players are playing a game of nerves by driving towards each other or towards a cliff edge or some variation on this theme. The player who swerves first loses face and the player who stays on course the longest wins the glory. But if neither swerves the consequences are disastrous. The game is widely associated with the classic 1955 film *Rebel Without a Cause* starring James Dean in which the main characters play a variant of this chicken game.

3 The two Nash equilibria are {stag, stag} and {hare, hare} but the first Nash equilibrium Pareto dominates the second. The rationale is as follows: the stag is bigger and the group is small enough so that a share in the stag is preferred to the whole hare. The situation where both players join in the stag hunt is therefore Pareto superior to the situation where both shoot their own hare.

## Notes

1   A series of games like political ambition are analysed in Gates and Humes (1997: Chapter 3).

2   See Haywood (1954) for an analytical discussion or www.combinedfleet.com/bismksea.htm for more general information.

3   See Roth (1995: 21–3) for a brief summary of the objectives of experimental research. See Mirowski (2002: 545–51) for a critique of the experimental approach.

4   Deleting weakly dominated strategies may also result in the deletion of a Nash equilibrium.

5   All references to Nash equilibria in this chapter are to pure strategy Nash equilibria. Remember from Chapter 1 that if a player chooses a pure strategy they choose just one of the alternative strategies that are available to them. If a game doesn't have an equilibrium in pure strategies it can still have one in mixed strategies as you will see in Chapter 6. Choosing a mixed strategy involves randomising between some or all of the player's available strategies. A pure strategy can be viewed as a special mixed strategy for which the respective pure strategy is played with probability one and any other strategy with probability zero.

6   Gibbons (1992: 9) calls this a 'brute-force approach' to finding a game's Nash equilibrium.

7   A classic coordination game with assurance is Rousseau's *stag hunt*. *See* Problem 3 at the end of this chapter.

8   Schelling (1960) showed that in many situations where formal theorising doesn't appear to offer much guidance people are still able to coordinate their actions by focusing independently on some particular feature of the situation.

9   See Ochs (1995) for a summary of the related experimental literature.

10  This kind of communication is sometimes called cheap talk as any commitments made are not binding.

11  Sometimes the title of this game is changed, for example to the dating game (*see* Gibbons, 1997: 132) because the original title is considered politically incorrect.

12  Battle of the sexes is like the friends game but the players have different preferences in relation to the choice of venues.

13  Another example of a game of chicken is played when two swimmers are swimming in the same lane in a crowded pool. When they are swimming towards each other they face a simultaneous choice of swerving in order to avoid the other or not swerving. If neither swerves there will be an uncomfortable collision. But swerving may set a precedent and is inconvenient. Alternatively, if one of them decides to swim backstroke he can commit to not swerving because he will be unable to see the other.

14  The Hutton Inquiry investigated the roles of the British Government and the BBC in the death of a senior civil servant who had made claims concerning the contents of a government dossier on weapons of mass destruction in Iraq.

15  *See*, for example, Hargreaves Heap and Varoufakis (1997) or Mirowski (2002).

# 3

# PRISONERS' DILEMMA

## Concepts and techniques

- Prisoners' dilemma
- Generalised pay-offs
- Pareto efficiency
- Public goods
- Open-access resources
- Binding contracts.

After working through this chapter you will be able to:

- Explain what is implied by a prisoners' dilemma
- Construct a pay-off matrix for a prisoners' dilemma game
- Show that the dominant-strategy equilibrium of the prisoners' dilemma is not Pareto-efficient
- Generalise the pay-offs of the prisoners' dilemma
- Describe prisoners' dilemmas in a variety of situations
- Show how prisoners' dilemma games can be used to analyse problems relating to the provision of public goods and the over-harvesting of open-access resources
- Reflect on some suggestions about ways to resolve prisoners' dilemmas.

# Introduction

Only one game is examined in this chapter. That game is the prisoners' dilemma.[1] The prisoners' dilemma is a truly classic game in the sense that it has been analysed in countless academic publications and is almost always discussed in introductory reviews of game theory. Its renown has also spread beyond academic circles. This is not surprising as strategic situations that can be characterised as a prisoners' dilemma are ubiquitous. Applications include oligopoly collusion, international trade and investment, environmental problems, wage inflation and public goods. The prisoners' dilemma game is interesting not only because of its wide applicability but also because it poses some interesting questions about the underlying assumptions of game theory, specifically in relation to the definition of rationality that the theory employs.[2] Some of these questions are discussed in this chapter.

This chapter begins with the original application of the prisoners' dilemma from which the name of the game is derived.[3] The dilemma is then generalised and applied in a range of contexts in Sections 3.2 to 3.4. Some related policy questions that arise in connection with public goods and the free-rider effect are discussed in Sections 3.5 to 3.6 and a macroeconomic application is discussed in Section 3.7. Some questions raised by the dilemma are discussed in Section 3.8.

## 3.1 Original prisoners' dilemma game

In the original prisoners' dilemma two suspects are being interviewed by the police in relation to a major crime. They are being interviewed in separate cells and neither knows how the other's interview is progressing. The moves of the game are therefore hidden and it is appropriate to model the situation as a simultaneous-move game (even if the prisoners are not actually being interviewed exactly at the same time). An implicit assumption of the game is that the prisoners did in fact commit the crime that they are being questioned about. The suspects can either confess to the crime or deny their involvement in it. If neither prisoner confesses the police are not able to convict either for the major crime but are able to secure a conviction against both of them in relation to a lesser crime. However, if just one of them confesses to the major crime they can both be convicted. The dilemma for the prisoners is that if one of them confesses but the other does not the one who confesses receives a much shorter sentence than the other (his reward for acting as an informer or 'grass').

 Take a look at the prisoners' dilemma represented by the pay-off matrix in Matrix 3.1. In Matrix 3.1 the pay-offs represent the prison sentences that the suspects face as a result of their actions. In this prisoners' dilemma if one suspect confesses and the other denies the confessor is released while the other receives a ten-year sentence. If neither suspect confesses they both receive short one-year sentences. If both confess they both spend five years in prison. What do you think will be the outcome of this game?

**Matrix. 3.1** Prisoners' dilemma

|  |  | prisoner 2 | |
| --- | --- | --- | --- |
|  |  | **deny** | **confess** |
| **prisoner 1** | **deny** | -1, -1 | -10, 0 |
|  | **confess** | 0, -10 | -5, -5 |

If you apply the methodology of Chapter 2 you will see that game theory makes a clear prediction about the game's outcome since it has a dominant-strategy equilibrium. You can see this by looking at the pay-off matrix in Matrix 3.1.1 where the prisoners' pay-offs corresponding to their best responses are underlined. For both prisoners confess is the best response to either deny or confess by the other implying that each player's dominant strategy is to confess. The dominant-strategy equilibrium is therefore {confess, confess} and the game theoretic prediction is that faced with these strategy choices and pay-offs both prisoners will confess.

**Matrix. 3.1.1** Dominant-strategy equilibrium of the prisoners' dilemma

|  |  | prisoner 2 | |
| --- | --- | --- | --- |
|  |  | **deny** | **confess** |
| **prisoner 1** | **deny** | -1, -1 | -10, <u>0</u> |
|  | **confess** | <u>0</u>, -10 | <u>-5, -5</u> |

The dilemma for the players is that they could both have higher pay-offs if they both denied. Since the {confess, confess} equilibrium is Pareto-dominated by {deny, deny} it is not Pareto-efficient. Both prisoners can work out that {confess, confess} is not an efficient outcome (as can the police) but the rational, self-interested dominant strategy is clearly to confess. This paradoxical result is not resolved by a pre-negotiated agreement to deny as once the police start to question the prisoners they each have an incentive to break the agreement. This will still be true even if they believe that the other will stick to the agreement. The dilemma for the prisoners is that by acting rationally, that is by choosing their strategies to maximise their pay-offs, they are worse off than if they had acted in some other presumably 'irrational' way . This is clearly a perverse result. It implies that the players could do better by acting altruistically or even randomly than by acting in their own self-interests. But with the pay-offs as they are in Matrix 3.1 the players will only deny if a prior agreement to deny is somehow enforceable.

> ### Pareto efficiency
>
> - In a two-player game an outcome is Pareto-efficient if it is not possible to improve one player's pay-off without at the same time lowering the pay-off of the other.

Making a prior agreement to deny would clearly be in the prisoners' joint interests and we could call this jointly rational behaviour[4] because it would make sense if the players were trying to maximise their total rather than their individual pay-offs. But the logic of game theory[5] assumes that individual players choose their strategies to maximise their individual not their joint pay-offs and with this assumption it is not clear how such an agreement could be enforced.[6] And unless the agreement to deny is enforced in some way the incentive for both prisoners to confess is so strong that neither can trust the other to keep to any such agreement. One possibility is that an agreement to deny could be enforced by a threat to punish confession after the event (this could involve a third party in prison or outside). If the punishment for confession was very severe denial could become a dominant strategy (*see* Problem 2 at the end of the chapter). But then the game would no longer be a prisoners' dilemma suggesting that changing the pay-offs in this way is a circumvention of the problem rather than a solution.

## 3.2 Generalised prisoners' dilemma

The prisoners' dilemma is not restricted to the scenario described above as played out in many crime dramas on TV and in films. It is therefore useful to characterise the problem in a more general way in order to capture the salient features of the game. Matrix 3.2 shows a generalised pay-off matrix for the prisoners' dilemma game in Matrix 3.1. A game is a prisoners' dilemma if the preferences of the players over the pay-offs (a), (b), (c) and (d)

are such that (c) is preferred to (a), (a) is preferred to (d) and (d) is preferred to (b) which, as more is assumed to be preferred to less, implies that $c > a > d > b$ as indicated below.[7] In Matrix 3.2. I have underlined the pay-offs that correspond to each player's best responses. As you can see, confess is still a dominant-strategy for both prisoners. The dominant-strategy equilibrium is therefore for both prisoners to confess but as $a > d$ both of them would be better off if they could both deny.

**Matrix. 3.2** Generalising the pay-offs in the prisoners' dilemma

|  | | prisoner 2 | |
| --- | --- | :---: | :---: |
| | | **deny** | **confess** |
| **prisoner 1** | **deny** | a, a | b, $\underline{c}$ |
| | **confess** | $\underline{c}$, b | $\underline{d}$, $\underline{d}$ |

$c > a > d > b$

Any game with the pay-off structure of Matrix 3.2 is a prisoners' dilemma. The players do not have to be prisoners and their strategy choices will rarely be between outright denial and confession. To encompass all these different possibilities the deny strategy is generally referred to as the cooperative strategy and the confess strategy is referred to as the defect strategy. By cooperating the players can achieve a mutually beneficial outcome. Defection, on the other hand, can be mutually harmful. If the prisoners in the original example both denied they would be cooperating or colluding with each other in order to achieve a shorter sentence. By confessing a prisoner is defecting from the cooperative strategy. A prisoners' dilemma with these generalised strategies and generalised pay-offs is shown in Matrix 3.3. The dominant-strategy equilibrium of the game in Matrix 3.3 is {defect, defect} even though both players would be better off if they could both cooperate.

**Matrix 3.3** Generalising the strategies as well as the pay-offs in the prisoners' dilemma

|  | | player column | |
| --- | --- | :---: | :---: |
| | | **cooperate (with row)** | **defect** |
| **player row** | **cooperate (with column)** | a, a | b, c |
| | **defect** | c, b | d, d |

$c > a > d > b$

> ## Exercise 3.1
>
> Construct a pay-off matrix for a prisoners' dilemma game using the gen-
> eralised strategies in Matrix 3.3 and any positive numbers between 1
> and 20 for the pay-offs.

## 3.3 Prisoners' dilemma and oligopoly collusion

Many of the strategic issues facing managers of firms in oligopoly markets can
be modelled using game theory and one of the most cited examples is a prisoners' dilemma. The application of the prisoners' dilemma to oligopoly theory
refers to the problem for firms[8] of sustaining cartels or more implicit collusion
over prices, output or other competitive weapons such as spending on advertising. These kinds of agreements stifle competition and are not usually in the
interests of consumers but they are desirable from the firms' perspective
because they can raise profits.[9] Consider the strategic situation described by the
pay-off matrix in Matrix 3.4.

In the game of oligopoly collusion represented in Matrix 3.4 Ash and Birch are
the only two firms producing wood flooring in Jesmania. The wood flooring
market is therefore an oligopoly or more precisely a duopoly. Ash and Birch can
raise their profits by colluding to maintain a high market price. If they do this
they each make profits of 7 billion units of Jesmanian money. The dilemma for
the firms is that if one of them cheats on the agreement by lowering their price
the cheat's profits rise to 10 billion while the other loses custom (to the cheat)
and profits fall to 3 billion. If both firms cheat by cutting price neither firm gains
customers from the other and the profits of both firms fall to 5 billion.

**Matrix 3.4** Oligopoly collusion

|       |         | Birch |       |
|-------|---------|---------|--------|
|       |         | collude | cheat  |
| Ash   | collude | 7, 7    | 3, 10  |
|       | cheat   | 10, 3   | 5, 5   |

With the firms' pay-offs as depicted in Matrix 3.4 do you think that collusion
between the firms is likely to be sustained? Game theory suggests that the
answer to this question is no. You should be able to see this by working out
that cheating is a dominant strategy for both firms and therefore the game

theoretic prediction is that both firms will cheat. This is a prisoners' dilemma for the firms as they could both make higher profits by colluding. Unfortunately the individual incentives for the firms to cheat are too strong. This prediction can be generalised. It implies that whenever there are strong individual incentives to cheat oligopolistic collusion will be difficult to sustain.[10] A real-world example of a collusive agreement breaking down is provided by Sotheby's and Christie's. These two international auction houses operated a price-fixing cartel for most of the 1990s until early 2000 in order to reduce the competition between them. The cartel broke down when Christie's blew the whistle on the cartel and handed over evidence to the European Commission. Christie's escaped without a fine as a reward for 'confessing' while Sotheby's were fined nearly £13 million.[11]

However, the incentive to cheat or defect from a collusive agreement won't always be as strong as it is in Matrix 3.4. If the market share of one firm is considerably larger than that of the other or others then the incentive of the larger firm to cheat may be weakened. Consider what happens if Birch is very large relative to Ash. In this case the pay-off matrix for the game could look like the one in Matrix 3.4.1. In this asymmetric oligopoly game cheating is no longer a dominant strategy for Birch. Birch is so large relative to the market as a whole that breaking the collusive agreement has a negative effect on its own as well as Ash's profits.[12] This is true whether Ash also breaks the agreement or not. Ash's situation hasn't changed so cheating is still a dominant strategy for the smaller firm. The dominant strategy equilibrium of this asymmetric game is for Ash to cheat and Birch to collude. This equilibrium outcome is Pareto-efficient as neither firm can improve their pay-off without worsening the position of the other. Consequently the game is no longer a prisoners' dilemma.

**Matrix 3.4.1** Asymmetric oligopoly collusion

|  | | Birch | |
| --- | --- | --- | --- |
|  | | collude | cheat |
| **Ash** | **collude** | 7, 40 | 3, 18 |
|  | **cheat** | 10, 20 | 5, 10 |

An example of cooperation being sustained at least partly through the actions of a dominant supplier is OPEC's ability in the early 1980s to keep oil prices high by restricting output. The OPEC strategy was helped considerably by the willingness of Saudi Arabia, a major player, to withhold production in order that other OPEC members with contrary objectives or in vulnerable political positions (specifically Libya, Iran, Iraq and Nigeria) could exceed their quotas. However, in 1985 Saudi Arabia became unwilling to maintain this position and Saudi production expanded rapidly leading to a virtual collapse of the cartel and a fall in oil prices.

## ◔ 3.4 International trade

Prisoners' dilemmas are also found in the arena of international trade. The theory of comparative advantage shows that trade can be mutually beneficial for countries but it is still tempting for governments[13] to try to protect domestic producers from foreign competition by imposing tariffs on imported goods. A tariff helps domestic producers by raising import prices. It will also raise revenue for the government but tariffs will mean higher prices for consumers. A government may be inclined to introduce a tariff if it believes that the benefits of the tariff to domestic industry outweigh the losses to consumers. However, it will still need to take into account the possibility of retaliatory action by other countries. In an extreme case this could escalate into a trade war. Imposing a tariff unilaterally is one thing but if two countries in a trading relationship impose tariffs on each other's exports, the gains to domestic producers may be outweighed by the revenue losses to domestic exporters. Retaliation of this kind is not uncommon. In 2003 there were fears that a trade war between the USA and Europe would be re-ignited when the USA rejected a final ruling from the World Trade Organisation that its protectionist tariffs on foreign steel were illegal. In retaliation the European Union threatened to impose sanctions on a range of US goods including Harley Davidson motorcycles and Ray-Ban sunglasses.[14]

This kind of scenario is modelled in the international trade game represented in Matrix 3.5. Jesmania and Rosatia are trading partners and each is deciding whether to impose a tariff on imports from the other country or not.[15] If one country imposes a tariff unilaterally then that country makes a significant net gain while the other loses. If both countries impose a tariff then both lose. If neither country imposes a tariff then both make moderate gains from trade. The pay-offs in Matrix 3.5 represent net effects (in billions of euros).

**Matrix 3.5** International trade 1

|  |  | Rosatia | |
|---|---|:---:|:---:|
|  |  | **no tariff** | **impose tariff** |
| **Jesmania** | **no tariff** | 10, 10 | -1, 15 |
|  | **impose tariff** | 15, -1 | 2, 2 |

In the international trade game in Matrix 3.5 the dominant-strategy equilibrium is for both countries to impose a tariff even though they would both be better off if neither imposed a tariff. The game as described here is a prisoners' dilemma for the two countries. The situation might be different if either or both of the countries were small relative to the market for the traded goods. In this case reduced demand due to a tariff might have little effect on import prices.[16] If import prices do not fall the negative effect of a tariff on consumers is more likely to outweigh the positive effects on domestic producers and government revenue. A country in this position has little incentive to unilaterally impose a tariff. This possibility is illustrated in Matrix 3.6 where both countries are assumed to be small and neither has an incentive to impose a tariff.

**Matrix 3.6** International trade 2

|  |  | Little Rosatia | |
| --- | --- | --- | --- |
|  |  | no tariff | impose tariff |
| Little Jesmania | no tariff | 10, 10 | –1, 8 |
|  | impose tariff | 8, –1 | –2, –2 |

International trade 2 is not a prisoners' dilemma. The dominant-strategy equilibrium of this game is for neither country to impose a tariff, the free trade alternative or mutual cooperation. This result suggests that trade wars are unlikely between small countries that are at the mercy of world markets. Small countries stand to lose more than they gain by imposing tariffs. On the other hand the analysis suggests that trade conflicts will be much more likely to flare up between large countries and large trading blocks like the European Union (EU) and the North American Free Trade Area (NAFTA).

### Exercise 3.2

In International trade 3 in Matrix 3.7 one country, Little Rosatia, is assumed to be much smaller relative to the world market than the other, Greater Jesmania. What is the dominant-strategy equilibrium of International trade 3? Can you give an interpretation of this version of the international trade game?

**Matrix 3.7** International trade 3

|  |  | Little Rosatia | |
| --- | --- | --- | --- |
|  |  | no tariff | impose tariff |
| Greater Jesmania | no tariff | 10, 10 | –1, 8 |
|  | impose tariff | 15, –1 | 2, –2 |

## 3.5  Prisoners' dilemma and public goods

The economic definition of a pure public good[17] is a good that is both non-excludable and non-rival in consumption. Non-rivalry means that one person's consumption does not reduce the supply of the public good to other potential consumers. This implies that supply of the good is non-divisible and the extra cost of supplying it to additional consumers is zero. An example is the security provided by the local police or the protection to sea-going vessels provided by a lighthouse. Non-excludability means that once a good or service becomes available anyone and everyone can use it. That is, no one can be excluded from its consumption. An example is clean air in an unpolluted environment. Most market goods have neither feature. They are private goods meaning that they are both excludable and rival in consumption. If a good is rival then one person's consumption is at the expense of another's and the incremental or marginal cost of supplying the good to an additional consumer is therefore positive. If a good is excludable then the owner of the good can exclude anyone and everyone else from using it. In this case the owner of the good is said to have property rights with respect to the good concerned. Some goods are neither purely public nor purely private but lie somewhere in between. In fact many so called public goods are only non-excludable and non-rival up to a point. For instance the security provided by the local police may become rival if there is a riot or major criminal event of some kind. Goods that are neither purely private nor purely public are called mixed goods or impure public goods. Table 3.1 gives some examples. Goods in the top left-hand quadrant are private goods because they are both excludable and rival. Goods in the bottom right-hand quadrant are public goods that are both non-excludable and non-rival. The goods in the other two quadrants are mixed goods. They are either non-excludable but rival or non-rival but excludable.

**Table 3.1** Non-rivalry and non-excludability

|  | Rival | Non-rival |
|---|---|---|
|  | **Pure private goods** | **Mixed goods** |
| **Excludable** | • Cornflakes<br>• Cars<br>• Chocolate | • Pay per view TV<br>• Toll bridges<br>• Private roads |
|  | **Mixed goods** | **Pure public goods** |
| **Non-excludable** | • State education<br>• Public health<br>• Open access resources such as ocean fishing fields, city streets and town parks | • National defence<br>• Lighthouses<br>• A clean environment<br>• Very large national parks |

National defence is a public good because it is non-excludable and non-rival. It is non-excludable because once a country has committed to defending itself no citizen can be excluded from the protection it offers; either all are defended or none. It is non-rival because one person's safety is not secured at the expense of another's. A lighthouse is a classic public good because no ship can be excluded from the warning it provides and the warning received by one passing ship does not diminish the warning received by the next. Public goods like national defence and the police tend to be provided by governments but not all goods that are provided by governments are pure public goods. Often they are merit goods. Merit goods like state-funded education and the National Health Service in the UK are impure public goods that are funded by governments because they are assumed to have wide-ranging benefits for society.[18] Merit goods are usually rival but state provision makes them non-excludable.

Economic theory predicts that the provision of public goods is likely to be problematic. The supply problem stems directly from the non-excludability and non-rivalry characteristics that generate free-rider effects. Free-riders are people who benefit from the provision of a good or service without paying. In the case of a public good the free-rider problem is endemic because no one can be excluded from consumption and one person's consumption has no effect on another's. Consequently there are limited private incentives to pay for provision. These free-rider effects can be modelled as a prisoners' dilemma[19] although in most cases more than two players will be involved making the dilemma an n-player game with $n > 2$.

Consider a situation where there are two neighbouring communities that both value a threatened natural habitat that has the non-excludable and non-rival characteristics of a public good. The communities are independently considering whether to finance the conservation of the threatened habitat. The habitat can be saved if one of the communities acts unilaterally or by both communities sharing the costs of conservation. Because the habitat has the characteristics of a public good, if only one of the communities supports the habitat, both gain. Whether the habitat will be conserved depends on the costs of conservation relative to the benefits. If the costs of conserving the habitat are so high that the expense of a unilateral commitment outweighs the benefits the problem is a prisoners' dilemma.

This scenario is represented in Matrix 3.8 where the pay-offs for two communities, Arleston and Waremouth, are the net benefits of conservation converted into monetised units. The value to each community of saving the habitat is 100 units. The cost of saving the habitat is 150 units. If the habitat is saved its benefits are non-excludable and non-rival and therefore both communities fully benefit regardless of who pays. If one community pays all of the 150 conservation costs, its net benefits are negative. If the costs are shared equally both communities gain. If neither community acts to save the habitat then neither gains and their net benefits are zero. What do you think will be the outcome of the conservation game represented in Matrix 3.8?

**Matrix 3.8** Conservation

|  |  | Community of Waremouth | |
|---|---|---|---|
|  |  | conserve | not conserve |
| Community of Arleston | conserve | 25, 25 | −50, 100 |
|  | not conserve | 100, −50 | 0, 0 |

The conservation game is a prisoners' dilemma for the two communities. Each community's dominant strategy is not to conserve and therefore the dominant-strategy equilibrium is {not conserve, not conserve} even though both communities would be better off if they both conserved. This is the theoretical prediction of the outcome of the game. The conservation game illustrates how the free-rider effect impacts on the provision of public goods. It shows that if the parties who stand to gain from the provision of a public good act in their own self-interest the public good is unlikely to be supplied. Non-excludability and non-rivalry reduce the private incentives to contribute towards the provision of public goods and therefore intervention by government may be necessary to ensure their supply. The example of conservation was not chosen by accident. Many environmental problems such as pollution and threats to biodiversity are exacerbated because the benefits that derive from improvements in environmental quality are often both non-excludable and non-rival. Because of this private incentives to improve (or refrain from harming) the environment are weak. Environmental problems like pollution are the result.[20]

## 3.6 Prisoners' dilemma and open-access resources

Ocean fisheries and the large tracts of tropical rain forest in South America and East Asia are effectively non-excludable resources since they are virtually impossible to police. Resources that are non-excludable in this way are called open-access resources. Open-access resources are not public goods since they are invariably rival. Fish caught by one group of fishermen cannot be caught again and once an area of forest has been logged it is unavailable to other would-be loggers (or any other users of the forest). When a resource is non-excludable but rival potential users face a prisoners' dilemma but not in relation to supply, instead the issue is one of over-harvesting or over-exploitation. This problem was first analysed in relation to common land with open access grazing rights to local sheep farmers.[21] For this reason the problem itself is often referred to as the 'tragedy of the commons'.[22] Fisheries, forests and grass for grazing are renewable resources but not all open-access resources are renewable. An example of a non-renewable open-access resource is a public road. Roads are effectively non-excludable but they are definitely rival – traffic congestion provides ample evidence of that.[23]

The example considered here is that of ocean fisheries. Take a look at the fishing game represented in Matrix 3.9. In this game the players are two fishing fleets from two different countries, fleet Cody and fleet Kippen. The fleets are rivals for the stock of fish in the sea. Fishing yields per trawler are assumed to be higher per sailing the greater the stock of fish in the sea. Fishing costs will therefore be lower and profits higher, the greater the stock.[24] The pay-offs in Matrix 3.9 reflect the profits from selling the fish that are caught over a fixed time period. Restrained fishing by both fleets generates a sustainable yield of fish and a reasonable level of profits for both fleets. Non-excludability implies that if fishing is unrestrained a fleet will trawl as long as there are positive profits to be made from fishing. Rivalry means that unrestrained fishing by one or both fleets depletes the stock of fish in the sea, lowers yields, raises fishing costs and lowers profits for both fleets. If one fleet shows restraint but the other does not the yields and profits of the fleet showing restraint will be lower than if neither or both had showed restraint. The yields and profits of the fleet not showing restraint will be higher.

**Matrix 3.9** Fishing game

|  | | Fleet Kippen | |
| --- | --- | --- | --- |
|  | | restrained fishing | unrestrained fishing |
| Fleet Cody | restrained fishing | 100, 100 | 25, 150 |
|  | unrestrained fishing | 150, 25 | 30, 30 |

If Cody and Kippen want to maximise their profits their dominant strategy is to fish indiscriminately. In the long term this may lead to non-sustainable yields and over-harvesting of the fisheries, possibly to extinction if the stock of fish is harvested beyond its critical minimum size (the level at which reproduction rates are so low that the stock is non-viable). Yet both fleets could make higher profits (probably for longer) if they could somehow agree to show restraint. The problem is a prisoners' dilemma for the fleets. By acting in their own self-interest they both are worse off than if they had managed to cooperate.

The prisoners' dilemma in ocean fisheries arises because access to the resource is open or non-excludable. The dilemma could therefore be solved in principle by restricting access. This may be easier in some situations than others. For example, property rights to fisheries closer to shores and where only a limited number of countries are affected should be easier to establish. One example where fishing rights have been restricted by quotas and more sustainable fishing practices have been the result is in Port Lincoln in South Australia. In this remote corner of South Australia there are no international border disputes to worry about and a combination of restricted access and self-regulation has generated high incomes for licensed fisherman and sustainable stocks of bluefin tuna, rock lobster and king prawn.[25]

## 3.7 **Macroeconomics**

Prisoners' dilemmas can also arise in the macroeconomic environment when the actions of individual agents acting in their own self-interest have damaging effects on the macroeconomy. When this is a possibility acting in what appears to be self-interest can be self-defeating. Consider the case of a trade union leader negotiating a wage increase. From the perspective of the union leader it makes sense to try to secure a wage increase for the union membership that is as large as possible. The problem for the trade union leader is that if other trade union leaders act in the same way, implying a wages free-for-all, the overall negative effects on the economy in terms of rising inflation or higher unemployment are likely to outweigh the positive effects of any given wage increase. This situation is illustrated in the wages game shown in Matrix 3.10. The pay-offs in the wages game are the utility pay-offs of the trade union leaders. Their utility depends on the welfare of their members and this depends on the real value of their wages and whether they have a job or not.[26]

In the wages game one of the players (TU leader 1) is a representative leader of a major trade union in a national labour market. The trade union leader chooses between making either high or moderate wage demands. Although each trade union leader in the economy acts independently their decisions impact on each other. Because all the leaders of the major trade unions are in an identical position each of them is effectively playing against a collective of all the others. This is modelled by letting the 'other' player in the game be a conglomeration of all the other trade union leaders. This is a useful simplification when there are more than two players in a game but, in terms of their strategies and relative pay-offs, they are identical.

**Matrix 3.10** Wages game

|  |  | all other TU leaders | |
| --- | --- | --- | --- |
|  |  | high wage demands | moderate wage demands |
| TU leader I | high wage demands | -5, -5 | 15, -10 |
|  | moderate wage demands | -10, 15 | 10, 10 |

In this instance the game is an n-player prisoners' dilemma. If all the leaders make high wage demands this triggers an upward inflationary spiral in the economy or massive redundancies or both. Either is disastrous for workers. If this is the only alternative the workers are better off if all the unions show restraint. But if one trade union leader makes a high wage demand while all the others show restraint the members of the first trade union benefit from high wage increases. The inflation this triggers leaves all the other union members worse off. Similarly, if one trade union leader shows restraint while all the others make high demands the economy still suffers but the employed members of the first trade union are not compensated by higher wages, so they are worse off. Unfortunately for the economy as a whole it is rational for every leader to go for high wages. This is not in their collective interests but to secure moderate wage demands all round requires some kind of deal on mutual restraint. The question then is how, if at all, could such a deal be instigated?

The wages game shows that where there are many players in a game, the interaction between them can still constitute a prisoners' dilemma. In a prisoners' dilemma, actions motivated by self-interest are not mutually beneficial, they are mutually harmful. Consequently, when interactions are characterised by a prisoners' dilemma Adam Smith's invisible hand may require some assistance in order to achieve a socially desirable outcome.

## 3.8 Resolving the prisoners' dilemma

One of the questions addressed in the vast literature on the prisoners' dilemma relates to evidence of collusion and cooperative behaviour in situations that can be characterised as prisoners' dilemmas. Clearly such behaviour contradicts the theoretical prediction. For example, large firms can and do collude. If they did not, there would be no rationale for governments and supranational organisations like the EU to regulate these kinds of activities by firms. Clearly there is a perceived need for this type of regulation as embodied by antitrust policy in the USA, as enforced by the Office of Fair Trading and the Competition Commission[27] in the UK and as encompassed in Article 81 of the European Community Treaty of Amsterdam.[28]

In addition, there is considerable experimental evidence to suggest that people playing one-shot prisoners' dilemma games will cooperate at least some of the time. In the experiments that have been conducted, of which there have been a large number, subjects playing one-shot prisoners' dilemma games[29] have been found to cooperate about half of the time (Camerer, 2003: 46). Similarly, subjects playing one-shot public good games have been shown to exhibit a systematic tendency not to free ride (Ledyard, 1995: 121). Changes in the relative pay-offs so that the pay-off from unilateral defection is less or the pay-off from unilateral (and multilateral) cooperation is more both increase the chances of cooperation in prisoners' dilemma games and, equivalently, the rate of provision in public good games. Communication between the players can also raise the rate of cooperation or contribution. Evidence of this kind contradicts the theoretical predictions in the same way as cooperative behaviour observed in the real world, outside the laboratory.

How then can such behaviour be explained other than by dismissing it as irrational? A number of possible answers to this question have been suggested in the academic literature. First of all it may be possible for the players to make enforceable or binding agreements to secure the cooperative outcome. Agreements could be enforced by the threat of punishment, possibly through a third party as discussed at the end of Section 3.1. Punishments could also be imposed through the legal system if for instance contracts are broken, or through government imposed penalties. Threats that work though informal networks of associates can also be effective. When threats to punish are credible they lower the pay-offs from non-cooperative behaviour. If the punishments are hard enough (so that in Matrix 3.3 $c < a$ and $d < b$) then they can make cooperation a dominant strategy. In this case there is no dilemma.

Second, if a prisoners' dilemma is repeated then, intuitively, the players should have more incentive to cooperate as their pay-offs are collected not just once but however many times the game is played. Repetition means that players need to choose long-term strategies that take into account their future pay-offs. They also have time to learn about the game and each other. If there are enough repetitions of the game then the possibility of higher pay-offs in the future as a result of earlier cooperative behaviour could outweigh the short-term gains from defection. This is what some analysts refer to as 'the shadow of the future' influencing decisions made today.

Lastly, if one or both of the players is unsure about the other's pay-offs then this could also change the outcome of the game. If, for instance, one of the players is not sure that non-cooperation is a dominant strategy for the other then it could make sense for the first player to choose the cooperative strategy but only if the prisoners' dilemma is repeated.

All of these possibilities point to ways of resolving prisoners' dilemmas without weakening the strong rationality assumptions that are integral to game theory. They can also help to reconcile the game theoretic predictions with both real-life observations and experimental evidence. All of them are given attention later in this book. The idea of a credible threat is developed in Chapter 4 and the possibility of making binding contracts is discussed in Chapter 9. Repeated prisoners' dilemma games are analysed in Chapter 8.

## Summary

This chapter has focused on just one game, the prisoners' dilemma. The dominant-strategy equilibrium of the prisoners' dilemma is not Pareto-efficient as both players could do better by choosing their dominated strategies. This equilibrium is unsettling because it suggests that rational play can be self-defeating which raises some interesting questions about the definition of rationality used in game theory.[30] After all, how rational is rational if non-rational choices result in higher pay-offs? The assumption that human beings are motivated only by self-interest can also be criticised. If this were a true reflection of human nature it would be difficult to explain why people give to charity, leave tips in restaurants they are unlikely to revisit, look after their children or care for their elderly relatives. This kind of behaviour suggests that people are not selfish all the time – but of course they are not altruistic all the time either.[31]

Rabin (1993) suggests instead that people engage in a type of reciprocal fairness: they are nice to people who are nice to them, but not so nice to people who are unkind to them. This idea can be incorporated into game theory by adding fairness bonuses or subtracting penalties from pay-offs. In the prisoners' dilemma fairness bonuses raise both players' pay-offs when they both cooperate and unfairness penalties lower the pay-offs of a player who defects when the other cooperates. If the fairness bonus is high enough the dominant strategy equilibrium of a prisoners' dilemma adjusted in this way is for both players to cooperate (see Camerer and Thaler, 2003: 162). Thus allowing for a shared sense of fairness can resolve the one-shot version of the prisoners' dilemma. But people do not always want to be nice to each other or expect other people to be nice to them and in these cases the prisoners' dilemma is less likely to be resolved by shared beliefs about fairness. Nevertheless, behavioural approaches of this kind offer some interesting answers to the questions raised by the prisoners' dilemma and game theory more generally. These questions are worth addressing because, as you have seen, there are numerous applications of the prisoners' dilemma – it is not restricted to prisoners.

## Answers to exercises

3.1

One possibility is the one illustrated in Matrix 3.11:

**Matrix 3.11**

|  |  | player 2 | |
| --- | --- | --- | --- |
|  |  | **cooperate** | **defect** |
| **player 1** | **cooperate** | 6, 6 | 1, <u>8</u> |
|  | **defect** | <u>8</u>, 1 | <u>5, 5</u> |

The game represented in Matrix 3.11 is a prisoners' dilemma because the dominant strategy of both players is to defect yet in the dominant-strategy equilibrium {defect, defect} the players' pay-offs are less than if they had both cooperated.

## 3.2

**Matrix 3.7** International trade 3

|  |  | Little Rosatia | |
| --- | --- | :---: | :---: |
|  |  | **no tariff** | **impose tariff** |
| **Greater Jesmania** | **no tariff** | 10, 10 | -1, 8 |
|  | **impose tariff** | 15, -1 | 2, -2 |

In international trade 3 the dominant-strategy equilibrium is for Little Rosatia not to impose a tariff and for Greater Jesmania to impose a tariff. This suggests that in trading relations between small and large countries tariffs are more likely to be raised by the latter. An example is the tariff wall erected by the EU against agricultural imports from smaller, developing countries as part of its Common Agricultural Policy (CAP).

## Problems

1 In the pay-off matrix below use numbers between –8 and –2 to write pay-offs for Alf and Bert such that {confess, confess} is a dominant-strategy equilibrium but not a Pareto-efficient one. Is the game you have created a prisoners' dilemma? If so explain why and if not explain why not.

|  |  | Bert | |
| --- | --- | :---: | :---: |
|  |  | **hold out** | **confess** |
| **Alf** | **hold out** |  |  |
|  | **confess** |  |  |

2 Imagine that the prisoners playing the prisoner's dilemma game represented in Matrix 3.1.1 (p. 59) have secured the services of a professional hit man in an attempt to enforce an agreement to deny. Show in a pay-off matrix how this could affect the prisoners' pay-offs? Is the game you have constructed still a prisoners' dilemma?

1 Describe three or more examples of prisoners' dilemmas that are faced by real people (acting individually or in groups) in real life.

2 How, if at all, are the prisoners' dilemma problems, described in the examples you have outlined in answer to Problem 1, resolved? If they are not resolved in practice how do you think they might be resolved?

3 In what sense is the Nash equilibrium of the prisoners' dilemma unsatisfactory?

**Answers to problems**

1 The pay-off matrix below shows one possibility. The dominant-strategy equilibrium is {confess, confess} but it is Pareto-dominated by {hold out, hold out}. The game in the matrix is a prisoners' dilemma as the pay-offs satisfy the conditions that $c > a > d > b$ where $c = -2$, $a = -3$, $d = -6$ and $b = -8$.

**Bert**

|  |  | hold out | confess |
|---|---|---|---|
| **Alf** | **hold out** | -3, -3 | -8, -2 |
|  | **confess** | -2, -8 | -6, -6 |

2 Matrix 3.1.1 is shown again below. If the prisoners secured the services of a hit man who agreed, for a fee, to kill a close relative of any one of them who confessed (whether the other confessed or not) the pay-offs could look like those in Matrix 3.1.2. Note that the pay-offs in Matrix 3.1.2 take into account more than the length of the possible prison sentences. They also incorporate how the prisoners' might feel about the death of their relative. I am assuming that this makes them very unhappy. The pay-offs in Matrix 3.1.2 make {deny, deny} the dominant-strategy equilibrium of the game. This is a Pareto-efficient outcome and the game is no longer a prisoners' dilemma even though it is still being played by prisoners.

**Matrix. 3.1.1** Prisoners' dilemma

|  |  | prisoner 2 | |
| --- | --- | --- | --- |
|  |  | deny | confess |
| **prisoner 1** | **deny** | -1, -1 | -10, 0 |
|  | **confess** | 0, -10 | -5, -5 |

**Matrix 3.1.2** Hiring a hit man to resolve the prisoners' dilemma

|  |  | prisoner 2 | |
| --- | --- | --- | --- |
|  |  | deny | confess |
| **prisoner 1** | **deny** | -1, -1 | -10, -100 |
|  | **confess** | -100, -10 | -105, -105 |

## Notes

1   Or the prisoner's dilemma, which one seems to be a matter of personal preference but as there are two prisoners and the dilemma is shared by both, the former representation is used here.

2   For a detailed discussion *see*, for example, Hargreaves Heap (1989) or, specifically in relation to the prisoners' dilemma, Rapoport (1974).

3   The prisoners' dilemma game is attributed either to Tucker (1950) or Flood (1952). *See* Roth (1995a: 87 note 12) for a brief discussion of the origins of the prisoners' dilemma and a review of initial experiments with prisoners' dilemma games. *See* Mirowski (2002: 357–60) for a full discussion.

4   Or collectively rational behaviour which as defined by Rapoport (1974: 18) is behaviour that prescribes a course of action to both players simultaneously. In a prisoners' dilemma collectively rational behaviour would result in both players being better off than if they had acted in their own self-interest that is in accordance with individual rationality.

5   Specifically non-cooperative game theory. The distinction between cooperative and non-cooperative game theory is returned to in Chapter 9.

6   Simply assuming that the players can make agreements that are truly binding changes the game from a non-cooperative one to a cooperative game. Cooperative games of this kind are discussed in Chapter 9. You should try not to confuse the idea of a cooperative game as defined in Chapter 1, Section 1.6 with the idea of cooperation as a strategy option for the players in a prisoner's dilemma as shown in Matrix 3.3.

7   Usually the pay-offs in a prisoners' dilemma are symmetric (the game is the same from the perspective of either player) but a game can still be a prisoners' dilemma even if it is not symmetric. All that is required is that each player's pay-offs satisfy the inequalities $c > a > d > b$ in Matrix 3.2.

8   Or countries as in the case of the oil cartel formed by the Organisation of Petroleum Exporting Countries (OPEC).

9 When firms collude to maximise their joint profits they are effectively acting as a monopoly and are therefore able to extract higher (monopoly) profits from the industry.

10 *See* Hutton (1994: 250–1) for a more general discussion of the prisoners' dilemma and its implications for cooperative behaviour in a market economy.

11 The European Commission made its ruling on 30 October 2002 *see* http://europa.eu.int/comm/archives.

12 If the collusive agreement is one that maintains a high price by restricting output and a large firm raises output by a significant proportion, the consequent fall in the market price could hurt the defector as much as its competitor. In this situation the large firm has no incentive to break the collusive agreement and even though a small firm has, the larger firm may be able and willing to compensate the other in order to sustain the agreement.

13 Or supranational confederations like the European Union.

14 'Fear of trade war after US steel tariffs ruled illegal', Andrew Osborne and David Gow in the *Guardian*, 11 November 2003.

15 Trade implies the exchange of one product for another thus the tariffs imposed by Jesmania and Rosatia would be on different commodities. In reality, unless either Rosatia or Jesmania has a monopoly in one or other of the traded commodities, a tariff imposed by either of them would affect exporters in other countries. For simplicity the pay-offs and strategies of these countries are ignored.

16 Beneficial terms of trade effects can arise when there is a reduction in the price of the imported good as a result of reduced demand due to the tariff. This positive effect is likely to be more significant for larger countries because a fall in import demand in a country like the USA, for instance, is likely to have a greater (downward) influence on world prices than an equivalent fall in a country like Lithuania (*see* the literature on optimal tariffs, e.g. Venables 2003: 412–13).

17 *See* a microeconomics text book such as Pindyck and Rubinfeld (2001: Chapter 18) for a fuller discussion of public goods.

18 Wide-ranging benefits that extend beyond the individual consumer of a good or service (such as education or health) are known as positive externalities. In the case of education and health the benefits of an educated and healthy workforce extend beyond the individual worker to the rest of society. These kinds of benefits are both non-rival and non-excludable.

19 Public goods may also be analysed as a chicken game (Ledyard, 1995: 144–5) or a stag hunt game (Camerer, 2003: 377).

20 *See* an environmental economics text such as Field and Field (2002: Chapter 4) for a more detailed discussion of these issues.

21 Resources like these, with group access rights are often referred to as common property resources.

22 The term was popularised by Hardin (1968).

23 *See* an environmental economics text such as Hanley, Shogren and White (2001: Chapter 7) or Van Kooten and Bulte (2000) for a more detailed analysis of open access resources.

24 If there are more fish in the sea they are easier, quicker and therefore cheaper to catch. As long as prices do not fall in line with costs as catches increase, profits per catch will be higher.

25 *Guardian*, 20 April 2001. For more information *see* the Australian Bureau of Agriculture and Resource Economics web site at www.abare.gov.au/research/fisheries.

26 *See* a labour economics text such as Sapsford and Tzannatos (1993: Chapter 10) or a text on the economics of trade unions such as Booth (1996) for a more detailed discussion of trade union utility functions.

27 *See* www.oft.gov.uk or www.competition-commission.org.uk.

28 Originally Article 85 of the Treaty of Rome. *See*, for example, Martin (2001).

29 Many of the prisoners' dilemma games that subjects are asked to play in experiments are repeated games (*see* Roth, 1995a: 27). This evidence is discussed in Chapter 8.

30 Mirowski (2003: 458) quotes Simon (1982: 2,487–8) who states that 'the main product of the very elegant apparatus of game theory has been to demonstrate quite clearly that it is virtually impossible to define an unambiguous criterion of rationality for this class of situations'.

31 For an introduction to this debate *see*, for example, Frank (2003: Chapters 7 and 8). For a discussion on economic rationality in relation to a specific example *see* Basu (2003: 896–7).

# TAKING TURNS

## Concepts and techniques

- Sequential moves
- Dynamic games
- Subgame perfect Nash equilibrium
- Backward induction
- Credible threats
- Extensive forms, game trees.

After working through this chapter you will be able to:

- Analyse games in which the players move sequentially
- Explain the difference between simultaneous and sequential moves and use extensive forms or game trees to illustrate sequential games
- Explain why moves might not be the same as strategies in dynamic games
- Complete strategic forms for sequential-move games
- Explain what is meant by a credible threat
- Show that sequential games can have Nash equilibria that are not supported by credible threats
- Explain what is implied by backward induction

- Define the concept of a subgame perfect Nash equilibrium
- Use examples to show how to derive a subgame perfect Nash equilibrium in a sequential-move game.

## Introduction

In the games analysed in this chapter one player moves first and the other sees the first player's move before making his or her move. Games where players move sequentially in this way are called sequential-move or dynamic games. In these kinds of games the concept of a Nash equilibrium as defined in Chapter 2 is not sufficient to ensure that players' strategies prescribe moves that are best responses to each other at every decision point in the game. Remember that a player's strategy for a game needs to map out their plan of action, their moves, for the entire game, taking into account all eventualities. Not all the eventualities will actually be realised. Which are, and which are not will depend on the moves of the players in the game. This means that a player's strategy for the game may need to specify moves that are never actually made. Consequently a player can threaten (or promise) to make a move in order to secure a preferred outcome but if the other player takes the threat seriously they will not need to carry the threat out. However, a threat or a promise will only be credible if it would actually be carried out by a rational player if required to do so. A threat will be credible if it would be in a player's best interest to carry it out in these circumstances. If a threat or a promise is not credible in this sense then it cannot be a best response to the other player's move at that particular point in the game. An equilibrium strategy for the whole game needs to specify moves that are best responses at all stages of the game. Therefore, if a threat or a promise involves a move that is not a best response at some decision point in the game it cannot be part of an equilibrium strategy for the whole game.

In dynamic games, Nash equilibria as defined in the previous chapter that incorporate non-credible threats or promises can exist. Therefore the concept of a Nash equilibrium needs to be refined. The analysis in this chapter shows that the idea of a subgame perfect Nash equilibrium is a more appropriate equilibrium concept for games in which the order of moves matters since this refinement of Nash equilibrium rules out strategy combinations that involve non-credible threats. The method of backward induction is used to show this and to determine the subgame perfect Nash equilibrium of the games analysed.

In Sections 4.1 to 4.3 three different games with sequential moves are examined in detail. The concept of a subgame perfect Nash equilibrium is defined and backward induction is used to determine the subgame perfect Nash equilibrium of each game. In Section 4.4 an entry deterrence game is analysed to explore some ideas relating to credibility and in Section 4.5 the centipede game is used to illustrate some of the limitations of the backward induction method.

## 4.1 Foreign direct investment game

The example developed in this section is called foreign direct investment (FDI). It is a variation on the foreign investment game you saw in Chapter 2. In this version of the game the two companies are Alpha and Beta. Alpha moves first and only Alpha is in a position to consider the option of making a foreign direct investment by opening a subsidiary in another country, Jesmania.[1] Alpha is currently exporting to Jesmania and can continue to export for the next 10 years (the expected life of its product) or engage in FDI by opening a subsidiary. Exporting is less costly but leaves Alpha's market share vulnerable to competition. If Alpha opens a subsidiary, by employing Jesmanians and developing links with the Jesmanian community it creates customer loyalty for its product and its market share is more secure. If there is no strategic threat from Beta then Alpha will choose the less costly option of exporting and will not engage in FDI. Alpha's profits when there is no strategic threat are shown in Matrix 4.1 in billions of euros.

**Matrix 4.1** Alpha's profits with no strategic threat from Beta

| | | |
|---|---|---|
| **Alpha's** | FDI | 40 |
| **moves** | export only | 60 |

Beta is not currently exporting but is considering expanding the market for its product by developing an export market in either Jesmania or at home. If it decides to export to Jesmania it will be in direct competition with Alpha and its profits will depend on whether Alpha is exporting or has chosen FDI. If Beta decides to export to Jesmania then Beta's profits will be higher if Alpha has not directly invested in Jesmania. In this case Beta's profits will also be higher than if it doesn't export and simply expands its domestic market. But if Alpha invests directly in Jesmania then Beta cannot compete with Alpha. In these circumstances Beta will incur major costs if it tries to enter the market but will only secure a small market share as a result, making a net loss overall. Therefore when Alpha invests directly in Jesmania, Beta's profits are higher if it doesn't export and instead expands production at home. Beta's pay-offs are shown in billions of euros in Matrix 4.2.

Matrix 4.2  Beta's pay-offs (contingent on Alpha's move)

|  |  | Alpha's moves | |
| --- | --- | --- | --- |
|  |  | FDI | export only |
| Beta's moves | export | -5 | 30 |
|  | not export | 10 | 10 |

If Beta decides to export to Jesmania then Alpha's profits will also be lower. If Alpha is only exporting to Jesmania it has no alternative but to passively share its export market. If it has chosen direct investment then it engages in a costly campaign to retain its monopoly position. This campaign is partially successful in that Alpha remains the market leader in Jesmania but the challenge by Beta weakens its monopoly of the market by opening up the market to domestic and other foreign competition. Alpha's pay-offs if Beta exports to Jesmania are shown in billions of euros in Matrix 4.3. With these pay-offs Alpha still prefers the export only option even if Beta enters the Jesmanian market.

Matrix 4.3  Pay-offs to Alpha if Beta exports to Jesmania

| Alpha's moves | FDI | 25 |
| --- | --- | --- |
|  | export only | 30 |

If the firms moved simultaneously then the pay-off matrix for the game would look like the one in Matrix 4.4. In Matrix 4.4 {export only, export} is the only Nash equilibrium in pure strategies. Export only is a best response for Alpha to Beta's move of exporting to Jesmania and if Alpha only exports to Jesmania then exporting to Jesmania is a best response for Beta. This Nash equilibrium seems to confirm that Alpha will choose the export only strategy regardless of whether there is a competitive threat from Beta or not. However, this way of representing the game ignores the sequence of moves.

Matrix 4.4  Pay-off matrix for FDI with simultaneous moves

|  |  | Beta | |
| --- | --- | --- | --- |
|  |  | export | not export |
| Alpha | FDI | 25, -5 | 40, 10 |
|  | export only | 30, 30 | 60, 10 |

In the FDI game Alpha actually moves first and chooses between FDI and export only. Beta moves last and chooses between exporting to Jesmania or not. But Beta sees Alpha's move and therefore Beta's choice of move is contingent on Alpha's move. This means that there is an important difference between the strategies of Alpha and Beta. Remember that a strategy is a plan for playing a game; it should give a complete description of what a player plans to do during the game and the more complex the game the more detailed a player's plan needs to be.

Because Alpha moves first, its plan for playing the game only needs to specify its preferred choice between FDI and export only. Alpha's available strategies are therefore the same as its available moves: a straight choice between FDI or export only. For Beta the situation is more complex. Beta's plan for the whole game needs to specify moves that are contingent on Alpha's choice. This is easiest to see in the extensive form or game tree for the FDI game shown in Figure 4.1.

In the game tree Alpha moves first at the decision node labelled A and chooses between FDI and export only. If Alpha chooses FDI the game moves to $B_1$ where Beta chooses between export and not export. If Alpha chooses not export at the decision node labelled A the game moves to $B_2$ where again Beta decides between export and not export. The extensive form shows the pay-offs of the firms written at the terminal nodes. It should be clear from the way the game tree is drawn that while Alpha simply chooses between FDI and export only Beta's choices are more complicated. A strategy for Beta needs to specify a choice at both $B_1$ and $B_2$ as Beta can't be sure before Alpha moves what Alpha will choose; Beta needs to have a full set of contingency plans.

More specifically, a strategy for Beta needs to specify what Beta's move should be if Alpha chooses FDI and what it should be if Alpha chooses export only. Because a strategy for Beta needs to map out a plan for all eventualities Beta actually has four possible strategies from which to choose:

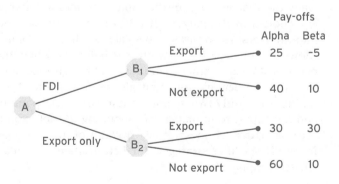

**Figure 4.1** Extensive form or game tree for FDI

1 Export to Jesmania whatever Alpha does (export, export).

2 Not export to Jesmania whatever Alpha does (not export, not export).

3 Export if Alpha chooses FDI and not export if Alpha chooses export only (export, not export).

4 Not export if Alpha chooses FDI and export if Alpha chooses export only (not export, export).

If you are finding it difficult to understand why Beta has four strategies instead of two, imagine that the boss of Beta has to go into hospital for an operation and leaves her deputy in charge of the firm. Alpha is expected to make its decision about whether to undertake FDI while Beta's boss is in hospital. Beta's boss wants to leave her deputy with precise instructions about what to do in response to Alpha's choice when Alpha makes it. She writes down her chosen strategy to cover all contingencies and expects the deputy to carry out her instructions precisely. If she writes down simply export or not export, the deputy will either export or not export whatever Alpha does. Simply writing export or not export corresponds to export whatever Alpha does and not export whatever Alpha does, that is (export, export) and (not export, not export). If Beta's boss wants to do anything different then she will have to be more specific. For example, if she wants Beta to export if Alpha chooses FDI but not export if Alpha chooses export only then she can write this down as (export, not export). Alternatively, if she wants Beta to not export if Alpha chooses FDI but export if Alpha chooses export only, then she can write this as (not export, export) as shown. Thus Beta's boss needs to write down one of four possible strategies.

In Matrix 4.4 the pay-offs correspond only to the firms' moves and for Beta these are not the same as its fully defined strategies. In dynamic games where one player's moves are conditional on another's this will always be the case and therefore a pay-off matrix corresponding to moves – a move matrix – is not really the strategic form of the game as it does not accurately depict the strategy choices of the players. It follows that any Nash equilibrium found by indicating best responses to moves alone is likely to be misspecified. Matrix 4.5 shows the fully specified pay-off matrix for FDI where the players' choices are between strategies rather than moves (although these are the same for Alpha). In Matrix 4.5 Beta has four strategies from which to choose while in the move matrix it has only two: export to Jesmania corresponding to (export, export) and not export to Jesmania corresponding to (not export, not export). This is because Matrix 4.4 does not take account of the sequence of moves and therefore only specifies strategies for Beta that involve making the same move whatever Alpha does.

**Matrix 4.5** Strategic form for FDI with sequential moves

**Beta**

|  |  | export, export | not export, not export | export, not export | not export, export |
|---|---|---|---|---|---|
| **Alpha** | **FDI** | 25, –5 | 40, 10 | 25, –5 | 40, 10 |
|  | **export only** | 30, 30 | 60, 10 | 60, 10 | 30, 30 |

### Exercise 4.1

Use the underlining (or equivalent) method to identify two Nash equilibria in Matrix 4.5 where the strategies of Beta are now fully specified.

The two Nash equilibria in Matrix 4.5 are {export only, (export, export)} and {FDI, (not export, export)}. In the first of these, Beta chooses export whatever Alpha chooses and Alpha chooses export only. In the second equilibrium Beta chooses not export if Alpha chooses FDI and export if Alpha chooses export only. As Alpha chooses FDI, Beta chooses not export. The first Nash equilibrium corresponds to the Nash equilibrium found in the simple moves matrix: {export only, export}. The second Nash equilibrium is not represented in the moves matrix. Can you see that the second Nash equilibrium, {FDI, (not export, export)}, is preferred by Alpha while the first is preferred by Beta? In the second Nash equilibrium Alpha's pay-off is 40, in the first it is only 30. In the first Nash equilibrium Beta's pay-off is 30, in the second it is only 10.

You should also be able to see that in the strategic form different strategies by Beta can lead to the same combination of moves and pay-offs for both players depending on what Alpha does. For example, {FDI, (export, export)} and {FDI (export, not export)} both result in Alpha undertaking FDI and Beta exporting. This gives Alpha a pay-off of 25 and Beta a pay-off of –5. Beta's strategies are different but the outcome is the same. This is one reason why it is important to think about an equilibrium in terms of the players' strategies rather than their pay-offs since the same pay-offs can result from different strategy pairs.

Now take a look at the two Nash equilibria that have been identified in the strategic form of the game. Do you think that both are equally feasible? Or do you think that either or both of them could embody moves that are not credible because they are not best, that is Nash responses to a move by the other player at some point in the game? In game theory this question is answered by identifying whether the Nash equilibria are also subgame perfect Nash equilibria. By definition, the players' strategies in a subgame perfect Nash equilibrium specify moves that are best responses at all the decision points or nodes in the game.

To find a subgame perfect Nash equilibrium for this game we can use backward induction.[2] Backward induction is used to choose between multiple Nash equilibria by checking that the players' moves are best responses to each other at every decision node. This process often amounts to checking the credibility of threats. To use backward induction start at an end point or terminal node of the game in its extensive form and work back through the game analysing subsets or subgames of the whole game independently. A subgame is a subset of the whole game that starts at some decision node where there is no uncertainty[3] and branches out from that node. Subgames end at nodes that are terminal nodes of the whole game.[4] In the FDI game there are two proper subgames: the subgame beginning at $B_1$ in Figure 4.1 and the subgame beginning at $B_2$. After identifying the subgames you can check if the players' strategies specify moves that are best responses in every subgame. If they are not, then a player's threat or promise to make such a move is not credible so can be ignored. Only threats or promises that are in a player's self-interest are credible. (If you are still unsure about the idea of a subgame you can test your understanding in Problem 1 at the end of this chapter.)

---

### A subgame

- A piece of a game that begins at a decision point where there is no uncertainty and ends at decision nodes that are terminal nodes of the whole game.

---

For a Nash equilibrium to be subgame perfect it has to specify a combination of credible moves in every subgame: moves that are best responses at every decision node. In the actual equilibrium that is played out some decision nodes will not be reached. Such nodes are said to be off the equilibrium path of the game. But players still need to specify their moves at these points as threatened actions off the equilibrium path influence other players' strategy choices on it. In a subgame perfect Nash equilibrium any threat to follow a given strategy, in order to enforce a particular strategy choice by other players, needs to be credible. To be credible a threat must be in a player's best interest to carry out if called upon to do so.[5] Backward induction involves working back through the game checking that the players' strategies specify moves that constitute a Nash equilibrium in every subgame. If the players' strategies are best responses in every subgame then they are playing rationally by acting in their own self-interest throughout the game.

> ## Subgame perfect Nash equilibrium
>
> ● A combination of strategies that yield a Nash equilibrium in every subgame, whether these subgames are reached in equilibrium or not. If players' strategies constitute a Nash equilibrium in every subgame they specify moves that are best responses to each other in every subgame.

## 4.1.1 Using backward induction to find the subgame perfect Nash equilibrium of the FDI game

In the FDI game there are two proper subgames: the subgame beginning at $B_1$ in Figure 4.1 and the subgame beginning at $B_2$. Using backward induction in this case means working back from the terminal nodes to the subgames beginning at $B_1$ and $B_2$ and checking that Beta's strategy specifies moves that are best responses to Alpha's move.[6] We can check each subgame in turn.

*The subgame beginning at $B_1$*

In order to have reached the subgame beginning at $B_1$ Alpha must have chosen FDI. At $B_1$ Beta chooses between export and not export. If Beta chooses not export Beta's pay-off is 10. If Beta chooses export Beta's pay-off is –5.

Consequently, not exporting is Beta's best response at $B_1$ to FDI by Alpha and exporting is not a best response. It is not rational for Beta to choose export if Alpha chooses FDI because by exporting Beta's pay-off is less than it would be if it chose not to export to Jesmania. Therefore if Alpha chooses FDI and Beta is rational, Beta will choose not export, as not exporting is a best response to FDI by Alpha. This means that any threat by Beta to export if Alpha chooses FDI is not credible. Because Beta's pay-offs are common knowledge Alpha knows this. It follows that Alpha knows that if it chooses FDI its pay-off will be 40. We can illustrate this in the game tree by highlighting the relevant branches of the tree as I have done in Figure 4.1.1. In Figure 4.1.1 the thickened branches show that if Alpha chooses FDI Beta's best response at $B_1$ is not to export.

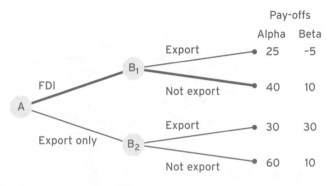

**Figure 4.1.1** Beta's best response at $B_1$

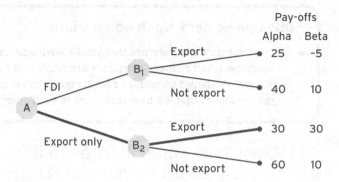

**Figure 4.1.2** Beta's best response at B₂

## The subgame beginning at B₂

In order for the game to have reached B₂ Alpha must have chosen export only. At B₂ Beta chooses between export and not export. If Beta chooses export Beta's pay-off is 30. If Beta chooses not export Beta's pay-off is 10.

At B₂ choosing export is a rational response to Alpha's move. By exporting Beta's pay-off is 30 and otherwise it is only 10. Therefore Beta will choose export at B₂ and Alpha's pay-off will be 30. Alpha knows this and so can predict that if it chooses export only its pay-off will be 30. This is indicated in Figure 4.1.2 where the thickened branches show that if Alpha chooses not export Beta's best response at B₂ is to export.

The backward induction procedure shows that Beta's best response at B₁ is not export and at B₂ it is export. This implies that (not export, export) is Beta's only rational strategy. Only this strategy can be part of a subgame perfect Nash equilibrium and we can rule out all Beta's other alternatives. This is shown in Figure 4.1.3 where the thickened branches show Beta's best responses at each of Beta's decision nodes.

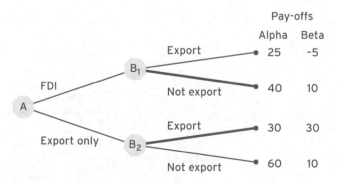

**Figure 4.1.3** Beta's best responses at B₁ and B₂

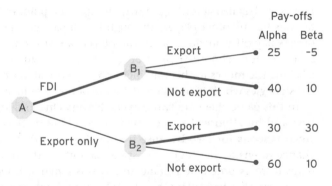

**Figure 4.1.4** Alpha's best response to (not export, export) by Beta

### Alpha's choice at A

Having analysed Beta's choices it is now possible to work back from $B_1$ or $B_2$ to the beginning of the game where Alpha is choosing between FDI and export only. Common knowledge means that Alpha knows that if it chooses FDI Beta will choose not export and Alpha's pay-off will be 40 (following the thickened branch from $B_1$ in Figure 4.1.3). But if Alpha chooses export only Beta will choose to export as well and Alpha's pay-off will only be 30 (following the thickened branch from $B_2$ in Figure 4.1.3). Thus FDI is a best response by Alpha to Beta's only credible strategy of (not export, export). This implies that the only subgame perfect Nash equilibrium of the FDI game is {FDI, (not export, export)}as illustrated by the thickened branches in Figure 4.1.4.

{FDI, (not export, export)} is the only Nash equilibrium in which Beta's strategy specifies moves that are best responses in both subgames. It is therefore the only subgame perfect Nash equilibrium of the game. This is Alpha's preferred Nash equilibrium outcome and Beta's least preferred. It appears that in this game Alpha has a first-mover advantage since Alpha's costly FDI strategy deters Beta from entering the Jesmanian market. Alpha's commitment to FDI is rational as Beta's implicit threat to export if Alpha commits to FDI is not credible.

In the next section a more abstract dynamic game is examined in order to highlight a number of different possibilities in games like FDI. In Sections 4.3 and 4.4 further examples are examined. The structure of these games is different but the method for finding the subgame perfect Nash equilibrium by ruling out non-credible threats or promises is the same.

## 4.2  Nice–not so nice game[7]

In this section we examine another sequential move game. It is similar to the FDI game in that there are two players and one moves first. However, the players' moves are labelled according to whether they are potentially more or less advantageous for the other player. Although the impact of one player's choice on the other's pay-off is made explicit, the players are still rational and self-interested and therefore choose their strategies in their own best interests. However, labelling the moves in this way highlights the threat–promise nature of the players' strategies which is an inherent feature of many sequential move games.

In this game there are two players: Players One and Two. Player One moves first and he chooses between two moves. One of these is potentially more advantageous for Two because if One chooses this move Two will have the chance to ensure her highest possible pay-off (in the discussion that follows it helps if we assume One is male and Two is female). If One chooses this move we can say that he is being nice to Two and if he does not then he is being not so nice to Two. Thus he has a choice between two moves: nice (to Two) and not nice (to Two). Two moves second after seeing One's move. Whether One has chosen his nice strategy or not Two makes a choice between two moves one of which is relatively more advantageous for One. Thus Two similarly chooses between a nice (to One) and a not so nice (to One) move. Although the impact of one player's move on the other's possible pay-off is common knowledge neither player cares about the other's pay-off, only their own. To summarise, One moves first and chooses between nice and not so nice. Two sees One's move and chooses between nice and not so nice.

Because One moves first, his strategies correspond to his moves as he has a simple choice between nice and not so nice. Because Two moves after One her strategies are more complex as they are contingent on One's move. Two has four possible strategies:

1  (nice, nice): always choose nice.

2  (not so nice, not so nice): always choose not so nice.

3  (nice, not so nice): choose nice if One chooses nice; choose not so nice if One chooses not so nice.

4  (not so nice, nice): choose not so nice if One chooses nice; choose nice if one chooses not so nice.

The extensive form for this version of nice–not so nice is shown in Figure 4.2. The fully specified pay-off matrix is shown in Matrix 4.6.

The extensive form shows clearly that there is conflict in this game. Two would prefer One to choose nice at decision node 1 so that she can secure her maximum pay-off of 6. However, One achieves his maximum pay-off of 5 by choosing not so nice as long as Two chooses nice at $2_B$. But Two may be able to deter One from choosing not so nice by threatening to choose not so nice at $2_B$ and by promising to choose nice if One also chooses nice. But is this threat and promise strategy by Two credible?

**Matrix 4.6** Strategic form for nice–not so nice 1

<table>
<tr><td></td><td></td><td colspan="4" align="center">**Two**</td></tr>
<tr>
<td></td>
<td></td>
<td>**nice, nice**</td>
<td>**not so nice, not so nice**</td>
<td>**nice, not so nice**</td>
<td>**not so nice, nice**</td>
</tr>
<tr>
<td rowspan="2">**One**</td>
<td>**nice**</td>
<td>2, 6</td>
<td>–1, 0</td>
<td>2, 6</td>
<td>–1, 0</td>
</tr>
<tr>
<td>**not so nice**</td>
<td>5, 2</td>
<td>–6, 3</td>
<td>–6, 3</td>
<td>5, 2</td>
</tr>
</table>

An examination of the strategic form in Matrix 4.6 shows that {nice, (nice, not so nice)} is the only Nash equilibrium of the game (you should check this by highlighting the best response pay-offs of both players). But is {nice, (nice, not so nice)} also a subgame perfect Nash equilibrium?

To answer this question we can use backward induction to work back from the terminal nodes in Figure 4.2 to the subgames beginning at $2_A$ and $2_B$. By doing this we can check whether (nice, not so nice) is potentially a subgame perfect Nash equilibrium strategy for Two. At $2_A$ Two's pay-off is 6 if she chooses nice and 0 otherwise. Since 6 > 0 nice is her best response to One's choice of nice at decision node 1. At $2_B$ Two's pay-off is 2 if she chooses nice and 3 otherwise. Since 3 > 2 her best response to One's choice of not so nice is to similarly choose not so nice. This implies that (nice, not so nice) is entirely rational for Two and I have highlighted the corresponding branches of the game tree in Figure 4.2.1.

Since (nice, not so nice) is a rational strategy for Two her threat to play not so nice if One chooses not so nice is credible and her promise to play nice if One chooses nice can also be trusted. If we can work this out so can One. One will assume that if he chooses nice at decision node 1 his pay-off will be 2. If he chooses not so nice his pay-off will be –6. Therefore One will choose nice. One's choice of nice is a best response to (nice, not so nice) by Two and therefore {nice (nice, not so nice)}, the Nash equilibrium identified in the strategic form, is the only subgame perfect Nash equilibrium of the game. The subgame perfect Nash equilibrium defines the players' moves through the game along the equilibrium path as illustrated in Figure 4.2.2 by the thickened branches.

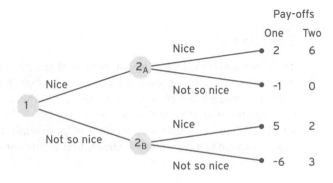

**Figure 4.2** Extensive form for nice–not so nice 1

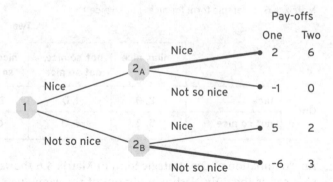

**Figure 4.2.1** Two's best responses

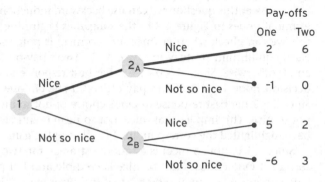

**Figure 4.2.2** The equilibrium path of nice–not so nice 1

Because Two's threat to play not so nice at $2_B$ is a credible threat, Two does not actually have to play not so nice in the equilibrium. One chooses nice and decision node $2_B$ is never reached. But Two's threat to play not so nice at $2_B$ is still part of her equilibrium strategy and it induces One's choice of nice. This shows how threatened moves off the equilibrium path can support a subgame perfect Nash equilibrium but to do so they need to be credible.

### Exercise 4.2

The extensive form of a different version of the nice–not so nice game, nice–not so nice 2, is shown in Figure 4.2.3. What is the subgame perfect Nash equilibrium of nice–not so nice 2? In this version of the game is Two's threat to play not so nice at $2_B$ credible? If so, why, and if not, why not? Does One gain any advantage by moving first in this game? Did One gain any advantage by moving first in nice–not so nice 1?

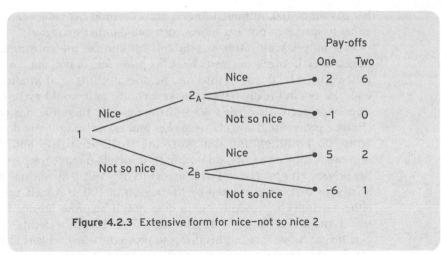

**Figure 4.2.3** Extensive form for nice–not so nice 2

## 4.3 Trespass

The two players in this game are a landowner, Bert, and a hiker, Angela. Bert owns some land by a river in a beautiful part of the English countryside. Angela likes to ramble in the countryside and would like to walk through Bert's land beside the river instead of walking along the tarmac road around Bert's land. Bert doesn't want walkers on his land and he moves first by putting up a large sign threatening to prosecute trespassers who come onto his land. Angela sees the sign and chooses between trespassing on Bert's land or not. If she defers to Bert's threat by not walking over his land he is satisfied but she is not. If she doesn't cross his land Bert doesn't prosecute, he effectively does nothing except perhaps smugly repaint his sign. If Angela challenges his threat to prosecute by crossing Bert's land Bert then has to choose between carrying out his threat to prosecute or not. If he prosecutes the law is such that if Angela has merely walked over his land he loses – in England there is no criminal law against trespassing unless the trespasser commits criminal damage of some kind. Assuming Angela doesn't commit any criminal damage, the whole procedure will be a waste of time and money for both of them. The players' pay-offs for this game are shown in Matrix 4.7.

If Angela is deterred by Bert's threat and chooses not trespass she loses the respect of other walkers including her friends in the rambling club and has feelings of inadequacy. This is represented by her pay-off of –10. If she decides to trespass on Bert's land and Bert prosecutes, she is greatly inconvenienced even if she doesn't end up losing in court. This possibility is represented by her pay-off of –100. If Bert doesn't prosecute she is personally satisfied and also wins respect from other hikers who are likely to follow her example. This is represented by her pay-off of 100. Although Angela moves second her choices are simple. She either trespasses or not; her moves correspond to her strategies.

Bert moves again after Angela and his choices are contingent on what Angela does. If Angela trespasses he either prosecutes or not. But if Angela doesn't trespass then he doesn't prosecute, he does nothing, and in effect the game ends. He doesn't really have to make a choice as it would make no sense for him to prosecute if Angela doesn't trespass. He therefore has two strategy choices: prosecute if Angela trespasses and do nothing if she doesn't, (prosecute, do nothing), and not prosecute if she trespasses and do nothing otherwise, (not prosecute, do nothing). If Angela doesn't trespass Bert retains his privacy and his control over access to his land. This satisfactory state of affairs for Bert is represented by his pay-off of 100. If Angela trespasses Bert either attempts to prosecute her or does not. If he prosecutes he is doomed to failure and this is represented by his pay-off of –100. If he decides not to prosecute he just looses face but his threat to prosecute other walkers in the future is considerably weakened. This is represented by his pay-off of –10.

**Matrix 4.7** Strategic form for trespass

|  |  | Angela | |
| --- | --- | --- | --- |
|  |  | **trespass** | **not trespass** |
| **Bert** | **prosecute, do nothing** | -100, -100 | 100, -10 |
|  | **not prosecute, do nothing** | -10, 100 | 100, -10 |

In Matrix 4.7 the best responses of the players are identified by underlining the corresponding pay-offs. Two Nash equilibria are identified:

- Nash equilibrium (1): {(not prosecute, do nothing), trespass}.

- Nash equilibrium (2): {(prosecute, do nothing), not trespass}.

The first of these is preferred by Angela (she trespasses but Bert doesn't prosecute) and the second by Bert (Angela doesn't trespass). The second Nash equilibrium is supported by Bert's threat to prosecute if Angela trespasses. But is this threat credible? We can answer this question by checking whether either of the two Nash equilibria are subgame perfect. The extensive form of the game is shown in Figure 4.3. Bert moves first by putting up his 'trespassers will be prosecuted' sign. Angela then decides whether to trespass or not at A. If she does Bert decides between prosecution or not at $B_1$. If she doesn't trespass the game moves to $B_2$ and Bert does nothing.

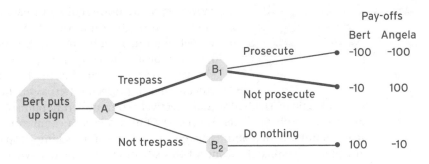

**Figure 4.3** Extensive form for trespass

To check whether either of the Nash equilibria identified in the strategic form is also subgame perfect we can use backward induction to work back to Bert's decision node at $B_1$ (we know that at $B_2$ he does nothing). Nash equilibrium (1) is {(not prosecute, do nothing), trespass}. In this equilibrium Bert doesn't prosecute at $B_1$. This is a rational response for Bert. His pay-off is $-10$ if he doesn't prosecute but $-100$ if he does.

Nash equilibrium (2) is {(prosecute, do nothing), not trespass}. In this equilibrium Bert prosecutes if Angela trespasses. However, Bert's threat to prosecute is not tested as Angela is deterred from trespassing. But as we have seen Bert's pay-offs mean that prosecuting is not a best response for him if Angela does trespass. Therefore the threat to prosecute by Bert is not credible; it is an empty threat. With common knowledge Angela can work this out so she will not be deterred by Bert's threat. Instead she will trespass on Bert's land. By trespassing she receives a pay-off of 100 but if she doesn't trespass her pay-off is $-10$. Because Bert's threat to prosecute is not credible only Nash equilibrium (1), {(not prosecute, do nothing), trespass}, is subgame perfect. The path of this equilibrium is indicated by the thickened branches in Figure 4.3.

The analysis of trespass shows how the concept of a subgame perfect Nash equilibrium rules out outcomes supported by empty threats – in this case the threat by Bert to prosecute. There are other empty threat situations that can be modelled as games. For instance, the threat by an employee to resign from his job if he is not given a rise is likely to be an empty one in a recession or when there are no other employers looking for his particular skills in the locality. Similarly the threat by a union to strike may not be credible if the union has only limited strike funds. The threat by a wife to leave her husband (or vice versa) may also be empty if she (or he) has nowhere else to go (*see* Chapter 9, Section 3). On the international stage the threat to invade a country may not be credible if the decision makers of the invading force are divided.

 However, some non-credible threats can be made credible through commitment. You will see this modelled formally in the next section but in trespass Bert may be able to commit to punishing Angela if she trespasses by changing his threat. Instead of threatening to prosecute trespassers he could put a bull in his field. The bull would effectively commit Bert to punishing trespassers and would probably deter Angela. The bull works as a commitment as the bull itself is not worried about the consequences of attacking trespassers so will attack indiscriminately. Contrast this situation with the one where Bert himself ups the ante by threatening to shoot trespassers. The law in a country like the UK is unlikely to make this a best response[8] and therefore it would not be a credible threat.

## 4.4 Entry deterrence

The structure of the entry deterrence game considered here is very similar to that of trespass. However the question of entry deterrence in relation to market structure and competition policy has been considered in depth in the industrial organisation literature and has wider implications.[9] The two players in the entry deterrence game are an incumbent monopolist and a firm that is a potential entrant into the monopolist's market. The entrant chooses between entering the market or not. The entrant will enter the market if by doing so it can make positive profits. If the entrant enters the market the monopolist will no longer be in a monopoly position and consequently its profits will be lower. The monopolist tries to deter entry by threatening to fight entry should it occur by engaging in some kind of aggressive market action.[10] For example, the monopolist may threaten to engage in an expensive advertising war or refuse to share the market by maintaining output. The latter action, sometimes called predatory pricing, would mean that prices would fall if the entrant entered and if they fell low enough this could prevent the entrant from making positive profits. Whatever strategy it threatens to adopt it will be costly for the monopolist as well as the entrant. Three questions are raised by this game. First of all, is the threat to fight entry by the monopolist a credible threat? Second, will it deter entry? Lastly, if the threat to fight doesn't deter entry is there a way for the monopolist to make the threat to fight credible? We will try to answer each of these questions using game theory.

To model this game we can make some simplifying assumptions about the market. Let's assume that the total market is worth 10 to the monopolist and if the monopolist concedes to the entrant by sharing, each firm's pay-off is 5. If the monopolist fights entry both make negative profits of −1. If the entrant doesn't enter its pay-off is zero. The entrant moves first and decides between entry and staying out of the market. If the entrant enters the monopolist decides between fighting entry and conceding by sharing the market. If the entrant stays out the monopolist does nothing – in effect the game ends. The monopolist has two strategies: concede if the entrant enters and do nothing otherwise (concede, do nothing) and fight if the entrant enters and do nothing otherwise (fight, do nothing). These pay-offs and strategies are shown in the strategic form in Matrix 4.8. In Matrix 4.8 the pay-offs corresponding to the best responses of both players to each other's strategies are underlined.

**Matrix 4.8** Strategic form of the entry deterrence game

|  |  | monopolist | |
|---|---|---|---|
|  |  | concede, do nothing | fight, do nothing |
| entrant | enter | <u>5</u>, <u>5</u> | -1, -1 |
|  | stay out | 0, <u>10</u> | <u>0</u>, <u>10</u> |

There are two Nash equilibria in this game. They are:

- Nash equilibrium (1): {enter, (concede, do nothing)}.

- Nash equilibrium (2): {stay out, (fight, do nothing)}.

In Nash equilibrium (1) the monopolist concedes if the entrant enters and the entrant duly enters. In Nash equilibrium (2) the monopolist fights if there is entry and therefore the entrant stays out. Nash equilibrium (1) is preferred by the entrant. The monopolist prefers Nash equilibrium (2) which is sustained by the threat to fight entry. To check whether either of these Nash equilibria are subgame perfect we need to examine the extensive form of the game. This is shown in Figure 4.4. In the game tree the entrant decides whether to enter or not at decision node E. If the entrant enters the monopolist decides between fighting and conceding at $M_1$.

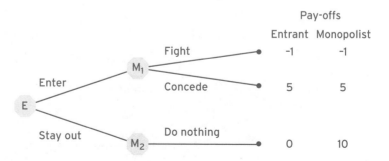

**Figure 4.4** Extensive form of the entry deterrence game

At $M_1$ the monopolist's best response is to concede; by conceding the monopolist's pay-off is 5 but it is –1 if the monopolist fights. Therefore conceding is a best response by the monopolist to entry. The entrant's pay-off from not entering the market is zero. Since the monopolist concedes if there is entry the entrant's pay-off from entry is 5. The entrant will therefore enter at E. This means that only Nash equilibrium (1), {enter, (concede, do nothing)}, incorporates moves that are best responses by the players at all the decision points in the game. In Nash equilibrium (2) the entrant is deterred from entry by the monopolist's threat to fight at $M_1$. But fighting at $M_1$ is not a credible threat and therefore Nash equilibrium (2) is not subgame perfect. Because the threat to fight is not credible only Nash equilibrium (1) is subgame perfect. Figure 4.4.1 highlights the equilibrium path through entry deterrence; at E the entrant enters and at $M_1$ the monopolist concedes.

## 4.4.1  Making the threat to fight credible

The theoretical prediction following from the analysis of the game represented in Figure 4.4.1 is that the entrant will always enter and the monopolist will always concede. In the first paragraph of the previous section three questions were posed in relation to this game. The theoretical prediction suggests that the answer to the first two is no: the threat to fight is not credible and entry will not be deterred. But what about the third question? Is there any way to make the threat to fight credible? In this subsection we consider the possibility that the monopolist is able to invest in some commitment to fight which can do just that. Such a commitment could take the form of a non-recoverable or sunk cost that makes fighting optimal but has no benefit for the monopolist otherwise (Dixit, 1980 and 1981). For example, the monopolist could invest in excess capacity. An investment of this sort would only be useful to the monopolist in the event of entry. If the entrant entered the monopolist could increase output at minimal cost. This would lower prices and reduce the profits of the potential entrant. Alternatively, it could invest in goodwill or generating customer loyalty. With a strong customer base the monopolist could confidently start an

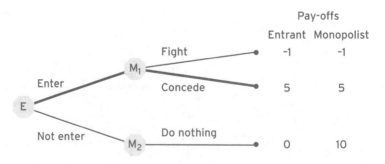

**Figure 4.4.1** Equilibrium path through entry deterrence

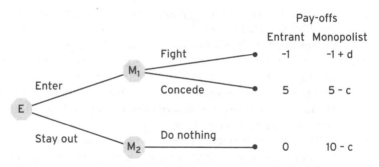

**Figure 4.4.2** Extensive form of entry deterrence with commitment

advertising war in the event of entry.[11] Making this kind of commitment would alter the monopolist's pay-offs. We can model this by assuming that the commitment costs c but generates net benefits of d if there is entry and the monopolist fights. The extensive form of the entry deterrence game with these changes is shown in Figure 4.4.2.

Using backward induction to work back to the decision node at $M_1$ we can see that if the entrant enters the monopolist will fight entry if condition (4.1) holds:

$$-1 + d > 5 - c \tag{4.1}$$

If condition (4.1) holds the pay-off to the monopolist from fighting $(-1 + d)$ is greater than the pay-off from conceding $(5 - c)$. As a result, fighting is a best response for the monopolist. This makes the threat to fight credible since it is in the monopolist's self-interest to carry out the threat of fighting if entry occurs. In these circumstances the entrant will stay out and the monopolist's pay-off will be $10 - c$. Depending on c this may be less than the monopolist's pay-off of 5 from concession in the game without commitment. Since the monopolist concedes if no commitment is made, it is only worthwhile for the monopolist to make the costly commitment if condition (4.2) also holds:

$$10 - c > 5 \tag{4.2}$$

The commitment should only be made if both conditions (4.1) and (4.2) are satisfied. If condition (4.1) is satisfied the commitment deters entry and if condition (4.2) is also satisfied the cost of deterring entry is worth paying. Combining conditions (4.1) and (4.2) leads to condition (4.3):

$$5 > c > 6 - d \tag{4.3}$$

If condition (4.3) is satisfied then fighting is credible and the commitment that makes it credible is worth investing in. In these circumstances {stay out, (fight, do nothing)} is not only a Nash equilibrium but also a subgame perfect Nash equilibrium. This shows that in some circumstances (where condition (4.3) or its equivalent is satisfied) a monopolist may be able to invest in a commitment to fighting that makes the threat to fight credible and thereby deters entry. So the answer to the question 'can the threat to fight be made credible?' is a qualified yes. And as we shall see in Chapter 7 if there is uncertainty about the monopolist's pay-offs the monopolist may not actually need to make the costly commitment in order to deter entry.

The entry deterrence game is another classic game in game theory. In some form or other it invariably appears in textbook introductions to game theory and in economic analyses of imperfect competition in product markets. It will appear without fail in courses in industrial economics or industrial organisation and will very probably make an appearance in courses in managerial and business economics. The game's defining characteristics are that (i) moves are made sequentially, (ii) one player makes a threat in order to deter some action by a second player, and (iii) the action in question is potentially advantageous to the second player but damaging to the first. Games with these characteristics have many applications outside the theory of industrial organisation. Applications hinge around the question of whether a player's threat is credible and therefore deters the relevant action of the other. Trespass and the FDI game (where Beta implicitly threatens to export if Alpha undertakes FDI) are both games with this kind of structure. There are other examples that we could examine. For example, a union's threat to strike in support of a wage demand (*see* Problem 3 at the end of this chapter) or one person's threat to sue another could be analysed using the methodology of this section.

In the examples we have looked at in this chapter most of the threats made were not credible; nice–not so nice 1 was an exception in this respect. However, you have seen that players may be able to make their threats credible by investing in some commitment to carry out the threat. For example, in the FDI game Beta could make a commitment to export (possibly by investing in capacity). This could deter Alpha from making the direct foreign investment. In wage negotiations a union could make the threat to strike credible by holding and winning a pre-strike vote. But for a commitment of this kind to be made the potential gains must outweigh the costs.

## 4.5 Centipede games

In this section we look at a family of games commonly called centipede games (because of the way they are represented diagrammatically (*see* Figure 4.5.2) and some questions will be raised about the backward induction method. For a more detailed discussion of centipede games[12] and the implications of these games for backward induction and subgame perfect Nash equilibrium see the analysis in Kreps (1993: 110–11) on which this section draws or Rosenthal (1981).

Take a look at the extensive form of the baby centipede game in Figure 4.5. In baby centipede there are two players, A and B. A moves first at $A_1$ and decides between down (D) and right (R). If A chooses down the game ends and both players receive a pay-off of 3. If A chooses right then B chooses between down (d) and right (r). If B chooses down the game ends and A receives a pay-off of 10 and B's pay-off is 0. If B chooses right then A chooses again between down and right at A2. If A chooses down A's pay-off is 1 and B's pay-off is –10. If A chooses right A's pay-off is 2 and B's pay-off is 1.

Working back from the end of the game A's best option at $A_2$ is to choose right. Anticipating this B will choose (r). In further anticipation of B's move A should choose down at $A_1$. Thus the subgame perfect Nash equilibrium is that A chooses D at the start of the game as A anticipates that B would choose r given the chance and therefore the most A can hope for by choosing right at $A_1$ is 2. The only reason for A to choose right at $A_1$ would be if A expected B to choose down but if B expects A to choose right at $A_2$ then B has no reason to choose down. Therefore if both players are rational and believe the other to be the same the game will end at $A_1$. Given the pay-offs this subgame perfect Nash equilibrium doesn't appear unduly problematic.

Now consider the mini-centipede game in Figure 4.5.1. Does this centipede game look familiar? It should do. From A's decision node at $A_2$ mini-centipede is the same as baby centipede. Knowing this you should be able to work out that the subgame perfect Nash equilibrium of mini-centipede still has A choosing down, D, at the start. This is because A anticipates that B would choose r at $B_1$ given the chance, in the further anticipation that A will choose D at $A_2$ (A's subgame perfect Nash equilibrium move in baby centipede). In other words A doesn't expect B to choose d at $B_1$ which would be a reason for A to choose right instead of down. However, the extra complexity in mini-centipede makes this subgame perfect Nash equilibrium somewhat less intuitive than that of baby centipede. To see this ask yourself what would B think if instead of choosing down at the start of the game A chose right (R)? Would B still be as confident that A would choose down at $A_2$? Maybe not. And if not could B rely on A choosing right at $A_3$? If B has any doubts about A's future moves then B could choose down at $B_1$ if A chooses right at $A_1$. If A attaches a high probability[13] to this possibility then it would be entirely rational for A to choose right at $A_1$.

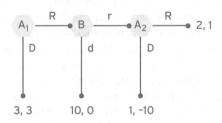

**Figure 4.5** Baby-centipede

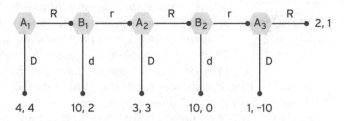

Figure 4.5.1 Mini-centipede

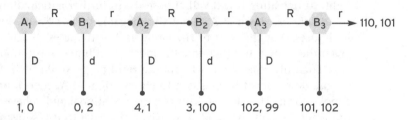

Figure 4.5.2 Centipede game

This kind of reasoning weakens the prediction that A will choose down at the start of the game. Now consider a more standard representation of the centipede game in Figure 4.5.2.

 Working backwards from the end of the centipede game you should find that once again the subgame perfect Nash equilibrium move for A is to choose D from the start. But this equilibrium is clearly Pareto inefficient. Both players would be better off if the game moved beyond B's first decision point at $B_1$ with B choosing right. And what should B think if A chooses R at $A_1$? Has A made a mistake or has A deviated with a purpose, and if so what purpose? Can B rely on A choosing R again at $A_2$? If A could be relied on to choose R at $A_2$ this would give B an incentive to choose r at $B_1$ in which case both A and B could benefit by B choosing r at $B_2$. The possibility of A choosing R at $A_1$, even if by mistake, suggests that a completely different outcome for the game is possible, one in which both players are potentially much better off. Consequently, the subgame perfect Nash equilibrium may not be the best prediction of this game. This possibility suggests that there are some limitations of the subgame perfect Nash equilibrium concept and the backward induction method. Experimental evidence tends to support this conclusion. A typical finding is that subjects rarely choose the equivalent of down (take in experiments) straightaway. However, the observed probability of choosing down (or take) does tend to rise as the game progresses, and perhaps surprisingly when the stakes are higher (*see*, for example, McKelvey and Palfrey, 1992 or Camerer, 2003: 94–5, 218–21 for a summary of this evidence).

## Summary

In this chapter you have seen how dynamic or sequential-move games are modelled. Five games were analysed in detail: the FDI game, nice–not so nice, trespass, entry deterrence and the centipede game. You saw how there is not always a one-to-one correspondence between a player's moves and strategies in sequential-move games. If one player moves after another, their moves are contingent on the moves of the other player. The strategies of the player will therefore need to allow for all eventualities. This means that players' strategies will sometimes have to specify moves at decision nodes that are never actually reached in the equilibrium of the game.

You used backward induction to make a theoretical prediction about the outcome of games with sequential moves. Backward induction allows the analyst to rule out strategies that incorporate non-credible threats. A non-credible threat is a threat that a player would not carry out if called upon to do so as it would not be in the player's self-interest so to do. Ruling out non-credible threats ensures that strategies specify moves that are a Nash equilibrium in every subgame of the whole game. Only strategies that meet this requirement can be part of a subgame perfect Nash equilibrium.

The role of credibility and commitment in sequential games was further highlighted in the analysis of the entry deterrence game from industrial organisation theory. In the entry deterrence game an incumbent monopolist is threatened by entry. In order to deter entry the monopolist threatens to fight entry should it occur. But if the threat to fight is not credible the entrant will enter. However, the monopolist may be able to make a commitment that makes fighting entry a best response. In these circumstances the threat to fight is credible and entry will be deterred. Because games with the same or a similar structure to entry deterrence are so ubiquitous, you will see this game again when we allow for more of the complexities of life in later chapters. In the last section of this chapter you saw how the subgame perfect Nash equilibrium of the centipede game is Pareto inefficient. This possibility suggests that the subgame perfect Nash equilibrium of a game might not always be the best prediction of the game's outcome.

## Answers to exercises

### 4.1

**Matrix 4.5.1** Best responses of Alpha and Beta underlined

|  |  | Beta | | | |
| --- | --- | --- | --- | --- | --- |
|  |  | export, export | not export, not export | export, not export | not export, export |
| **Alpha** | FDI | 25, -5 | 40, <u>10</u> | 25, -5 | <u>40</u>, <u>10</u> |
|  | **export only** | <u>30, 30</u> | <u>60</u>, 10 | <u>60</u>, 10 | 30, <u>30</u> |

The Nash equilibria are {export only, (export, export)} and {FDI, (not export, export)}.

### 4.2

The subgame perfect Nash equilibrium of nice–not so nice 2 is {not so nice, (nice, nice)}, the corresponding branches are highlighted in Figure 4.2.4. Any threat by Two to play not so nice at $2_B$ in order to persuade One to choose nice is not credible because at $2_B$ Two's best response is to choose nice. By choosing nice at $2_B$ her pay-off is 2 while if she chooses not so nice her pay-off is only 1. In this version of the nice–not so nice game One has an advantage by moving first. One can choose not so nice and then rely on Two being nice which gives One his maximum pay-off of 5.

One's position in nice–not so nice 2 can be contrasted with his position in nice–not so nice 1. In nice–not so nice 1, even though One still moves first, this does not give him such an advantage because Two's threat to play not so nice at 2B is credible. One cannot secure his maximum pay-off by choosing not so nice and does better by being nice to Two.

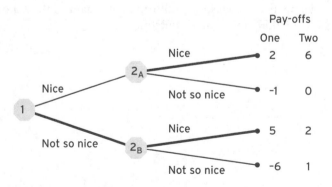

**Figure 4.2.4** Extensive form for nice–not so nice 2

## Problems

1 The game in Figure 4.6 is played between players A and B. A moves first and chooses between north, east, west or south at A. B moves second and chooses between left and right. How many proper subgames does the sequential move game in Figure 4.6 have and what is the subgame perfect Nash equilibrium of this game?

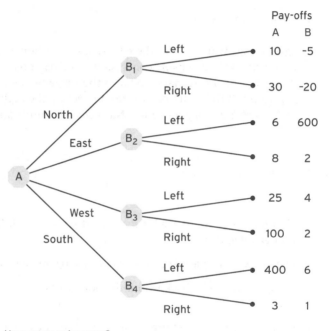

**Figure 4.6** How many subgames?

2 Consider the following scenario: a single firm monopolises a market. When faced by the possibility of entry into the market the monopolist threatens to fight should entry occur. Use game theory to analyse this scenario and to characterise the circumstances when the threat by the monopolist to fight entry (a) is not credible and (b) is credible.

3 In the wage demands game represented in Figure 4.7 a union is negotiating with a firm and trying to secure a wage increase for its members, the firm's employees. The union (U) has to decide between making a high or a low wage demand. The firm (F) will definitely accept the low wage demand (at $F_l$) but may reject a high wage demand at $(F_h)$. If the firm rejects the high demand the union and the employer enter into a long, drawn-out bargaining phase that is expensive for them both (it may for instance involve a work-to-rule, strike or even a lockout). At the end of this phase the

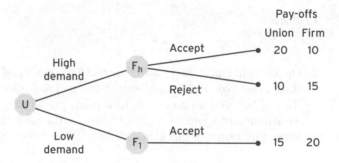

**Figure 4.7** Wage demands

agreed wage will lie somewhere between the original high and low demands; both sides will have made concessions. The pay-offs in Figure 4.7 are illustrative of this scenario. What is the subgame perfect Nash equilibrium of this game? If the firm's pay-off from rejecting the high demand is 5 instead of 15 does the subgame perfect Nash equilibrium change?

## Questions for discussion

1 How does the idea of a subgame perfect Nash equilibrium rule out non-credible threats?

2 Explain why all Nash equilibria are not subgame perfect.

3 What is implied by backward induction? Does backward induction always make sense?

4 In games like entry deterrence how can the threat to fight entry or its equivalent be made credible?

5 What is the centipede game and why is the subgame perfect Nash equilibrium of the centipede game somewhat unsatisfactory?

## Answers to problems

1 The game in Figure 4.6 has 4 proper subgames: the subgames beginning at the decision nodes labelled $B_1$, $B_2$, $B_3$ and $B_4$. The subgame perfect Nash equilibrium is {south, (left, left, left, left)}. B will always choose left so A should choose south.

2 See Sections 4.4 and 4.4.1. For part (a) you can model a game with the same pattern of relative pay-offs as those in Figure 4.4. For part (b) the relative pay-offs should have the same pattern as those in Figure 4.4.2.

3 In the subgame perfect Nash equilibrium of this game the union makes the low wage demand and the firm accepts it: {low demand, (reject, accept)}. The union makes the low wage demand because the firm's threat to reject is credible; the firm's equilibrium strategy is (reject, accept). The pay-offs imply that rejection and concession (on both sides) hurts the firm less than passive acceptance of the high demand. If the firm's pay-off from rejecting the high demand was 5 instead of 15 (implying that the firm's negotiating costs are higher) the firm's threat to reject would no longer be credible and in the subgame perfect Nash equilibrium the union would make the high demand and the firm would accept: {high demand, (accept, accept)}.

## Notes

1 The strategic role of FDI or multinational investment has been considered by a long line of authors probably beginning with Knickerbocker (1973). Smith (1987) and Horstmann and Markusen (1987) develop early models where overseas production is undertaken, in preference to exporting, in order to deter entry as domestic firms in a foreign country become more efficient.

2 Or rollback as Dixit and Skeath (1999) call it.

3 The significance of the qualification will be made clearer in Chapter 5, Section 5.1.

4 Gibbons (1997: 135) defines a subgame as a 'piece of an original game that remains to be played, beginning at any point at which the complete history of the play of the game thus far, is common knowledge'. *See* Bierman and Fernandez (1998: Section 6.5) or Montet and Serra (2003: 104) for a more formal definition.

5 Katz and Rosen (1998, Chapter 15: 513) call this the 'credibility condition'.

6 In FDI the subgames starting from $B_1$ and $B_2$ and ending at terminal nodes are proper subgames. The game starting at A is the whole game and technically the whole game is also a subgame as it starts at a node where there is no uncertainty and ends at a terminal node, but it is only a subgame in a trivial sense.

7 Nice–not so nice is similar to the trust game analysed in Gibbons (1997).

8 The law as it stands in England will heavily punish this kind of action if it is deemed unreasonable force. This was demonstrated when Tony Martin, a householder who shot dead a would-be burglar, received a five year prison sentence (*see* www.tonymartinsupportgroup.org).

9 *See* Vickers (1985) for an early introduction.

10 The economic literature relating to entry deterrence generally (*see*, for example, Bain, 1968, 1956 and Sylos-Labini, 1962) and strategic entry deterrence in particular (*see*, for example, Spence, 1977) is large.

11 In trespass Bert's purchase of a bull would constitute a 'strategic' investment of this kind.

12 Centipede games have some of the features of the nice–not so nice game as both games require an element of trust for the players to be 'nice' to each other. But in centipede games the players face multiple decision nodes.

13 *See* Rosenthal (1981) for a more rigorous discussion along these lines.

# HIDDEN MOVES AND RISKY CHOICES

- Explain how and why evidence of common consequence and common ratio effects weakens the descriptive claims of expected utility theory

- Explain what is implied by the axiom of transitivity

- Explain how and why evidence of preference reversal weakens the descriptive claims of expected utility theory.

## Introduction

In Section 1.8 of Chapter 1 it was stated that the outcome of a game will depend on the information that the players have. In the games considered so far, all the players have had the same information, they knew where they were in the game and who they were playing. In this chapter you will see how to model situations where there is less shared information than this. First, you will see how simultaneous-move games can be modelled as dynamic games with hidden moves. I have already claimed that these two possibilities are equivalent in game theoretic terms and in Section 5.1 you will see why this is the case. In Section 5.2, risk is modelled by incorporating probabilities in individual decision-making problems. Using probabilities allows the analyst to calculate either expected values or expected utilities. The latter usage is generally considered the more versatile but expected utility theory is not without its critics. Some of the criticisms of expected utility theory are supported by experimental evidence and this will be examined in detail in Section 5.3.

## 5.1 **Hidden moves**

We will start by considering the battle of the sexes game in Matrix 5.1. This game was first analysed in Chapter 2 in Matrix 2.19 and you should verify that it has two Nash equilibria in pure strategies: {pub, pub} and {party, party}. In Chapter 2 the players were assumed to move simultaneously or if the players moved at different times their moves were hidden. I've claimed that these two possibilities are equivalent and intuitively it is not difficult to see why this might be; if a move is hidden to a player then it cannot really matter when it was made. Here we can use the methodology of Chapter 4 to argue this point more forcibly. We will do this by analysing a sequential-move version of the battle of the sexes game. Two possibilities are considered: a sequential-move game with seen moves and one with hidden moves.

**Matrix 5.1** Battle of the sexes

Janet

|  |  | pub | party |
|---|---|---|---|
| **John** | **pub** | 3, 2 | 1, 1 |
|  | **party** | −1, −2 | 2, 3 |

Let's first consider the battle of the sexes game as a sequential-move game in which John moves first but there are no hidden moves. Figure 5.1 illustrates this case; John moves first and Janet observes John's move. In this version of the game if John chooses pub Janet makes a decision at Janet$_1$ and if he chooses party then she makes a decision at Janet$_2$. Because Janet's move is contingent on John's she has four pure strategies: (pub, pub), (pub, party), (party, pub) and (party, party). The players' pay-offs are such that if John chooses pub, so will Janet, but if John chooses party she will choose party. Thus only (pub, party) is rational for Janet. John knows this and as he prefers the pub the subgame perfect Nash equilibrium of this dynamic version of battle of the sexes is {pub, (pub, party)} which implies that both of them go to the pub. This is what I meant in Chapter 2 Section 2.4.3 when I said that the game had a first mover advantage; if the moves are seen, then whoever moves first can secure their preferred outcome. To show that this is true when Janet has the first move draw the game tree with Janet moving first. You should be able to use backward induction to argue that the subgame perfect Nash equilibrium now has both players going to the party. This shows that, unlike the simultaneous-move game, there is a unique equilibrium outcome when one of the players moves first and their move is observed by the other. This is not the case when the player's move is hidden.

We can see this by examining Figure 5.2 which shows how the game-tree looks when John moves first but his move is hidden from Janet. The dotted line between Janet's decision nodes, Janet$_1$ and Janet$_2$, is a simple illustrative device that is used to signify that Janet doesn't know whether she is at Janet$_1$ or

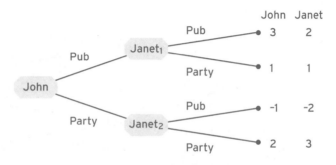

**Figure 5.1** Battle of the sexes with John moving first and his move is seen by Janet

Janet$_2$. Broken lines either joining or around a player's decision-nodes are used in this way. They indicate that the player with the move doesn't know which of the nodes joined by or, enclosed within, the broken lines, he or she is at. In this case Janet doesn't know whether she is at Janet$_1$ or Janet$_2$ because she hasn't seen John's move.

In the version of the game depicted in Figure 5.2 we cannot use backward induction to analyse Janet's moves at Janet$_1$ and Janet$_2$ because the games beginning at these nodes are not proper subgames of the whole game. Remember from Chapter 4 that the definition of a subgame is a subset of the whole game that starts at a decision-node where there is no uncertainty. As Janet doesn't see John's move she doesn't know whether she is at Janet$_1$ or Janet$_2$ so there is clearly some uncertainty for her at each of these decision-nodes. This implies that there are no proper subgames of this version of the game and backward induction cannot be used. Furthermore, as Janet's moves are not contingent on John's move – they can't be as she doesn't see John's move – she has only two pure strategies: pub and party. As John moves first there is no possibility of him seeing Janet's move and therefore he too has only two pure strategies: pub and party. It follows that unless Janet has some information about John's moves the sequential version of this game with hidden moves is analytically equivalent to the simultaneous-move version. Each player has two pure strategies, neither player has an advantage and there are two Nash equilibria. Since each prefers a different equilibrium neither is more likely than the other.

This indeterminacy is borne out in experiments with battle of the sexes games in which subjects tend to choose randomly and there are many mismatches (Camerer, 2003: 353–67). As you have seen, the theoretical prediction changes if John moves first and Janet sees his move. In experiments this is modelled by allowing one player to announce in advance their intended choice. When this happens the announcing player secures their preferred outcome as predicted. Interestingly, subjects also tend to coordinate on the first mover's preferred outcome even when the second-mover doesn't know what the first-mover has done. Camerer (2003: 367) attributes this to 'a tacit – almost telepathic – first-mover advantage'. Telepathy isn't assumed in game theory. Instead a first-mover advan-

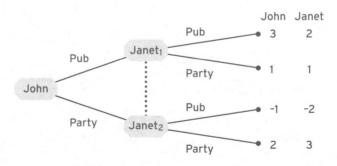

**Figure 5.2** Game tree for battle of the sexes with hidden moves

tage of this kind would be explained by assuming that the second-mover, Janet in Figure 5.2, had some information about the likelihood of John choosing pub. This information would be reflected in her beliefs and these are modelled by probabilities. We have not dealt with probabilities yet but now you are going to see how they can be incorporated into the analysis.

## 5.2  Risk and probabilities

As noted in Chapter 1 not all risky situations are strategic ones and the analysis of risk and uncertainty extends beyond game theory to decision theory more generally (see, for example, Watson and Bude, 1987: Part 1 or Biswas, 1997: Chapters 1–2). In order to keep the analysis simple we can start by considering some situations where there is risk but it is non-strategic. When risk is non-strategic the decision maker has no influence or possible impact on how the risk is resolved.

For example, when you plan your next holiday you will have to make a number of decisions concerning your destination, the timing of your holiday and so forth. You will make these decisions in the knowledge that there is some risk that your plans will be disrupted, perhaps because of a luggage handlers' strike or your cat being ill, or that the holiday is a disaster for some other reason (for example if the weather is awful). But your choice concerning your holiday doesn't actually have any effect on any of these possibilities; they will occur or not occur whatever you decide. The luggage handlers, your cat or the weather don't sit down and think about where or if you are going on holiday and then make a decision about whether to strike, be ill or organise a freak hurricane. The chance of a strike taking place, your cat being ill or the weather being bad is therefore independent of how you actually choose and this means that the luggage handlers, your cat and the weather are not playing a strategic game with you. Other examples of instances where there is non-strategic risk are lotteries, a football match from the standpoint of a supporter and games of chance like roulette. In all of these cases there is only one player, i.e. the decision maker herself, and therefore no strategic interaction of the kind you have been looking at in the previous chapters. People who are superstitious in these circumstances think that the weather, the outcome of the lottery, the match or the spin of the roulette wheel are in some way influenced by what they do. That is, they think they are playing some kind of strategic game but they are not.

## Exercise 5.1

In the examples (a) to (g) below only the last two could easily be represented as strategic games. Can you say why? (Hint: who are the decision makers in the examples, are there more than one and if so do they both make their decisions by taking into account what they think the other is likely to do?)

(a) Betting on the outcome of a horse race or a cricket match that hasn't to your knowledge been fixed.

(b) Gambling on a fair roulette wheel at a casino.

(c) Deciding whether to take an umbrella with you when you go out for the day in England.

(d) Deciding whether to take out insurance against the risk of your home being burgled.

(e) A smoker deciding whether to continue smoking or not.

(f) A thug thinking about whether to punch someone in a bar who has annoyed him but who might be a karate expert.

(g) A firm deciding whether to enter a new industrial sector where one firm has a monopoly position but it is unclear whether the incumbent will resist entry or not.

The first example of non-strategic risk you are going to look at is the decision faced by Mr Punter on a day out at the races. He is deciding whether or not to bet in the last race of the day on a horse owned by his friend Mr Lucky. Mr Lucky has inside knowledge about his horse and the other horses in the race. He assures Mr Punter that his horse has a 1 in 10 (a 0.1 or $\frac{1}{10}$) chance of winning the race.[1] Mr Punter has €M left in his pocket. If he bets €c on the horse winning the race and the horse wins Mr Punter wins €z making a net gain of €z – c which we can call €w. If he makes the bet and the horse loses he will take home €M – c. If he doesn't make the bet he takes home the whole €M. (€M is the amount of money he starts with, c is the cost of the bet and w is his net win if the horse wins.) In making his decision whether to bet on the horse or not Mr Punter knows that there are only two ways in which the uncertainty can be resolved:[2]

- The horse wins (probability 0.1).

- The horse loses (probability 0.9).

However, there are three possible outcomes from Mr Punter's perspective:

- He bets €c and wins €z so that his total wealth is €M + (z – c) = €M + w.

- He bets and loses €c so that his total wealth is €M – c.

- He doesn't bet and retains his original monetary wealth €M.

The outcomes, €M + w, €M − c and €M are Mr Punter's contingent pay-offs. They are contingent on Mr Punter's initial decision and how the uncertainty is resolved. The decision problem for Mr Punter is represented by the diagram in Figure 5.3.

Figure 5.3 is a decision-tree showing the choice problem for Mr Punter. It is not a game-tree as such, as Mr Punter is not involved in a strategic game but the two forms are very similar. Figure 5.3 shows that Mr Punter moves first by deciding to bet on the horse or not. After he has made his decision the race is run and either his horse wins or it doesn't. As far as Mr Punter is concerned whether his horse wins is decided by *chance* or *nature* (a pseudo player) as he has no influence on the outcome. The chance move is depicted by the probabilities written beside the branches of the decision-tree attached to the right of the decision-nodes labelled chance. Chance determines whether the horse wins or not and it wins with probability 0.1 and loses with probability 0.9. The chance move is the same whether Mr Punter bets or not – it is not contingent on his move. Mr Punter's pay-offs are written at the terminal-nodes of the decision-tree. Only his pay-offs are shown as he is the only proper player in the game. The horse, for instance, is not.

Should Mr Punter bet on the horse? Assuming Mr Punter prefers more money to less his decision will depend on the expected pay-off from betting relative to the expected pay-off from not betting. The simplest way to calculate expected pay-offs is to calculate the expected value of the pay-offs from betting and not betting respectively. The expected value of the pay-off from taking a particular decision is the average of the pay-offs associated with all the possible outcomes of that decision. The average is calculated by weighting (or multiplying) each pay-off by the probability that it will occur. The expected value of Mr Punter's

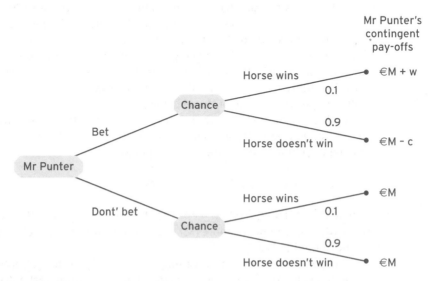

**Figure 5.3** Mr Punter's decision-tree

pay-off from betting is the sum of the weighted pay-offs from winning and losing and each pay-off is weighted by the probability that it occurs. Thus if he bets the expected value of his pay-off is:

- $0.1(€M + w) + 0.9(€M - c)$

This formulation says that the expected value of betting is the probability of winning (0.1) multiplied by the pay-off from betting and winning (€M + w) plus the probability of losing (0.9) multiplied by the pay-off from losing (€M − c). If he doesn't bet then his wealth is the same whether the horse wins or not therefore his expected pay-off from not betting is:

- €M

That is €M with certainty, a sure thing. If Mr Punter prefers more money to less, then he could decide to bet on the horse if the expected value of betting is greater than the expected value of not betting or:

- $0.1(€M + w) + 0.9(€M - c) > €M$

which simplifies to $€w > €9c$.

If Mr Punter chooses to bet because w is greater than 9c this implies that his utility or satisfaction from the expected pay-off of betting is greater than his utility from the expected pay-off of not betting. We can write Mr Punter's subjective utility for a given monetary pay-off as $U(€)$ where $U(€)$ is the function that determines how a given monetary sum translates into units or levels of satisfaction in Mr Punter's mind. For example, if the monetary sum is €100 then U(100) is the subjective utility value to Mr Punter of €100. If Mr Punter prefers more money to less then the function $U(€)$ will reflect this so that, for example, $U(€100) > U(€10) > U(€5)$. But the amount by which $U(€100) > U(€10)$ will depend on Mr Punter's preferences which will be unique to him. He may, for example, value €100 more than, less than or exactly ten times as much as €10. His utility function will reflect his preferences in this regard as well (some different possibilities are outlined below).

With this notation the condition that his utility from the expected pay-off of betting is greater than his utility from the expected pay-off of not betting can be written in mathematical shorthand as:

- $U(0.1(M + w) + 0.9(M - c)) > U(M)$

where $U(0.1(M + w) + 0.9(M - c))$ is Mr Punter's utility from the expected value of betting on the horse and U(M) is his utility from €M which is the expected value of not betting.

This formulation has the advantage of simplicity in that it implies that if the expected value of one option is greater than another then the decision maker should simply choose the former. However, because some very risky options can have the same expected value as other very safe options this formulation fails to take into account differing attitudes to risk. It implies that all the decision maker cares about is the overall expected value of a given choice and not the probabilities that are implicit in that relevant expected value calculation. For example, it implies that an individual would be indifferent between a sure payment of €1000 and a lottery ticket with a 1 in 1000 (0.001 or $\frac{1}{1000}$) chance of winning €1 000 000. This is because if there is a 1 in 1000 chance of winning with the lottery ticket there is also a 999 in 1000 chance of losing, that is winning nothing. The expected value of the lottery gamble is therefore (0.001 × 1 000 000 + 0.999 x 0) = €1000, the same as the sure payment of €1000. Would you be indifferent between these two options, or prospects[3] as they are sometimes called? Even if you are most people would not be. For instance, some people are risk averse which means that they don't really like risk and others, like Formula One racing car drivers and bungee jumpers, appear to love it and actively seek it out. Alternatively you may not fit into either of these categories because you neither worry about nor enjoy risk – in this case you are risk neutral.[4] A further complication is that some people might like to take small risks, for instance by buying lottery tickets, but they might not be so keen to take large risks, for example with their lives.

## 5.2.1 Expected utility

 One way of taking these different attitudes to risk into account is to calculate the expected utility,[5] as opposed to the expected value, of taking a particular gamble. The expected utility of accepting a particular gamble (or prospect) is the average utility derived from the associated contingent pay-offs. It is calculated by finding the utility of each of the possible contingent pay-offs, weighting each by the probability that it occurs and then summing to come up with the overall average. This can be contrasted with the expected value calculation which probability weights the contingent pay-offs themselves, not the utility or satisfaction that they potentially bring to the decision maker. These two formulations sound, on the face of it, very similar. But the differences between them mean that the expected utility of a gamble or prospect will only equal the utility of the expected value if the decision maker doesn't care about risk (he or she is risk neutral) or there is in fact no risk (the gamble is a sure thing). We can see this by looking at some examples and I'll start by reconsidering the decision problem faced by Mr Punter.

As you have already seen the expected value of betting for Mr Punter is 0.1(M + w) + 0.9(M – c). Letting U(€) define Mr Punter's utility for money his utility from the expected value of betting is given by:

- Utility of the expected value of the bet, UEV: $U(0.1(M + w) + 0.9(M - c))$.

while the expected utility of betting is determined by probability weighting the utilities of each of the contingent pay-offs $(M + w)$ and $(M - c)$. This leads to:

- Expected utility of the bet, EU: $0.1U(M + w) + 0.9U(M - c)$.

This is in effect the expected value of the utility of betting while the utility of the expected value is the utility of the expected monetary value of betting. The two definitions may look and sound very similar but, as noted above, they will only be equal if Mr Punter is risk neutral. Otherwise, by separately probability weighting the utilities of the alternative pay-offs the expected utility formulation will reflect either his aversion to, or love of, risk.

More specifically the theoretical assumptions that underlie the expected utility calculation[6] imply that if he is risk averse the expected utility of betting, EU, will be less than the utility of the expected value, UEV. If he is risk-loving the opposite will be true. More generally if a risky alternative has the same expected value as a sure thing a risk-averse person will prefer the sure thing because the expected utility of the gamble will be less. On the other hand a risk-loving person will prefer the gamble. The expected utility formulation also implies that, if two gambles have the same expected value but one is relatively more risky than the other, a risk-loving person will prefer the more risky gamble, a risk-averse person will prefer the safer gamble and a risk-neutral person will be indifferent between the two prospects. A gamble could be riskier than another that had the same expected value if the probability of losing in the risky gamble is higher but there is also a bigger chance of winning a larger prize.

It follows that Mr Punter (and anyone else who is facing a risky choice) won't necessarily choose the option with the highest expected value. Instead, if they are either risk-averse or risk-loving[7] they will choose the option with the highest expected utility which may or not be the option with the highest expected value. This doesn't mean that a risk-averse person will never gamble, just that they will only choose risky options if they have a high enough expected value relative to the expected value of choosing some less risky or risk-free alternative.

To summarise, the expected utility of a gamble is the probability weighted average of the utilities of the pay-offs corresponding to the alternative outcomes that characterise the gamble (the horse winning or losing in Mr Punter's case). To generalise a little assume that an action has two possible outcomes corresponding to the contingent pay-offs x and y. The probability of x occurring is p and the probability of y occurring is therefore $(1 - p)$. The expected utility from making the decision to take the action will be:

- $EU = pU(x) + (1 - p)U(y)$

If there is a third possible outcome corresponding to the contingent pay-off z and the probability of z occurring is q then the expected utility of this prospect will be:

- $EU = pU(x) + (1 - p - q)U(y) + qU(z)$

If there are more than three possible outcomes then the expected utility formulation is extended accordingly.

> ## Expected value and expected utility
>
> - Expected utility, EU: the expected utility of a gamble is the (probability weighted) *average of the utilities of the pay-offs* corresponding to the alternative outcomes that characterise the gamble.
>
> - Expected value, EV: the expected value of a gamble is the (probability weighted) *average of the pay-offs* corresponding to the alternative outcomes that characterise the gamble.
>
> - Utility of expected value, UEV: the utility of the expected value of a gamble is the utility of the (probability weighted) average of the pay-offs corresponding to the alternative outcomes that characterise the gamble.

## 5.2.2 Expected values, expected utilities and attitudes to risk

To illustrate some of these points consider the gambles A and B described by the following probabilities and prizes.

*Gamble A*

- You win €100 000 with probability 0.01.
- You win nothing with probability 0.99.

*Gamble B*

- You win €2000 with probability 0.5.
- You win nothing with probability 0.5.

Ask yourself which gamble you prefer (assume that entry is costless) and make a note of your answer. The decision-tree corresponding to this choice problem is illustrated in Figure 5.4.

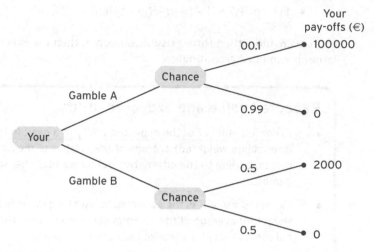

**Figure 5.4** Choice between gambles A and B

The expected value of gamble A is $0.01 \times 100\,000 + 0.99 \times 0 = 1000$ and the expected value of gamble B is $0.5 \times 2000 + 0.5 \times 0 = 1000$. As the expected values of the two gambles are the same the utilities of the expected values of the two gambles will also be the same. This means that if you don't attach any value (positive or negative) to risk you should be indifferent between the two gambles. But were you? Possibly not. Gamble B has a higher probability of winning a reasonable prize than gamble A although the prize in gamble A is larger. This means that gamble B is a relatively safer gamble and if, like me, you would prefer gamble B you are, at least in relation to these gambles, risk-averse. If you prefer gambler A you are risk-loving.

With the expected utility formulation we can take account of these different possibilities. To see this, suppose that your utility function, $U(€y)$, for an amount of money y is $y^2$ ($U(€y) = y^2$). Then the utility you would derive from €10 would be worth 100 (units of utility), the utility you derive from €100 would be 10 000 and so on. With this utility function the utilities of the expected values of the two gambles are:

- Utility of the expected value of gamble A: $UEV(A) = U(0.01 \times 100\,000 + 0.99 \times 0)$
$$= U(1000) = 1000^2 = 1\,000\,000.$$

- Utility of the expected value of gamble B: $UEV(B) = U(0.5 \times 2000 + 0.5 \times 0)$
$$= U(1000) = 1000^2 = 1\,000\,000.$$

The utilities of the expected values are the same for both gambles because their expected values are the same. Now let's look at the expected utility formulations. The expected utility of gamble A is:

- Expected utility of gamble A: $EU(A) = 0.01U(100\,000) + 0.99U(0)$

With $U(\text{€}y) = y^2$ we can calculate precisely the expected utility of gamble A as:

- Expected utility of gamble A: $EU(A) = 0.01(100\,000^2)$
$$= 100\,000\,000.$$

and the expected utility of gamble B is:

- Expected utility of gamble B: $EU(B) = 0.5U(2000) + 0.5U(0)$
$$= 0.5(2000)^2 = 2\,000\,000$$

With the utility function $U(\text{€}y) = y^2$ the expected utility of gamble A is higher than that of gamble B even though the expected values of the two gambles are the same. An individual with this utility function would therefore choose gamble A (the more risky gamble) in preference to gamble B (the relatively safer gamble). Such a person is risk-loving; he or she prefers a risky option to a safer option with the same expected value. The expected value formulation couldn't take these kinds of preferences into account but you have seen that the expected utility formulation can.

Now consider the position of Ms Careful whose utility for money is described by the function $U(\text{€}y) = \sqrt{y}$ (or $y^{\frac{1}{2}}$). With this utility function the utility Ms Careful derives from €100 is $U(\text{€}100) = 10$ and the utility she derives from €4 is $U(\text{€}4) = 2$ and so on. The expected values of gambles A and B haven't changed, both are still 1000, but the utility of these expected values and the expected utilities of the gambles will be different since the utility function is different. As the expected value of gambles A and B are both 1000 Ms Careful's utility from the expected value of gambles A and B is:

- Utility of the expected value of gamble A: $UEV(A) = U(1000) = \sqrt{1000} = 31.623$

- Utility of the expected value of gamble B: $UEV(B) = U(1000) = \sqrt{1000} = 31.623$

For Ms Careful the expected utility of gamble A is $0.01U(100\,000) + 0.99U(0)$ and with her utility function this implies:

- Expected utility of gamble A: $EU(A) = 0.01\sqrt{100\,000} + 0.99\sqrt{0}$
$$= 0.01(316.23) = 3.1623$$

and the expected utility of gamble B is $0.5U(2\,000) + 0.5U(0)$ or:

- Expected utility of gamble B: $EU(B) = 0.5\sqrt{2\,000} + 0.5\sqrt{0}$
$$= 0.5(44.72) = 22.36$$

So for Ms Careful the expected utility of gamble B is higher than that of gamble A and therefore, if she is aiming to maximise her expected utility, she will

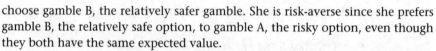

choose gamble B, the relatively safer gamble. She is risk-averse since she prefers gamble B, the relatively safe option, to gamble A, the risky option, even though they both have the same expected value.

This exercise has shown that the expected value formulation won't always reflect people's different subjective valuations of risky pay-offs. The expected utility formulation, on the other hand, by probability weighting the utilities of the contingent pay-offs can take better account of people's different attitudes to risk. This is why I said in Section 1.8 of Chapter 1 that the expected utility formulation was potentially a more useful way of calculating a player's expected pay-off.

---

## The expected utility and the expected value of a gamble

Ms Flutter is deciding whether to take a gamble with a 0.75 chance of winning €100 and a 0.25 chance of winning €20:

- expected value of the gamble is: $0.75€100 + 0.25€20 = €80$;

- expected utility of the gamble is: $0.75U(€100) + 0.25U(20)$;

- utility of the expected value of the gamble is: $U(0.75€100 + 0.25€20) = U(€80)$.

Ms Flutter's utility function for an amount of money €M is $U(€M) = M^2$. With this utility function:

- expected utility of the gamble = $0.75U(€100) + 0.25U(€20)$
$$= 0.75 \times 100^2 + 0.25 \times 20^2 = 7{,}500 + 100 = 7{,}600$$
- utility of the expected value of the gamble = $U(€80) = 80^2 = 6400$

Ms Flutter is risk-loving: the expected utility of the gamble is higher than the utility of the expected value of the gamble.

---

The following lottery example shows in a stark way how important attitudes to risk can be. In this example you are offered a choice between two lottery tickets. One is for a midweek lottery and the other is for a Saturday lottery. The prizes and the probabilities of winning in the two lotteries are as follows.

### Midweek lottery

- 50 per cent chance of winning €10 000.

- 50 per cent chance of winning nothing.

### Saturday lottery

- 100 per cent chance of winning €5000.

The expected values of these two lotteries are the same, €5000, but the midweek lottery is risky – there is a good chance that you will win nothing – while the Saturday lottery is completely safe – you are guaranteed €5000. In these circumstances I would be very surprised if you were indifferent between these two lotteries. Most people would prefer the certainty of the Saturday lottery (which is not really a lottery at all, it is a sure thing). This would imply that they were risk-averse; they prefer a sure thing to a risky prospect with the same expected value. If you prefer the midweek lottery you are risk-loving; you prefer a risky prospect to a sure thing with the same expected value. If you are indifferent between the two lotteries then you are risk neutral. The expected value formulation cannot take account of these different possibilities but the expected utility formulation can.

## Attitudes to risk

- Risk love: risk lovers prefer a gamble to a sure thing with the same expected value.

- Risk aversion: risk-averse people prefer a sure thing to a gamble with the same expected value.

- Risk neutrality: risk-neutral people are indifferent between a sure thing and a gamble with the same expected value.

If two gambles have the same expected value but one is riskier than the other because there is a higher probability of winning the lowest valued prize but also a higher probability of winning the highest valued prize:

- Risk lovers prefer the riskier gamble.

- Risk-averse people prefer the safer gamble.

- Risk-neutral people are indifferent between the two gambles.

If one gamble has a higher expected value than another then:

- Risk lovers and risk-neutral people will always choose the gamble with the higher expected value.

- Some risk-averse people may choose the gamble with the lower expected value if it appears less risky.

## Exercise 5.2

You are offered the choice of a free ticket to enter lottery 1 or a free ticket to lottery 2. In lottery 1 and lottery 2 the prizes and the probabilities of winning are as follows:

*Lottery 1*
- 10 per cent chance of winning €5000.
- 70 per cent chance of winning €2500.
- 20 per cent chance of winning nothing.

*Lottery 2*
- 40 per cent chance of winning €5000.
- 20 per cent chance of winning €2500.
- 40 per cent chance of winning nothing.

Which lottery do you prefer? What are the expected values of the tickets for these two lotteries? If you prefer lottery 1 are you risk-averse, risk-neutral or risk-loving in relation to the two lotteries?

To summarise, if outcomes are uncertain people won't necessarily choose between prospects according to their expected value. Instead, if people care about risk the choices they make may be more consistent with the expected utility hypothesis. The expected utility formulation can better account for people's attitudes to risk because the utility of a contingent pay-off (rather than the pay-off itself) is weighted by the probability that it will occur. This means that the overall weighting given to a contingent pay-off depends not just on the probability that it will occur but also on the utility function of the individual concerned. An outcome that has a lower probability of occurring is still given a lower weight but the relative worth of a larger pay-off will be magnified or diminished according to the individual's utility function.

A person whose utility function is such that he or she attaches more and more incremental (or marginal) value to equal increases in income will be more willing to gamble on higher and higher prizes. Such a person is a risk-lover. Similarly, a person who attaches less and less incremental value to equal increases in income will be less willing to gamble. This kind of person is risk-averse. Someone who values equal gains in income equally is risk-neutral. This implies that the expected utility of a gamble will be less than the utility of the expected value of the gamble if the individual is risk-averse. The opposite will be true if the individual is a risk-lover like Ms Flutter in the boxed example. The two calculations will be equal if the individual is risk neutral.

More formally risk-loving people have increasing marginal utility, risk-averse people have diminishing marginal utility and risk-neutral people have constant marginal utility. This can be made more precise by using some mathematical terminology. In general, if an individual's utility function is given by $U(y) = y^z$, where y is a monetary (or other objectively valued) pay-off and $z > 0$ then if $z = 1$ the individual's marginal utility is constant, it is increasing if $z > 1$ and diminishing if $z < 1$. Thus the individual is risk-neutral if $z = 1$, risk-loving if $z > 1$ and risk-averse if $z < 1$.[8] The two examples that were used above were $U(y) = y^2$ and $U(y) = \sqrt{y} = y^{1/2}$. In the first case $z = 2 > 1$ and in the second $z = \frac{1}{2} < 1$. We showed above that with $U(y) = y^2$ an individual's choices would reflect those of a risk-lover and in the second case, that of Ms Careful, her choices were consistent with risk aversion.

The kinds of examples we have looked at show that attitudes to risk are important. In general people don't like risk and that they commonly take action to avoid risk, for example by buying insurance or diversifying. On the other hand many people who buy insurance also gamble. Often the gambles they take are unfair[9] in that they favour the individual or institution that offers them. This implies they are risk-loving, but buying insurance implies they are also risk-averse. It seems strange that people can be risk-averse and risk-loving at the same time but one explanation is that people have different attitudes to risk in different situations and over different sums of money. If this is true then they will have a utility function that has both risk-averse and risk-loving regions.[10] Alternatively people may gamble for reasons that are unrelated to whether they are risk-loving or not – for example they may enjoy gambling (it is a form of entertainment) or they are mistaken about the element of risk involved (they think the gambles they accept are fair or favour them).

## 5.3 Limitations of expected utility theory

Expected utility theory implies that when individuals choose between risky alternatives they will choose the one with the highest expected utility. This hypothesis is widely used to determine equilibrium strategies in games where there is uncertainty for one or more of the players (you will see examples of this in Chapters 7 and 8). However, the expected utility hypothesis relies on a number of underlying assumptions about the ways in which people make choices between risky prospects and these assumptions have been criticised. For a detailed exposition of these assumptions and a formal derivation of the expected utility hypothesis *see* Starmer (2000: 334–6) or Camerer (1995: 617–20)

The criticisms levelled at expected utility theory suggest that its applicability maybe limited and as such these limitations should be born in mind when drawing insights from theoretical arguments that rely on the expected utility formulation. The criticisms of the theory fall into two main groups: theoretical and descriptive. Theoretical considerations arise when expected utility theory is unable to capture important elements of an individual's choice problem. The descriptive limitations follow from experimental evidence of violation of the underlying assumptions of expected utility theory.

## 5.3.1 Theoretical limitations[11]

The theoretical limitations of expected utility theory include evidence of portfolio effects and issues associated with the temporal resolution of uncertainty.

### 5.3.1.1 Portfolio effects

Critics argue that the expected utility formulation ignores 'other gambles' that are already faced by the individual but may be relevant. Consider the position of Ms Investor who is offered shares in either Marks & Spencer or Manchester United. If she already holds shares elsewhere her choice is likely to be affected by her existing portfolio of holdings. For instance, if she already holds shares in Tottenham Hotspur she may prefer to diversify away from English football. If she prefers to diversify then she will take the Marks & Spencer shares. This consideration implies that the probability distributions of gambles under consideration will not always be sufficient descriptions of the choice problem.

### 5.3.1.2 Temporal considerations

The expected utility formulation does not take into account the timing of any resolution of uncertainty but this can matter to people. To see this imagine you are offered a choice between €500 for sure or a lottery ticket with a 40 per cent chance of winning a million euros and a 60 per cent chance of winning nothing. A possible drawback of the lottery option is that if you win you won't get the money until a year from today. However, this is not so much the issue here. What I'd like you to consider is whether your choice between the €500 for sure or the lottery ticket is affected by the timing of the resolution of the uncertainty. By this I mean the time at which you find out whether you have or have not won the lottery. Consider the following possibilities:

(a) The lottery is drawn today and you find out whether you have won or not today.

(b) The lottery is drawn a year from today and you find out whether you have won or not a year from today.

(c) The lottery is drawn today and you find out whether you have won or not a year from today.

If you, like me and many others, would prefer (a) and you are indifferent between (b) and (c) then getting the information sooner is valuable to you. This could be because you can only plan your life properly if you have the relevant information or it may be because you just don't like not knowing. Whatever the explanation, uncertainty has a negative value for you if you prefer (a). Furthermore indifference between (b) and (c) implies that the important time is when the uncertainty is resolved for *you*, not when the uncertainty is 'physically' resolved. Expected utility theory is unable to handle these kinds of issues. As Kreps (1990: 114) says, the problem is one 'of a partial or incomplete model' of the choice problem. Furthermore, people in general don't like uncertainty and the expected utility formulation cannot really take this possibility into account. Of course you may not prefer (a). Maybe you like uncertainty? Perhaps it makes your life more exciting? But expected utility theory cannot incorporate preferences like these either.

## 5.3.2 Descriptive limitations

The logic of expected utility theory follows from a number of underlying assumptions or axioms (see Machina, 1989: 17 or Camerer, 1995: 618–19 for a summary). But experimental evidence suggests that people's behaviour is not always consistent with two of these: the independence axiom and the axiom of transitivity. This evidence weakens the descriptive claims of expected utility theory, that is its claims to be able to accurately predict what people will actually do when confronted with risk. However, this doesn't automatically mean that the prescriptive or normative claims of the theory are similarly weakened; we might still want to recommend that people act in accordance with the theory even if they don't always conform to the theory's predictions in practice. Nevertheless the evidence that people do not always act in ways that are consistent with the axioms of independence and transitivity represents a serious attack on the validity of expected utility. We are going to examine some of that evidence here first in relation to the independence axiom and secondly in relation to the axiom of transitivity. For a more detailed discussion you could look at Kahneman (2003), Starmer (2000), Camerer (1995) or Machina (1987 or 1989).

### 5.3.2.1 The independence axiom

The independence axiom of expected utility theory says that the choice between risky gambles or prospects should not be affected by elements that are the same in each. Consider gambles A and B below where x, y, z, v and w are monetary prizes:

- Gamble A: 0.5x + 0.25y + 0.25z

- Gamble B: 0.5v + 0.25w + 0.25z

Gamble A has a 0.5 probability of winning the prize x, a 0.25 probability of winning the prize y and a 0.25 probability of winning the prize z. Gamble B offers a 0.5 probability of winning the prize v, a 0.25 probability of winning w and, just as in gamble A, a 0.25 chance of winning z. Thus the gambles have a common element or consequence, z, and a common probability of winning it. The independence axiom claims that your choice between gambles A and B should be independent of this common consequence and the probability of winning it and therefore your choice should not be affected by either the probability of winning z or the value of z. This does not seem unreasonable but in experiments where individuals are asked to choose between risky prospects behaviour consistent with the independence axiom is not consistently observed.

Before we consider this experimental evidence consider the gambles on offer in choice problems A and B below. In each case you should make a choice between the gambles you are offered. Make a note of the gambles you prefer in A and B and we will return to them later.

> **Choice problem A.** a and b are two gambles. Gamble a has a certain pay-off of €1 000 000 and gamble b will give you a 10 per cent chance of winning €5 000 000, an 89 per cent chance of winning €1 000 000 and a 1 per cent chance of winning nothing. **Which gamble do you prefer, a or b?**

> **Choice problem B.** e and f are two gambles. Gamble e will give you €700 with certainty. Gamble f will give you an 80 per cent chance of winning €1100 and a 20 per cent chance of winning nothing. **Which gamble do you prefer, e or f?**

Evidence of violations of the independence axiom is commonly divided into two effects known as (i) common consequence and (ii) common ratio effects.

## (i) Common consequence effects

Consider an illustrative choice problem between two options S and R where:

- Option S: pb + qb + ra + sb
- Option R: pa + qc + ra + sb

a, b and c are three monetary prizes such that a < b < c and a = 0. p, q, r, s are the probabilities of winning in S and R. If r > 0 then s = 0 and if s > 0 then r = 0. The common consequence in the two options is therefore a if s = 0 and b if r = 0. As a = 0 the gambles are both riskier when s = 0 and r > 0.

Thus if r > 0 (in which case s = 0) by choosing S you have a (p + q) chance of winning b, and an r chance of winning nothing, that is a. If you choose R you have a (p + r) chance of winning nothing, i.e. a, but a q chance of winning the bigger prize of c. If s > 0 (in which case r = 0) then S represents a sure thing, a certain prize of b, while R is a p chance of nothing, a q chance of c and an s chance of b. In either case S is the relatively safer option because with S there is less chance of loosing (winning a). But the biggest prize, c, can only be won by choosing R. The choice between S and R is illustrated in Matrix 5.2 which shows the pay-offs and probabilities corresponding to the two options. This type of matrix is sometimes called a state contingent matrix.

**Matrix 5.2** The S and R options

<table>
<tr><td></td><td></td><td colspan="4" align="center">**Probabilities**</td><td></td></tr>
<tr><td></td><td></td><td align="center">p</td><td align="center">q</td><td align="center">r</td><td align="center">s</td><td></td></tr>
<tr><td>**Options**</td><td>S</td><td align="center">b</td><td align="center">b</td><td align="center">a</td><td align="center">b</td><td>**Pay-offs**</td></tr>
<tr><td></td><td>R</td><td align="center">a</td><td align="center">c</td><td align="center">a</td><td align="center">b</td><td></td></tr>
</table>

$0 = a < b < c$
If $s > 0$ then $r = 0$ and the common consequence is b
If $r > 0$ then $s = 0$ and the common consequence is $a = 0$

The independence axiom implies that an individual's choice between S and R should be independent of r and s and therefore independent of whether $r = 0$ or $s = 0$. Letting $r = 0$ or $s = 0$ simply amounts to scaling up or down the common consequence and should have no affect on people's choices. But when gambles like S and R have been presented to people in experiments researchers have found that there is a systematic tendency for them to (i) prefer S when $r = 0$ and the common consequence is greater than zero and (ii) prefer R when $s = 0$ and the common consequence is zero. Such behaviour violates the independence axiom because it implies that people's choices are affected by the value of common consequences. Evidence of the common consequence effect was first discovered by Maurice Allais (1953) and was originally referred to as the Allais paradox. Before examining in detail the example Allais used to illustrate this paradox consider the gambles in choice problem A* below. Make a choice between the gambles you are offered and make a note of your choice.

> **Choice problem A\*.** c and d are two gambles. Gamble c will give you an 11 per cent chance of winning €1 000 000 and an 89 per cent chance of winning nothing. Gamble d will give you a 10 per cent chance of winning €5 000 000 and a 90 per cent chance of winning nothing. **Which gamble do you prefer, c or d?**

Allais' example is represented here by attaching specific values to the prizes and probabilities in the S and R gambles in Matrix 5.2 as shown in Matrices 5.2.1 and 5.2.2. In Allias' example S and R are offered in two different situations. In situation 1 $r = 0$ and $s = 0.89$ and in situation 2 $r = 0.89$ and $s = 0$. As shown in Matrix 5.2.1 in situation 1 the choice between S and R is between 1 million for sure if you choose S and a 0.89 chance of 1 million, and a 0.1 chance of 5 million and a 0.01 chance of nothing if you choose R. In situation 2 represented in Matrix 5.2.2 S offers a 0.11 chance of 1 million and a 0.89 chance of nothing while R is a 0.1 chance of 5 million and a 0.9 chance of nothing.

**Matrix 5.2.1** Situation 1 (r = 0, s = 0.89)

Probabilities

|  |  | 0.01 | 0.1 | 0 | 0.89 |  |
|---|---|---|---|---|---|---|
| Options | S | 1m | 1m |  | 1m | Pay-offs |
|  | R | 0 | 5m |  | 1m |  |

**Matrix 5.2.2** Situation 2 (s = 0, r = 0.89)

Probabilities

|  |  | 0.01 | 0.1 | 0.89 | 0 |  |
|---|---|---|---|---|---|---|
| Options | S | 1m | 1m | 0 |  | Pay-offs |
|  | R | 0 | 5m | 0 |  |  |

You should ask yourself whether you prefer S or R in each case. In situation 1 S is a safe option, a sure thing and R is relatively risky although there is a chance of winning 5 million. After choosing between S and R in situation 1 ask yourself whether you would make the same choice in situation 2? Again S is safer than R but S is no longer a sure thing.

According to the independence axiom your choice between R and S in situation 1 should be independent of the 0.89 chance of winning 1 million as this is a common consequence. Similarly your choice in situation 2 should be independent of the 0.89 chance of winning nothing. As S and R are otherwise identical, the independence axiom implies that if you choose S when r = 0 in situation 1 then you should also choose S in situation 2 when s = 0. Did you conform to this prediction? Maybe you did, maybe not. You can check again by looking at your choices in response to A and A*. The choice problems A and A* are in fact the same as those represented in Matrices 5.2.1 and 5.2.2 (*see* Machina, 1989: 22). Gambles a in A and c in A* correspond to the S options in situations 1 and 2 respectively while gambles b and d correspond to the R options in situations 1 and 2. Choices consistent with expected utility theory and the independence axiom are either a in A and c in A* or b in A and d in A*. If you chose b in A and c in A* or a in A but d in A* then you violated the independence axiom.

If your choices were not consistent with the independence axiom don't worry, you are in good company. There is in fact considerable evidence that people systematically prefer S in situation 1 (or a in A) when r = 0 but they prefer R in situation 2 (i.e. d in A*) when s = 0. Similar violations of the independence axiom have been found to occur in other examples where r and s are large relative to q. In the Allais example when r = 0, S is totally safe and R is relatively risky but when s = 0 both S and R are risky and S is only marginally safer than R. In these circumstances, choices in violation of the independence axiom can be defended on the grounds that when r = 0, S is clearly the safest option but when s = 0, as both options are very risky and R is only marginally more risky than S, it's worth having a gamble on R.

Evidence of behaviour that violates the independence axiom weakens the descriptive claims of expected utility theory. However, the normative claims of the theory are also weakened if people continue to violate the independence axiom after the axiom has been explained to them and its logic justified. Unfortunately, for expected utility theory there is evidence that people do just that. That is, they continue to violate the independence axiom even after it has been explained to them (*see* Slovic and Tversky, 1974). In fact anyone who read the first part of this section and then violated the independence axiom in their responses to A and A$^*$ also did so after the independence axiom had been explained to them.

### (ii) The common ratio effect

The independence axiom implies that choices should also be independent of the probability of a common consequence but there is experimental evidence that contradicts this prediction. Consider options S′ and R′ where:

- Option S′ = $\lambda Px_2 + (1 - \lambda)Px_2 + (1 - P)c$
- Option R′ = $\lambda Px_3 + (1 - \lambda)Px_1 + (1 - P)c$

In S′ and R′ c, $x_1$, $x_2$ and $x_3$ are prizes, c = $x_1 < x_2 < x_3$ and often in experiments c = $x_1$ = 0. $\lambda P$, $(1 - \lambda)P$ and $(1 - P)$ are the probabilities of winning the prizes where $0 < \lambda < 1$, $0 < P \leq 1$. The common ratio in question is the ratio of the probabilities of winning $x_2$ or $x_3$ in S′ and R′, namely:

$$\frac{\text{Prob. of winning in S'}}{\text{Prob. of winning in R'}} = \frac{P}{\lambda P} = \frac{1}{\lambda} \tag{5.1}$$

The independence axiom implies that choices between S′ and R′ should be independent of (1 − P) and therefore P. However, there is evidence that people systematically prefer S′ when P is high and prefer R′ when P is low.[12]

Before examining a numerical example consider the choice problem in B$^*$ below. Without looking back at choice problem B, make a choice between g and h and note which gamble you prefer:

> **Choice problem B$^*$.** g and h are two gambles. Gamble g will give you a 20 per cent chance of winning €700 and an 80 per cent chance of winning nothing. Gamble h will give you a 16 per cent chance of winning €1100 and an 84 per cent chance of winning nothing. **Which gamble do you prefer, g or h?**

The choice problems in B and B* can be written in the same way as options S' and R'. In B and B* $\lambda = 0.8$, $c = x_1 = 0$, $x_2 = €700$, $x_3 = €1100$. But P = 1 in choice problem B and P = 0.2 in choice problem B*. The common ratio is 1.25 (i.e. $\frac{1}{0.8}$ when P = 1 in B and $\frac{0.2}{0.16}$ when P = 0.2 in B*. Gambles e and f in B correspond to S' and R' and are defined as follows:

- Option S' = gamble e = 0.8€700 + 0.2€700 = €700 for sure.

- Option R' = gamble f = 0.8€1100 + 0.2€0 = 0.8€1100, i.e. a 0.8 or an 80 per cent chance of winning €1100 and a 20 per cent chance of nothing.

Thus when P = 1 e is the safe gamble corresponding to option S' and f is the risky gamble corresponding to option R'. In choice problem B* P = 0.2 and gambles g and h correspond to S' and R' and are given by:

- Option S' = gamble g = $(0.8 \times 0.2)€700 + (0.2 \times 0.2)€700 + 0.8€0 = 0.2€700$ i.e. a 0.2 or 20 per cent chance of winning €700 and an 80 per cent chance of nothing.

- Option R' = gamble h = $(0.8 \times 0.2)€1100 + (0.2 \times 0.2)€0 + 0.8€0 = 0.16€1100$, i.e. a 0.16 or 16 per cent chance of 1100 and an 84 per cent chance of nothing.

Thus when P = 0.2 g is the safe gamble corresponding to option S' and gamble h is the risky gamble corresponding to option R'.

The independence axiom implies that your choice between gambles e and f and gambles g and h should be independent of the value of P. But gambles e and g and gambles f and g are the same other than that P = 1 in gambles e and f and P = 0.2 in gambles g and h. Consequently, the independence axiom implies that if you chose gamble e when P = 1 in B then that you should have chosen gamble g in B* when P = 0.2. Similarly if you prefer gamble f when P = 1 in B you should prefer gamble h in B* when P = 0.2. Were your choices consistent with the independence axiom? Maybe they were but once again you would not be alone if they were not.[13] Experiments have shown that in examples like this people have a systematic tendency to choose option S' when P = 1 and S' is a sure thing but to choose option R' when P < 1.

Systematic evidence of common consequence and common ratio effects in experiments suggests that the independence axiom does not always reflect what people do.[14] This evidence weakens the claims of expected utility theory to be a descriptive theory. These claims are further weakened by evidence of violations of the transitivity axiom.

### 5.3.2.2 Transitivity

The axiom of transitivity implies that if A is preferred to B and B is preferred to C then A will be preferred to C. This claim appears entirely uncontroversial. For example, if you prefer chocolate to beer and beer to apple pie then you should prefer chocolate to apple pie. But it seems that when choices are over risky prospects there are instances were the axiom of transitivity is systematically violated. Examples of behaviour that contradict transitivity are usually referred to as instances of preference reversal. Before examining a generalised problem consider the specific choices in problem C below and make a note of your answers to (i) and (ii).

> **Choice problem C.** P and $ are two gambles. Gamble P will give you an 80 per cent chance of winning $100 and a 20 per cent chance of winning nothing. Gamble $ will give you a 40 per cent chance of winning $500 and a 60 per cent chance of winning nothing.
> (i) Which gamble do you prefer, gamble P or gamble $?
> (ii) How much would you be willing to pay to take part in each of the gambles P and $?

Now consider the following example characterised by two gambles or bets: a P bet and a $ bet. The P bet and the $ bet are defined as follows:

- The P bet: a p chance of winning X and a $(1 - p)$ chance of winning x.

- The $ bet: a q chance of winning Y and a $(1 - q)$ chance of winning y.

Where X, x, Y and y are prizes, p and q are probabilities and $X > x$, $Y > y$, $Y > X$ and $p > q$.

The P bet offers a higher chance of winning the smaller prize, X, but the $ bet offers a smaller chance of winning the bigger prize, Y. The choice problem in C is a numerical example of this kind. In C, $X = \$100$, $Y = \$500$, $x = y = 0$, $p = 0.8$ and $q = 0.4$. In experiments involving similar P and $ bets subjects are asked to choose between the P bet and $ bet and to value the P and $ bets (as you were asked to do in C). In effect both tasks amount to answering the same question, namely which of these two bets do you prefer? The axiom of transitivity implies that whichever bet you prefer (in your answer to part (i)) you should assign a higher value to it (in your answer to part (ii)). However, researchers have found a systematic tendency for people to choose the P bet in these circumstances and put a higher value on the $ bet. This has been interpreted in terms of intransitive preferences or preference reversal.[15]

To see this we can consider separately the implications of placing a higher value on the $ bet but stating a preference for P (*see* Machina, 1989: 32). If a subject's valuation of the P bet is $CE_p$ and their valuation of the $ bet is $CE_\$$ then the subject is:

(a)  indifferent between the P bet and some sure or certain amount[16] $CE_p$ implying that P *Indf* $CE_p$ where *Indf* is shorthand for saying that the individual is indifferent between P and $CE_p$.

(b) Indifferent between the $ bet and some sure value $CE_\$$ implying that $ *Indf* $CE_\$$.

And if the subject puts a higher value on the $ bet this implies:

(c) $CE_\$$ is greater than $CE_P$ which if the individual concerned prefers more money to less implies that he or she prefers $CE_\$$ to $CE_P$ or $CE_\$$ *PT* $CE_P$ where *PT* is shorthand for preferred to.

However, if the subject chooses P over $ then they:

(d) strictly prefer P to $. That is, P is preferred to $ or P *PT* $.

As (a) says that P *Indf* $CE_P$ and (b) says that $ *Indf* $CE_\$$ then if P *PT* $ it must also follow that $CE_P$ *PT* $CE_\$$. But (c) says that $CE_\$$ *PT* $CE_P$ which is a contradiction and (a)–(d) together imply that:

(e) $CE_P$ *Indf* P *PT* $ *Indf* $CE_\$$ *PT* $CE_P$ *Indf* P.

(e) simultaneously implies that P is preferred to $, P *PT* $ and $ is preferred to P, $ *PT* P which is inconsistent with transitivity and instead implies intransitive preferences or preference reversal.[17] An alternative interpretation favoured by psychologists is in terms of response mode or framing effects. This interpretation suggests that people respond differently to analytically equivalent questions that are framed differently or have different reference points. For instance, in the P and $ bet example the same question is asked in terms of first choice and then valuation and it is conceivable that choice and valuation invoke different mental responses. Framing effects of this kind have been observed in other experiments where different aspects of the same problem are highlighted, for example when subjects are asked to make decisions in relation to monetary losses or gains or survival and mortality (Kahneman and Tversky, 1979; Tversky and Kahneman, 1981; and *see* Kahneman (2003) for a recent review of framing effects).

Experimental evidence of preference reversal and violations of the independence axiom clearly weaken the descriptive claims of expected utility theory but to what extent? How meaningful are these experimental results which are after all conducted in a laboratory? Some of the experiments conducted relate to very specific cases, for example where the probability of the common consequence is very large as in Allais' famous example. Nevertheless the evidence is difficult to ignore and it should be no surprise that a number of alternative theories of choice under risk have been developed such as prospect theory (Kahneman and Tversky, 1979; Kahneman, 2003), generalised expected utility theory (Machina, 1982) and regret theory (Loomes and Sugden, 1986).

# Summary

In Section 5.1 of this chapter extensive forms were used to model uncertainty about where a player is in a game. A simple device of a broken line linking decision-nodes was used to illustrate uncertainty for players about where they are in a game. This technique was used to show that hidden-move games can be analysed as simultaneous-move games.

In Section 5.2 the idea of non-strategic risk was considered. Risk is incorporated in decision-making problems by specifying the likelihood of different events in terms of probabilities. Individuals are then assumed to choose between gambles or prospects on the basis of their expected pay-offs. Two alternative ways of calculating an expected pay-off were considered: expected value and expected utility. Examples were used to show that only the expected utility formulation can incorporate individuals' attitudes to risk. Individuals may be risk-averse, risk-neutral or risk-loving. Since not everyone is risk-neutral the expected utility formulation is potentially more useful when analysing decision problems characterised by risk. This conclusion will also apply to strategic games. If players' pay-offs in games are formulated in terms of their utility then the calculation of an expected pay-off will automatically generate an expected utility. An expected pay-off calculated in this way will take into account a player's attitude to risk. If the players' pay-offs are written in terms of some objective measure, such as units of money, they won't do this since the calculation of the expected pay-off will only yield an expected value.

Expected utility theory is not without its critics and in Section 5.3 some of the limitations of expected utility theory were considered. Experimental evidence of violations of the underlying assumptions of expected utility theory weakens the descriptive claims of the theory. As you will see in subsequent chapters expected utility theory is fundamental to game theoretic analysis when information is incomplete. It follows that experimental evidence of the kind discussed in Section 5.3 must also weaken the descriptive claims of game theory. A question remains as to why people don't automatically conform to the rules proscribed by expected utility theory. Perhaps in some instances they are just mistaken or ill informed and in such cases the normative or prescriptive claims of expected utility theory (and game theory by assumption) are less affected. However, you should be aware that experimental evidence has raised some challenging questions about the validity of expected utility in particular and game theory more generally. These questions have not been resolved although behavioural game theorists are making inroads in this area (*see*, for example, Kahneman, 2003 or Camerer, 2003).

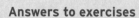 

## Answers to exercises

### 5.1

In the examples given only the last two could easily be represented as strategic games. In examples (a) to (e) the risk faced by the decision maker is independent of the choice made. For example, in (b) the outcome of the spin of the roulette wheel is unaffected by a punter's decision to bet or not (what happens, happens). But in example (f) if the thug decides to punch the other man this will clearly affect him and therefore the other man may wish to take some sort of preventative action, whether he is a karate expert or not (a game like this is analysed in Chapter 7). In example (g) the potential entrant needs to think about the likely response to entry of the incumbent firm and the latter's profits will depend not only on whether there is entry or not but also on what the incumbent does if there is entry. This is a classic game theoretic scenario and you saw it modelled in Chapter 4. You will see it again in Chapters 7 and 8 where the extra element of uncertainty suggested here is considered.

### 5.2

You were offered the choice of a free ticket to enter lottery 1 or a free ticket to lottery 2. In lottery 1 and lottery 2 the prizes and the probabilities of winning are as follows:

**Lottery 1:**

- 10 per cent chance of winning €5000.
- 70 per cent chance of winning €2500.
- 20 per cent chance of winning nothing.

**Lottery 2:**

- 40 per cent chance of winning €5000.
- 20 per cent chance of winning €2500.
- 40 per cent chance of winning nothing.

The expected values of lottery 1 is:

- EV(1) = 0.1€5000 + 0.7€2500 + 0.2€0 = €500 + €1750 = €2250.

The expected value of lottery 2 is:

- EV(2) = 0.4€5000 + 0.2€2500 + 0.4€0 = €2000 + €500 = €2500.

The expected value of lottery 2 is higher but lottery 2 is riskier; there is greater chance of winning nothing even though there is a higher probability of winning the larger prize. If you prefer lottery 1 you must be risk-averse. If you are risk-loving or you are risk-neutral you will choose lottery 2.

## Problems

1  What is the expected value of a gamble where you toss a coin and win €100 if it lands heads and lose €50 if it lands tails?

2  A bloke in an English pub is trying to exchange his Scottish pound notes for English pound notes. Legally a Scottish pound note is worth exactly the same as an English pound note. However, there is 10 per cent chance that the Scottish notes are forgeries. If I am risk-neutral how much should I be willing to pay for a Scottish pound note?

Questions 3 to 7 refer to the following scenario: Mr X is aiming to maximise his expected utility (he is an expected utility maximiser). His utility for money is given by the function $U(€y) = y^{1/2}$ where y is a monetary pay-off. Mr X's total income is €10 000. He is offered a bet on the outcome of the toss of a fair coin where, if the coin comes up heads, he loses all his income, but if it comes up tails he doubles it (by winning an extra €10 000).

3  What is Mr X's expected utility if he takes the bet?

4  What is Mr X's expected utility if he rejects the bet?

5  Will he take the bet?

6  Mr X is now offered a bet where if a fair coin comes up heads he again loses everything, but if it comes up tails he wins €40 000, taking his total income to €50 000. Will he take the bet?

7  Is Mr X risk-averse, risk-loving or risk-neutral?

## Questions for discussion

1  How well does expected utility theory hold up as either (a) a descriptive theory or (b) a prescriptive (or normative) theory in the light of experimental evidence contradicting the independence and transitivity axioms?

2 Consider the following choice problem attributable to Tversky and Kahneman (1981):

*You have to make a decision for yourself or a close friend between surgery or radiation therapy. You are given the following information:*

**Surgery:** of 100 people having surgery 90 live through the post-operative period, 68 are alive at the end of the first year and 34 are alive at the end of 5 years.

**Radiation therapy:** of 100 people having radiation therapy all live through the treatment, 77 are alive at the end of one year and 22 at the end of 5 years.

Which treatment would you choose? Would you choose differently if the problem was phrased as follows?

*You have to make a decision for yourself or a close friend between surgery or radiation therapy. You are given the following information:*

**Surgery:** of 100 people having surgery 10 die during surgery or the post-operative period, 32 die by the end of the first year and 66 die by the end of 5 years.

**Radiation therapy:** of 100 people having radiation therapy none die during treatment, 23 die by the end of one year and 78 die by the end of 5 years.

If your choice changes why do you think this might be? If your choice doesn't change can you explain why in experiments researchers have observed a systematic tendency for less people to choose radiation when the problem is phrased in terms of survival than when it is phrased in terms of mortality?

## Answers to problems

1 The expected value of the gamble is $\frac{1}{2}$(€100) − $\frac{1}{2}$ (€50) = €25.

2 The expected value of a Scottish note is 0.9 English pounds (90 pence). I should be willing to pay 90 pence for each note.

3 Mr X's expected utility if he takes the bet is $\frac{1}{2}.0 + \frac{1}{2}(20\,000^{1/2}) = 70.71$.

4 Mr X's expected utility if he doesn't take the bet is $10\,000^{1/2} = 100$.

5 Mr X will not take the bet. His expected utility if he doesn't take the bet is 100. If he takes the bet his expected utility is only 70.71.

6 His expected utility if he takes the new bet is $\frac{1}{2} (50\,000^{1/2}) = 111.8$. If he doesn't take the bet his expected utility is still 100. Since 111.8 > 100 he will take the new bet.

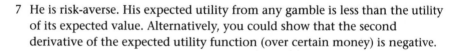

7 He is risk-averse. His expected utility from any gamble is less than the utility of its expected value. Alternatively, you could show that the second derivative of the expected utility function (over certain money) is negative.

## Notes

1 The probabilities in Mr Punter's decision problem are objectively given to him by the horse's owner. When probabilities are determined in this way the situation is said to be one of risk. An alternative possibility is that Mr Punter has no inside knowledge and instead bases his decision on his own subjective assessment of the horse's chance of winning the race. In this case the probabilities in Mr Punter's decision problem would be subjectively determined and technically speaking this would imply that the situation was one of uncertainty rather than risk (*see* Starmer, 2000: 334 for an exact distinction between these two terms).

2 These alternative possibilities are sometimes referred to as states of nature or the world. This terminology is more usual when the decision-making problem is characterised by uncertainty rather than risk (*see* previous note).

3 Starmer (2000) defines a prospect as a list of consequences with associated probabilities.

4 If you want to know more about attitudes to risk, expected values and expected utilities you could start by consulting the relevant chapter in a microeconomics textbook for example Katz and Rosen (1998: Chapter 6, pp. 167–8) or Frank (2003: Chapter 6, pp. 212–15).

5 Expected utilities are often referred to as von Neumann-Morgenstern utility functions after the originators of expected utility theory. For a precise formulation see Starmer (2000). For a less formal introduction consult a microeconomics textbook such as Katz and Rosen (1998: Chapter 6, Section 4).

6 For a detailed exposition of these assumptions and a formal derivation of the expected utility hypothesis *see* Starmer (2000: 334–6).

7 That is they care about risk and by assumption are choosing to maximise expected utility rather than expected value.

8 The individual's marginal utility is given by differentiation as $zy^{z-1}$ and the rate of increase (or decrease) in marginal utility is $(z - 1)zy^{(z-2)}$. The latter will equal zero if $z = 1$ implying constant marginal utility, it is positive if $z > 1$ implying increasing marginal utility and it is negative if $z < 1$ implying diminishing marginal utility.

9 Fair gambles have a zero expected value, for example a game where if a coin comes down heads you win €10 and you lose €10 otherwise. The expected value of this game is $[\frac{1}{2}10 - \frac{1}{2}10] = 0$. The expected value of your wealth if you accept this gamble is the same as the certain value of your wealth if you refuse the gamble. For example, if your initial wealth is €40 then the expected value of your wealth if you take the gamble is $[\frac{1}{2}(40 + 10) + \frac{1}{2}(40 - 10)] = \frac{1}{2}50 + \frac{1}{2}30 = 40$. By definition risk-averse people always refuse fair gambles, risk-neutral people are indifferent about fair gambles and risk-lovers always accept fair gambles (see Frank, 2003,: Chapter 6 for a more detailed discussion). The gambles offered by the gambling industry must be unfair in this technical sense or the industry could not expect to make profits.

10 *See*, for example, Kemp (1988).

11 *See*, Kreps (1990, Chapter 3: Section 5) for a more detailed discussion of these issues.

12 *See*, for example, Starmer and Sugden (1989), Machina (1989: 25–6) or Camerer (1995: 623–4) for further discussion.

13 If your choices were consistent with the independence axiom would they still be if the prizes were in tens of thousands of euros?

14 Apparently, it is not just humans who violate the independence axiom. Battalio, Kagel and MacDonald (1985) found that in experiments with rats some of their non-human subjects exhibited common ratio effects.

15 This pattern of violation was first observed by Lichentenstein and Slovic (1971) and Lindman (1971). *See* Tversky and Thaler (1990) for a review of the related evidence.

16 CEp is called the certainty equivalent of P.

17 *See* Loomes and Sugden (1983), Machina (1989) or Camerer (1995) for a more detailed discussion.

# 6

# MIXING AND EVOLVING

## Concepts and techniques

- Mixed strategy Nash equilibrium
- Evolutionary game theory
- Evolutionary stable equilibrium.

After working through this chapter you will be able to:

- Analyse games in which players choose mixed strategies
- Explain the difference between a pure strategy and a mixed strategy
- Derive the mixed strategy equilibrium of a two-player simultaneous-move game
- Analyse evolutionary games
- Explain what is meant by an evolutionary stable strategy
- Derive the evolutionary stable equilibrium of evolutionary games like hawk–dove and stag hunt
- Show that a dominant strategy in a static game will also be a stable strategy in an evolutionary game.

## Introduction

In this chapter the analytical tools developed in previous chapters (and Chapter 5 in particular) are used to examine two different kinds of games. The games that we are going to look at first are all simultaneous-move games that you have seen before. But now you are going to see what can happen in these games if the players randomise between their available pure strategies. When players randomise they are using mixed strategies and the related solution concept is that of a mixed strategy Nash equilibrium. The other games we are going to look at are evolutionary games where players' strategies (or behaviours) can change over time. In these kinds of games the relevant solution concept is that of an evolutionary stable equilibrium.

Simultaneous-move and evolutionary games are conceptually quite different. They are together in this chapter because in some evolutionary games the evolutionary stable equilibrium looks very much like a mixed strategy Nash equilibrium. This suggests that evolutionary game theory can provide a rationale for the mixed strategy Nash equilibrium concept. However, the insights that follow from evolutionary game theory go beyond that of mixed strategy Nash equilibrium. Evolutionary game theory has been used extensively to explore ideas relating to natural selection and the development of social conventions. Some of these insights are touched on in this chapter using examples like the chicken game which in an evolutionary context is analysed as a hawk–dove game.[1]

## 6.1 Nash equilibrium in mixed strategies

If players choose mixed strategies they are choosing a combination of pure strategies on the basis of a probabilistic distribution. For example, if a player is choosing between two strategies called left and right, one possible mixed strategy would be to choose left with probability $\frac{1}{4}$ and right with probability $\frac{3}{4}$ (or left a quarter of the time and right three-quarters of the time[2]). The player could operationalise a strategy like this by randomly choosing a card from a pack and then choosing left if it is a diamond and down if it is a club, a spade or a heart. This particular mixed strategy could then be written in shorthand either as {left; $\frac{1}{4}$, right; $\frac{3}{4}$} or {left, right; $\frac{1}{4}$, $\frac{3}{4}$}.

Mixed strategies can make intuitive sense in zero and constant-sum games if none of the players have dominant strategies. In games of this kind if one player can predict the other's behaviour then the first player has more chance of winning. Players therefore have an incentive to behave unpredictably and mixing up their pure strategies can help them to do this. Think about a footballer taking a penalty: if he always kicks the ball to the left he makes life easy for goalkeepers. Choosing a mixed strategy by randomising between kicking to the left, the right or straight ahead would be a way of behaving unpredictably and making it more difficult for the goalkeeper to save the penalty. Randomising may also be a useful way of deterring another player from choosing an action that is costly for you. For example, a monopolist might deter entry by randomising between fighting or conceding to entry, should entry occur (*see* Chapter 4, Section 4 and Chapter 8, Section 4). Choosing a mixed strategy might also be a rational way of dealing with uncertainty about what you think the other player is likely to be doing, for example if neither of you have a dominant strategy or if there are multiple pure strategy Nash equilibria. However, even when it is rational for players to randomise, mixed strategies will only be optimal if they are best responses to each other.

In this section you will see how to derive equilibrium mixed strategies, mixed strategies that are best responses to each other, in two-person simultaneous-move games where there is no uncertainty about pay-offs. In Chapters 7 and 8 the methodology used here will be extended to simultaneous, sequential and repeated-move games where there is more uncertainty.

Take a look at the chicken game in Matrix 6.1 where the two players are Tough and Duff and they are choosing between challenging the other to a fight or not. Neither really wants to fight but nor do they want to lose face by backing down. You saw a chicken game like this in Chapter 2, Section 2.4.3. Chicken games have two Nash equilibria in pure strategies and in this chicken game the two Nash equilibria are {backdown, challenge} and {challenge, backdown}. However, as you saw in Chapter 2, a feature of chicken games is that each player prefers a different Nash equilibrium. Here, Tough prefers the equilibrium in which Duff backs down but Duff prefers Tough to backdown. In these circumstances it is not clear how, or if, the players will manage to coordinate their strategy choices. One solution to this coordination problem might be for the players to choose mixed strategies.

**Matrix 6.1**  Tough and Duff chicken

|  |  | Duff | |
|---|---|:---:|:---:|
|  |  | **backdown** | **challenge** |
| **Tough** | **backdown** | 1, 1 | 0, 2 |
|  | **challenge** | 2, 0 | -3, -3 |

A mixed strategy is essentially a rule that prescribes certain action choices according to a probability distribution. When a player is playing against another player who is using a mixed strategy then the first player's pay-off is contingent on the mixed strategy of his opponent. For example, if Duff chooses backdown half of the time then if Tough chooses backdown he will get 1 half of the time (when Duff chooses backdown) and 0 half of the time (when Duff chooses challenge). Tough's pay-off from choosing backdown is therefore an expected pay-off equal to $\frac{1}{2}(1) + \frac{1}{2}(0) = \frac{1}{2}$. Tough's expected pay-off from choosing challenge is calculated in an analogous way as $\frac{1}{2}(2) + \frac{1}{2}(-3) = -\frac{1}{2}$. If the pay-offs in Matrix 6.1 are units of utility then these expected pay-offs are expected utilities which, as you saw in Chapter 5, means that Tough's attitude to risk is accounted for and we don't need to make any further allowances in this respect. If Tough similarly adopts a mixed strategy then Duff's expected pay-offs can be calculated in the same way (see below).

For the players' mixed strategies to be optimal they need to be best responses to each other. For example, if Tough chooses backdown with probability $p_t$ and challenge with probability $1 - p_t$ while Duff chooses backdown with probability $p_d$ and challenge with probability $1 - p_d$, then for $p_t$ and $p_d$ to constitute a mixed strategy Nash equilibrium they must be best responses to each other. We will examine two equivalent ways of solving for mixed strategies that constitute a mixed strategy Nash equilibrium. Method 1 is intuitive. Method 2 relies rather more on mathematical logic.

### Method 1

The intuitive argument goes like this: if either player chooses a mixed strategy then they must be indifferent between playing either of their pure strategies. If not, then one pure strategy would be preferred and they would choose that rather than randomising. According to this logic for a mixed strategy to be part of a Nash equilibrium for Tough, he must be indifferent between choosing challenge or backdown. If this is the case his expected pay-off from choosing challenge must be the same as his expected pay-off from choosing backdown. Similarly, if Duff chooses a mixed strategy, his expected pay-off from choosing challenge must be the same as his expected pay-off from backdown.

Let's look at the game first from Tough's perspective. Tough's expected pay-off from choosing backdown depends on Duff's strategy. If Duff chooses backdown with probability $p_d$ and challenge with probability $1 - p_d$ then Duff is choosing a mixed strategy. In this case Tough's expected pay-off from choosing backdown is:

$$\text{Tough's expected pay-off from backdown} = p_d 1 + (1 - p_d)0 \qquad (6.1)$$

Tough's expected pay-off from choosing challenge if Duff is choosing a mixed strategy is:

$$\text{Tough's expected pay-off from challenge} = p_d 2 + (1 - p_d)(-3) \qquad (6.2)$$

Setting these two expected pay-offs equal yields:

$$p_d1 + (1 - p_d)0 = p_d2 + (1 - p_d)(-3) \tag{6.3}$$

which solves for $p_d = \frac{3}{4}$ where $p_d$ is the probability that Duff chooses backdown. In other words it is rational for Tough to choose a mixed strategy if Duff chooses backdown with probability $\frac{3}{4}$ (or is choosing backdown three-quarters of the time).

Now looking at the game from Duff's perspective, his expected pay-off from choosing backdown if Tough is choosing a mixed strategy is:

$$\text{Duff's expected pay-off from backdown} = p_t1 + (1 - p_t)0 \tag{6.4}$$

His expected pay-off from choosing challenge is:

$$\text{Duff's expected pay-off from challenge} = p_t2 + (1 - p_t)(-3) \tag{6.5}$$

Setting these two expected pay-offs equal yields:

$$p_t1 + (1 - p_t)0 = p_t2 + (1 - p_t)(-3) \tag{6.6}$$

which solves for $p_t = \frac{3}{4}$ where $p_t$ is the probability that Tough chooses backdown. This means that if $p_t = \frac{3}{4}$ it makes sense for Duff to choose a mixed strategy.

Equations (6.1)–(6.6) imply that if $p_d = \frac{3}{4}$ it is rational for Tough to choose a mixed strategy and if $p_t = \frac{3}{4}$ it is rational for Duff to choose a mixed strategy. If $p_d = \frac{3}{4}$ and $p_t = \frac{3}{4}$ then Duff and Tough's mixed strategies will be best responses to each other since they can do no better by choosing something else. Therefore, the mixed strategies $p_d = \frac{3}{4}$ and $p_t = \frac{3}{4}$ are Nash equilibrium strategies. We can write this mixed strategy Nash equilibrium as {(Tough: backdown; $\frac{3}{4}$, challenge; $\frac{1}{4}$)(Duff: backdown; $\frac{3}{4}$, challenge; $\frac{1}{4}$)}.

### Method 2

More formally, if a strategy is a Nash equilibrium strategy then it is a best response to the equilibrium strategy of the other player. For a strategy to be a best response it should generate the highest possible or maximum pay-off for the player concerned. Therefore we can find Tough and Duff's equilibrium mixed strategies by finding the strategies that maximise their expected pay-offs.

Tough's expected pay-off from choosing $p_t$ as a mixed strategy, $\text{EPO}_{\text{Tmixed}}$, if Duff chooses $p_d$ is:

$$\text{EPO}_{\text{Tmixed}} = p_t [p_d1 + (1 - p_d)0] + (1 - p_t)[p_d2 + (1 - p_d)(-3)] \tag{6.7}$$

Duff's expected pay-off from choosing $p_d$ as a mixed strategy, $\text{EPO}_{\text{Dmixed}}$, if Tough chooses $p_t$ is:

$$\text{EPO}_{\text{Dmixed}} = p_d \, [p_t 1 + (1 - p_t)0] + (1 - p_d)[p_t 2 + (1 - p_t)(-3)] \tag{6.8}$$

To find each player's optimal mixed strategy we can use calculus. This involves differentiating (6.7) and (6.8) with respect to $p_t$ and $p_d$. We can then solve for the optimal values of $p_t$ and $p_d$ from the first order conditions. By differentiating (6.7) with respect to $p_t$ and setting the resulting expression equal to zero we obtain the following condition:

$$[p_d 1 + (1 - p_d)0] - [p_d 2 + (1 - p_d)(-3)] = 0 \tag{6.9}$$

rearrangement of (6.9) leads to:

$$p_d 1 + (1 - p_d)0 = p_d 2 + (1 - p_d)(-3) \tag{6.10}$$

Equation (6.10) solves for $p_d = \frac{3}{4}$ as in Method 1.

Equation (6.10) shows that the first order condition for utility maximisation for Tough requires that Tough's expected pay-off from choosing backdown equals his expected pay-off from choosing challenge. Equation (6.10) should look familiar to you. Can you see that it is the same as equation (6.3) above? This coincidence means that the intuitive argument in Method 1 is implied by the mathematical derivation in Method 2. In other words, the mathematics of Method 2 simply formalises the intuition of Method 1.

Applying the same methodology to Duff's pay-off by differentiating (6.8) with respect to $p_d$ leads to:

$$[p_t 1 + (1 - p_t)0] - [p_t 2 + (1 - p_t)(-3)] = 0 \tag{6.11}$$

rearrangement of (6.11) leads to:

$$p_t 1 + (1 - p_t)0 = p_t 2 + (1 - p_t)(-3) \tag{6.12}$$

Equation (6.12) solves for $p_t = \frac{3}{4}$ as in Method 1. Equation (6.12) should also look familiar to you. It is the same as equation (6.6). This coincidence confirms that the intuition of Method 1 is consistent with the mathematical logic of Method 2.

Using either method, the mixed strategy Nash equilibrium of the game is {(Tough: backdown; $\frac{3}{4}$, challenge; $\frac{1}{4}$)(Duff: backdown; $\frac{3}{4}$, challenge; $\frac{1}{4}$)}. As Methods 1 and 2 lead to the same result you can use either to solve for the equilibrium mixed strategies. This is a general result. It means that if you want to find a player's equilibrium mixed strategy you can do so by simply setting their expected pay-offs from their pure strategies equal.

In the mixed strategy Nash equilibrium of Tough and Duff's chicken game each player's expected pay-off is $\frac{3}{4}$. This is found by substituting for $p_t = p_d = \frac{3}{4}$ in equations (6.7) and (6.8) (you should check this). In the mixed strategy Nash equilibrium each player is indifferent between challenge or backdown and their expected pay-offs are greater than or equal to their pay-offs from following any other strategy given that the other is following their equilibrium mixed strategy. For example if Tough challenges for sure but Duff follows his equilibrium mixed strategy then Tough's expected pay-off, $EPO_{Tchallenge,}$ is:

$$EPO_{Tchallenge} = p_d2 + (1 - p_d)(- 3) = \frac{6}{4} - \frac{3}{4} = \frac{3}{4} \tag{6.13}$$

And if Tough always chooses backdown but Duff follows his equilibrium mixed strategy then Tough's expected pay-off, $EPO_{Tbkdown,}$ is:

$$EPO_{Tbkdown} = p_d1 + (1 - p_d)0 = \frac{3}{4} \tag{6.14}$$

If both players follow one or other of their pure strategies then they either get 0, 1, 2 or –3 depending on which strategy they and the other player choose.

## Exercise 6.1

In the simplified Penalty – taking game in Matrix 6.2 below the striker can only kick to the left or the right and therefore the goalkeeper only moves either to the left or the right. If the striker and the goalkeeper choose the same direction (looking at the game from either the striker's or the goalie's perspective) the goalkeeper saves the penalty and otherwise the striker scores. Derive the mixed strategy Nash equilibrium of this game.

Matrix 6.2  Penalty taking

|  |  | goalkeeper | |
| --- | --- | --- | --- |
|  |  | left | right |
| striker | left | 0, 1 | 1, 0 |
|  | right | 1, 0 | 0, 1 |

Mixed strategies have a certain appeal when players are trying to be unpredictable as in games of pure conflict like penalty taking. They also make sense when one player is trying to deter some action by another, for instance in quality control exercises in which auditors make random checks to discourage malpractice (or encourage good practice). The random checks made by officials at customs controls are another example of this kind. It would be impractical to search everyone's bags – there are too many people and not enough customs officials. Officials also make random ticket checks at some events. For example, at the Wimbledon tennis championships there is excess demand for tickets but the organisers want to deter ticket holders from selling on their tickets to touts. Again, it would be impractical to check everyone's ticket. Mixed strategies may also be rational when a player just doesn't know what else to do.

But mixed strategies won't always make sense even if neither player has a dominant strategy. For example, in coordination games like the Battle of the sexes, players really want to coordinate their actions even if they have different preferences. In these circumstances rational players may be more likely to search for alternatives by pre-committing or by looking for focal points (*see* Schelling, 1960). In a game theoretic context focal points are strategy combinations that stand out in some way for all the players and therefore they can choose to coordinate their actions around them. For example, in the Battle of the sexes game that you saw in Chapter 2 (Section 2.4.3), party might become a focal point if both players were fans of a famous footballer who had also been invited to the party.

Even if mixed strategies appeal to the players in a game one problem with the mixed strategy Nash equilibrium concept in practice is that players somehow need to work out each other's mixed strategies in order to make it operational. This will not always, if ever, be easy. One possibility is that players can learn to play mixed strategies if a game is repeated enough times. But in a mixed strategy Nash equilibrium the expected pay-off of a player from using their equilibrium mixed strategy is, by assumption, the same as their pay-off from choosing a pure strategy. Consequently, there is no extra incentive to randomise or maintain a randomising strategy in preference to choosing a pure strategy. Nevertheless, even if individual players are choosing pure strategies a mixed strategy Nash equilibrium could be played out among a group of players if an equilibrium fraction of the group chooses one pure strategy while the rest of the group chooses another.

The predictive validity of mixed strategy Nash equilibria in zero-sum and constant-sum games has been tested in a long line of experiments that began in the 1950s. This research is discussed in detail in Camerer (2003: Chapter 3). To summarise Camerer, some of the earlier studies provided support for the mixed strategy Nash equilibrium concept and in particular the argument that a mixed strategy Nash equilibrium can be learned (Kaufman and Becker, 1961 and Malcolm and Lieberman, 1965). More recent studies have found that the frequencies with which players choose their pure strategies in zero-sum games are often very close to the mixed strategy Nash equilibrium prediction (*see*, for example, O'Neill, 1987). However significant deviations from the mixed strategy Nash equilibrium frequencies have also been observed. In some experiments where subjects are explicitly allowed to randomise most do not choose mixtures corresponding to the mixed strategy Nash equilibrium and subjects often choose pure strategies (for example, Bloomfield, 1994). However, the mixture of strategies chosen within groups of subjects is often close to the mixed strategy Nash equilibrium predictions (Camerer, 2003: 142). This evidence is consistent with the idea noted above of a mixed strategy Nash equilibrium being played out among a group of people. This possibility is explored in Section 6.2 below.

Field studies of the mixed strategy Nash equilibrium concept have also been conducted. For example, Walker and Wooders (2001) and Hsu, Huang and Tang (2003) have examined the direction of serves in professional tennis and Palacios-Huerta (2003) has studied penalty taking in association football. These studies have tended to confirm (less so in the case of Hsu et al.) that professional players in tennis and association football can successfully employ equilibrium mixed strategies. This may be less true for subjects in laboratory experiments but they have less incentive to practise.

## 6.2 **Evolutionary games**

One scenario where mixed strategies of a kind can make sense is in evolutionary games. Evolutionary game theory has its origins in biology where it is acknowledged that in any animal population some behavioural patterns will be more successful than others. For example, a particular behavioural strategy may represent a more efficient way of securing resources that are necessary for survival. From the biological perspective more successful strategies, or phenotypes as they are called, will be fitter. Being fitter means that they will have more reproductive success and become more numerous. If one type of behaviour in a population is becoming more numerous, while another is becoming less numerous, the existence of the less successful phenotype is threatened and it is not, in biological terms, evolutionary stable. Evolutionary game theory seeks to identify patterns of behaviour in populations that are evolutionary stable.

### 6.2.1 Hawks and doves

We can explore these ideas further by examining the hawk–dove game in Matrix 6.3. This game looks like a chicken game between two players who choose between strategies called hawk and dove but it has a different, evolutionary interpretation. In the evolutionary version of this game a population of animals (not necessarily birds) is made up of two types; hawks and doves. Hawk and dove are two patterns of animal (possibly human) behaviour or phenotypes that, from a strictly biological perspective, are genetically determined. Hawks are aggressive and prefer to fight while doves are more peaceful by nature and prefer not to fight. Hawks and doves meet up and interact randomly. The pay-offs represent shares of some scarce resource that is necessary for survival, e.g. food, water or perhaps oil. The average pay-off of hawks and doves will reflect their share of the scarce resource. The greater their share of the scarce resource the higher will be their chances of survival and the higher their reproduction rates.[3]

Matrix 6.3  Hawk–dove 1

|  | hawk | dove |
|---|---|---|
| hawk | -4, -4 | 12, 0 |
| dove | 0, 12 | 6, 6 |

There are three possible pairings in this game: hawk with hawk, dove with dove and hawk with dove. If a hawk interacts with another hawk they fight over the resource injuring themselves and destroying most of the resource in the process receiving a pay-off of –4 each. If two doves interact they peacefully share the resource and both receive a pay-off of 6. If a dove pairs with a hawk the hawk secures all of the resource and the dove receives nothing.

There are also three possible outcomes in terms of the survival of hawks and doves in the population: only hawks survive; only doves survive; both doves and hawks survive. The resulting population will not be stable if the entry or invasion of one or more of either type raises the average pay-off of the invading type over that of the other. If this happened the reproductive rate of the invader would be higher than that of the other type and the latter's survival would be threatened. In these circumstances the population is not stable because it is vulnerable to invasion. Additionally a population composed of both hawks and doves would only be stable if the average pay-off of the hawks or the doves was the same. If this were not the case the reproductive rate of one type would be higher than that of the other and the survival of one behavioural type would be threatened. But if (i) neither hawks nor doves stand to gain by invasion and (ii) their reproduction rates are equal where they coexist then the population mix will be stable. A population satisfying these conditions constitutes an evolutionary stable equilibrium as defined by the biologist Maynard Smith (1982).

In the hawk–dove game in Matrix 6.3 what kind of population mix of hawks and doves would be evolutionary stable? We can start to answer this question by initially considering a population where half are hawks and the other half doves. In this situation the probability of a hawk being paired with another hawk, or a dove interacting with another dove is $\frac{1}{2}$ as is the probability of a hawk being paired with a dove. The average pay-offs of hawks and doves will be:

Average pay-off of a hawk: $APO_H = \frac{1}{2}(-4) + \frac{1}{2}(12) = 4$    (6.15)
Average pay-off of a dove: $APO_D = \frac{1}{2}(0) + \frac{1}{2}(6) = 3$    (6.16)

(6.15) and (6.16) imply that when the population is half hawks and half doves the average pay-off of hawks is higher. According to the biological interpretation hawks will therefore have higher survival rates and reproduce faster. As a result, the population will become more hawkish. Thus a mix of $\frac{1}{2}$ hawks and $\frac{1}{2}$ doves is not a stable equilibrium as the percentage of hawks in the population will be growing.

But if the population is made up of only hawks then $APO_H = -4$. This is not a stable situation either as the entry of one dove would only marginally raise $APO_H$ and the pay-off of the dove, $APO_D$, would be 0 which is considerably greater than −4. Therefore doves could invade the population and doves would reproduce faster than hawks. This means that a population consisting only of hawks is not evolutionary stable either.

What if the population consisted only of doves? The average pay-off of the doves would be 6 but if one hawk invaded its pay-off would be 12 and the average pay-off of the doves would fall. Therefore hawks could invade the population and if they did they would reproduce faster than the doves. Therefore a population consisting only of doves is not stable either.

The only possible evolutionary stable equilibrium is therefore one where doves and hawks both coexist but not in equal numbers. For stability we require that the average pay-offs of hawks and doves are equal. That is, $APO_H = APO_D$. If this condition is satisfied the reproduction rates of hawks and doves will also be equal.

To find the stable mix of hawks and doves where $APO_H = APO_D$ let h be the fraction of hawks (the probability of a random member of the population being a hawk). Then the average pay-offs of hawks and doves will be:

Average pay-off of a hawk: $APO_H = h(-4) + (1-h)12 = 12 - 16h$    (6.17)
Average pay-off of a dove: $APO_D = h(0) + (1-h)6 = 6 - 6h$    (6.18)

Setting $APO_H = APO_D$ leads to:

$$APO_H = 12 - 16h = 6 - 6h = APO_D$$    (6.19)

or:

$$h = \frac{6}{10}$$    (6.20)

$h = \frac{6}{10}$ or 0.6 implies that 60 per cent of the population are hawks and 40 per cent are doves. This mix of doves and hawks is stable because if hawk numbers increase $APO_H$ will fall relative to $APO_D$ and if the population is invaded by doves

APO$_D$ falls relative to APO$_H$. Therefore neither hawks nor doves can mount a successful invasion; the invader always ends up with a lower average pay-off than the invaded type. This means that the invader's reproduction rate will be lower and its numbers will fall until the average pay-offs of both types are equal and the 60:40 mix is restored. The 60:40 hawk–dove ratio is therefore evolutionary stable and constitutes an evolutionary stable equilibrium. This stable equilibrium is shown diagrammatically in Figure 6.1 where APO$_H$ and APO$_D$ are plotted against the fraction of hawks in the population.

In Figure 6.1 the average pay-offs of hawks and doves are measured along the vertical axis and the fraction of hawks is measured along the horizontal axis. The lines corresponding to APO Dove and APO Hawk chart the average pay-offs of doves and hawks in relation to the fraction of hawks in the population. When this fraction is 0.6 the two lines cross signifying that the average pay-offs of doves and hawks are equal when 60 per cent of the population are hawks. To the right of this point the fraction of hawks is higher but APO$_H$ is less than APO$_D$. Consequently, doves reproduce faster than hawks signifying that the population is not vulnerable to invasion by hawks. To the left of the intersection point the percentage of doves in the population is higher than 40 per cent but APO$_D$ is less than APO$_H$. As a result hawks reproduce faster than doves. This signifies that the population is not vulnerable to invasion by doves either.

$h = 0.6$ also corresponds to the mixed strategy Nash equilibrium of the equivalent chicken game. That is, if we interpret the hawk–dove game in a strictly non-evolutionary way then the mixed strategy Nash equilibrium of that game would be {(hawk: $\frac{3}{5}$, dove: $\frac{2}{5}$)(hawk: $\frac{3}{5}$, dove: $\frac{2}{5}$)}. If you are not sure about this let $p_h$ be the probability of choosing hawk as a strategy for one of the players. Then set the expected pay-off from hawk equal to the expected pay-off from dove for the other. Solving for $p_h$ will give you $p_h = 0.6$.

Thus the evolutionary approach gives a rationale for the Nash equilibrium concept and in this particular case the idea of a Nash equilibrium in mixed strategies. The strictly biological interpretation also suggests that natural selection depends on individual pay-offs, not the pay-off of the population as a whole.

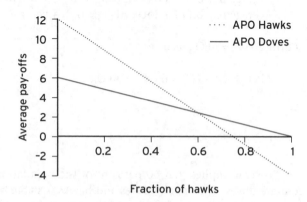

**Figure 6.1** Average pay-offs of hawks and doves

This is clear in the hawk–dove game as the population as a whole would be better off if there were no hawks but a population of all doves would not be stable as it would be vulnerable to invasion by hawks.

## Exercise 6.2

Find the evolutionary stable equilibrium of the hawk-dove game in Matrix 6.3.1. Why do you think the equilibrium fraction of hawks is higher in hawk-dove 2 than in hawk-dove 1?

**Matrix 6.3.1**  Hawk-dove 2

|      | hawk | dove |
|------|------|------|
| hawk | 1, 1 | 6, 2 |
| dove | 2, 6 | 3, 3 |

## 6.2.2 Socio-evolutionary games

An alternative to the strictly biological interpretation is to consider behaviour in terms of preferences or strategies rather than predetermined types. Then the evolution of behavioural strategies can be interpreted in terms of learning rather than genetically programmed adaptation. For example, hawk and dove could represent two behavioural preferences in a society: aggressive and peaceful. In this scenario members of the society would benefit if they could avoid simultaneous hawk-like behaviour but there is conflict as the benefits of cooperation are distributed differently between hawks and doves. According to this socio-evolutionary interpretation people will learn which strategies are more successful and adapt by consciously adopting strategies that achieve higher pay-offs. They will adopt more hawkish or more dovish behaviour depending on the usefulness of each. However, the usefulness of a preference for a certain type of behaviour or strategy will depend on the frequency others are using the same strategy since being hawkish will only be a good idea if there are enough doves in the population. The stable mix of behavioural strategies will be one where there is no incentive for members of the society to switch strategies. Thus the evolutionary approach can suggest ways in which social rules and cultural conventions become established over time.

In order to develop these arguments further[4] consider the stag hunt game in Matrix 6.4 (you saw this game earlier in Problem 3 of Chapter 2). In stag hunt the choice is between hunting for stag and hunting for hare. Stag hunting requires cooperation but a hunter acting alone can successfully kill a hare. However, the stag is bigger and a share in a stag is preferred to a whole hare. In the simultaneous-move version of this game there are two Nash equilibria in pure strategies: {stag, stag} and {hare, hare}. Since stag hunt is a coordination game with assurance (*see* Chapter 2, Section 2.4) one of the equilibria is Pareto superior. Can you see that the Pareto superior equilibrium is {stag, stag}, the equilibrium in which everyone joins in the stag hunt? There is also a mixed strategy Nash equilibrium in which both players choose stag with probability $\frac{1}{5}$ or 0.2.

**Matrix 6.4** Stag hunt

|  | stag | hare |
|---|---|---|
| **stag** | 5, 5 | 0, 1 |
| **hare** | 1, 0 | 1, 1 |

In the socio-evolutionary version of this game people in a large population are assumed to fall into two groups. They either follow a social convention of cooperation and working together or they act on their own. The first group of people will choose stag hunting and the second group hunting for hare. Over time people can switch between strategies but they will only do so if they expect to make a higher return by doing so. They can learn which strategy is likely to do better from social interactions with acquaintances and friends. People's hunting partners though are chosen randomly. If a stag hunter is paired with an individualistic hare hunter the latter does better but if two stag hunters are paired together they do better than two hare hunters. If the proportion of cooperating stag hunters in the population is s then the average pay-off of stag hunters is:

$$\text{Average pay-off of stag hunters: } APO_S = s5 + (1 - s)0 = 5s \qquad (6.21)$$

And the average pay-off of hare hunters is:

$$\text{Average pay-off of hare hunters: } APO_H = s1 + (1 - s)1 = 1 \qquad (6.22)$$

The expected pay-off from stag hunting is therefore higher when $5s > 1$ or $s > \frac{1}{5}$ = 0.2. When $s < 0.2$ the proportion of stag hunters in the population is not high enough and hare hunting is more beneficial. When $s = 0.2$ the expected pay-off from stag hunting is the same as it is from hunting hare.

As before there are three possible outcomes in terms of the population mix: a population composed solely of stag hunters, a population composed of only hare hunters and a population where both types of hunting are practised. However, the last possibility could not persist and therefore cannot constitute an evolutionary stable equilibrium. To see this consider what happens if 20 per cent of the population are stag hunters (s = 0.2). The average pay-offs of both types of hunter would be the same but if just one person decided to switch from hare hunting to stag hunting the average pay-off of stag hunters, 5s, would increase (as s would have increased). Furthermore, since s > 0.2 $APO_S$ is higher than $APO_H$ and so more hare hunters will switch to stag hunting. Eventually no hare hunters will be left as the whole population will have switched to stag hunting. Similarly if s = 0.2 but one stag hunter switches to hare hunting the average pay-off of hare hunters would stay the same but the average pay-off of stag hunters would fall below that of hare hunters (s is less than 0.2 so 5s < 1). Once other stag hunters learn what had happened they too will switch to hare hunting which would lower the expected pay-off from stag hunting still further. Eventually only hare hunters would be left in the population. Thus a population composed of both types of hunters cannot survive.

What makes a population of both types stable in the hawk–dove game but unstable in the stag hunt game? Well, in the hawk–dove game the average pay-off of each type is higher the rarer it becomes but the opposite happens in the stag hunt game. In the stag hunt game the average pay-off associated with either strategy is higher the more people employ it. This is shown in Figure 6.2 which you can compare with Figure 6.1. Figure 6.2 shows the average pay-offs of stag and hare hunters plotted against the fraction of people in the population who are using the stag hunting strategy. When this fraction is 0.2 the average pay-offs are equal. In contrast to Figure 6.1, when the fraction of stag hunters rises above 0.2 the average pay-off of stag hunters increases. The number of stag hunters in the population will therefore continue to increase. On the other hand, when the fraction of stag hunters falls below 0.2 the average pay-off of stag hunters falls. In this case the number of stag hunters will continue to decrease.

However, a population consisting solely of either stag hunters or hare hunters will be stable. To see this consider a population consisting only of stag hunters: if one person were to switch to hare hunting that person's pay-off would be 1 but as long as the percentage of stag hunters is greater than 20 per cent the average pay-off from stag hunting is higher than 1. In Figure 6.2 this is shown by the lower average pay-off of hare hunters when the fraction of stag hunters in the population is between 1 and 0.2. Similarly, in a population consisting only of hare hunters if one or two people switched to stag hunting then their average pay-off would be less than 1.[5] This will be true as long as the percentage of stag hunters is less than 20 per cent, in which case the expected pay-off from stag hunting is less than that from hare hunting. In Figure 6.2 this is shown by the lower average pay-off of stag hunters when the fraction of stag hunters in the population is between 0 and 0.2.

Consequently, there are two evolutionary stable equilibria: either the population is composed solely of stag hunters or there are only hare hunters. Either possibility will be a stable outcome. The first evolutionary stable equilibrium where there are only stag hunters corresponds to the {stag, stag} Nash equilibrium

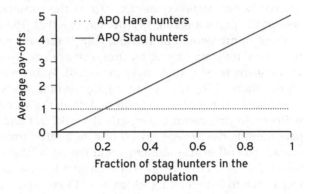

**Figure 6.2** Average pay-offs of hunters

in the static version of the game. The all hare hunter evolutionary stable equilibrium corresponds to the {hare, hare} Nash equilibrium. But there is no evolutionary stable equilibrium corresponding to the mixed strategy Nash equilibrium of the static game. Which evolutionary stable equilibrium will result will depend on the initial mix of hunting strategies. This will in turn depend on the social conventions in the population (or society). It is therefore entirely plausible that different evolutionary equilibria could evolve in different societies facing the same evolutionary issues. However, should two previously isolated populations with different hunting strategies come into contact a new evolutionary stable equilibrium could established in which both populations follow the same strategy. But the fact that in the stag hunting equilibrium the pay-offs are higher does not guarantee that this will be the outcome.

The analysis in the previous section showed how the evolutionary stable equilibrium of the evolutionary hawk–dove game corresponds to the mixed strategy Nash equilibrium of the equivalent simultaneous move or static game. Similarly, the evolutionary equilibria of the stag hunt game correspond to the two pure Nash equilibria of the static stag hunt game. In fact all evolutionary equilibria are Nash equilibria. Hence evolutionary theory provides some rationale for the Nash equilibrium concept generally and the mixed strategy Nash equilibrium in particular.

However, as you have seen, not all Nash equilibria are evolutionary stable (the mixed strategy equilibrium of stag hunt for example). But if the Nash equilibrium of a static game is also a dominant strategy equilibrium there will be an evolutionary equivalent. We can see this by looking at the conservationists' dilemma in Matrix 6.5 (you saw a different version of this game in Section 3.5 of Chapter 3).

**Matrix 6.5** The conservationists' dilemma

|  | conservation | exploitation |
|---|---|---|
| **conservation** | 25, 25 | –50, 100 |
| **exploitation** | 100, –50 | 0, 0 |

In this game the players choose between conservationist and exploitative strategies. The static version of the conservationists' dilemma is a prisoners' dilemma and exploitation is a dominant strategy. The dominant strategy equilibrium is therefore {exploitation, exploitation} even though the players would have higher pay-offs if they could agree to conserve. In a socio-evolutionary context conservation and exploitation are alternative strategies employed by people that interact randomly. If the proportion of conservationists is c then the average pay-off of conservationists is c25 – (1 – c)50 = 75c – 50 but the average pay-off of exploiters is c100 + (1 – c)0 = 100c. Since 100c is greater than 75c – 50 for all positive values of c the average pay-off of conservationists will always be less than that of exploiters. This means that whatever the initial value of c conservationists will want to switch strategies until c = 0 and everyone is an exploiter. If c = 0 the population is stable because even if only one exploiter switched to conservation their expected pay-off would fall. Thus exploitation is the evolutionary stable strategy of the game. This result illustrates a general proposition that dominant strategies in static games are stable strategies in an evolutionary context.

## Summary

In this chapter you have seen how to derive the mixed strategy Nash equilibrium of two-person simultaneous-move games. When a player chooses a mixed strategy they choose a mix of their pure strategies on the basis of some probabilistic rule. For example, imagine a game where a player has two pure strategies: up and down. A possible mixed strategy would be to choose up with probability $\frac{1}{2}$ and down with probability $\frac{1}{2}$. The player could operationalise this mixed strategy by tossing a coin. If it came up heads the player could decide to choose up and if it came up tails she could choose down.

In a mixed strategy Nash equilibrium the players mixed strategies are best responses to each other. In some zero and constant sum games there may be no Nash equilibrium in pure strategies but there will always be a mixed strategy Nash equilibrium. In these games mixed strategies also have a certain intuitive appeal as players are more likely to win if they behave unpredictably and choosing mixed strategies is one way of doing just that. There are other types of games where players could use mixed strategies. For example, in games like chicken and battle of the sexes, where there is more than one Nash equilibrium in pure strategies, the players might think about randomising. However, mixed strategies may be difficult to operationalise in practice and in some circumstances they may be undesirable.

One interpretation of a mixed strategy Nash equilibrium that has met with some success is in terms of a population of player types. For example, individual players in a population may be choosing pure strategies but a mixed strategy Nash equilibrium could be played out if an equilibrium fraction of the group chooses one pure strategy while the rest of the group chooses the other. This possibility was considered in the context of evolutionary game theory. Two different evolutionary standpoints were explored. The hawk–dove game was initially analysed from a strictly biological standpoint where the idea of natural selection is paramount and then re-interpreted in a socio-evolutionary context. Socio-evolutionary game theory explores ideas relating to the development of social conventions and cultural norms. This approach was used to examine two more games: the Stag hunt coordination game and the conservationists' version of the prisoners' dilemma. Evolutionary game theory is an interesting and relatively new branch of game theory. It offers many new insights of which some have been touched on in this chapter.

## Answers to exercises

6.1

**Matrix 6.2** Penalty taking

<table>
<tr><td></td><td></td><td colspan="2">goalkeeper</td></tr>
<tr><td></td><td></td><td>left</td><td>right</td></tr>
<tr><td rowspan="2">striker</td><td>left</td><td>0, 1</td><td>1, 0</td></tr>
<tr><td>right</td><td>1, 0</td><td>0, 1</td></tr>
</table>

If the probability the striker kicks to the left is $p_s$ and the probability the goalkeeper dives to the striker's left is $p_g$ then if the striker kicks to the left his expected pay-off is:

$$\text{Striker (left)} = p_g 0 + (1 - p_g)1 \tag{i}$$

If he kicks to the right his expected pay-off is:

$$\text{Striker (right)} = p_g 1 + (1 - p_g)0 \tag{ii}$$

Setting these two equal implies:

$$p_g 0 + (1 - p_g)1 = p_g 1 + (1 - p_g)0 \qquad \text{(iii)}$$

(iii) solves for $p_g = \frac{1}{2}$. As this game is symmetric setting the goalkeeper's expected pay-offs from diving left and right equal solves for $p_s = \frac{1}{2}$. Thus the mixed strategy Nash equilibrium is {(striker: left; $\frac{1}{2}$, right; $\frac{1}{2}$) (goalkeeper: left; $\frac{1}{2}$, right; $\frac{1}{2}$)}.

6.2

**Matrix 6.3.1** Hawk–dove 2

|       | hawk | dove |
|-------|------|------|
| **hawk** | 1, 1 | 6, 2 |
| **dove** | 2, 6 | 3, 3 |

Let h equal the fraction of hawks in the population then $APO_H = h1 + (1 - h)6 = 6 - 5h$ and $APO_D = h2 + (1 - h)3 = 3 - 1h$. $APO_H = APO_D$ when $6 - 5h = 3 - 1h$ or $h = \frac{3}{4} = 0.75$. In Hawk–dove 1 the equilibrium fraction of hawks was 0.6 which is clearly less. The equilibrium fraction of hawks is lower in hawk–dove 1 because the costs for a hawk of being paired with another hawk and the gains for a dove from being paired with another dove are both higher.

## Problems

1  Consider the penalty game in Matrix 6.5. This game is a version of the Penalty-taking game in Matrix 6.2. In this version of the game the striker derives more pleasure when he scores by kicking to the left (perhaps because this is naturally more difficult for him). What is the mixed strategy Nash equilibrium of this version of the penalty-taking game? Why is the mixed strategy Nash equilibrium of the asymmetric penalty game different from the mixed strategy Nash equilibrium of the symmetric version?

**Matrix 6.5** Asymmetric penalty taking

|         |       | goalkeeper | |
|---------|-------|------|-------|
|         |       | **left** | **right** |
| **striker** | **left** | 0, 1 | 2, 0 |
|         | **right** | 1, 0 | 0, 1 |

2  Derive the mixed strategy equilibrium of the zero-sum game described in Matrix 6.6. Do you recognise this game? If you do try playing it with a friend and try to observe what kind of strategy works best for you (or your friend).

**Matrix 6.6**  Paper, scissors, stone

|  |  | Player 2 | | |
|---|---|---|---|---|
|  |  | stone | paper | scissors |
| **Player 1** | **stone** | 0, 0 | −1, 1 | 1, −1 |
|  | **paper** | 1, −1 | 0, 0 | −1, 1 |
|  | **scissors** | −1, 1 | 1, −1 | 0, 0 |

3  In the simultaneous move game in Matrix 6.7 players either share or grab:

**Matrix 6.7**  Share or grab

|  |  | Y | |
|---|---|---|---|
|  |  | share | grab |
| **X** | **share** | 3, 3 | 1, 5 |
|  | **grab** | 5, 1 | 0, 0 |

(a)  Derive the pure strategy Nash equilibria of this game.

(b)  Derive the mixed strategy equilibrium of this game.

(c)  Explain how this game might be interpreted in an evolutionary context.

(d)  Show that the evolutionary stable equilibrium of the version of the game described in part (c) is mathematically equivalent to the mixed strategy equilibrium derived in part (b).

(e)  What would the evolutionary stable equilibrium of the game be if the pay-offs changed so that when two grabbers meet they each received a pay-off of 2 (but this was the only change)? Explain your answer.

## Questions for discussion

1  How likely do you think it is that players in games with no Nash equilibrium in pure strategies choose mixed strategies?

2  How can the ideas underlying evolutionary game theory be used to explain how cultural preferences for different types of behaviour have emerged in different societies?

## Answers to problems

1  The mixed strategy Nash equilibrium of asymmetric penalty taking is
   {(striker: left; $\frac{1}{2}$, right; $\frac{1}{2}$)(goalkeeper: left; $\frac{2}{3}$, right; $\frac{1}{3}$). To see this let $g_l$ equal
   the probability that the goalkeeper moves to the left then the expected pay-
   off to the striker from kicking the ball to the left is $g_l0 + (1 - g_l)2$. His
   expected pay-off from kicking the ball to the right is $g_l1 + (1 - g_l)0$. These
   expected pay-offs are equal when $g_l = \frac{2}{3}$. If $s_l$ is the probability that the striker
   kicks to the left then the expected pay-off to the goalkeeper from moving to
   the left is  $s_l1 + (1 - s_l)0$. The goalkeeper's expected pay-off from moving to
   the right is $s_l0 + (1 - s_l)1$. These pay-offs are equal when $s_l = \frac{1}{2}$.
     In this version of the penalty-taking game the equilibrium mixed
   strategy of the striker is the same as in the symmetric version but the mixed
   strategy of the goalkeeper has changed. Because the striker gains more
   satisfaction from scoring to the left he will only randomise if the goalkeeper
   moves to the left more often than he moves to the right.

2  The mixed strategy Nash equilibrium is for each player to choose each
   strategy with the same probability: $\frac{1}{3}$. To solve let let $p_s =$ the probability that
   player 1 chooses stone, $p_p$ equal the probability that she chooses paper and
   then $(1 - p_s - p_p)$ is the probability that she chooses scissors. Set player 2's
   expected pay-offs from stone, scissors and paper equal to each other and
   solve for $p_s$ and $p_p$ and then $(1 - p_s - p_p)$. The game is symmetric so the
   equilibrium mixed strategies of the players are the same. Note that this is
   another zero-sum game with a first-mover disadvantage.

3  The answers are as follows:

   (a)  {share, grab} and {grab, share}.

   (b)  Let $p_s$ equal the probability that Y shares then X's expected pay-off from
        sharing is $p_s3 + (1 - p_s)1 = 2p_s + 1$ and his pay-off from grabbing is $p_s5 +
        (1 - p_s)0 = 5p_s$. Setting these equal solves for $p_s = \frac{1}{3}$. As the game is
        symmetric the mixed strategy Nash equilibrium is {(X: share; $\frac{1}{3}$, grab; $\frac{2}{3}$
        )(Y: share; $\frac{1}{3}$, grab; $\frac{2}{3}$)}.

   (c)  Share or grab is a chicken or hawk–dove game. In a socio-evolutionary
        context grabbers are hawks and sharers are doves.

   (d)  Letting s equal the fraction of sharers in the population and setting the
        average pay-off of sharers equal to the average pay-off of grabbers solves
        for $s = \frac{1}{3}$ and the evolutionary stable equilibrium is that $\frac{1}{3}$ of the
        population are sharers and $\frac{2}{3}$ are grabbers. This is a stable mix because if
        the fraction of grabbers increases their average pay-off will be less than
        that of sharers and vice versa.

(e)   If the pay-offs change in this way then the pay-off matrix becomes:

**Matrix 6.7**  Share or grab

|  |  | Y | |
| --- | --- | --- | --- |
|  |  | **share** | **grab** |
| **X** | **share** | 3, 3 | 1, 5 |
|  | **grab** | 5, 1 | 2, 2 |

Now the game is a prisoners' dilemma and grabbing is a dominant strategy
so that in the evolutionary version of the game the only evolutionary
stable strategy is grab. In other words, the only evolutionary stable
equilibrium is one in which the population is composed solely of grabbers.
This is true even though the population as a whole would be better off if
everyone was a sharer.

## Notes

1   For a full discussion of evolutionary game theory *see* Maynard Smith (1982).

2   Thinking about mixed strategies in this way implicitly assumes that there are multiple
    opportunities for choosing strategies, that is, the game is repeated and for a quarter of the
    repetitions the player chooses left. In this chapter we will treat these two alternative ways of
    thinking about mixed strategies as equivalent.  Repeated games are analysed in detail in Chapter 8.

3   In Maynard Smith's (1982) original example hawks and doves are two animals contesting a
    resource of value V. The resource could be territory in a favourable habitat. Animals that breed in
    the favourable habitat produce more offspring.  In the contest over the resource, hawks 'escalate'
    the contest and continue until injured or their opponent retreats while doves only 'display' and
    retreat at once if their opponent escalates.

4   For a more detailed discussion *see* Ridley (1996).

5   Unless there are less than five people in the population, but the initial assumption was that the
    population was large.

# MYSTERY PLAYERS

## Concepts and techniques

- Bayesian Nash equilibrium

- Perfect Bayesian Nash equilibrium

- Bayes' rule

- Signalling.

After working through this chapter you will be able to:

- Analyse games in which one or more players are unsure about the pay-offs of the other

- Define the concept of a Bayesian Nash equilibrium

- Explain how to use Bayes' rule to update beliefs

- Explain the role of signalling in games with incomplete information

- Derive the Bayesian equilibrium of static and dynamic games with incomplete information.

## Introduction

In all the games in this chapter information is incomplete and asymmetric because at least one of the players is unsure about the other's pay-offs. Games in which players are incompletely informed in this way are known as Bayesian games. In Bayesian games the Nash equilibrium concept needs to be refined in order to take account of players' beliefs. A Nash equilibrium that does this is called a Bayesian Nash equilibrium, or more simply a Bayesian equilibrium. In a Bayesian equilibrium the actions of players need to be optimal or best responses given their expectations about the other player. Players' expectations depend on the knowledge they have and their beliefs. An extra restriction in dynamic games is that the players' strategies need to be best responses in every subgame, even those that are not actually played out in the equilibrium. In these circumstances the Bayesian equilibrium is perfect.

The procedure for finding a Bayesian equilibrium in games with asymmetric information is somewhat more complex than any you have seen before. It involves first proposing a strategy combination and then calculating the beliefs generated by those strategies. The proposed strategies then need to be checked to ensure that they are optimal given the players' beliefs. Beliefs in game theory are characterised by probabilities and are conditional on the 'type' of the player about whom there is doubt. A player's type is determined by his pay-offs. Since in any game a player's choice of strategy also depends on their pay-offs, players' strategies in Bayesian games will be conditional on their type. If moves are observed information may be revealed about a player's type and the beliefs of the other player(s) may be updated. This updating process uses a rule of probability theory known as Bayes' rule.

These ideas are explored by examining four games in detail. In all of these games there is asymmetric information about one or both players' pay-offs. In Section 7.1 you will see another version of the friends or enemies game that you first analysed in Chapter 2. In the version of the game analysed here Ms Row is unsure about Mr Column's preferences, specifically whether he is a party lover or not. Friends or enemies is a static game and in Sections 7.2 to 7.5 two games with sequential moves are analysed. The game examined in Section 7.2 is the entry deterrence game that you saw in Chapter 3 but here there is uncertainty for the potential entrant about the pay-offs of the incumbent monopolist. In Sections 7.3 and 7.4 the entry deterrence game is extended by allowing for the possibility that the monopolist can signal its type. Signals[1] are actions taken by players to convey information. They represent an attempt by one player to communicate with another. For example, a potential employee might signal her productivity by investing in education. Alternatively, a second-hand car dealer could signal the quality of his cars by offering a three-month warranty. The possibility of signalling adds another layer of realism to game theory and makes the analysis of games with asymmetric information very interesting. Signals are explicit in the game examined in Section 7.5 which is a version of the Cho and Kreps (1987) beer and quiche game. In this game one of the players, a man, sends a signal about his type which is either tough or wimpy and the other player, a bully, decides whether to fight the man on the basis of the signal sent. In Section 7.6 a battle of the sexes game is analysed. In this version of the game both players are uncertain about the pay-offs of the other.[2]

## 7.1 Friends or enemies again

The game considered in this section is played by Mr Column and Ms Row. They are playing a friends or enemies game like the ones examined in Chapter 2. Here Mr Column and Ms Row have both received invitations for two different New Year's Eve events. They are independently choosing between spending a relatively quiet evening at a local hotel or having a much wilder night by going to a party. The key features of the game in Chapter 2 are retained in that one player wants to match the action choice of the other while the other player wants to avoid matching and one or both players has a preference for one or other of the actions available to them. Here Ms Row simply wants to avoid Mr Column but he would like to see her. Mr Column also has a strong preference for one of the venues. However, in this version of the game asymmetric information is an added ingredient. The problem for Ms Row in that she is unsure about Mr Column's preferences. Mr Column is either a *party-lover* or he is not. If Mr Column is a party lover his dominant strategy is to go the party but if he is not a party-lover his dominant strategy is to go to the hotel. This is an important gap in Ms Row's knowledge as she wants to avoid Mr Column. The information in the game is asymmetric because although Mr Column knows his own preferences and pay-offs Ms Row does not.

The game is represented by pay-off matrices 7.1.1 and 7.1.2. Pay-off Matrix 7.1.1 describes the game when Mr Column is a party-loving type and Matrix 7.1.2 describes the game when he is not. Mr Column knows which matrix is appropriate but Ms Row does not.

**Matrix 7.1.1** Mr Column is a party lover

|  |  | Mr Column | |
|---|---|---|---|
|  |  | **party** | **hotel** |
| **Ms Row** | **party** | 2, 3 | 4, 0 |
|  | **hotel** | 3, 2 | 0, 1 |

**Matrix 7.1.2** Mr Column is not a party-lover

**Mr Column**

|  |  | party | hotel |
|---|---|---|---|
| **Ms Row** | **party** | 2, 1 | 4, 2 |
|  | **hotel** | 3, 0 | 0, 3 |

Since Ms Row doesn't know whether Mr Column is a party-lover or not she cannot be sure which pay-off matrix is appropriate. But she does know two very important things. One of these is the probability that Mr Column is a party lover – this is common knowledge and is given by P. She also knows from the pay-offs in Matrices 7.1.1 and 7.1.2 that if he is a party-lover Mr Column will choose party so she should choose hotel and if Mr Column is not a party lover then he will choose hotel so Ms Row should choose party (you should verify that if Ms Row knows Mr Column's type and he is a party-lover the Nash equilibrium is {hotel, party} and if he is not a party lover the Nash equilibrium is {party, hotel}).

The equilibrium of this game needs to specify the following:

(i)   A strategy for Mr Column that is conditional on Mr Column's type (party-lover, or not) and optimal given his expectations about Ms Row's actions.

(ii)  A strategy for Ms Row that is optimal given her beliefs about Mr Column and her expectations about his actions.

(i) implies that the equilibrium strategy of Mr Column (the player about whom there is uncertainty) needs to specify actions that are conditional on his type. More generally if there is uncertainty about any player in a game then the equilibrium strategy of that player needs to specify actions that are conditional on their type.[3] (i) and (ii) together imply that the equilibrium strategies of each player will be conditional on their expectations or beliefs about the other. In a simultaneous-move or static game, an equilibrium that incorporates beliefs in this way is called a Bayesian Nash equilibrium or Bayesian equilibrium. In a Bayesian equilibrium the strategies of the players specify actions that are consistent with their type and their beliefs about the actions of the other player.

## Bayesian Nash equilibrium

- A combination of the players' strategies such that each player's strategy is a best response to the equilibrium strategies of all the other players, whatever the player's type and whatever the type of the other players.

The Bayesian equilibrium is relatively easy to determine in this game because one of the player's, Mr Column, has a dominant strategy.[4] The Bayesian equilibrium for this game can be derived in four steps:

**Step 1:** Propose a strategy for Mr Column conditional on his type:

- The party-loving Mr Column: Party is a dominant strategy so he always chooses party.

- The non-party-loving Mr Column: Hotel is a dominant strategy so he always chooses hotel.

**Step 2:** Calculate beliefs for Ms Row that are consistent with Mr Column's strategy as defined in Step 1 and probability, $P$, that Mr Column is a party lover. Consistent beliefs for Ms Row are that:

- With probability $P$ Mr Column is a party lover and will always choose party.

- With probability $(1 - P)$ Mr Column is not a party lover and will always choose hotel.

**Step 3:** Propose a strategy for Ms Column that is consistent with her beliefs about Mr Column:

Ms Row should choose hotel if her expected pay-off from choosing hotel, $EPO_{hotel}$, is greater than her expected pay-off from choosing party $EPO_{party}$. She should choose party if $EPO_{party} > EPO_{hotel}$. If $EPO_{party} = EPO_{hotel}$ she might as well randomise between her two pure strategies.

Whether $EPO_{hotel} > EPO_{party}$ depends on $P$. There is a critical value of $P$, which we shall call $P^*$, such that if $P > P^*$, $EPO_{hotel} > EPO_{party}$ but if $P < P^*$ $EPO_{hotel} < EPO_{party}$ and if $P = P^*$, $EPO_{hotel} = EPO_{party}$. Thus a strategy for Ms Row that is consistent with her beliefs is:

- Choose hotel if $P > P^*$.

- Choose party if $P < P^*$.

To fully specify Ms Row's strategies $P^*$, the critical value of $P$ needs to be determined. $P^*$ is defined by the condition that if $P = P^*$ then $EPO_{hotel} = EPO_{party}$ where:

$$EPO_{hotel} = P(3) + (1 - P)0 = 3P \qquad (7.1)$$

Ms Row's pay-off if she chooses hotel and Mr Column chooses party is 3. If she chooses hotel there is a $P$ probability of this happening. She gets zero if they both choose hotel and if she is choosing hotel there is a $(1 - P)$ probability of this happening. Her expected pay-off from choosing party is:

$$\text{EPO}_{\text{party}} = P(2) + (1 - P)4 = 4 - 2P \tag{7.2}$$

Her pay-off is 2 if she chooses party and Mr Column also chooses party. There is a P chance of this happening if she goes to the party. Her pay-off is 4 if she chooses party and Mr Column goes to the hotel and he goes to the hotel with probability $(1 - P)$. $\text{EPO}_{\text{hotel}} = \text{EPO}_{\text{party}}$ if:

$$3P = 4 - 2P \tag{7.3}$$

which solves for:

$$P = \tfrac{4}{5} = P^* \tag{7.4}$$

Thus $P^*$, the critical value of P, equals $\tfrac{4}{5}$. If $P > \tfrac{4}{5}$ Ms Row's expected pay-off is higher if she chooses hotel and if $P < \tfrac{4}{5}$ her expected pay-off is higher if she chooses party. Thus $P^* = \tfrac{4}{5}$ defines Ms Row's strategy:

- Choose hotel if $P > \tfrac{4}{5} = P^*$.
- Choose party if $P < \tfrac{4}{5} = P^*$.

If $P = \tfrac{4}{5}$ Ms Row is indifferent between hotel and party and we can assume that she chooses randomly between the two venues.

**Step 4** Check that the players' strategies are optimal, that is best responses to each other and consistent with their beliefs:

*Mr Column*

Party-lover: chooses party.

Non-party-lover: chooses hotel.

These are optimal strategies for Mr Column as party is a dominant strategy for the party-lover and hotel is a dominant strategy for the non-party-lover.

*Ms Row*

If $P > \tfrac{4}{5}$ choose hotel.

If $P < \tfrac{4}{5}$ choose party.

If $P = \tfrac{4}{5}$ randomise.

Ms Row expects the party-loving Mr Column to choose party and the other Mr Column to choose hotel. She knows that the probability that Mr Column is a party lover is P. As shown in Step 3, $\tfrac{4}{5}$ is the critical value of P such that if $P > \tfrac{4}{5}$. $\text{EPO}_{\text{hotel}} > \text{EPO}_{\text{party}}$ and the inequality is reversed if $P < \tfrac{4}{5}$. If $P = \tfrac{4}{5}$ she is indifferent between her two pure strategies and therefore she might as well randomise between them. These strategies are therefore optimal for Ms Row given her expectations about Mr Column.

As the strategies defined here are optimal and consistent with the players' beliefs they constitute a Bayesian equilibrium for this game which is written in terms of the players strategies as:

### Mr Column

Party-lover always chooses party.

Non-party-lover always chooses hotel.

### Ms Row

If $P > \frac{4}{5}$ chooses hotel.

If $P < \frac{4}{5}$ chooses party.

If $P = \frac{4}{5}$ randomises between hotel and party.

Where P is the common knowledge probability that Mr Column is a party-lover. Thus in the Bayesian equilibrium of this game Ms Row only chooses hotel if the probability that Mr Column is a party-lover is high enough (higher than $\frac{4}{5}$, the critical value of P) and she chooses party (or randomises) otherwise.

## Exercise 7.1

In the friends and enemies game described by Matrices 7.2.1 and 7.2.2 Ms Row doesn't know whether Mr Column is a party-lover or not. Nothing has changed for Mr Column but now Ms Row's preferred outcome is that she goes to the hotel and Mr Column goes to the party. The worst possible outcome for her is that she goes to the party and so does Mr Column. The probability that Mr Column is a party-lover is p. How does the change to Ms Row's preferences alter the Bayesian equilibrium of the game?

Matrix 7.2.1 Mr Column is a party-lover

|  |  | Mr Column | |
| --- | --- | --- | --- |
|  |  | party | hotel |
| | party | 0, 3 | 3, 0 |
| Ms Row | hotel | 4, 2 | 2, 1 |

## Exercise 7.1 (Continued)

**Matrix 7.2.2** Mr Column is not a party-lover

|  |  | Mr Column | |
|---|---|:---:|:---:|
|  |  | party | hotel |
| Ms Row | party | 0, 1 | 3, 2 |
|  | hotel | 4, 0 | 2, 3 |

## 7.2 Entry deterrence with incomplete information

In this section we are going to analyse a version of the entry deterrence game that you first saw in Chapter 4, Section 4.4. In the version examined here the entrant is unsure about the pay-offs of the incumbent monopolist. The entrant is aware that the monopolist may have invested in a sunk cost that makes it optimal to fight entry (as discussed in Chapter 3, Section 4.4.1) but doesn't know if the incumbent has made this investment or not. If the monopolist has made this investment then fighting is a best response to entry, otherwise it is not. The incumbent is therefore one of two types: a *strong* monopolist for whom fighting is an optimal strategy or a *weak* monopolist for whom conceding to entry is a best response. The entrant knows that a strong monopolist will always fight and a weak monopolist will always concede but doesn't know which of the two the monopolist is. The entrant knows only $P_s$, the prior or initial probability that the monopolist is strong. $P_s$ is common knowledge.[5]

Entry deterrence is a sequential-move game and the extensive form of this version of the game with asymmetric information is shown in Figure 7.1. The pay-offs of the weak monopolist and the entrant are the same as the game analysed in Chapter 4 (*see* Figure 4.4). The strong monopolist has invested in a commitment to fighting entry that costs 2 but generates a net benefit of 5 if there is entry and the incumbent fights.[6] Because this game is a little more complex than the version examined in Chapter 4 it will be helpful to refer to the incumbent as a he and the entrant as a she. If you are not sure about this then imagine that the managing director of the incumbent monopoly is a man and the managing director of the firm that is a potential entrant is a woman.

The extensive form in Figure 7.1 shows that a chance move determines whether the monopolist is strong with probability $P_s$ or weak with probability $(1 - P_s)$. The entrant doesn't see the chance move and decides between entry or not at either $E_1$ or $E_2$. The broken line between $E_1$ and $E_2$ indicates that the entrant doesn't know which of the decision nodes $E_1$ or $E_2$ actually applies. The incumbent knows his type and, if the entrant enters, decides between fighting or not. If the monopolist is strong then entry moves the game to $M_{s1}$ where the strong monopolist will choose fight (the pay-off from fighting is 4 while the pay-off from conceding is only 3). If the monopolist is weak entry moves the game to $M_{w1}$ where concession is the weak incumbent's best response (the pay-off from fighting is –1 while the pay-off from concession is 5). Can you see from Figure 7.1 that if the entrant knew the monopolist's type there would be entry only if the monopolist were weak? But with asymmetric information about the monopolist's type the entrant needs to work out the expected pay-offs of entering and staying out before making a move. The crucial part of this decision-making process for the entrant is the determination of $P_s^*$, the critical value of $P_s$ such that if $P_s > P_s^*$ the expected pay-off from staying out is higher than that of entering.

The equilibrium of this game is defined in the same way as in Section 7.1 in terms of the strategies and beliefs of the players but here the players' strategies also need to be best responses in every subgame. The equilibrium therefore needs to be subgame perfect, that is a perfect Bayesian Nash equilibrium or, more simply, a perfect Bayesian equilibrium.

As you saw in Chapter 4 subgame perfectness in the entry deterrence game rules out equilibria in which the entrant stays out because the weak monopolist threatens to fight entry. Such a threat is not credible because it is not in the weak monopolist's self interest to carry out and therefore it is not a best

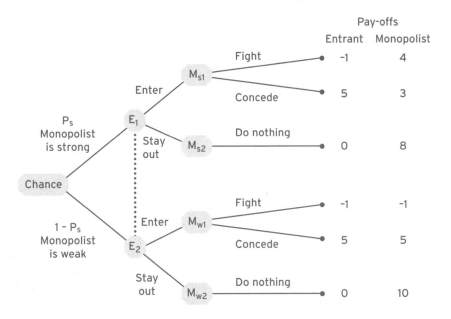

**Figure 7.1** Extensive form of entry deterrence with asymmetric information

response in the subgame starting at $M_{w1}$. In the asymmetric entry deterrence game the monopolist's equilibrium strategy is conditional on type: the strong monopolist will always fight and the weak monopolist will always concede. These strategies are consistent with the entrant's belief that the monopolist is strong and always fights with probability $P_s$.[7]

---

### Perfect Bayesian Nash equilibrium

- A combination of strategies and beliefs such that:

  (i) the players' strategies specify actions that are conditional on their type, constitute a Nash equilibrium given the players' beliefs and specify moves that are best responses in every subgame.

  (ii) the players' beliefs are consistent with the equilibrium strategies of the players and their commonly held prior beliefs and where possible beliefs are updated using Bayes' rule.

---

To fully determine the perfect Bayesian equilibrium of this game $P_s^*$, the critical value of $P_s$, needs to be defined. $P_s^*$ is defined by the condition that the entrant's expected pay-off from staying out is equal to the expected pay-off of entering. The entrant's expected pay-off from staying out, $EPO_{SO}$ is zero whatever the monopolist's type. The expected pay-off of entering, $EPO_E$, depends on $P_s$ where:

$$\text{Expected pay-off of entering: } EPO_E = (1 - P_s)5 + P_s(-1) = 5 - 6P_s \qquad (7.5)$$

The entrant should stay out if:

$$EPO_{SO} > EPO_E \qquad (7.6)$$

that is:

$$0 > 5 - 6P_s \qquad (7.7)$$

(7.7) solves for;

$$P_s > \tfrac{5}{6} = P_s^* \qquad (7.8)$$

Thus $P_s^* = \tfrac{5}{6}$ is the critical value of $P_s$ such that if $P_s > \tfrac{5}{6}$ the entrant should stay out of the market and the entrant should enter if this inequality is reversed.[8] This calculation allows us to fully determine the Bayesian equilibrium of the game as follows:

*Strategy of incumbent monopolist*

Strong monopolist always fights entry.
Weak monopolist always concedes to entry.

*Strategy of entrant*

Stay out if $P_s > \frac{5}{6}$.

Enter if $P_s < \frac{5}{6}$.

Randomise if $P_s = \frac{5}{6}$.

## 7.3 Entry deterrence with signalling

You may be wondering whether the monopolist can do anything about $P_s$. After all, the higher $P_s$ the less chance that the entrant will enter and therefore both strong and weak incumbents have an incentive to raise $P_s$ if initially $P_s < \frac{5}{6}$. A strong monopolist will clearly want to reveal his true strength in some way and a weak incumbent would like to convey a false impression of strength. Both might be possible if the monopolist can send a signal by taking an action that is cheaper for the strong monopolist and therefore less likely to be taken by the weak monopolist. For example, the monopolist could launch a targeted marketing or publicity campaign or make a special offer to its existing customers. Either of these would be more costly for a weaker monopolist that had a less secure and less well identified customer base. If the signal is not more expensive for the weak monopolist then it won't convey any information since a weak monopolist would be just as likely to send it as a strong monopolist. Think about the warranties offered by firms selling computers. Longer warranties are a signal that the product they are selling is less likely to break down. A signal like this is effective only because manufacturers of unreliable computers cannot afford to offer similar terms – too many customers would make claims against them.

In the entry deterrence game if the entrant sees a signal that she believes is more likely to be sent by the strong monopolist then she learns something about the monopolist. She should therefore incorporate the extra information implicit in the signal in her decision-making process. We can model her decision using probability theory, specifically Bayes' rule, to update $P_s$. If the updating procedure raises $P_s$ enough, so that it is more than $\frac{5}{6}$, entry will be deterred.

### Updating $P_s$

If a signal is sent then in a perfect Bayesian equilibrium the entrant's beliefs need to be updated using Bayes' rule. According to Bayes' rule the updated value of $P_s$ is the conditional probability that the monopolist is strong given that the signal, which we can abbreviate to SIG, has been sent. Bayes' rule says that this conditional probability, which I am going to write as $P_{rob}(M_s|SIG)$, equals the probability that the monopolist is strong *and* sends the signal divided by the probability that the signal is sent. The probability that the monopolist is strong is $P_s$ and the probability that the strong monopolist sends the signal is another conditional probability: the probability that the signal is sent given that the monopolist is strong. I am going to write this conditional probability as $P_{rob}(SIG|M_s)$. Therefore the probability the monopolist is strong *and* sends the signal is $P_{rob}(SIG|M_s)P_s$. The probability that the signal is sent is the probability that the monopolist is strong and sends the signal *plus* the probability that the monopolist is weak and sends the signal. The probability that the monopolist is strong and sends the signal is $P_{rob}(SIG|M_s)P_s$ as before. The probability that the monopolist is weak and sends the signal is equivalently given by $P_{rob}(SIG|M_w)(1 - P_s)$ where $P_{rob}(SIG|M_w)$ is the conditional probability that the weak monopolist sends the signal and $(1 - P_s)$ is the probability that the monopolist is weak. Using this terminology Bayes' rule[9] says that the updated value of $P_s$, $P_{rob}(M_s|SIG)$, is given by:

$$\text{Updated } P_s = \text{Prob}(M_s|SIG) = \frac{P_{rob}(SIG|M_s)P_s}{P_{rob}(SIG|M_s)P_s + P_{rob}(SIG|M_w)(1 - P_s)} \qquad (7.9)$$

To keep things simple we shall assume that the signal is free for the strong monopolist so that a strong monopolist will always send the signal. In this case the probability that a strong monopolist sends the signal, the conditional probability that the signal is sent given that the monopolist is strong, $P_{rob}(SIG|M_s)$, is equal to 1. This implies that the probability that the monopolist is strong *and* sends the signal is just $P_s$. However, if the signal is costly for a weak monopolist he may or may not send the signal. The conditional probability that a weak monopolist sends the signal is $P_{rob}(SIG|M_w)$ which, for simplicity, we can abbreviate to $w_s$. $w_s$ is likely to be less than 1 as sending the signal is costly for the weak monopolist. With these assumptions the expression for the updated value of $P_s$ can be simplified to:[10]

$$\text{updated } P_s = \frac{P_s}{P_s + (1 - P_s)w_s} \qquad (7.10)$$

Expression (7.10) looks a lot simpler than (7.9). It should be easier for you to see in (7.10) that in order to raise $P_s$ the weak monopolist needs to send the signal with some probability greater than zero but less than one. To see this think about what happens to $P_s$ if the entrant sees the signal but $w_s = 0$. In this case the entrant knows the monopolist is strong and from (7.10) $P_s = 1$. If $w_s = 1$ then if the entrant sees the signal and updates $P_s$ this leads to $P_s = \frac{P_s}{P_s + (1 - P_s)} = P_s$ so nothing is learned from the signal and $P_s$ is unchanged. But if $0 < w_s < 1$ then the updating procedure raises $P_s$.

## Exercise 7.2

If the entrant observes the signal and the initial value of $P_s = \frac{1}{2}$ what will the updated value of $P_s$ be according to Bayes' rule if $w_s = \frac{1}{4}$ ? What will the updated value of $P_s$ be if $w_s = \frac{1}{2}$?

Allowing for the possibility of signals changes the perfect Bayesian equilibrium of this game. If a strong incumbent monopolist always sends the signal and a weak monopolist can also send the signal but at a cost the perfect Bayesian equilibrium becomes:

### Strategy of incumbent monopolist

Strong monopolist always sends the signal and always fights entry.

Weak monopolist sends the signal with some probability if initially $P_s < \frac{5}{6}$; concedes if there is entry.

### Strategy of entrant:

Enters if doesn't see the signal since $P_s = 0$.

If the entrant sees the signal $P_s$ is updated using Bayes' rule and the entrant:

- enters if the updated value of $P_s < \frac{5}{6}$.

- stays out if the updated value of $P_s > \frac{5}{6}$.

- randomises if the updated value of $P_s = \frac{5}{6}$.

Whether the weak monopolist sends a signal or not will depend on the costs of sending the signal relative to the expected gains from deterring entry. This is easiest to see by looking at a numerical example.

## 7.4 Numerical example of entry deterrence with signalling

Assume that the initial value of $P_s$ is $\frac{1}{2}$ as in Exercise 7.2. This is less than $\frac{5}{6}$ so if there is no signalling entry will definitely take place. If a signal of strength is available at zero cost to the strong monopolist but at a positive cost to the weak monopolist then the strong monopolist will send the signal. Bayes' rule implies that the weak monopolist needs to randomise between sending the signal or not in order to raise $P_s$. Specifically the weak monopolist needs to randomise with just enough chance of not sending the signal so that the updated $P_s \geq \frac{5}{6}$ (you should have seen from working through Exercise 7.2 that the higher $w_s$ the less $P_s$ is raised by the signal). Thus there is a critical value of $w_s$, $w_s^*$, such that when $w_s = w_s^*$ the updated value of $P_s = \frac{5}{6}$. We can solve for $w_s^*$ by substituting for $P_s = \frac{1}{2}$ into equation (7.10). Doing this leads to:

$$\text{updated } P_s = \frac{\frac{1}{2}}{\frac{1}{2} + \frac{1}{2} w_s} \tag{7.11}$$

The weak monopolist needs to set $w_s$ so that the updated value of $P_s = \frac{5}{6}$. Setting $P_s = \frac{5}{6}$ solves for $w_s^*$, the critical value of $w_s$. Setting $P_s = \frac{5}{6}$ leads to:

$$\text{updated } P_s = \frac{\frac{1}{2}}{\frac{1}{2} + \frac{1}{2} w_s} = \frac{5}{6} \tag{7.12}$$

(7.12) solves for $w_s^* = \frac{1}{5} = 0.2$.[11] If $w_s = \frac{1}{5}$ and the entrant observes the signal $P_s$ will be updated so that $P_s = \frac{5}{6}$. In this case the entrant will be indifferent between entering or not and will randomise between entry and staying out. If $w_s > \frac{1}{5}$ the updated value of $P_s$ will be less than $\frac{5}{6}$ and the entrant will enter. If $w_s < \frac{1}{5}$ the updated value of $P_s$ will be greater than $\frac{5}{6}$ and the entrant will stay out but the lower $w_s$ the less chance the signal will actually be sent and if it isn't sent the entrant will enter, so not sending the signal is costly for the weak monopolist.

But sending the signal is also costly for the weak monopolist and it will be optimal to incur signalling costs only if the resulting probability of entry is low enough. In order to fully determine the perfect Bayesian equilibrium of the signalling version of the entry deterrence game we therefore need to be a little more specific about the entrant's strategy.

The weak monopolist will send the signal only if the expected pay-off from sending the signal, $EPO_{sig}$, is high enough relative to the expected pay-off of not sending the signal, $EPO_{nsig}$. The weak monopolist's expected pay-offs depend on the probability of no entry, which I will call y. $EPO_{nsig} = 5$ for the weak monopolist because if there is no signal the entrant knows the incumbent is weak and there will be entry. If there is entry the weak monopolist concedes and receives a pay-off of 5 (*see* Figure 7.1). $EPO_{sig}$ depends on the weak monopolist's signalling costs and the strategies of the entrant which are characterised by the probability of no entry, y.

The expected pay-off from signalling for the weak monopolist is at most 10 less the costs of signalling (that's if there is no entry for sure when the signal is sent). Hence if signalling costs are greater than 5 $EPO_{sig} < 5$ and the weak monopolist does better by not sending the signal and simply conceding. Let's assume that the weak monopolist's signalling costs are 3. In this case the weak monopolist's pay-off will be 2 in the event of entry and 7 if there is no entry. Accordingly $EPO_{sig}$ is given by:

$$EPO_{sig} = (1 - y)2 + y7 = 2 + 5y \qquad (7.13)$$

Equality between $EPO_{sig}$ and $EPO_{nsig}$ defines the critical value of y, $y^*$, such that if $y = y^*$ the weak monopolist is indifferent between sending the signal or not. Setting these two expected pay-offs equal we obtain:

$$EPO_{sig} = 2 + 5y = 5 = EPO_{nsig} \qquad (7.14)$$

(7.14) solves for $y^* = \frac{3}{5}$ or 0.6.

If you look back at (7.13) and (7.14) you will see that we solved for the critical value of y, the probability that the entrant enters, by examining the strategies and expected pay-offs of the weak monopolist . If you look back at (8.8) and (7.12) you will see that we solved for the critical value of $w_s$, the probability that the weak monopolist sends the signal, in a similar way by examining the beliefs and strategies of the entrant. This procedure is analogous to the one we used in Chapter 6 to solve for the mixed strategy Nash equilibrium of the battle of the sexes game. In Chapter 6 we solved for each players' optimal mixed strategy by setting the expected pay-offs of the other player from each pure strategy equal. We have clearly done something very similar here and this is no coincidence because the weak monopolist is following a mixed strategy;[12] in order to raise $P_s$ the weak monopolist needs to randomise between sending and not sending the signal so that $0 < w_s < 1$. If the weak monopolist is randomising then intuitively (*see* Method 1 in Chapter 6) the weak monopolist must be indifferent between sending and not sending the signal. If this were not true the weak monopolist would choose whichever pure strategy was preferred. Equation (7.14) implies that the weak monopolist will be indifferent between sending and not sending the signal only if $y = y^* = \frac{3}{5}$. Thus $0 < w_s < 1$ can only be an equilibrium strategy for the weak monopolist if $y = y^*$. But if $y = \frac{3}{5}$ the entrant is also following a mixed strategy which can only be a best response if the entrant's expected pay-off from entering is the same as her expected pay-off from staying out. Equations (7.8), (7.10), (7.11) and (7.12) show that this will be the case only if the updated value of $P_s$ is exactly equal to $\frac{5}{6}$ which requires that $w_s = w_s^* = \frac{1}{5}$.

The argument in the preceding paragraph shows that if $w_s = w_s^*$ and $y = y^*$ the mixed strategies of the weak monopolist and the entrant are best responses to each other. In other words, the critical values of $w_s$ and y determine the equilibrium strategies of the entrant and the weak monopolist. Accordingly, when the initial or prior value of $P_s$ is $\frac{1}{2}$ and the costs of signalling for the weak monopolist are 3, the perfect Bayesian equilibrium of the entry deterrence game with signalling is defined as follows:

### Strategy of monopolist

The strong monopolist always sends the signal and always fights entry.

The weak monopolist sends the signal with probability $\frac{1}{5}$ and concedes if there is entry.

### Strategy of entrant

Enters if there is no signal.

If the signal is sent, enters with probability $\frac{2}{5}$, stays out with probability $\frac{3}{5}$.

In the equilibrium of this asymmetric information entry deterrence game the entrant may stay out if a signal is sent even though the initial value of $P_s$ is less than $\frac{5}{6}$. For signalling to be effective it needs to be more costly for the weak monopolist who randomises between sending and not sending the signal. In the perfect Bayesian equilibrium of this game the probability that the weak monopolist sends the signal, $w_s$, is $\frac{1}{5}$ and if a signal is sent then the updated value of $P_s$ is $\frac{5}{6}$ and the entrant is indifferent between entering and staying out. The entrant may still enter in these circumstances but there is a positive probability that she will stay out. If no signal is sent then the updated value of $P_s$ will be 0 and the entrant will enter for sure. Thus a weak monopolist can deter entry without being strong if there is enough initial uncertainty about the incumbent's pay-offs. If not the monopolist may still be able to deter entry by sending a signal that is more costly for a weak monopolist.

You may be wondering what sort of signal could be effective in the sense outlined in this section. A number of alternatives such as a marketing campaign or a highly visible investment programme are possible. But to signal strength in terms of a commitment to fight entry the costs of the signal need to be higher for a weak monopolist. An alternative possibility is that the monopolist might have fought entry on a previous occasion. However, this would make the game a repeated game and the version of entry deterrence considered here is not repeated. A repeated version of entry deterrence is analysed in Chapter 8 and in that model the possibility of fighting entry in a previous repetition of the game in order to deter entry in later rounds is analysed.[13]

In the game considered in the next section one of the players chooses between two alternative signals. Not sending a signal for this player is not an option as it was for the weak monopolist in the entry deterrence game but the player does have a preference for one of the signals and his preference depends on his type.

## 7.5 The beer and quiche signalling game

In this game, based on the Cho and Kreps (1987) model, there is both asymmetric information and signalling. There are two players: a man and a bully. The bully is unsure about the disposition of the man who is either a *wimp* or *tough* and this uncertainty is a concern for the bully as he is thinking about whether or not to start a *fight* with the man. The bully only really wants to fight the man if the latter is a wimp. But he doesn't know the man's type and has to make his decision on the basis of a signal sent by the man. The signal is that the man either eats quiche or drinks beer. The wimp would rather eat quiche and the tough man prefers to drink beer. Both types of men prefer not to get into a fight with the bully. The man and the bully make their moves sequentially with the man moving first.

We are going to look at a version of this game that has well defined pay-offs.[14] The probability, $p_t$, that the man is tough is also common knowledge and is equal to $\frac{1}{3}$. In the perfect Bayesian equilibrium of this version of the beer and quiche game if the wimp drinks beer the bully may be deterred from fight-ing. Drinking beer is a costly strategy for the wimp (relative to eating quiche) but less costly than fighting.

The bully's pay-off is 1 if he fights the wimp or defers to the tough man and 0 otherwise. The wimp gains 1 by eating quiche and receives a bonus of 2 if the bully defers to him. The tough man also receives a bonus of 2 if the bully defers and gains an extra 1 by drinking beer. Figure 7.2 illustrates the game if the man is tough for sure. Figure 7.3 is the extensive form of the game if the man is definitely a wimp. Figure 7.4 brings Figures 7.2 and 7.3 together and illustrates the beer and quiche game with incomplete information for the bully about the man's type.

In the game in Figure 7.2 there is no asymmetry of information. The bully knows that the man is tough and so the bully's best response to either quiche or beer is to defer (for a pay-off of 1 rather than a pay-off of 0). The optimal strategy of the man is therefore to drink beer (for a pay-off of 3 instead of a pay-off of 2). In the subgame perfect Nash equilibrium of this version of the beer and quiche game the man will therefore drink beer and the bully will defer.

In the quiche game in Figure 7.3 information is also complete; the bully knows the man is a wimp. The bully's best response to either quiche or beer is to fight (for a pay-off of 1 rather than 0). The optimal strategy of the man is therefore to eat quiche (a pay-off of 1 rather than a pay-off of 0). The wimp has nothing to gain by drinking beer in order to look tough as the bully will fight regardless. It follows that in the subgame perfect Nash equilibrium of this ver-sion of the quiche game where the bully knows that the man is a wimp, the man will eat quiche and the bully will fight.

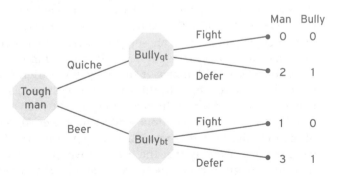

**Figure 7.2** The man is tough for sure

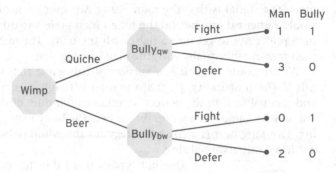

**Figure 7.3** The man is a wimp for sure

In the beer and quiche game illustrated in Figure 7.4 information is incomplete and asymmetric. In this version of the game a chance move determines whether the man is tough or a wimp. The man is tough with probability $\frac{1}{3}$ and a wimp with probability $\frac{2}{3}$. The man knows his own type but the bully does not. The bully sees only the signal. The dotted lines between the bully's decision nodes $Bully_{qt}$ and $Bully_{qw}$ and his decision nodes at $Bully_{bt}$ and $Bully_{bw}$ indicate that he is unsure which of these nodes he is at: whether he faces a wimp or the tough man when he sees the man eating quiche or drinking beer. If he sees quiche he could be at either at $Bully_{qt}$ or $Bully_{qw}$. Similarly if he sees the man drinking beer he could be at either $Bully_{bt}$ or $Bully_{bq}$. All the bully knows is the initial or prior probability, $p_t$, that the man is tough since it is common knowledge that $p_t = \frac{1}{3}$.

The obvious question to ask in relation to the beer and quiche game with incomplete information is whether or in what circumstances there is an incentive for the wimp to drink beer in order to convince the bully that he is tough. The wimp doesn't like beer but it may be worth sacrificing the quiche if this deters the bully from fighting with a high enough probability. In game theoretic terms this amounts to asking whether there is a perfect Bayesian equilibrium of the game in which the wimp drinks beer and avoids a fight.

One thing to note right away is that in the quiche game with asymmetric information there is no perfect Bayesian equilibrium in which the bully chooses a pure strategy response to *both* quiche and beer (either fight or defer). Can you see why this is? To be part of a perfect Bayesian equilibrium a strategy must prescribe moves that are subgame perfect, that is best responses in every subgame, even those that are not actually reached in the suggested equilibrium. Now, consider what happens if the bully always fights in response to quiche but defers if he sees beer. In this case both types of men will choose beer (the bonus pay-off to the man from avoiding a fight is 2 which is greater than the benefit of 1 that he derives from sending his preferred signal). But if both types of men choose beer it is not a best response for the bully to defer at beer because the probability that the man is a wimp is higher than the probability that he is tough.[15] Therefore the strategy to fight in response to quiche and

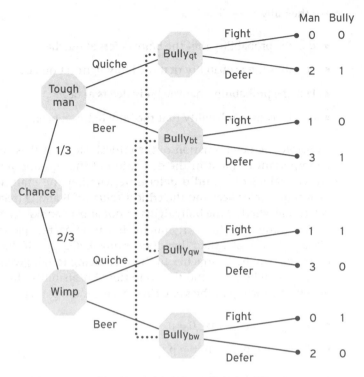

**Figure 7.4** Quiche game with asymmetric information about the man

defer in response to beer cannot be part of a perfect Bayesian equilibrium. What happens if the bully always fights regardless? Well then the wimp will eat only quiche and the tough man will drink only beer in which case fighting is not a best response to beer. You should be able to apply the same kind of reasoning to rule out the bully's other two pure strategy choices: always defer whatever signal is sent and fight at beer but defer at quiche. It follows that in any perfect Bayesian equilibrium of this game the bully must be randomising at either quiche or beer or both.

The perfect Bayesian equilibrium of the quiche game is defined as before in terms of the strategies and beliefs of the players. In order to determine the equilibrium beliefs and strategies of the players it is helpful to adopt some simplifying terminology. Loosely following Binmore (1992) we can define the strategies of the man as follows:

- $B$ is the probability that the tough man drinks beer.

- $(1 - B)$ is the probability that the tough man eats quiche.

- $Q$ is the probability that the wimp eats quiche.

- $(1 - Q)$ is the probability that the wimp drinks beer.

For the bully:

- d is the probability that the bully defers at quiche.
- $(1 - d)$ is the probability that the bully fights at quiche.
- D is the probability that the bully defers at beer.
- $(1 - D)$ is the probability that the billy fights at beer.

As before the determination of the critical values of these probabilities will be an important element in the derivation of the equilibrium of this game. The critical values of D and d determine whether the man, whatever his type, prefers quiche or beer and the critical values of B and Q (relative to each other) determine whether the bully fights or not at beer and quiche.

The bully will fight at quiche if the expected pay-off from fighting, $EPOq_{Bfight}$, is greater than that of deferring, $EPOq_{Bdefer}$. If the conditional probability that the bully attaches to the man being tough given that he's seen the man eat quiche is $p_{tq}$ and the conditional probability that he attaches to the man being a wimp in the same circumstances is $p_{wq}$ then:

- $EPOq_{Bdefer} = p_{tq}1 + p_{wq}0 = p_{tq}.$
- $EPOq_{Bfight} = p_{wq}1 + p_{tq}0 = p_{wq}.$

Thus the bully will defer at quiche if $p_{tq} > p_{wq}$ and fight if the inequality is reversed. The conditional probabilities $p_{tq}$ and $p_{wq}$ are calculated using Bayes' rule. Bayes' rule says that $p_{tq}$ is equal to the probability that the man is tough *and* eats quiche divided by the probability that quiche is eaten (by either type of man). The probability that the man is tough *and* eats quiche is calculated by multiplying the probability that he is tough, $\frac{1}{3}$, by the probability that the tough man eats quiche, $(1 - B)$. This product equals $\frac{1}{3}(1 - B)$. $p_{wq}$ is equal to the probability that the man is a wimp *and* eats quiche divided by the probability that quiche is eaten. The probability that the man is a wimp *and* eats quiche is calculated by multiplying the probability that he is a wimp, $\frac{2}{3}$, by the probability that the wimp eats quiche, Q. This product equals $\frac{2}{3}Q$. The probability that quiche is eaten is the sum of $\frac{1}{3}(1 - B)$ and $\frac{2}{3}Q$. Thus;

$$p_{tq} = \frac{\frac{1}{3}(1 - B)}{\frac{1}{3}(1 - B) + \frac{2}{3}Q} \tag{7.15}$$

$$p_{wq} = \frac{\frac{2}{3}Q}{\frac{1}{3}(1 - B) + \frac{2}{3}Q} \tag{7.16}$$

The bully defers at quiche if $p_{tq} > p_{wq}$ which from (7.15) and (7.16) requires that $\frac{1}{3}(1 - B) > \frac{2}{3}Q$ or $2Q < (1 - B)$. Thus the condition $2Q < (1 - B)$ determines the critical values of Q and B relative to each other such that if 2Q < (1 – B) the bully defers at quiche.

Similarly the bully will fight at quiche if $p_{wq} > p_{tq}$ which requires that $\frac{2}{3}Q > \frac{1}{3}(1 - B)$ or 2Q > (1 – B). And the bully will be indifferent between fighting and deferring and therefore randomise by assumption if 2Q = (1 – B). To summarise the analysis implies that:

(a)  The bully defers at quiche if: 2Q < (1 – B).

(b)  The bully fights at quiche if: 2Q > (1 – B).

(c)  The bully randomises at quiche if: 2Q = (1 – B).

The game is symmetric and so similar analysis at beer leads to the following predictions:

(d)  The bully defers at beer if: B > 2(1 – Q).

(e)  The bully fights at beer if: B < 2(1 – Q).

(f)  The bully randomises at beer if: B = 2(1 – Q).

Thus B > 2(1–Q) defines the critical values of B and Q relative to each other. If this condition is satisfied the bully will defer at beer.

As argued above in any equilibrium the bully must be randomising at either beer or quiche or both and this implies that either (c) 2Q = (1 – B) and/or (f) B = 2(1 – Q) must hold. We can check each of these conditions in turn to see whether either is feasible.

Beginning with (c) the condition that 2Q = (1 – B). This condition can be rearranged to obtain B = 1 – 2Q or B = $2(\frac{1}{2} - Q)$. $2(\frac{1}{2} - Q)$ must be less than 2(1 – Q) and therefore condition (c) implies that B = $2(\frac{1}{2} - Q) < 2(1 - Q)$. That is, B < 2(1 – Q). But B < 2(1 – Q) is the condition for the bully to fight at beer (condition (e)). This means that if condition (c) is satisfied so that the bully is randomising at quiche then he must always fight at beer. In these circumstances the wimp has no incentive to drink beer and so will always eat quiche. Thus Q, the probability that the wimp eats quiche equals 1. But if Q = 1 then substituting for Q into condition (c) gives 2 = (1 – B) and this is impossible (a probability cannot be greater than 1).[16] This impossibility means that condition (c) cannot hold and therefore the bully must be either fighting or deferring at quiche and not randomising.

Turning now to (f) the condition that B = 2(1 – Q). This condition can be rearranged to obtain 2Q = 2 – B. 2 – B is clearly greater than 1 – B and 2Q > 1 – B is the condition for the bully to always fight at quiche. So if condition (f) is satisfied so that the bully is randomising at beer, the bully must always fight at quiche. In these circumstances the tough man has no incentive to eat quiche so will always drink beer. Thus B = 1. Substituting for B = 1 into condition (f) leads to 1 = 2(1 – Q) which solves for Q = $\frac{1}{2}$. This is certainly feasible. Q = $\frac{1}{2}$ indicates that the wimp is randomising between beer and quiche which is not unreasonable if the bully is randomising at beer but fighting at quiche. However, the wimp's mixed strategy needs to be more than reasonable to be part of an equilibrium: it also needs to be a best response to that of the bully.

To discover the conditions in which this will be the case we need to find the critical value of D, the probability that the bully defers at beer, such that the wimp is just indifferent between beer and quiche. The wimp will be indifferent between beer and quiche if his expected pay-off from quiche, $EPO_q$, and his expected pay-off from drinking beer, $EPO_b$, are equal. If the bully is fighting at quiche then $EPO_q = 1$. $EPO_b$ depends on the randomisation strategy of the bully:

- $EPO_b = 0(1 - D) + 2D$.

Setting $0(1 - D) + 2D$ equal to 1, the wimp's pay-off from eating quiche, solves for $D = \frac{1}{2}$.

$D = \frac{1}{2}$ is therefore the critical value of D such that if $D = \frac{1}{2}$ the wimp is indifferent between drinking beer and eating quiche and randomises between them. If Q also equals $\frac{1}{2}$ then as we have seen the bully will randomise between fighting and deferring at beer but will fight at quiche (d = 0). Thus $Q = \frac{1}{2}$ and $D = \frac{1}{2}$, d = 0 are best responses to each other and B = 1 (the tough man always drinks beer) is also a best response to $D = \frac{1}{2}$ and d = 0. These values for Q, D, d and B define the perfect Bayesian equilibrium of this game as follows:

### The man's strategy

The tough man drinks beer for sure.

The wimp eats quiche with probability $\frac{1}{2}$ and drinks beer with probability $\frac{1}{2}$.

### The bully's strategy

If the man eats quiche; fights for sure.

If the man drinks beer; fights with probability $\frac{1}{2}$ and defers with probability $\frac{1}{2}$.

In this equilibrium[17] the wimp can avoid a fight by drinking beer. If he eats quiche the bully always picks a fight but if the wimp drinks beer he has a 50:50 chance of not getting into a fight. Drinking beer means that the wimp sends a costly signal to the bully that he is tough. Because a tough man would always drink beer the bully cannot be sure if the man he sees drinking beer is tough or a wimp and he therefore randomises between fighting and deferring. If the wimp is lucky he avoids a fight but the price is having to drink the beer. In more general terms this analysis confirms that incomplete and asymmetric information can completely change the outcome of a game. If a player can send a costly signal some (more costly) action by the other player may be deterred. In the beer and quiche game the wimp has an incentive to drink beer in order to deter the bully from fighting. On the other hand the wimp drinking beer gives the bully a reason to fight at beer which is not such a good result from the perspective of the tough type of man.

## 7.6 Asymmetric information for both players in the battle of the sexes

In this section we examine a situation in which neither player is sure about the pay-offs of the other in a battle of the sexes game.[18] The two players are Jess (a guy) and Rosy (a girl). Jess has a preference for the pub while Rosy has a preference for the party. The pay-off matrix for this battle of the sexes game with no asymmetry of information is shown in Matrix 7.3.1.

In the game in Matrix 7.3.1 there are two Nash equilibria in pure strategies: {pub, pub} and {party, party}. There is also a Nash equilibrium in mixed strategies: {(Jess: pub; $\frac{3}{4}$, party; $\frac{1}{4}$ ), (Rosy: pub; $\frac{1}{4}$, party; $\frac{3}{4}$)}. Matrix 7.3.2 illustrates a version of this game in which there is incomplete information for both players about each other's pay-offs. In the game in Matrix 7.3.2 both players have an extra incentive to choose their preferred venue but neither knows how great the other's incentive is.[19]

**Matrix 7.3.1** Battle of the sexes with complete information

|  |  | Rosy | |
| --- | --- | --- | --- |
|  |  | **pub** | **party** |
| **Jess** | **pub** | 3, 2 | 1, 1 |
|  | **party** | 0, 0 | 2, 3 |

**Matrix 7.3.2** Battle of the sexes with asymmetric information

|  |  | Rosy | |
| --- | --- | --- | --- |
|  |  | **pub** | **party** |
| **Jess** | **pub** | 3 + bj, 2 | 1, 1 |
|  | **party** | 0, 0 | 2, 3 + br |

In Matrix 7.3.2 if Jess goes to the pub with Rosy he gets a bonus of bj. He doesn't get this bonus if he goes to the pub alone. bj gives Jess an extra incentive to choose pub. The asymmetric information arises because only Jess knows bj. If

Rosy goes to the party with Jess she also gets a bonus. Her bonus is br but she gets it only if Jess also goes to the party. br represents an extra incentive for her to choose party. Only Rosy knows br.

However, both players know that bj and br are independent (or unrelated) random values drawn from a uniform distribution between 0 and 1. This means that the probability that br (or bj) takes one particular value between 0 and 1 is the same as the probability that it takes any other value between 0 and 1 (the probability that br = 0.1 is the same as the probability that br = 0.2 or br = 0.25).[20] As there are an infinite number of possible values that br and bj can take between 0 and 1, it follows that the probability that br or bj takes some particular value between 0 and 1 is infinitesimally small and therefore we can really only determine cumulative[21] probabilities. An example of a cumulative probability is the probability that br is less than or equal to 0.2 ($P_{rob}$br ≤ 0.2) from which the probability that br is greater than 0.2 ($P_{rob}$br > 0.2) can be determined as $1 - P_{rob}$br ≤ 0.2.

In the Bayesian equilibrium of this simultaneous-move game the strategies of the player will depend on bj and br as follows:

### Jess's strategy

pub if bj > $j^*$.

party if bj ≤ $j^*$.

Where $j^*$ is the critical value of bj such that if bj > $j^*$ Jess's expected pay-off from going to the pub ($EPOJ_{pub}$) is greater than his pay-off from going to the party ($EPOJ_{pty}$).

### Rosy's strategy

party if br > $r^*$.

pub if br ≤ $r^*$.

Where $r^*$ is the critical value of br such that if br > $r^*$ Rosy's expected pay-off from going to the party ($EPOR_{pty}$) is greater than her expected pay-off from going to the pub ($EPOR_{pub}$).

In order to define the Bayesian equilibrium of this game the beliefs of the players and the critical values of $j^*$ and $r^*$ need to be determined.

Given Jess' strategy as outlined above Rosy predicts that the probability that Jess goes to the pub is equal to the probability that bj > $j^*$ and the probability that he goes to the party is equal to the probability that bj ≤ $j^*$. Because bj is a draw from a uniform distribution between 0 and 1 the probability that bj ≤ $j^*$ is equal to $j^*$ and the probability that bj > $j^*$ is $1 - j^*$. Therefore, Rosy predicts that the probability that Jess goes to the pub is given by $1 - j^*$ and the probability that he goes to the party is $j^*$.[22]

Jess's predictions about Rosy are defined in an equivalent way. He will predict that the probability that she goes to the pub is $r^*$ and the probability that she goes to the party is $1 - r^*$.

With these probabilities it is possible to determine the expected pay-offs of the players as follows. Jess's expected pay-off from going to the pub is:

- $EPOJ_{pub} = r^*(3 + bj) + (1 - r^*)1 = r^*(2 + bj) + 1$

where $r^*(3 + bj)$ is the probability that Rosie goes to the pub, $r^*$, multiplied by Jess's pay-off if he also goes to the pub. $(1 - r^*)1$ is the probability that Rosy goes to the party, $(1 - r^*)$, multiplied by Jess's pay-off if he goes to the pub and she goes to the party. Jess's expected pay-off from going to the party is:

- $EPOJ_{pty} = r^*(0) + (1 - r^*)2 = 2 - 2r^*$

These pay-offs imply that going to the pub is an optimal strategy for Jess if $r^*(2 + bj) + 1 > 2 - 2r^*$ or:

$$bj > 1/r^* - 4 = j^* \tag{7.17}$$

$j^* = 1/r^* - 4$ since $j^*$ is the critical value of bj such that if $bj > j^*$ Jess's expected pay-off from going to the pub is greater than his expected pay-off from going to the party.

Rosy's expected pay-off if she goes to the pub is:

- $EPOR_{pub} = (1 - j^*)2 + j^*(0) = 2 - 2j^*$

If she goes to the party her expected pay-off is:

- $EPOR_{pty} = (1 - j^*)1 + j^*(3 + br) = j^*(2 + br) + 1$

Going to the party is optimal for her if $j^*(2 + br) + 1 > 2 - 2j^*$ or:

$$br > 1/j^* - 4 = r^* \tag{7.18}$$

where $r^*$ is the critical value of br such that if $br > r^*$ she prefers to go to the party. Equations (7.17) and (7.18) imply that $j^* = 1/r^* - 4$ and $r^* = 1/j^* - 4$ which is only possible if $j^* = r^*$. Substituting for $r^* = j^*$ in (7.18) and multiplying through by $j^*$ leads to:

$$(j^*)^2 + 4j^* - 1 = 0 \tag{7.19}$$

(7.19) solves for:[23]

$$j^* = r^* = \frac{-4 + \sqrt{16 + 4}}{2} = \frac{-4 + \sqrt{20}}{2} \tag{7.20}$$

This is approximately equal to 0.2361 (or $\approx$ 0.2361). To fully define the Bayesian equilibrium all we need to do now is substitute for $j^*$ and $r^*$ into the strategies and beliefs of the players:

### Jess's strategy

Choose pub if $bj > j^* \approx 0.2361$.

Choose party if $bj \leq j^* \approx 0.2361$.

### Rosy's strategy

Choose party if $br > r^* \approx 0.2361$.

Choose pub if $br \leq r^* \approx 0.2361$.

These strategies are optimal given the following beliefs for Jess and Rosy:

$$\text{Probability that Jess goes to the pub} = 1 - j^* = 1 - \frac{-4 + \sqrt{20}}{2} \approx 0.7639.$$

$$\text{Probability that Rosy goes to the pub} = r^* = \frac{-4 + \sqrt{20}}{2} \approx 0.2361.$$

An interesting implication of this analysis is that as the upper limit of the uniform distribution from which $bj$ and $br$ are drawn approaches zero the informational incompleteness disappears and $j^*$ and $r^*$ approach 0.25, i.e. $\frac{1}{4}$.[24] As noted at the beginning of this section the mixed strategy Nash equilibrium of the game with no informational asymmetry is that Jess goes to the party and Rosy goes to the pub with probability $\frac{1}{4}$. Thus as the information becomes more symmetric the Bayesian equilibrium of this game approaches the mixed strategy Nash equilibrium of the original game with complete information. This is a general result originally attributed to Harsanyi (1973). It suggests that the mixed strategy Nash equilibrium of a simultaneous-move game with complete information can be interpreted as the Bayesian Nash equilibrium of a related game with a little amount of incomplete information. As Gibbons (1997: 140) puts it 'the crucial feature of a mixed strategy Nash equilibrium is not that player j chooses a strategy randomly, but rather that player i is uncertain about player j's choice; this uncertainty can arise either because of randomisation or (more plausibly) because of a little incomplete information'. Thus the Bayesian Nash equilibrium concept provides some rationale for the idea of a mixed strategy equilibrium in simultaneous-move games.

# Summary

In this chapter four games with asymmetric information about one or both players' pay-offs were analysed. In each case a Bayesian equilibrium was derived. In each of these equilibria the actions of the players were optimal or best responses given their expectations about the other player. Their expectations were shown to depend on their beliefs and their beliefs were constructed from their knowledge about the other player's type.

In the two dynamic games analysed there was also scope for signalling as beliefs can be updated using Bayes' rule if moves are observed. Signals are actions players take to convey information about their type. They represent an attempt by one player to communicate with another. Allowing for the possibility of signals adds an extra element of realism to games with asymmetric information. In Section 7.3 the possibility of the monopolist signalling his type in the entry deterrence game was considered and in Section 7.4 the circumstances in which this might be an optimal strategy for a weak monopolist were analysed using a numerical example. Signals are explicit in the beer and quiche game examined in Section 7.5 where the possibility of a player choosing a costly signal in order to deter some action by the other player was examined.[25] For signals to be effective in this way they need to be more affordable for one type of player (so that they convey information) but not prohibitively expensive for the other type.

In Section 7.6 a static battle of the sexes game with asymmetric information about both players was analysed. You saw that as the information became more symmetric in this game, the Bayesian equilibrium approached the mixed strategy Nash equilibrium of the original game with complete information. This suggests that a mixed strategy Nash equilibrium can be interpreted as an equilibrium of a game in which the players are uncertain about the actual choices of their rivals. This uncertainty gives rise to beliefs that correspond to the players' equilibrium mixed strategies.

All of the games analysed in this chapter were two-player games. However, many strategic situations characterised by incomplete information involve more than two players. For example, auctions can be analysed as games of incomplete information in which a single seller is incompletely informed about the valuations of more than one interested buyer.[26] Other trading and contracting transactions are similarly characterised by incomplete information of one kind or another, but not all such transactions are easily characterised as games.

## Answers to exercises

### 7.1

In the friends and enemies game represented in Matrices 7.2.1 and 7.2.2 (reproduced below) party is a dominant strategy for the party-loving Mr Column and hotel is a dominant strategy for the Mr Column who is not a party-lover. Ms Row doesn't know whether Mr Column is a party lover or not. She should choose hotel if her expected pay-off from choosing hotel, $EPO_{hotel}$, is greater than her expected pay-off from choosing party $EPO_{party}$, and she should randomise or choose party otherwise. Whether $EPO_{hotel} > EPO_{party}$ depends on p.

Let $p^*$ be the critical value of p such that if $p > p^*$ $EPO_{hotel} > EPO_{party}$. A strategy for Ms Row that is consistent with her beliefs is choose hotel if $p > p^*$ and choose party if $p < p^*$. To determine $p^*$, set Ms Row's expected pay-offs from hotel and party to be equal. In this game her expected pay-offs are $EPO_{hotel} = p(4) + (1 - p)2 = 2 + 2p$ and $EPO_{party} = p(0) + (1 - p)3 = 3 - 3p$. $EPO_{hotel} = EPO_{party}$ if $5p = 1$ or $p = \frac{1}{5}$. Thus $p^*$, the critical value of p, equals $\frac{1}{5}$. If $p > \frac{1}{5}$ Ms Row's expected pay-off is higher if she chooses hotel and if $p < \frac{1}{5}$ her expected pay-off is higher if she chooses party. Thus $p^* = \frac{1}{5}$ defines Ms Row's strategy.

**Matrix 7.2.1** Mr Column is a party-lover

|  |  | Mr Column | |
|---|---|:---:|:---:|
|  |  | **party** | **hotel** |
| **Ms Row** | **party** | 0, 3 | 3, 0 |
|  | **hotel** | 4, 2 | 2, 1 |

**Matrix 7.2.2** Mr Column is not a party-lover

|  |  | Mr Column | |
|---|---|:---:|:---:|
|  |  | **party** | **hotel** |
| **Ms Row** | **party** | 0, 1 | 3, 2 |
|  | **hotel** | 4, 0 | 2, 3 |

The Bayesian equilibrium of this asymmetric information version of friends or enemies is given by:

### Strategy of Mr Column

Party lover always chooses party.

Non-party lover always chooses hotel.

### Strategy of Ms Row

If $p > \frac{1}{5}$ chooses hotel.

If $p < \frac{1}{5}$ chooses party.

If $p = \frac{1}{5}$ randomises between hotel and party.

In the first example of this game represented in Matrices 7.1.1 and 7.1.2, Ms Row's worst possible outcome was that both players went to the hotel and her perferred outcome was that she went to the party and Mr Column went to the hotel. In the version of the game in this exercise, Ms Row's worst possible outcome is that both players go to the party and her preferred outcome is that she goes to the hotel and he goes to the party. Ms Row therefore has more incentive to go to the hotel and in this Bayesian equilibrium she is more likely to choose the hotel. She will only choose the party when the probability that Mr Column chooses party, p, is relatively small (less than $\frac{1}{5}$) and the probability that he chooses hotel is correspondingly high.

### 7.2

Substituting for $P_s = \frac{1}{2}$ and $w_s = \frac{1}{4}$ into equation (7.10) gives: updated $P_s = P_s/[P_s + (1 - P_s) w_s] = \frac{1}{2} /[\frac{1}{2} + \frac{1}{2} \cdot \frac{1}{4}] = \frac{4}{5}$ or 0.8.

 If $w_s = \frac{1}{2}$ then the updated value of $P_s$ is $\frac{1}{2} /[\frac{1}{2} + \frac{1}{2} \cdot \frac{1}{2}] = \frac{2}{3}$ or 0.666. Note that the higher $w_s$ the less $P_s$ is raised. The higher $w_s$ the less the entrant learns from seeing the signal and the less extra credence she attaches to the possibility that the monopolist is strong. If $w_s = 1$ nothing is learned and $P_s$ is not raised by the signal. But not sending the signal is risky for the entrant as if no signal is sent the entrant will know the monopolist is weak and enter for sure. On the other hand sending the signal is costly as well. These considerations should all enter into the weak monopolist's decision-making process.

## Problems

1  In the game described in Figure 7.5 what is the critical value of $P_s$, the probability that the monopolist is strong, such that the entrant is indifferent between entry and staying out?

 Note that in the entry deterrence game illustrated in Figure 7.5 the pay-offs of the entrant and the monopolist are generalised pay-offs. Using pay-offs

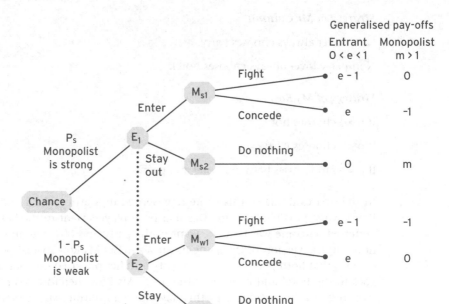

**Figure 7.5** Extensive form of entry deterrence with incomplete information and generalised pay-offs: $0 < e < 1$, $m > 1$

like these means that the results of the analysis can be generalised to other games in which the relative pay-offs of the players satisfy the conditions that $0 < e < 1$, and $m > 1$. The actual values of the pay-offs can vary. For example, $m = 4$, $m = 5$ or $m = 5000$ all satisfy the condition that $m > 1$ and $e = \frac{5}{6}$ and $e = \frac{1}{2}$ both satisfy the condition that $0 < e < 1$. This is a useful feature and you will be seeing this version of the entry deterrence game again in Chapter 8.[27]

2  In the game represented in pay-off Matrix 7.4 a and b are randomly drawn from a distribution over the interval (0, 1). Only Apex knows the value of a and only Bortex knows the value of b. Can you characterise the Bayesian equilibrium of this simultaneous-move game in terms of the critical values of a and b? If $a = b = 0$ so that there is no asymmetric information what is the mixed strategy Nash equilibrium of this game?

**Matrix 7.4** Asymmetric information for Apex and Bortex

|  |  | Bortex | |
|---|---|---|---|
|  |  | **raise** | **lower** |
| **Apex** | **raise** | a, b | a, −1 |
|  | **lower** | 1, b | −1, 3 |

1 How does incomplete information about players' pay-offs change the theoretical prediction of the outcome of games like entry deterrence?

2 What is the role of signalling in games with incomplete information?

3 Under what kinds of circumstances is signalling likely to be effective from the perspective of the signaller? Under what kinds of circumstance might signalling be ineffective or even lead to undesired results?

**Answers to problems**

1 Other than the generalisation of the pay-offs, the essential features of the game in Figure 7.5 are the same as those of the entry deterrence game represented in Figure 7.1. As e is greater than 0 but less than 1 the pay-off to the entrant from staying out, 0, is less than the pay-off from entry followed by concession, e, and higher than the pay-off from entry followed by fight, (e − 1), which is less than 0. Accordingly, the entrant's preferred outcome is entry followed by concession and her least preferred outcome is entry followed by a fight.[28]

For the monopolist as m is greater than 1, no entry is still preferred to entry and, if there is entry, concession is still a best response for the weak monopolist but fighting is a best response for the strong monopolist.[29] Thus in the one-shot version of this game with complete information if there was entry the weak monopolist would concede (0 > −1) and the strong chain-store would fight. Since (e − 1) < 0 the entrant will only enter if the monopolist is weak.

If there is asymmetric information about the monopolist's pay-offs the entrant will be indifferent between entering and staying out if the expected pay-offs of the entrant from entering, $EPO_E$, and staying out, $EPO_{SO}$, are equal. As $EPO_{SO} = 0$, $P_s^*$ is defined by the condition that:

$$EPO_E = (1 − P_s)e + P_s (e − 1) = EPO_{SO} = 0 \qquad (i)$$

Multiplying through leads to $e − eP_s + eP_s = P_s$. This solves for $P_s^* = e$.

Note that as before $P_s^*$ is equal to the entrant's pay-off from entry followed by concession, e, divided by e less the pay-off from entry followed by a fight, e − 1, that is $e/(e − (e − 1)) = e$.

2　Let $a^*$ be the critical value of a such that if $a > a^*$ the expected pay-off for Apex of raise, $EPOA_r$, is greater than that of lower, $EPOA_l$. Then Bortex will expect Apex to choose lower with probability $a^*$ and raise with probability $1–a^*$.

Let $b^*$ be the critical value of b such that if $B > b^*$ the expected pay-off for Bortex of raise, $EPOB_r$, is greater than that of lower, $EPOB_l$. Then Apex will expect Bortex to choose lower with probability $b^*$ and raise with probability $1 – b^*$.

With these expectations Apex's expected pay-offs are $EPOA_r = a$ and $EPOA_l = (1 – b^*)(1) + b^*(–1) = 1 – 2b^*$. Therefore Apex will choose raise when:

$$a > 1 – 2b^* = a^* \qquad\qquad (i)$$

For Bortex, $EPOB_r = b$ and $EPOB_l = (1 – a^*)(– 1) + a^*3 = 4a^*–1$. Therefore Bortex chooses raise if:

$$b > 4a^* –1 = b^* \qquad\qquad (ii)$$

Solving (i) and (ii) simultaneously for $a^*$ and $b^*$ leads to $a^* = \frac{1}{3}$ and $b^* = \frac{1}{3}$. The Bayesian equilibrium follows.

If $a = b = 0$ there is no asymmetric information for the players. There is no Nash equilibrium in pure strategies but there is a mixed strategy Nash equilibrium: {(Apex: raise; $\frac{3}{4}$, lower; $\frac{1}{4}$)(Bortex: raise; $\frac{1}{2}$, lower; $\frac{1}{2}$)}.

This game is a simplified version of a game analysed in Myerson (1991: 130). In the original game the asymmetric information is modelled by multiplying the pay-offs a and b by the same small number. As this number tends to zero the Bayesian equilibrium converges to the mixed strategy Nash equilibrium of the game with complete information for the players. This is a further illustration of the connection between the idea of a Bayesian equilibrium and a mixed strategy Nash equilibrium (*see* the last part of Section 7.6).

## Notes

1　The literature on signalling is large and originates with Spence (1973, 1974). *See* Rasmusen (2001: Chapter 11) or a microeconomics text such as Katz and Rosen (1998: Chapter 17) for a more detailed discussion of signalling and asymmetric information.

2　Some of the analysis in this chapter is quite technical. If you feel at all daunted by any of this material, you might be pleased to know that the first half of the next chapter on repeated games is technically less demanding and you will be able to understand most of it without reading any of this chapter. However, if you want to understand Sections 8.3 and 8.4 of Chapter 8 which looks at repeated games with asymmetric information it will help to work though at least Sections 7.1 and 7.2 of this chapter.

3 Gibbons (1997: 141) defines a strategy for player i in a Bayesian game as an action rule that specifies a feasible action for each of player i's types. Gibbons says that given this definition of a strategy in a static Bayesian game, the appropriate definition of an equilibrium, i.e. a Bayesian Nash equilibrium, is just the familiar Nash concept.

4 *See* Fudenberg and Tirole (1991: 209–11).

5 You could imagine that in the business world in which the monopolist and the potential entrant are operating a known proportion of monopolists, corresponding to $P_s$, are strong.

6 The costs of the commitment, c, and the net benefit, d, satisfy the conditions derived in Section 4.4.1 that $5 > c > 6 - d$ as $c = 2$ and $d = 5$ and $5 > 2 > 6 - 5 = 1$.

7 In a perfect Bayesian equilibrium the players not only hold 'reasonable' beliefs but also choose credible (subgame perfect) strategies (*see* Gibbons 1997: 142). For a more precise definition of a perfect Bayesian Nash equilibrium *see* Gibbons (1997: 144) or Montet and Serra (2003: 150).

8 Note that because $EPO_{SO} = 0$, expression (7.7) implies that $P_s^*$ is determined by the entrant's pay-off from entry followed by concession, 5, divided by the entrant's pay-offs from entry followed by concession, 5, minus the pay-off from entry followed by a fight, –1. That is, $\frac{5}{5-(-1)} = \frac{5}{6}$.

9 Or, using less mathematical shorthand and consequently more words, Bayes' rule says that the updated value of $P_s$, $P_{rob}(M_s|SIG)$ is given by the probability that the monopolist is strong and sends the signal divided by the probability that the signal is sent. The probability that the monopolist is strong and sends the signal can be written as $P_{rob}$ (strong monop sends signal).$P_{rob}$ (monop is strong). The probability that the signal is sent is the probability that the monopolist is strong and sends the signal plus the probability that the monopolist is weak and sends the signal. This can be written as $P_{rob}$(strong monop sends signal).$P_{rob}$(monop is strong) + $P_{rob}$(weak monop sends signal).$P_{rob}$(monop is weak). Using this terminology the updated value of $P_s$ is given by:

$$\frac{P_{rob}(\text{strong monop sends signal}).P_{rob}(\text{monop is strong})}{P_{rob}(\text{strong monop sends signal}). P_{rob}(\text{monop is strong}) + P_{rob}(\text{weak monop sends signal}).P_{rob}(\text{monop is weak})}$$

If the strong monopolist always sends the signal so that $P_{rob}$(strong monopolist sends signal) = 1 then $P_{rob}$(strong monopolist sends signal).$P_{rob}$(strong) = $P_{rob}$(strong) = $P_s$ and the expression simplifies to the one in (7.10).

10 If Bayes' rule still looks complicated to you then you may not be surprised to learn that in experiments designed to study Bayesian judgment subjects appear to make systematic departures from Bayes' rule (*see* Camerer, 1995: 596–8).

11 (7.12) implies $\frac{1}{2} = \frac{5}{6} \Big/ [\frac{1}{2} + \frac{1}{2} w_s]$ or $\frac{5}{12} w_s = \frac{1}{12}$ implying $w_s = \frac{1}{5}$.

12 Commonly called a behavioural strategy in a Bayesian game.

13 If the game analysed here had been played just once before, it would not have been in the weak monopolist's interest to fight entry the first time round. Fighting would have given the weak monopolist a pay-off of –1. If followed by no entry this would give the monopolist a total pay-off of 9. Two rounds of concession on the other hand give the weak incumbent a pay-off of 10. Thus fighting with certainty in the first round of a twice repeated entry deterrence game in which the weak monopolist's pay-offs are the same as those in Figure 7.1 cannot be an equilibrium strategy for the weak monopolist: it would be too costly. However, if the game is repeated more than twice this could change. This possibility is examined in Chapter 8.

14 For a generalised version which allows for more interesting cases see Gibbons (1997: 144–7) or Montet and Serra (2003: 183–4).

15 If both the tough man and the wimp choose beer then the bully's expected pay-off from deferring at beer is $\frac{1}{3}$ (1) + $\frac{2}{3}$ (0) = $\frac{1}{3}$ and his expected pay-off from fighting is $\frac{1}{3}$ (0) + $\frac{2}{3}$(1) = $\frac{2}{3}$ which is clearly greater than that from deferring.

16 The bully will be indifferent at quiche only if the probability that the tough man eats quiche is twice as high as the probability that the wimp eats quiche but this is impossible if the wimp definitely eats quiche, $Q = 1$.

17 In this equilibrium all the decision-nodes in the game are reached. There is therefore no need to think about beliefs off the equilibrium path (out off equilibrium beliefs). In other versions of the game in which the probability the man is a wimp is lower this may not be the case. If some decision-nodes are not reached incredible plans off the equilibrium path need to be ruled out in order to define an equilibrium. Cho and Kreps (1987) do this by evoking their 'intuitive criterion' (*see* Montet and Serra, 2003: 179). The intuitive criterion rules out actions off the equilibrium path that do not benefit informed players.

18 Because there is asymmetric information for both players in this game the analysis that follows is a little more complicated than that of the previous sections and you may want to work though this section only if you are reasonably confident about probability theory and solving simultaneous equations. Otherwise you might prefer to skip it. If you do skip it you will also want to skip Problem 2 at the end of the chapter. Nothing else in this book follows from the analysis in this section.

19 This way of modelling the uncertainty for the players follows Gibbons (1997: 138–40).

20 For a more formal definition of a uniform distribution *see* Rasmusen (2001: 400–1). See Greene (1993: Chapter 3) for a detailed discussion of probability and distribution theory.

21 Or probabilities within intervals between 0 and 1.

22 For example, if $j^* = 0.5$ then the probability that $bj \leq 0.5$ is 0.5; in a uniform distribution between 0 and 1 every value has an equal probability and therefore exactly half the possible values of $bj$ must be less than or equal to 0.5 and the other half must be greater than 0.5. Similarly if $j^* = 0.25$ then exactly a quarter of the values of $bj$ will be less or equal to $j^*$ and three-quarters will be greater than $j^*$. More generally if $bj$ and $br$ are draws from a uniform distribution between 0 and x (where $x > 0$ but could be greater than, equal to or less than 1) then the probability that $bj < j^*$ equals $j^*/x$ and the corresponding probability that $bj > j^*$ equals $1 - j^*/x$.

23 Using the standard formula that $j^* = \dfrac{-b \pm \sqrt{b^2 - 4ac}}{2a}$ where $a = 1$, $b = 4$ and $c = -1$ and noting that $\dfrac{-4 - \sqrt{16+4}}{2}$ is negative.

24 This can be seen by substituting x for the value 1 as the upper limit of the distribution (*see* Note 22). The quadratic in (7.19) then becomes $(j^*)^2 + 4j^* - x = 0$ and $j^* = r^* = \dfrac{-4 + \sqrt{16 + 4x}}{2}$. The probability that Jess goes to the party (Rosy goes to the pub) is $j^*/x$ and this equals $\dfrac{-4 + \sqrt{16 + 4x}}{2x}$. Substituting for smaller and smaller values of x in this expression generates values that tend closer and closer to 0.25.

25 However, a signal won't always have the desired result or even the expected result if a player for whom it is not meant receives it (*see* Carmichael, 2002 for a version of the beer and quiche game that incorporates this possibility).

26 *See*, for example, Gibbons (1992: 155–68), Binmore (1992: 526–36) or Montet and Serra (2003: 151–5).

27 The game in Figure 7.1 can also be analysed using these generalised pay-offs. *See* Notes 28 and 29 below.

28 The entrant's pay-offs in Figure 7.1 can be represented in terms of the generalised pay-offs in Figure 7.5 by dividing through each of the entrant's pay-offs by 6 (the pay-off from entry followed by concession plus one). This leaves the entrant's pay-off from staying out as 0 but her pay-off from entry followed by concession is 5/6 and her pay-off from entry followed by fight as –1/6, i.e. $e = 5/6$ and $e - 1 = -1/6$.

29 The strong monopolist's pay-offs in Figure 7.1 can be represented in terms of the generalised pay-offs in Figure 7.5 by subtracting 4 from each of his pay-offs. This generates a value of 4 for m. The weak monopolist's pay-offs can be generalised by letting his pay-off from no entry be the same as that for the strong monopolist (8) and obtaining the pay-offs from fighting and conceding by swapping round the strong monopolist's pay-offs.

# 8

# PLAYING AGAIN AND AGAIN . . .

## Concepts and techniques

- Finite, infinite and indefinite repetition
- Discounting
- Meta-strategies
- Trigger strategies
- Reputation.

After working through this chapter you will be able to:

- Analyse repeated games
- Find the subgame perfect Nash equilibrium of finitely repeated games
- Explain the paradox of backward induction in the context of a repeated prisoners' dilemma
- Explain the meaning of the chain store paradox
- Show how the paradox of backward induction can be resolved if there is uncertainty about when a repeated game ends
- Explain how uncertainty about players' pay-offs or their rationality can resolve the paradox of backward induction in the finitely repeated prisoners' dilemma and entry deterrence games.

## Introduction

Repeated games are games in which a one-shot or single-stage game is played a number of times. In repeated games the same players interact more than once. This means that there is likely to be scope for players not only to learn but also, potentially, to mislead. These kinds of considerations make the analysis of repeated games interesting and bring game theory closer to the complexities of real life where people quite often interact repeatedly. A closer approximation to reality necessarily adds a level of complication to the analysis, but most of the analytical tools used in this chapter, such as backward induction, expected pay-offs and Bayes' rule, you have seen before. In addition the games examined in this chapter are all repeated versions of one-shot games that we have analysed in detail elsewhere. The idea of repetition was briefly mentioned in Chapter 6 when we were looking at mixed strategies and again at the end of Section 7.4 in Chapter 7. Here we examine repeated games explicitly and in some of the games we are going to look at, one or more of the players either randomises or sends a signal or both.

In repeated games, players' plans for the game need to specify their moves in every repetition or stage of the game. Strategies that prescribe a set of moves in this way are called intertemporal or meta-strategies. As in a one-shot game a player's choice of strategy needs to take into account all the possible moves of the other players in the game and for a meta-strategy to be an equilibrium strategy it needs to be a best response to the equilibrium meta-strategies of the other players in the game. Meta-strategies need to specify responses to all the possible moves of the other players and can be used to enforce particular kinds of behaviour by incorporating punishments or rewards.

Repeated games may be played a finite number of times or played over an infinite or indefinite time horizon. If a game is repeated a finite number of times then this means that the number of times the players play the game is fixed and there is an end game. If there is an end game then we can use backward induction to make a prediction about the likely outcome of the game. If a game is repeated an infinite number of times then the players believe that there will never be an end game. If a game is repeated indefinitely then the players know that the game is finite but do not know exactly when it will end and therefore always believe that there is some probability that there will be another repetition or round of the game. If future pay-offs are discounted[1] in infinitely repeated games then infinite and indefinite repetition are analytically equivalent. But the analysis of finitely repeated games is very different from that of infinitely or indefinitely repeated games because, starting from the last play of the game, we can use backward induction to unravel the subgame perfect Nash equilibrium of the game. In infinitely or indefinitely repeated games this is not an option as there is no clearly identifiable end game.

In this chapter we are going to look at only two games: the repeated prisoners' dilemma and a repeated entry deterrence game. These two games are interesting to compare as the single-stage prisoners' dilemma is a simultaneous-move game and the single-stage entry deterrence game is a game with sequential moves. Initially we will consider finitely repeated versions of both these games. This analysis leads to a paradox of backward induction which is called the chain store paradox in entry deterrence games. This paradox can be resolved theoretically if there is some uncertainty in the game. The uncertainty may be with respect to the number of repetitions of the game or in relation to at least one of the players' pay-offs or, equivalently, their state of mind. In Sections 8.2 to 8.4 you will see how the finitely repeated prisoners' dilemma and the entry deterrence game can be developed in order to allow for both these kinds of uncertainty. Repeated games and repeated prisoners' dilemmas in particular have been the subject of a considerable amount of experimental work. The main results of this work are outlined in Section 8.5.

## 8.1 Finite repetition

For a player's strategy to be an equilibrium strategy in a repeated game it needs to be a best response to the other player's move in every repetition of the game. As each repetition is effectively a subgame of the whole game the appropriate equilibrium concept is that of a subgame perfect Nash equilibrium. In finitely repeated games there is a unique endgame and therefore we can use backward induction to find the subgame perfect Nash equilibrium of these kinds of games. In this section you will see how to use backward induction to find the subgame perfect Nash equilibrium of a finitely repeated prisoners' dilemma and a finitely repeated version of the entry deterrence game first seen in Chapter 4. As you saw in Chapter 3, the one-shot prisoners' dilemma has a unique Nash equilibrium, {defect, defect}. In Chapter 4 you saw that that the entry deterrence game analysed in Section 4.4 has a unique subgame perfect Nash equilibrium, {enter, (concede, do nothing)}. In the finitely repeated versions of these games backward induction leads us to the prediction that {defect, defect} will be the outcome in every repetition of the prisoners' dilemma and in every repetition of the entry deterrence game the entrant will enter and the monopolist will concede. This is a general result. It implies that if there is a unique (subgame perfect) Nash equilibrium in a one-shot game this equilibrium will be played out in every stage of the repeated game. Since this result can contradict intuitive predictions about the likely outcome of the game, it is referred to as a paradox of backward induction or, more specifically in relation to the entry deterrence game, the chain store paradox (Selten, 1978).

## 8.1.1 The finitely repeated prisoners' dilemma

Consider the prisoners' dilemma in Matrix 8.1. In the one-shot version of this game cooperation is not a Nash equilibrium strategy since it is not a best response to either of the other player's strategies. Instead defect is a dominant strategy and the theoretical prediction is {defect, defect}. To solve the finitely repeated version of this prisoners' dilemma we can use backward induction to predict what the players will do in the last stage, the last repetition of the game, and then work backwards through each stage of the game in the same way until we reach the first repetition of the game.

**Matrix 8.1** Prisoners' dilemma

|  |  | Joe Column | |
|---|---|---|---|
|  |  | cooperate | defect |
| John Row | cooperate | 1, 1 | –1, 2 |
|  | defect | 2, –1 | 0, 0 |

Let's assume that the game is repeated 30 times. Using backward induction means that we start by analysing the moves of the players in the 30th repetition, the last round of the game. If the players reach the last stage they know that they are not going to play the game ever again and therefore the game looks like a one-shot game. Rational players will treat it as such and will defect as {defect, defect} is the unique Nash equilibrium of the single-stage version of the game. In the penultimate stage (the 29th repetition) both players know that they will defect in the last stage so there is no incentive to cooperate at this stage and therefore to defect is a dominant strategy. Thus in the penultimate stage both players will defect. In the pre-penultimate round (the 28th repetition) both players know they will defect in the penultimate and last stages of the game so once again there there is no incentive to cooperate and both will defect. The same logic implies that both players will defect in the 27th, the 26th and the 25th repetition of the game and therefore they will defect in the 24th, the 23rd and so on right back to the 1st repetition of the game. Here, rational players will be able to reason that they will defect in all the other repetitions of the game and therefore both players' dominant strategy will be to defect. Consequently, both players will defect in the first stage and all the subsequent repetitions of the game. This reasoning implies that the subgame perfect Nash equilibrium of the repeated prisoners' dilemma is for both players to defect in all repetitions of the game. In other words, the strategy combination {defect, defect} is the equilibrium outcome in every stage of the game.

Does this result appear somewhat paradoxical to you? If so, you are not alone. For many people this result is contrary to their intuition which suggests that there should be scope for cooperation in the repeated prisoners' dilemma. As both players gain by cooperation it seems quite reasonable to expect them to be able to find a way of cooperating at least for some repetitions of the game. For instance, one or both players could cooperate at various points in the game in order to induce the other player to cooperate. After all, if this wasn't successful they could just revert back to defection. Although this kind of behaviour is not consistent with the theoretical prediction, it is consistent with much of the related experimental evidence. A common finding in experiments is that, at least for some of the time, both players cooperate. By cooperating they end up with higher pay-offs than they would in the subgame perfect Nash equilibrium of the game where neither ever cooperates (*see* Roth, 1995a: 26–8). This evidence is discussed in more detail in the last section of this chapter.

## 8.1.2 Repeated entry deterrence: the chain store game

In the repeated entry deterrence game the incumbent monopolist is assumed to be a chain store that has a store in a number of towns or localised markets. In each of these towns the chain store is a monopolist. A competitor is considering entering each of the local markets in which the chain store has a monopoly by opening one of its own stores. In each town where there is entry the incumbent monopolist decides whether to fight entry or concede by sharing the market. If there is no entry the monopolist does not have to do anything. This is a repeated game. In each stage the potential entrant decides whether to enter or not and if there is entry the incumbent decides whether to fight or not.

The extensive form of a single stage of the repeated game is shown in Figure 8.1. The pay-offs in Figure 8.1 are the same as those in the entry deterrence game we analysed in Section 4.4 of Chapter 4. In this version of the game, concession is the chain store's best response to entry. The chain store is therefore a weak monopolist, as defined in Chapter 7, and in the subgame perfect Nash equilibrium of the one-shot game the entrant enters and the monopolist concedes (there is no asymmetric information in this version of the game).

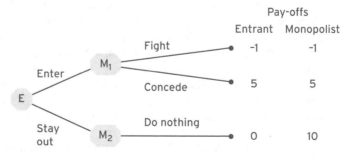

**Figure 8.1** A stage of the repeated entry deterrence game

To simplify things let's assume (like Selten, 1978) that the potential entrant decides whether to enter the market in each of the towns in a specific sequence[2] and that the chain store is a monopolist in only 20 towns. The 1st town represents the first local market in which entry may or may not take place and the 20th town is the last. To find the subgame perfect Nash equilibrium we can analyse what will happen in the 20th town and then use backward induction to work back from the 20th town to the 1st.

If the entrant enters in the 20th town the best response for the chain store is to concede. There is no incentive for the monopolist to do anything else as there are no more repetitions of the game. The entrant knows this and will therefore enter. Thus entry followed by concession is the subgame perfect strategy combination in the last repetition of the game. The 19th town is the penultimate local market where there is a threat of entry. Does the chain store have any incentive to fight entry here? To answer this question ask yourself if fighting in the 19th town would deter entry in the 20th? If not, there is no incentive for the chain store to fight entry. But both players know that entry would be followed by concession in the 20th town and therefore the entrant will enter the 20th town whatever the chain store does in the 19th. This means that there is no incentive for the chain store to fight entry in the 19th town and if the entrant enters the monopolist will concede. The entrant knows this and will therefore enter the 19th town and the monopolist will duly concede. In the 18th town, the pre-penultimate local market in which the entrant considers entry, the monopolist again has no incentive to fight if there is entry and therefore the entrant will enter and the monopolist will concede. Similarly in the 17th and the 16th towns the entrant will enter and the monopolist will concede so that there is no incentive to fight entry in the 15th repetition of the game either and therefore no incentive to fight in the 14th town. Using backward induction logic, the game unravels back to the first stage of the game which takes place in the first town in which the competitor considers entry. If the entrant enters in this town the monopolist will still have no incentive to fight as entry will be followed by concession in the next town and the town after that whether he fights or not. Therefore the entrant will enter in the first town and a rational monopolist will concede.

The logic of backward induction leads us to the unique subgame perfect Nash equilibrium of the game in which there is entry followed by acquiescence in every town. Do you think that this is a reasonable prediction of what might happen? Perhaps it seems more reasonable to you that the chain store will fight entry in one or more towns in the early stages of the game in order to build a reputation for 'toughness' which deters entry in later stages. This is an intuitive prediction that to many people including Selten (1978) appears more reasonable than the outcome predicted by game theory. This is another example of the paradox of backward induction which in relation to the repeated entry deterrence game is known, thanks to Selton (1978), as the chain store paradox.

This result, that the subgame perfect equilibrium of a repeated game in which there is a unique (subgame perfect) Nash equilibrium in the single-stage version is one in which the equilibrium of the one-shot game is played out in every repetition, is a general one. To see this consider any repeated game which has a unique (subgame perfect) Nash equilibrium in the single-stage version. To solve such a game we would use backward induction to unravel the game from its last repetition. In the last stage of the game the players are effectively playing a single-stage game as there is no repetition. They will therefore choose their best response or Nash strategies so that the predicted outcome in the last stage of the game will be the Nash equilibrium of the one-shot game. In the penultimate repetition the players know that they will choose their Nash strategies in the next repetition and therefore there is no incentive to do anything different here. In the pre-penultimate repetition the players will apply the same logic and therefore they will choose their Nash strategies again. It follows that at no stage of the game will either player have an incentive to choose any strategy other than their Nash strategy and consequently the Nash equilibrium strategy combination will result in every repetition of the game.

## 8.2  Infinite and indefinite repetition

The paradox of backward induction in finitely repeated games can be resolved by allowing for some uncertainty about the future in terms of when the game ends. The paradox can also be resolved if there is some asymmetry of information about one or more of the players' pay-offs or their rationality. In this section, the first possibility is examined by assuming that the players in a repeated prisoners' dilemma game are either not sure when the last play of the game will be played or they believe the game will go on for ever. This kind of uncertainty can make cooperation an equilibrium strategy for both players. However, another theoretical problem arises in that there is no unique equilibrium; instead there are multiple possibilities, a result commonly known as the Folk theorem (since it is not attributed to a single source[3]).

If a game is repeated either infinitely or indefinitely there is no well-defined end game and therefore backward induction cannot be applied. This means that a different type of calculation is needed to determine the equilibrium of the game. Instead of using backward induction the players have to look forward and evaluate each alternative strategy, its current and its future returns given the likelihood of repetition. In these circumstances credible threats and promises to secure a particular strategy, such as cooperation in the prisoners' dilemma, can be made.

Have another look at the prisoners' dilemma in Matrix 8.1. If this game is repeated indefinitely the players know that there is a last game but they do not know when it will be played. This is modelled by assuming that there is a fixed probability, $P$, that the game will continue into the next round. In this game the players can choose from an almost infinite number of possible intertemporal or meta-strategies. For instance, they could commit to a strategy that involves always cooperating or always defecting or they could decide to cooperate in the first three repetitions and defect thereafter. They could also choose more complicated strategies that depended on the actions of the other player. They could, for example, start by cooperating and thereafter cooperate in a given repetition of the game if the other player cooperated in the previous repetition but defect otherwise. This strategy is the tit-for-tat strategy in which a player chooses moves by mirroring the moves of the other player in the previous round. Tit-for-tat is a type of trigger strategy as a change in a player's choice of move is triggered by a particular choice of move by the other player. Another trigger strategy is the grim strategy. In a prisoners' dilemma a player playing a grim strategy would cooperate unless the other player defected in which case the player playing the grim strategy would defect for the rest of the game. Trigger strategies are sometimes called punishment strategies because in games like the prisoners' dilemma they can be used to punish non-cooperative behaviour. While the tit-for-tat strategy is a forgiving punishment strategy as a return to cooperation is reciprocated, the grim strategy is an unforgiving strategy.

Let's assume that Joe and John are unforgiving types[4] and announce[5] that they will choose grim strategies to play their repeated prisoners' dilemma. Do you think that these strategies could make it rational for both players to cooperate? If this were to happen, the grim strategies could be said to be self-enforcing in that they would have induced a cooperative outcome without any third-party interference or other changes in the rules of the game. To see whether this is a realistic possibility we need to look more closely at the players' pay-offs.

We can start by considering the game from Joe's perspective. If he believes that John is committed to the grim strategy then what should be his response? If Joe cooperates he will expect to get an initial pay-off of 1 and then 1 in each repetition of the game that is actually played out. The probability that the game will be played one more time is P. The probability that the game will be played two more times is $P^2$ (the probability that the game is played once more *and* then once more again). Similarly the probability that the game is played three more times is $P^3$ and, generalising, the probability that the game is played n more times is $P^n$. Joe's expected pay-off from cooperation, $EPO_{coopJoe}$ is therefore:

$$EPO_{coopJoe} = 1 + P + P^2 + P^3 + P^4 + \ldots P^n + \ldots = \sum_{n=0}^{n=\infty} P^n \tag{8.1}$$

This is an initial 1 followed by an infinite stream of 1s weighted by the probability of the game being repeated 1 more time, 2 more times, 3 more times and so on. The sum of an infinite stream[6] of 1s weighted in this way is $\frac{1}{1-P}$. Therefore Joe's expected pay-off from cooperation if John is playing a grim strategy is:

$$EPO_{coopJoe} = \frac{1}{1-P} \tag{8.2}$$

But if Joe defects his pay-off will be 2 then 0 for the rest of the game however long that is. Consequently, he should cooperate if $\frac{1}{1-P} > 2$ which requires $P > \frac{1}{2}$ and if this condition is satisfied Joe will have no incentive to defect. As the game is symmetric the condition for John to cooperate if Joe plays a grim strategy is the same.

In other words, if $P > \frac{1}{2}$ the gains from cooperation outweigh the gains from defection and both players should cooperate in every repetition of the game. $P = \frac{1}{2}$ is the critical value of P such that if $P > \frac{1}{2}$ the grim strategies of the players are best responses to each other and therefore neither player has an incentive to deviate. In these circumstances the grim strategies define a subgame perfect Nash equilibrium of the whole game in which there is cooperation at every stage.

This result can be generalised in terms of the prisoners' dilemma game in Matrix 8.2 that you first saw in Matrix 3.3 in Chapter 3.

**Matrix 8.2** Generalised prisoners' dilemma

|  |  | Player column | |
| --- | --- | --- | --- |
|  |  | **cooperate** | **defect** |
| **Player row** | **cooperate** | a, a | b, c |
|  | **defect** | c, b | d, d |

c > a > d > b

To keep things simple we shall assume that the probability that the game continues for at least one more round is P as before and both players again commit to grim strategies. With these assumptions if a player cooperates they can expect a pay-off of a until the game ends. This means that the expected pay-off from cooperation,[7] $EPO_{coop}$, is:

$$EPO_{coop} = a + aP + aP^2 + aP^3 + \ldots aP^n + \ldots = \sum_{n=0}^{n=\infty} aP^n = \frac{a}{(1-P)} \tag{8.3}$$

If either player cheats they receive a one-off gain of c then d until the game ends. This means that the expected pay-off from defection, $EPO_{defect}$, is:

$$EPO_{defect} = c + dP + dP^2 + dP^3 + \ldots dP^n + \ldots = c + \sum_{n=1}^{n=\infty} dP^n = c + \frac{dp}{(1-P)} \tag{8.4}$$

A reasonable decision rule for the players would be to cooperate if $EPO_{coop} > EPO_{defect}$ or:

$$\frac{a}{(1-P)} > c + \frac{dp}{(1-P)} \tag{8.5}$$

Rearranging (8.5) leads to:

$$a > c(1-P) + dP = c - cP + dP \tag{8.5.1}$$
$$a - c > P(d-c) \tag{8.5.2}$$

as $a - c < 0$ and $d - c < 0$ (8.5.2) simplifies to:

$$\frac{a-c}{d-c} < P \tag{8.6}$$

Condition (8.6) determines the critical value of P, $P^*$, such that if $P > \frac{a-c}{d-c} = P^*$ there is no incentive for either player to defect. If this condition is satisfied it is rational for both players to cooperate in all the repetitions of the game. Thus the grim strategies can self-enforce cooperation if P is large enough. In these circumstances there is a subgame perfect Nash equilibrium of the repeated prisoners' dilemma in which there is cooperation in every repetition.

The condition in (8.6) is a general condition that applies to all prisoners' dilemma games. To see this think about the pay-offs in the Prisoners' dilemma game in Matrix 8.1 where $a = 1$, $b = -1$, $c = 2$ and $d = 0$. Substituting these values into (8.6) defines the critical value of P as $(1 - 2)/(0 - 2) = \frac{1}{2}$ as we saw before.

If the generalised prisoners' dilemma in Matrix 8.2 is repeated infinitely rather than indefinitely then the players believe that there will always be another repetition of the game. But if the game goes on forever then in order to plan ahead the players need to work out the discounted present values of their pay-offs in the future as the game progresses. The value today,[8] the present value, of a sum of money €X received n years in the future is $X/(1 + r)^n$ where r is the rate of return (the interest rate) on money invested today (in the present) and $1/(1 + r)$ is the discount factor, F. This formulation[9] implies that the value to an individual of a sum of money like €X is less if they receive it in the future than if they receive it today; money today is worth more than money tomorrow. However, as long as future pay-offs are worth something (the value of the future is not discounted away) the benefits of infinite cooperation are likely to outweigh any short-term gains from defection. As in the case of indefinite repetition this intuitive prediction can be formalised by deriving the players' equilibrium strategies.

To see this assume once again that the players both commit to grim strategies. In the infinitely repeated version of the generalised prisoners' dilemma in Matrix 8.2 the expected pay-off from cooperation, $EPO_{coop}$, will be:

$$EPO_{coop} = a + a\,\frac{1}{1+r} + a\,\frac{1}{(1+r)^2} + a\,\frac{1}{(1+r)^3} + \ldots a\,\frac{1}{(1+r)^n} + \ldots \tag{8.7}$$

Substituting F for the discount factor $\dfrac{1}{1+r}$ leads to:

$$a + aF + aF^2 + aF^3 + \ldots aF^n + \ldots = \sum_{n=0}^{n=\infty} aF^n = \frac{a}{1-F} \qquad (8.7.1)$$

Take a look back at equation (8.3) and compare it with (8.7.1). Do they look similar? (8.7.1) is the same as (8.3) except that P has been replaced by F. Thus the infinite sum in (8.7.1) sums to $\frac{a}{1-F}$ instead of $\frac{a}{1-P}$. If either player defects they receive a one-off gain of c then the appropriately discounted value of d until the game ends. Thus the expected pay-off from defection in the infinitely repeated prisoners' dilemma in Matrix 8.2, $EPO_{defect}$, is:

$$EPO_{defect} = c + d\,\frac{1}{1+r} + d\,\frac{1}{(1+r)^2} + d\,\frac{1}{(1+r)^3} + \ldots d\,\frac{1}{(1+r)^n} + \ldots \qquad (8.8)$$

Or, after substituting F for $\frac{1}{1+r}$:

$$EPO_{defect} = c + dF + dF^2 + dF^3 + \ldots dF^n + \ldots = c + \sum_{n=1}^{n=\infty} aF^n = c + \frac{dF}{1-F} \qquad (8.8.1)$$

As you can see (8.8.1) is the same as (8.4) except that P has been replaced by F. Thus in the infinitely repeated prisoners' dilemma if both players choose grim strategies they should cooperate as long as:

$$\frac{a}{1-F} > c + \frac{dF}{1-F} \qquad (8.9)$$

which simplifies to:

$$\frac{a-c}{d-c} < F \qquad (8.10)$$

(8.10) confirms the intuitive prediction that if F is high enough, so that the future is not discounted away too quickly, there is an incentive for the players to cooperate. If both players choose grim strategies it will be rational for them to cooperate as long as $F > \frac{a-c}{d-c}$. In these circumstances, there is a subgame perfect Nash equilibrium of the infinitely repeated prisoners' dilemma in which both players cooperate in every repetition. Moreover, if pay-offs are discounted in the infinitely repeated prisoner's dilemma then the infinitely and indefinitely repeated games are formally equivalent.

You may need a little more convincing that the grim strategies in the examples we have looked at are subgame perfect strategies. In particular, you might be wondering whether the grim threat to defect forever in response to a defection by the other player is a credible threat. After all, if it is not a credible threat the grim strategies can't be part of a subgame perfect Nash equilibrium. If you have doubts in this regard, assume that the probability of continuation or the discount factor, whichever you prefer, is greater than its critical value as determined above. For the grim strategies to be subgame perfect the following must be true for both players in the infinite or indefinite game:

(a)  Cooperation is a best response to cooperation.

(b)  Defect is best response to defect.

Consider the game from John Row's perspective in the prisoners' dilemma in Matrix 8.1. We have already shown that (a) is true in the infinite/indefinite game given the assumption that the probability of continuation or the discount factor is greater than its critical value. But (b) is also true. It is true in any single-stage game as defect is a best, that is a Nash, response to defect. It is also true in the infinite/indefinite game because if Joe Column, who is meant to be playing a grim strategy defects without provocation then Joe can't be using a grim strategy unless he has defected by mistake. If Joe isn't playing grim then as John has no contrary information he will expect Joe to defect again. Therefore John might as well defect straight away in effect triggering the grim punishment by defecting forever. Regarding the second possibility that Joe Column has made a mistake, then even if Joe reverts to grim in the next repetition by cooperating, John's best response is still to defect. This is so because if John doesn't punish the mistake Joe will assume that John isn't playing grim and that John will defect again, in which case Joe, as he has no contrary information, should defect straightaway. John can reason this out and therefore he should also defect.

Thus the grim strategies are best responses to each other in the equilibrium of the game in which both players cooperate. They also incorporate credible threats. It follows that as long as the probability of continuation in the indefinite game or the discount factor in the infinite game is large enough it is possible to sustain cooperative behaviour in every repetition of a prisoners' dilemma.

But the grim strategies are not the only meta-strategy combination that can generate cooperation in the indefinitely or infinitely repeated prisoners' dilemma. The Folk theorem says that an infinite number of strategies can enforce any given outcome in an indefinitely or infinitely repeated game like the repeated prisoners' dilemma. For example, a more forgiving strategy like tit-for-tat that incorporates both an incentive to cooperate as well as a punishment for defection can also achieve a cooperative outcome.[10] Such strategies are sometimes referred to as 'stick and carrot' strategies. An infinite number of these can be constructed, for example strategies that punish defection for longer than tit-for-tat.[11]

The Folk theorem implies that indefinitely and infinitely repeated games have multiple equilibria and therefore it is almost impossible to make a clear prediction of what will actually happen in such games. The problem of multiple Nash equilibria that we first came across in Chapter 2 seems to have grown to nightmare proportions. Nevertheless, the analysis in this section has shown that in infinitely and indefinitely repeated prisoners' dilemma games we should expect cooperation at least some of the time. The introduction of some uncertainty for both players about the timing of the last repetition has completely changed the theoretical prediction about the outcome of the game. The players have more incentive to cooperate since defection in every repetition is no longer the unique subgame perfect equilibrium of the game.

## Exercise 8.1

Consider the prisoners' dilemma in Matrix 8.3 where in terms of the generalised prisoners' dilemma in Matrix 8.2, a = 3, b = 1, d = 2 and c = 5. Assume that this game is repeated indefinitely with probability Q of repetition at each stage and that the firms commit to grim strategies where they collude if there has been collusion in all previous repetitions and cheat otherwise. In these circumstances what is the critical value of Q, Q*, such that if Q > Q* there is a perfect Nash equilibrium of the game in which both firms collude in every repetition?

**Matrix 8.3**  Oligopoly collusion

|  |  | Jessup Inc | |
| --- | --- | :---: | :---: |
|  |  | collude | cheat |
| **Rosden Ltd** | collude | 3, 3 | 1, 5 |
|  | cheat | 5, 1 | 2, 2 |

## 8.3  Asymmetric information in the finitely repeated prisoners' dilemma

Another solution to the paradox of backward induction was proposed by Kreps, Milgrom, Roberts and Wilson (1982). They analysed a finitely repeated prisoners' dilemma with a definite end game but uncertainty for one of the players about the rationality or equivalently the pay-offs of the other.

Specifically one of the players, for example Column, is unsure about the other player's (Row's) approach to the game. While column is entirely rational and knows that in a finitely repeated prisoners' dilemma the subgame perfect equilibrium is for both players to defect in every repetition, Column is unsure whether Row is aware of this. Column believes that there is some chance that Row is not entirely rational (or has different pay-offs to Column) and will cooperate as long as row also cooperates, but defect otherwise. In other words, Column believes that there is some probability that Row is committed to a tit-for-tat strategy. If Row is indeed committed to tit-for-tat then cooperation may be a best response for Column, at least some of the time. However, Column isn't sure about Row. Row may after all be entirely rational and quite able to work out the subgame perfect equilibrium of the game. In this case Row is likely to defect in every repetition. Given this uncertainty, Column's optimal strategy will depend on Column's beliefs about Row and those beliefs need to be incorporated in the equilibrium of the game. A further complication is that a rational Row, who knows that Column is unsure of Row's true nature, may find it advantageous to act as if he were irrational (or had different pay-offs) in order to give Column an incentive to cooperate.

Thus a little uncertainty about the nature (or pay-offs) of one of the players makes it more difficult to work out what the best responses of the players should be. Is it rational for them to cooperate or not? Intuitively it seems at least possible that there is an equilibrium of the game which depends on Column's beliefs and in which both Column and a rational Row cooperate at least some of the time. Kreps et al. (1982) confirm this intuition and show that under certain conditions both Row and rational Column will both cooperate in all but the last two repetitions of the game. Where this happens, the paradox of backward induction in the prisoners' dilemma is resolved. To understand exactly how the this happens it is useful to work through an example. This is done in Section 8.3.1.[12]

## 8.3.1 Irrational play?

Consider the prisoners' dilemma in Matrix 8.4. The restrictions on the generalised pay-offs in Matrix 8.2 are that a = 1, b < 0, c > 1, d = 0 and c + b < 2 as in the original Kreps et al. (1982) article.

**Matrix 8.4** Row and Column play prisoners' dilemma

|  |  | Column | |
|---|---|:---:|:---:|
|  |  | **cooperate** | **defect** |
| **Row** | **cooperate** | 1, 1 | b, c |
|  | **defect** | c, b | 0, 0 |

c > 1, b < 0 and c + b < 2

In this example of the finitely repeated prisoners' dilemma there is a probability, P, that one player (Row) cooperates in response to cooperation but defects in response to defect, i.e. plays tit-for-tat. Such a strategy is not rational according to the game theoretic reasoning so we can call this player irrational or TFT Row.[13]

The pay-offs in Matrix 8.4 imply that Column's best response to TFT Row is to cooperate until the last game. To see this consider what happens if Column defects against TFT Row at any point in the game. Defection gives Column a pay-off of c but in the next stage Column's pay-off will be at most 0 as TFT Row will defect. If Column had waited until the next stage to defect his pay-off from these two stages would have been 1 + c which is greater than c + 0. This will be true at any point in the game implying that as long as there is one more repetition of the game Column should cooperate if he believes that Row is irrational.

However, Column doesn't know whether Row is irrational or not but if Row ever deviates from tit-for-tat then Column will know that Row is rational. If Column knows Row is rational then Column should defect. Since both rational and irrational Row benefit from cooperation by Column, rational Row has an incentive to mimic TFT Row. If rational Row can acquire or build a reputation for being irrational Column may cooperate. This intuition can be confirmed in four steps. At the first step we are going to consider a two-stage game. A three-stage game is analysed at the second step and a ten-stage game at the third step. The last step generalises the analysis of the ten-stage game to an n-stage game. This is possible because the last three stages of any n-stage game are the same as the last three stages of the ten-stage game.

**Step 1**  The two-stage (twice repeated) game

The two-stage prisoners' dilemma is analysed as in Section 8.1 using backward induction. In order that this analysis can be extended to consider a three-stage and eventually an n-stage game it is convenient to label the progress of the game in terms of the time remaining or more accurately the number of repetitions of the game that remain to be played. Using this formulation the first stage or first repetition of the game is labelled t = 2 since at the start of the game the players know that there are two repetitions of the game to be played. The second stage is the last stage of the two-stage game. It is labelled t = 1 as after the first stage has been played out there is only one repetition remaining to be played. The time line of the two-stage game is illustrated in Figure 8.2 and Table 8.1 sets out the moves of the players as the game progresses.

In the first stage of the game (at t = 2) TFT Row will definitely cooperate and rational Row will definitely defect; rational Row has no incentive to do anything else as backward induction shows that Column will definitely defect in the last stage of the game at t = 1. But in the first stage at t = 2 Column's move is unknown.[14] We can call this unknown move $M_{c2}$. Whatever Column's move is at t = 2 we know that TFT Row will mimic it at t = 1 and therefore TFT Row's move at t = 1, which we can call $M_{tft1}$, must equal $M_{c2}$.

1st stage | Last stage
t = 2 | t = 1

**Figure 8.2**  Time line of two-stage game

**Table 8.1** Moves in the two-stage game

|  | t = 2 | t = 1 |
|---|---|---|
| **irrational/TFT Row** | cooperate | $M_{tft1}$ |
| **rational Row** | defect | defect |
| **Column** | $M_{c2}$ | defect |

To make a prediction about what will happen in this two-stage game we need to determine $M_{c2}$ and $M_{tft1}$. Column has two alternatives at t = 2: $M_{c2}$ = cooperate and $M_{c2}$ = defect. We shall consider each of these in turn:

### (i) Column cooperates at t = 2

If $M_{c2}$ = cooperate then, in the next repetition, TFT's move, $M_{tft1}$, will be to cooperate. In this case Column's pay-off at t = 2 is P + (1 – P)b and Column's pay-off at t = 1 is Pc + (1 – P)0. Thus Column's pay-off for the whole game if Column cooperates in the first play of the game, $COL(EPO_{coop2})$, is:

$$COL(EPO_{coop2}) = P + (1 – P)b + Pc \qquad (8.11)$$

### (ii) Column defects at t = 2

If $M_{c2}$ = defect, Column defects at t = 2. In this case TFT will defect at t = 1 and $M_{tft1}$ = defect. In this case Column's pay-off at t = 2 will be Pc and his pay-off at t = 1 will be 0. Thus his pay-off for the whole game if he defects, $COL(EPO_{def2})$, will be:

$$COL(EPO_{def2}) = Pc + 0 = Pc \qquad (8.12)$$

Conditions (8.11) and (8.12) imply that in the two-stage game Column has an incentive to cooperate in the first repetition at t = 2 if P + (1 – P)b + Pc ≥ Pc or:

$$P + (1 – P)b \geq 0 \qquad (8.13)$$

**Step 2** The three-stage (three times repeated) game in which condition (8.13) is satisfied

The time line of the three-stage game is shown in Figure 8.3. Since the last two repetitions of the three-stage game are the same as in the two-stage game we can work out what will happen at t = 2 if condition (8.13) is satisfied and rational Row cooperates in the first repetition of the three-stage game at t = 3: Column will cooperate. But we need to work out whether or in what circumstances rational Row has an incentive to cooperate at t = 3. If both rational Row and Column cooperate at t = 3 this will resolve the paradox of backward induction in the three-stage game.

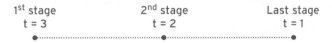

| 1st stage | 2nd stage | Last stage |
|---|---|---|
| t = 3 | t = 2 | t = 1 |

**Figure 8.3** Time line of three-stage game

First let's consider the possibilities from the perspective of rational Row. Rational Row will only cooperate at t = 3 if he believes that Column will also cooperate. But if Column does cooperate rational Row may still defect. There are therefore two possibilities from rational Row's perspective if Column cooperates at t = 3: he can cooperate or defect. We shall consider each of these possibilities in turn.

## (i) Rational Row defects at t = 3 (and Column cooperates)

If rational Row defects (and Column cooperates) at t = 3 Column will know that Row is rational, Row will know that Column knows this and therefore both will defect at t = 2 and t = 1. This implies that Row's expected pay-off from defection at t = 3, the first repetition of the three-stage game (if Column cooperates), is just c, the one-off gain from defection.

## (ii) Rational Row cooperates at t = 3 (and Column also cooperates)

If rational Row cooperates at t = 3, the first play of the game, given that condition (8.13) is satisfied Column will cooperate in the next repetition at t = 2. From our analysis of the two-stage game we know that rational Row will defect at t = 2 and both rational Row and Column will defect at t = 1 (the last repetition). In these circumstances rational Row's pay-offs will be 1 at t = 3, c at t = 2 and 0 in the last repetition. Thus rational Row's pay-off for the whole game will be 1 + c. This is clearly greater than c (rational Row's pay-off if he defects at t = 3) which means that rational Row should cooperate in the first repetition of the three-stage game as long as Column also cooperates.

This line of reasoning implies that if Column cooperates at t = 3 so will rational Row. But why should Column cooperate at t = 3? To answer this question let's consider the game from the perspective of Column. There are two possibilities: whether Column cooperates or he defects. Again we shall consider each of these in turn.

## (i) Column cooperates at t = 3

If Column cooperates at t = 3 then rational Row cooperates at t = 3 (but not at t = 2 or t = 1). As long as condition (8.13) holds, Column also cooperates at t = 2 but not at t = 1. In these circumstances Column's expected pay-off, $COL(EPO_{coop3})$, is:

$$\text{COL(EPO}_{coop3}) = 1 + P + (1 - P)b + Pc \qquad (8.14)$$

## (ii) Column defects at t = 3

If Column defects at t = 3 then TFT, rational Row and Column all defect at t = 2 and t = 1. In these circumstances Column's expected pay-off, COL(EPO$_{def3}$), is at most c (it is c if rational Row cooperates at t = 3). That is:

$$\text{COL(EPO}_{def3}) \leq c \qquad (8.15)$$

Combining (8.14) and (8.15) implies that Column has incentive to cooperate at t = 3 if:

$$1 + P + (1 - P)b + Pc \geq c \qquad (8.16)$$

If condition (8.13) is satisfied as we have assumed, then $P + (1 - P)b \geq 0$ and a sufficient condition for Column to cooperate at t = 3 is that:

$$1 + Pc \geq c \qquad (8.17)$$

Conditions (8.13) and (8.17) together define the critical value of P, $P^*$, such that if $P \geq P^*$ both Column and rational Row will cooperate in the first repetition of the three-stage game. If conditions (8.13) and (8.17) are both satisfied then Column cooperates at t = 3 and t = 2, rational Row cooperates at t = 3 only and irrational, TFT Row always cooperates. What this means is that as long as conditions (8.13) and (8.17) are satisfied both Row and Column will cooperate at t = 3 (the first repetition of the three-stage game) even if Row is in fact rational.

**Step 3** The ten-stage game

The last three repetitions of the ten-stage game are equivalent to the three-stage game already considered (*see* Figure 8.4). This means that if conditions (8.13) and (8.17) are satisfied rational Row and Column will both cooperate a t = 3 in the ten-stage game. If they cooperate at t = 3 it will be rational for them to cooperate at t = 4. If they cooperate at t = 4 it will also be rational for them to cooperate at t = 5 and at t = 6, t = 7, t = 8, t = 9 and t = 10, the first repetition of the game. Consequently, if conditions (8.13) and (8.17) are satisfied there will be cooperation in all but the last two repetitions of the game.

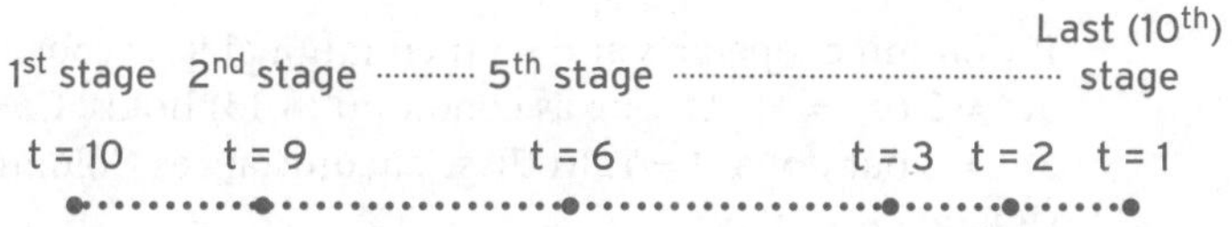

|  |  |  |  | Last (10th) |  |  |
|---|---|---|---|---|---|---|
| 1st stage | 2nd stage | ......... | 5th stage | ........................... | stage |  |
| t = 10 | t = 9 |  | t = 6 |  | t = 3  t = 2  t = 1 |  |

•••••••••••••••••••••••••••••••••••••••••••••

**Figure 8.4** Time line for ten-stage game

**Step 4** An n-stage game where n > 10

The last ten repetitions of any n-stage game are equivalent to the ten-stage game considered in Step 3. Therefore, if conditions (8.13) and (8.17) are satisfied rational Row and Column will both cooperate at t = 10 in the n-stage game (the first repetition of the 10-stage game). If they cooperate at t = 10 it will be rational for them to cooperate at t = 11 and if they cooperate at t = 11 it will also be rational for them to cooperate at t = 12 and at t = 13 and then in every repetition of the game prior to t = 13 including the first repetition at t = n.

The conclusion in Step 4 implies that in any n repeated prisoners' dilemma in which there is doubt about the rationality of one of the players, cooperation can be an equilibrium strategy by both players at every stage of the game except the last two. Cooperation will be a best response for both players in all but the last two stages as long as conditions equivalent to (8.13) and (8.17) are satisfied even if the player about whom there is doubt is in fact rational. To summarise:

● In any n repeated prisoner's dilemma where the pay-offs c and b and the probability P satisfy conditions equivalent to (8.13) and (8.17) there is an equilibrium of the game in which rational Row and Column cooperate until the penultimate repetition of the game at t = 2.

Whether cooperation is an equilibrium strategy or not will, therefore, depend on the players beliefs as characterised by P.

## 8.3.2 Implications of the analysis

The analysis in Section 8.3.1 shows that if there is asymmetric information about the objectives of one of the players in a finitely repeated prisoner's dilemma then, under certain conditions, there is a Bayesian equilibrium of the game in which both players cooperate until the penultimate repetition of the game.[15] This will be true even when both players are actually rational. Essentially what happens is that asymmetric information about Row's attitude to the game gives a rational Row an incentive to cooperate in order to keep doubt in Column's mind.[16] More precisely and using the terminology of Chapter 7, when Row cooperates, Bayesian updating by Column leads to an upward valuation of the probability that Row is irrational. If the updated value of P is high enough then Column's expected pay-off from cooperation will be large enough to induce cooperation. Although the precise details of the equilibrium in a game where there are more than three repetitions were not presented,[17] the analysis in Section 8.3.1 shows that that under certain conditions there is a limit (or upper bound) to the number of stages in which both players defect in the n-stage game. In fact P doesn't have to be very high to achieve this result and yet, if it is high enough, the theoretical prediction in relation to the outcome of the game completely changes. Something similar happens in the entry deterrence game examined in Section 8.4.

---

### Exercise 8.2

For what values of P, the probability that Ben is a tit-for-tat player, will Rosie and rational Ben both cooperate in all but the last two repetitions of a 20-stage prisoners' dilemma game in which the pay-offs in each stage are those in Matrix 8.5?

Matrix 8.5  Rosie and Ben play a repeated prisoners' dilemma

|  |  | Ben | |
|---|---|:---:|:---:|
|  |  | cooperate | cheat |
| Rosie | cooperate | 1, 1 | –1, 2 |
|  | cheat | 2, –1 | 0, 0 |

---

## 8.4  Resolving the chain store paradox

A solution to the backward induction paradox in the entry deterrence game was proposed by Kreps and Wilson (1982). The version of the entry deterrence examined here is very similar to the one outlined in Section 8.1.2. The chain store has a store in N towns or localised markets and in each of the towns in which it has a store it is a monopolist. A competitor is considering entering the market in each of the towns in which the chain store has a monopoly by opening one of its own stores. The potential entrant decides whether to enter the market in each of the N towns in a specific sequence. In each town where there is entry the chain-store monopolist decides whether to fight entry or concede by sharing the market. If there is no entry the monopolist doesn't have to do anything. The game is therefore an N repeated game where in each stage the potential entrant decides whether to enter or not and if there is entry the incumbent decides whether to fight or not.

In this version of the game there is incomplete information about the chain store's pay-offs. As in Chapter 7, Section 7.2, the entrant is unsure about the pay-offs of the incumbent monopolist. The entrant believes that there is a possibility that the monopolist has invested in a sunk cost that makes it optimal to fight entry. If the monopolist has made this investment then fighting is a best response to entry, otherwise it is not. The chain store is therefore either a *strong* monopolist for whom fighting is an optimal strategy or a *weak* monopolist for whom conceding to entry is a best response. The entrant knows that a strong monopolist will always fight and that in a one-shot version of the game a weak monopolist will always concede but doesn't know which of the two the monopolist is. The entrant only knows $P_s$, the probability that the monopolist is strong. We are going to follow Kreps and Wilson (1982) by analysing this game with the generalised pay-offs in Table 8.2.

**Table 8.2** Pay-offs in the repeated entry deterrence game with incomplete information about the chain store's pay-offs

| | Pay-offs for each repetition of the game | | |
|---|---|---|---|
| | **entrant** | **weak chain store** | **strong chain store** |
| **entry followed by fight** | e - 1 | -1 | 0 |
| **entry followed by concession** | e | 0 | -1 |
| **entrant stays out** | 0 | m | m |

m > 1, 0 < e < 1

The pay-offs in Table 8.2 are the same as those in Problem 1 in Chapter 7. Using generalised pay-offs like these means that the results of the analysis can be used to explain and predict outcomes in different strategic situations. This is useful here because we want to show that the chain store paradox can be resolved generally, not just for one specific case. As already noted in relation to Problem 1 in Chapter 7, nothing else has changed in relation to the game analysed in Chapter 7, Section 7.2 other than that here it is repeated. As e is greater than 0 but less than 1 the pay-off to the entrant from staying out is less than her pay-off from entry followed by concession and higher than her pay-off from entry followed by fight.[18] Therefore the entrant's preferred outcome is entry followed by concession and her least preferred outcome is entry followed by fight. From the perspective of the chain store, since m is greater than 1 no entry is still preferred to entry. If there is entry, concession is still a best response for the weak chain store and fighting is a best response for the strong chain store. In the one-shot version of this game with complete information if there was entry the weak monopolist would concede and the strong chain store would fight. As (e − 1) < 0 the entrant would only enter if the chain store were weak. The extensive form of a single stage of this game is shown in Figure 8.5. The broken line between $E_1$ and $E_2$ shows that the entrant does not know whether the chain store is strong or weak.

The analysis in Section 7.2 of Chapter 7 suggested that with incomplete information about the monopolist's pay-offs the entrant might be deterred from entry in the one-shot game. This could happen if $P_s$ is high enough, that is greater than or equal to some critical level $P_s^*$. As the last repetition of the repeated game is effectively a one-shot game it follows that in the last repetition

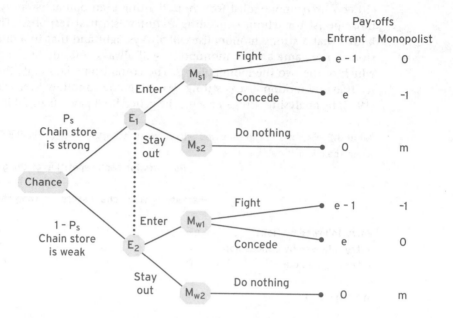

**Figure 8.5** Extensive form of a stage of the repeated entry deterrence game with asymmetric information

of the repeated game entry will be deterred if the value the entrant attributes to $P_s$ is greater than $P_s^*$, where, as before $P_s^*$, is determined by setting equal the entrant's expected pay-offs from entering and staying out. In the repeated game, as in the one-shot game, the weak chain store has no incentive to fight entry in the last repetition of the game and therefore the entrant's expected pay-offs from entering and staying out can be determined in exactly the same way as in Chapter 7.

With the pay-offs in Table 8.2 the entrant's expected pay-off from entering in the last local market will be $P_l(e - 1) + (1 - P_l)e$ where $P_l$ is the value the entrant attributes to the probability that the monopolist is strong in the last repetition of the game. As the entrant's expected pay-off from staying out is 0 we need to set $P_l(e - 1) + (1 - P_l)e$ equal to zero to solve for the critical value of $P_s$ in the last repetition of the game. Doing this solves for $P_l^* = e$.[19] This means that if the value the entrant attributes to $P_s$ in the last repetition of the game is greater than e the entrant will not enter in the last local market.

Furthermore, as we saw in Chapter 7, Section 7.3, if $P_s < P_s^*$ in the one-shot game, which is equivalent to the last repetition of the repeated game, the weak monopolist may find it worthwhile to send a signal that he is in fact strong. To deter entry the signal needs to raise $P_s$ to $P_s^*$. In the repeated game, the weak monopolist can send a signal that he is strong by fighting entry in a previous repetition. This will be worthwhile for the weak monopolist if fighting in an early repetition of the game deters entry in a sufficient number of the later stages of the game. In these circumstances, the threat to fight by the weak monopolist will be credible and entry will be deterred without the weak monopolist actually having to fight.

The analysis in Kreps and Wilson (1982) formalises this intuition and shows that, depending on $P_s$ and the entrant's pay-offs, there are equilibria of the game in which the entrant will only enter, if she enters at all, in the later stages of the game. This result implies that the chain store paradox can be resolved by allowing for some doubt in the entrant's mind about the chain store's pay-offs. To understand exactly how the paradox is resolved it is useful to work through some analysis in order to derive the equilibrium of the game described by the pay-offs in Table 8.2. This is done in Section 8.4.1.[20]

## 8.4.1 Repeated entry deterrence with an uncertain entrant

It is convenient to delineate the progress of the n-stage game from the perspective of the entrant as she considers whether to enter the nth market or not. From her perspective n is the number of potential markets remaining. Using this formulation the first stage or first repetition of the game is the Nth, since at the start of the game the entrant can enter at most N markets. The second stage is the N – 1th and at the last stage n = 1 since at this stage she can enter at most one market. The time line of the game, using this terminology, is illustrated in Figure 8.6.

In this game $P_s$ is the probability that the entrant attributes to the monopolist being strong at the start of the game. $P_s$ is common knowledge. However, as you saw in Chapter 7, in sequential-move games like this the entrant is likely to update this probability if she learns anything about the monopolist as the game progresses. She will learn something if she enters and the chain store responds by fighting. As fighting is costly for the weak monopolist the entrant is likely to raise the probability that she attributes to the monopolist being strong (see Section 7.3 in Chapter 7). In order to incorporate this possibility we need to distinguish between the value of $P_s$ at the start of the game, in the Nth repetition, which we can call $P_N$ and the updated values of $P_s$ as the game progresses. We can do this by letting $P_n$ be the updated value of $P_s$ in the nth repetition. Using this terminology $P_{n+1}$ is the updated value of $P_s$ in the round before n, $P_{n-1}$ is the updated value of $P_s$ in the round after n, $P_1$ is the updated value of $P_s$ in the last repetition and $P_2$ is the updated value of $P_s$ in the penultimate repetition. The time line in Figure 8.6 illustrates how $P_s$ is updated as the game progresses.

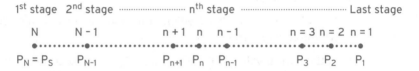

Figure 8.6 Time line for the N-stage entry deterrence game

Kreps and Wilson (1982) show that the equilibrium of the repeated entry deterrence game, with the pay-offs in Table 8.2, depends only on the updated value of $P_s$. The probability that the entrant attributes to the chain store being strong will be updated according to Bayes' rule. If entry is followed by a fight in the nth repetition Bayes' rule implies that $P_{n-1}$ should be updated as follows:[21]

$$P_{n-1} = \frac{P_n}{P_n + X_n(1 - P_n)} \tag{8.18}$$

In (8.18) $X_n$ is the probability that the weak monopolist fights in the nth repetition. Note that if $X_n$ equals 0 then $P_{n-1}$ equals 1; the monopolist must be strong if entry was fought but $X_n = 0$. If $X_n$ equals 1 both the weak and strong monopolists fight with the same probability and the entrant learns nothing from a fight. As a result $P_{n-1}$ equals $P_n$. This implies that to raise $P_n$ the weak monopolist needs to randomise between fighting and conceding so that $0 < X_n < 1$. If there is no entry the entrant learns nothing and $P_{n-1} = P_n$ but if entry is followed by concession the entrant knows the monopolist is weak, as the strong monopolist would never concede and the value of $P_{n-1}$ will be updated to 0. In this case the entrant enters at $n - 1$ implying that if entry is followed by concession in the nth local market the entrant will enter in the next and every subsequent local market. The first concession is therefore very costly for the weak monopolist.

When the weak chain store fights in the repeated entry deterrence game he is attempting to deter entry in the next repetition by sending a signal to the entrant that he is in fact strong. This is only possible because the entrant is unsure of the chain store's pay-offs. If the entrant believes that the probability that the monopolist is strong is high enough entry will be deterred. Signalling changes the equilibrium strategies of the players in much the same way as it did in Section 7.3 of Chapter 7 where signalling in the entry deterrence game was first discussed. If there is a positive probability $X_n$ that the weak monopolist fights then there is a perfect Bayesian equilibrium characterised by the following strategies:

### Strategies of chain store

*Strong chain store*: always fights.

*Weak chain store*: fights entry with probability $X_n$ in the nth round and concedes with probability $1 - X_n$.

### Strategy of entrant

If $P_n > P_n^*$ stay out.

if $P_n < P_n^*$ enter.

If $P_n = P_n^*$ randomise between entering and staying out, staying out in the nth round with probability $Y_n$.

$P_n^*$ is the critical value of $P_n$ such that if $P_n = P_n^*$ the entrant's expected pay-off from entering, $EPO_{enter}$, in the nth local market is equal to her expected pay-off from staying out, $EPO_{stayout}$.

To fully specify the equilibrium strategies $P_n^*$, $X_n$ and $Y_n$ need to be determined.

## Solving for $X_n$

If the weak chain store randomises in order to raise $P_n$ so that $P_n = P_n^*$ the entrant will also randomise since EPO$_{entry}$ will equal EPO $_{stay\ out}$.[22] The entrant's expected pay-off from staying out in any repetition of the game is zero. Setting the entrant's expected pay-off from entry in the nth local market equal to zero leads to:

$$\text{EPO}_{entry} = P_n(e - 1) + (1 - P_n)(1 - X_n)e + (1 - P_n)(X_n)(e - 1) = 0 \qquad (8.19)$$

$P_n(e - 1)$ is the probability that the chain store is strong multiplied by the entrant's pay-off if she enters and the chain store fights (which the strong monopolist does with certainty). $(1 - P_n)$ is the probability that the chain store is weak and e is the pay-off to the entrant when the weak monopolist concedes which he does with probability $1 - X_n$. The weak monopolist fights with probability $X_n$ and the entrant's pay-off in this event is $(e - 1)$. (8.19) can be rearranged to obtain:

$$(1 - X_n) = (1 - e)/(1 - P_n) \qquad (8.20)$$

or:

$$X_n = (e - P_n)/(1 - P_n) \qquad (8.21)$$

## Determining Pn*

We shall determine $P_n^*$ in three steps. In the first step we will solve for $P_1^*$. In the second step we will derive an expression for $P_2^*$. In the third step we will generalise the results of the first and second steps to derive an expression for $P_n^*$.

**Step 1** Solve for $P_1^*$ (the critical value of $P_s$ in the last repetition of the game)

Do you remember how to solve for $P_1^*$? You saw how to do this in the preceding section and in Problem 1 of Chapter 7. We need to set the expected pay-offs of the entrant from entering and staying out equal in the last repetition of the game. The expression for EPO$_{entry}$ in the last repetition of the game is simpler than that in (8.19) because $X_1 = 0$.[23] Since the weak chain store will concede for sure in the last stage of the game, the expected pay-off of the entrant from entering at n = 1 is just $P_1(e - 1) + (1 - P_1)e$. EPO $_{stay\ out}$ is zero as before. We can set these two expected pay-offs equal to obtain:

$$P_1(e - 1) + (1 - P_1)e = 0 \qquad (8.22)$$

(8.22) solves for $P_1 = e = P_1^*$.

**Step 2** Solve for $P_2{}^*$ using Bayes' rule

Having defined $P_1{}^*$ and an expression for $X_n$ we can use Bayes' rule to solve for $P_2{}^*$. Bayesian updating implies that:

$$P_1{}^* = \frac{P_2{}^*}{P_2{}^* + (1 - P_2{}^*)X_2} \tag{8.23}$$

Substituting in (8.23) for $P_1{}^* = e$ (from Step 1) and for $X_2 = (e - P_2{}^*)/(1 - P_2{}^*)$ from (8.21) solves for $P_2{}^* = e^2$.

**Step 3** Generalise from Steps 1 to 2 to obtain an expression for $P_n{}^*$

Step 1 solved for $P_1{}^* = e = e^1$ and Step 2 solved for $P_2{}^* = e^2$. The same procedure that we used in Step 2 could be used to obtain $P_3{}^* = e^3$, $P_4{}^* = e^4$ and eventually $P_N{}^* = e^N$. Accordingly the critical value of $P_n$ is given by $e^n$ where $N \geq n \geq 1$. Thus:

$$P_n{}^* = e^n \tag{8.24}$$

where $P_n{}^*$ is the critical value of $P_n$ such that if $P_n = P_n{}^*$ the entrant randomises between entering and staying out in the nth local market.

## Defining $Y_n$

It still remains to define $Y_n$, the probability that the entrant stays out in the nth round. If $0 < Y_n < 1$ the entrant must be randomising between entering and staying out but the entrant will only be indifferent between her two pure strategies if $P_n = P_n{}^*$. This condition will be satisfied if the weak chain store is also randomising. But the weak chain store will only randomise if he is indifferent between fighting and conceding. In this case his expected pay-off from concession, $EPO_{concede}$, must equal his expected pay-off from fighting, $EPO_{fight}$.

In the penultimate repetition of the game at $n = 2$ $EPO_{fight} = -1 + Y_1 m + (1 - Y_1)0$ and $EPO_{concede} = 0.^{24}$ If these two are equal then $-1 + Y_1 m + (1 - Y_1)0 = 0$. This solves for $Y_1 = \frac{1}{m}$. Repeating this procedure solves for $Y_n = \frac{1}{m}$.

The equilibrium values of $P_n{}^*$, $X_n$ and $Y_n$ define the perfect Bayesian Nash equilibrium of this finitely repeated entry deterrence game in terms of the players' strategies:

### Strategies of chain store

*The strong chain store*: always fights entry.

*The weak chain store*: fight entry if $P_n \geq e^{n-1}$.

Randomise between fighting and conceding if $P_n < e^{n-1}$, fighting with probability $X_n$ where $X_n = (e - P_n)/(1 - P_n)$.

Concedes if conceded before.

Concede in the last round.[25]

### The entrant

Stay out if $P_n > e^n$.

Enter if $P_n < e^n$.

Randomise between entering and staying out if $P_n = e^n$, staying out with probability $\frac{1}{m}$.

These strategies describe an equilibrium of the repeated game in which entry can be deterred as long as $P_n \geq P_n{}^* = e^n$. $P_n{}^*$ is the critical value of $P_n$ such that if $P_n = P_n{}^*$ the entrant is indifferent between entering and staying out. e is the critical value of $P_n$ in the last repetition of the game.

In the first local market, that is the first, the Nth, repetition of the game, $P_N{}^* = e^N$ and therefore entry will be deterred from the start of the game if $P_s$, the initial or prior probability that the monopolist is strong, is greater than $e^N$. This is important because e, the critical value of $P_s$ in the last repetition, is less than one[26] and therefore if N is large $e^N$ will be very small. Even if $P_s$ is also quite small, if N is large $e^N$ is likely to be smaller and in this case entry will be deterred from the start of the game. More generally, as $P_n{}^* = e^n$ and e < 1, $P_n{}^*$ is smaller at the start of the game and therefore entry is more likely to be deterred in earlier rounds. But as the game goes on $e^n$ will get larger as n gets smaller and therefore entry will become more likely.

To see this let e = 0.5, $P_s$ = 0.125 and N > 3. As $e^3$ = 0.125 and $e^4 < 0.125$, entry will be deterred in the first local market (the Nth) and in all subsequent local markets until the game reaches the pre-penultimate repetition (at n = 3) where $P_3{}^* = 0.125$. At this point as $P_s = P_3{}^*$ the entrant will randomise between entry and staying out. If $P_s$ were as small as 0.015625 then entry would still be deterred until n = 6 as $e^6 = 0.015625$. At this point the entrant will randomise between entering and staying out and if the entrant enters the weak chain store will randomise between fighting and conceding. If the weak chain store concedes the entrant will enter in every subsequent repetition of the game. A possible time line for this version of the entry deterrence game in which $P_s = 0.015625$ and N = 10 is illustrated in Figure 8.7.

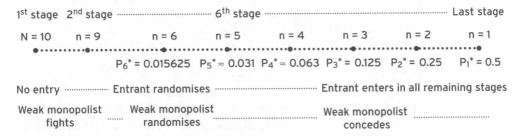

| 1st stage | 2nd stage | ······································ | 6th stage | ······································ | | | Last stage |
|---|---|---|---|---|---|---|---|
| N = 10 | n = 9 | n = 6 | n = 5 | n = 4 | n = 3 | n = 2 | n = 1 |

$P_6{}^* = 0.015625$   $P_5{}^* \approx 0.031$   $P_4{}^* \approx 0.063$   $P_3{}^* = 0.125$   $P_2{}^* = 0.25$   $P_1{}^* = 0.5$

No entry ·············· Entrant randomises ································· Entrant enters in all remaining stages

Weak monopolist      Weak monopolist ··································      Weak monopolist ························
     fights ······     randomises                                         concedes

**Figure 8.7** Possible time line for the repeated entry deterrence game: e = 0.5, N = 10, $P_n{}^* = (0.5)^n$ and $P_s$ = 0.015625

## 8.4.2  Implications of the analysis

The analysis in the previous section shows that in the repeated chain store game, and games like it, when there is imperfect information the entrant only enters for sure in the nth repetition of the game if the probability that the chain store is strong is less than the critical value $P_n^*$. The critical value $P_n^*$ depends on the entrant's relative pay-offs and also the stage at which the game is at. If the initial probability that the chain store is strong is greater than $P_N^*$, the critical value of $P_n$ at the start of the game when n = N (N is the number of times the game is repeated) there will not be entry in the first local market. But the critical value $P_n^*$ gets larger as the game progresses which means that entry will become much more likely. If the entrant enters (because $P_n \leq P_n^*$) the weak chain store will randomise between fighting and conceding in order to raise the updated value of $P_{n-1}$. But if the weak monopolist concedes, and as he is randomising there is a chance that he will, the entrant will enter in all the subsequent repetitions of the game.

The analysis predicts that the likely path of the game is one where initially the chain store is not challenged by entry as the probability that he will fight is too high. However, entry becomes more likely as the game progresses. If the entrant enters, the weak monopolist will randomise between fighting and concession. As long as the weak chain store fights, entry can be deterred in the next repetition but if he concedes just once the entrant will enter in all the subsequent repetitions of the game. This theoretical prediction is consistent with our earlier intuitive expectations that entry is likely to be deterred in early rounds by fighting or the threat of a fight – Kreps and Wilson (1982) call this the 'reputation effect'. But in later rounds the reputation effect is worth less to the chain store and concession is more likely. As noted by Kreps (1990: 542) only a little uncertainty about the entrant's pay-offs is needed to change the theoretical prediction completely and in so doing resolve the chain store paradox.

### Exercise 8.3

In an entry deterrence game described by the pay-offs in Table 8.3 the chain store is a monopolist in 20 local markets. The entrant is unsure about the chain store's pay-offs: the chain store is either strong or weak. The beliefs of the entrant are characterised by $p_n$, the probability that the chain store is strong in the nth repetition of the game. $p_n$ is updated using Bayes' rule. The initial probability that the entrant is strong, $p_{20}$, is $\frac{1}{2}$ and this is common knowledge. The entrant moves first and decides between entering or not in each of the local markets monopolised by the chain store. If the entrant enters the strong chain store fights for sure. The optimal strategy of the weak chain store depends on the number of repetitions left in the game and the updated beliefs of the entrant.

In the last repetition of the game what is the critical value of $p_1$, $p_1^*$, such that when $p_1 = p_1^*$ the entrant is indifferent between entering and staying out? Can you derive an expression for the critical value of $p_n$, $p_n^*$ such that when $p_n = p_n^*$ the entrant is indifferent between entering or staying out in the nth repetition the game? Will entry ever be deterred?

**Table 8.3** Pay-offs in a single stage of an entry deterrence game repeated 20 times

| | Pay-offs for each repetition of the game | | |
|---|---|---|---|
| | entrant | weak chain store | strong chain store |
| entry followed by fight | $-\frac{1}{6}$ | -1 | 0 |
| entry followed by concession | $\frac{5}{6}$ | 0 | -1 |
| entrant stays out | 0 | 4 | 4 |

## 8.5 Experimental evidence

There have been hundreds of documented experiments where subjects have played prisoners' dilemmas. Researchers have investigated whether demographic variables influence the likelihood of cooperation, for example whether women are more likely to cooperate than men (Mason, Phillips and Redington, 1991) or whether risk-averse subjects are more or less likely to cooperate (Sabater, Grande and Georgantiziz, 2002). Most of the experiments conducted have involved repeated plays of the game in one form or another. However, in any experiment the repeated game must terminate at some point and therefore the conditions corresponding to infinite repetition cannot be replicated. Roth and Murnighan (1978) argue that even if subjects are unsure about how many repetitions of the game will be played, subjects will make subjective assessments about the likelihood that any given game is the last. Thus in repeated games where the subjects are unsure about the number of repetitions that they will play the conditions approximate those of indefinite repetition. Roth and Murnighan (1978) conducted a repeated prisoners' dilemma experiment where the pay-off matrix was such that mutual cooperation could be part of an equilibrium along the lines outlined in Section 8.2 as long as the probability of continuing, P, was greater than $\frac{1}{3}$. Subjects played three games with varying probabilities of continuing. They found that cooperation was more likely when the probability of continuing was greater than $\frac{1}{3}$ but the difference was not that great. Roth (1995a) claims that such results are fairly typical and extend to finitely repeated games. He cites experimental work by Selten and Stoecker (1986) as illustrative of the later. In the repeated games constructed by Selten and Stoecker (1986) subjects played a series of 10 prisoners' dilemmas 25 times. The 25-times repeated game is called a supergame. Supergames like these give subjects scope for learning and in this case the opportunity to gain experience with the 10-times repeated game (*see* Camerer, 2003: Chapter 6). Selten and Stoecker found that in the 10-times repeated game, initial periods of mutual cooperation tended to be followed by an initial defection and mutual defection thereafter. However, in later rounds of the supergame (the 25-times repeated game) subjects tended to defect earlier suggesting that they learned the dangers of not defecting first. Results like those of Selten and Stoecker are consistent with the analysis of Kreps, Milgrom, Roberts and Wilson (1982) outlined in Section 8.3 if subjects initially cooperate because they are unsure about the motivation of their opponents (for example whether they have an inclination to cooperate perhaps by playing tit-for-tat or whether or not they understand the backward induction logic).

There have also been a number of exercises involving computer simulations of repeated prisoners' dilemmas. In these simulations the number of repetitions tends to be large. The well documented simulations initiated by Axelrod (1980a, 1980b and 1984) are an example. Axelrod ran a series of computer tournaments between strategies advocated by academics who had written on the prisoners' dilemma. The most successful strategy, in terms of the pay-offs that were accumulated, was tit-for-tat and the other highest scoring strategies similarly started with unilateral cooperation. Based on these results Axelrod suggests that a successful strategy needs to be nice, provokable and forgiving. A nice strategy is one that never defects first. A provokable strategy responds by defecting in response to defect and a forgiving strategy readily returns to cooperation if an opponent cooperates. Tit-for-tat satisfies all three criteria.

Maynard Smith (1982: 169–70) interprets Axelrod's results in an evolutionary context and derives conditions for the evolution of cooperative behaviour within or between species. First, there must be repeated interactions between individuals, second each individual must be able to retaliate against defection and lastly either individual recognition must be possible or the number of potential pairings must be small. He cites the example of reciprocal altruism between male olive baboons that have no known genetic relationship to show that in higher organisms cooperation can depend on individual recognition. He argues that this example can readily be modelled as a game that has tit-for-tat as an evolutionary stable equilibrium, but notes that 'the conclusion that cooperative behaviour is a stable outcome rests on the assumption that individuals who are in some sense successful pass their characteristics on to more "descendants" than those who are not'.

However, while Axelrod's results suggest that cooperative behaviour should emerge as a long-run strategy in repeated prisoners dilemma games the evidence from experiments is that the opposite is more likely. Roth (1995: 29) suggests that this difference is explained by the ability of subjects in experiments to learn and adapt as they gain experience with the game and the opponents they are playing.[27]

The kind of reputation effects analysed in Section 8.4 have been explored in a number of experiments. Jung, Kagel and Levin (1994) constructed a repeated entry deterrence game where the monopolist faces different entrants but subjects also play a supergame variant of an eight-times repeated game. In these experiments the monopolist is either strong or weak. The strong monopolist always chooses a predatory 'fight' response to entry but the weak monopolist prefers accommodation in a single stage of the game. Entry is only worthwhile for an entrant if the monopolist concedes (or accommodates). As the game progresses the entrant has to infer the monopolist's type on the basis of observed responses to previous entrants. The pay-offs in the Jung et al. experiments are such that when the initial probability that the monopolist is strong is one-third there is a Bayesian equilibrium in which the weak monopolist fights in early repetitions of the game and the entrant stays out. When experienced subjects (who had played more than 30 rounds of the supergame) played this game entrants rarely entered and if they did the predatory fight response by the weak monopolist was commonly observed in the first four repetitions of the eight-times repeated game. Entry followed by accommodation was observed more often in the sixth, seventh and eighth repetition. Similar results were observed by Cooper, Garvin and Kagel (1997) in a series of entry deterrence experiments where monopolists with high costs chose to raise output to deter entry under certain conditions. These results are generally supportive of Kreps and Wilson (1982).

Reputation effects in repeated games are not confined to games played between monopolists and potential entrants. Camerer and Weigelt (1988) constructed experiments to test the Kreps and Wilson (1982) model in relation to a 'trust' game. They describe the game as one played between a lender and a borrower where the latter is either honest or not. If she is dishonest then in a single stage of the game she prefers to default on the lender's loan and if she is honest she prefers to repay the loan. The monetary pay-offs are such that lenders would only want to loan to honest borrowers. Each experiment had 75–100 repetitions of an eight-stage game 'to give the subjects lots of experience' (Camerer and Weigelt, 1988: 4). There is a theoretical equilibrium of the eight-stage game along the lines outlined in Section 8.4.1 in which the lender will lend and the dishonest borrower repay in the nth repetition of the game if the probability that the borrower is honest is greater than $0.786^n$. Given an initial or prior probability of the borrower being honest equal to $\frac{1}{3}$ the lender should lend and the borrower repay in the first three repetitions of the game. In the fourth repetition, lenders and dishonest borrowers randomise and the probability of default rises as the last repetition approaches. This leads to the prediction that lending should drop off in the fifth repetition which in Camerer and Weigelt's experiments it did but not as sharply as predicted by the theory. Camerer and Weigelt (1988: 26) concluded that Krep's and Wilson's

(1982) model 'predicts reasonably well, given its complexity'. However, the theoretical prediction did not stand up for some periods of the game. Similar conclusions are arrived at by authors who have either replicated or extended Camerer and Weigelt's experimental work (see Camerer, 2003: 450–3).

## Summary

In this chapter you have seen how the subgame perfect equilibrium of a finitely repeated game with a unique equilibrium in the single-stage game is one in which the unique equilibrium of the one-shot game is played out in every stage of the repeated game. This result follows from backward induction logic but appears to be paradoxical in games like the repeated prisoners' dilemma and entry deterrence where a different result seems intuitively more plausible. This paradox can be resolved if there is uncertainty about the timing of the last repetition of the game or one (or both) of the player's pay-offs or their rationality. Resolving the paradox means that cooperation in the prisoners' dilemma and fighting entry or its equivalent in games like the chain store game can be equilibrium strategies.

The analysis in Section 8.2 showed that when the timing of the last repetition of the game is uncertain players can devise meta-strategies so that mutual cooperation is an equilibrium outcome in the prisoners' dilemma. The analysis in Sections 8.3 and 8.4 showed that even when the timing of the last repetition is clear, in repeated prisoners' dilemma games and games like the chain store game, players might choose actions that would be irrational in a single-stage version of the game. It will be rational for them to do this if by doing so they can either elicit (or deter) an action by the other player that is desirable (or undesirable) from the first player's perspective. This is a form of signalling. It can be effective if there is uncertainty about the type of player and one type has an incentive to mimic another in order to acquire a reputation for a particular kind of behaviour. Reputation effects of this kind can arise only in situations where interactions between players are repeated. An example is the lending scenario analysed by Camerer and Weigelt (1988) as a trust game. In a repeated version of the trespass game analysed in Chapter 4 it could also be rational for Bert to prosecute early trespassers like Angela in order to deter the rest of the rambling club from crossing his land. This would only work for Bert if there was uncertainty about the likely outcome of a court case. Similarly, in a repeated version of the political ambition game analysed in Chapter 2, it could make sense for a weak incumbent to stand in order to deter future challengers (see Exercise 2.3). Again this would only work for the incumbent if potential challengers were unsure about the incumbent's political vulnerability (see Gates and Humes, 1997: Chapter 6). Reputation effects might also be relevant in the interactions between government macroeconomic policy makers and the private sector, where the stated intentions of the former need to be credible to work,[28] or the annual negotiations over terms and conditions that take place between firms and their workers.[29]

## Answers to exercises

8.1

Matrix 8.3 Oligopoly collusion

|  |  | Jessup Inc | |
| --- | --- | --- | --- |
|  |  | collusion | cheat |
| Rosden Ltd | collusion | 3, 3 | 1, 5 |
|  | cheat | 5, 1 | 2, 2 |

In the indefinitely repeated version of this prisoners' dilemma both players are committed to grim strategies and the probability of another repetition at each stage is Q. You can substitute Q for P and for a = 3, b = 1, d = 2 and c = 5 into expression (8.4) to obtain;

$$EPO_{cheat} = 5 + 2Q/(1 - Q)$$

The expected pay-off from collusion is found by substituting into expression (8.3) to obtain:

$$EPO_{collusion} = 3/(1 - Q)$$

Thus the firms should always collude if:

$$3/(1 - Q) > 5 + 2Q/(1 - Q)$$

or:

$$(3 - 5)/(2 - 5) < Q$$

This solves for $Q > \frac{2}{3}$. Thus $Q = \frac{2}{3}$ is the critical value of Q such that if $Q > \frac{2}{3}$ and the players commit to grim strategies it is rational for them to collude in every repetition of the game.

8.2

The relative pay-offs in Matrix 8.5 satisfy the restrictions imposed in Matrix 8.4. You can therefore substitute for c = 2 and b = –1 into conditions (8.13) and (8.17) to solve for the critical value of P.

**Matrix 8.5**  Rosie and Ben play a repeated prisoners' dilemma

|  |  | Ben | |
| --- | --- | --- | --- |
|  |  | cooperate | cheat |
| Rosie | cooperate | 1, 1 | -1, 2 |
|  | cheat | 2, -1 | 0, 0 |

Condition (8.13) becomes:

$$P + (1 - P)(-1) \geq 0 \qquad \text{(i)}$$

or:

$$2P - 1 \geq 0 \qquad \text{(ii)}$$

(ii) solves for $P \geq \frac{1}{2}$. Condition (8.17) becomes:

$$1 + 2P \geq 2 \qquad \text{(iii)}$$

or:

$$2P \geq 1 \qquad \text{(iv)}$$

which again solves for $P \geq \frac{1}{2}$ implying that $P = \frac{1}{2}$ is the critical value of P. If P is greater than or equal to $\frac{1}{2}$ cooperation is an equilibrium strategy for both players in all but the last two repetitions of the game.

8.3

**Table 8.3**  Pay-offs in a single stage of an entry deterrence game repeated 20 times

| | Pay-offs for each repetition of the game | | |
| --- | --- | --- | --- |
| | entrant | weak chain store | strong chain store |
| entry followed by fight | $-\frac{1}{6}$ | -1 | 0 |
| entry followed by concession | $\frac{5}{6}$ | 0 | -1 |
| entrant stays out | 0 | 4 | 4 |

In the last stage of the entry deterrence game described by the pay-offs in Table 8.4, the 20th repetition, the weak chain store will definitely concede. Therefore the entrant's expected pay-off from entering, $EPO_{entry}$, is $p_1(-\frac{1}{6}) + (1 - p_1)\frac{5}{6}$. If the entrant is indifferent between entering and staying out then $EPO_{entry}$ must equal her expected pay-off from staying out which is zero. Thus $p_1$ is defined by setting $EPO_{entry} = 0$:

$$EPO_{entry} = p_1(-\tfrac{1}{6}) + (1 - p_1)\tfrac{5}{6} = 0 \tag{i}$$

(i) solves for $p_1{}^* = \frac{5}{6}$.

Substituting for $p_1 = \frac{5}{6}$ and $X_2 = (\frac{5}{6} - p_2)/(1 - p_2)$ (from expression (8.21)) into expression (8.23) solves for $p_2 = (\frac{5}{6})^2$. Generalising leads to $p_n{}^* = (\frac{5}{6})^n$ where $p_n{}^*$ is the critical value of $p_n$ such that if $p_n > p_n{}^*$ the entrant will not enter but if $p_n = p_n{}^*$ the entrant will randomise between entry and staying out and if $p_n < p_n{}^*$ the entrant will definitely enter.

$\frac{5}{6}$, $(\frac{5}{6})^2$ and $(\frac{5}{6})^3$ are all greater than $\frac{1}{2}$ but[30] $(\frac{5}{6})^4 < \frac{1}{2}$. Hence, $(\frac{5}{6})^n < \frac{1}{2}$ for all values of $n > 4$ including $n = 20$. The analysis in Section 8.4.1 implies that in these circumstances there is a perfect Bayesian equilibrium of the game in which the entrant stays out in the first and all the subsequent local markets until $n = 3$. At this point in the game there will be entry as $p_n = \frac{1}{2} < p_n{}^* = (\frac{5}{6})^3$. The weak chain store will randomise at this point between fighting and conceding and if the chain store concedes there will be entry for sure followed by concession at $n = 2$ and $n = 1$. But if the weak chain store fights[31] so that $p_2 = p_2{}^*$ the entrant will randomise between entry and staying out at $n = 2$. If there is entry the weak chain store should randomise between fighting and conceding. If the chain store concedes there will be entry followed by concession at $n = 1$. If the chain store fights $p_1$ will be updated and the entrant will randomise between entry and concession at $n = 1$. If there is entry the weak chain store concedes.

## Problem

1 What is the Nash equilibrium of the one-shot version of the game in Matrix 8.6? If the game is infinitely repeated what is the critical value of the discount factor, F, such that {work, work} in each repetition can be a perfect Nash equilibrium if both players commit to a grim strategy?

**Matrix 8.6** The temptation to free ride

|  |  | Luke | |
|---|---|---|---|
|  |  | **work** | **free ride** |
| **Darth** | **work** | 4, 4 | 0, 5 |
|  | **free ride** | 5, 0 | 1, 1 |

## Questions for discussion

1 What is paradoxical about the subgame perfect Nash equilibrium of the finitely repeated prisoners' dilemma? How can uncertainty about the timing of the last repetition of the game resolve this dilemma?

2 If the paradox of backward induction in the finitely repeated prisoners' dilemma can be resolved by allowing for some uncertainty about the rationality of one of the players, does this mean that the paradox can only be resolved if one of the players is irrational?

3 Why do you think that subjects in experiments sometimes cooperate in finitely repeated prisoners' dilemma games?

4 What is the chain store paradox and how can it be resolved?

## Answer to problem

1 The critical value of F is $\frac{1}{4}$. Luke and Darth have an incentive to work in every repetition of the game if $F > \frac{1}{4}$ and both players play a grim strategy of the kind: work if Darth and Luke have always worked in the past, otherwise choose free ride.

## Notes

1 Discounting allows for the possibility that money today is worth more to the individual than the same amount of money in the future. Over any reasonable period of time, this will be true for most people because money today can be invested and earn interest so that a sum of money received today is worth more than the same amount of money received in the future. To allow for this, the value of future money has to be discounted by the interest rate to arrive at its present value (its value today). Although, the economic literature on time discounting is not without controversy, in experiments even animals appear to discount future benefits, 'sometimes at alarmingly high discount rates' (Kagel, 1987: 177).

2 In Selten's original formulation (Selten, 1978) there are 20 towns, 20 potential entrants and unique entry dates are assigned to each town. For a discussion of Selten's formulation *see* Rosenthal (1981).

3 Although the most commonly quoted version is attributed to Friedman (1971).

4 Alternatively we could assume they played a strategy like tit-for-tat and derive a similar result but the analysis is more complicated (*see*, for example, Hargreaves Heap and Varoufakis, 1997: Chapter 6, Section 3).

5  Communication is not necessary but it does make the equilibrium outcome more plausible.

6  The sum of an infinite series like this can be found by multiplying through (8.1) by P to obtain:

$$\text{P. EPO}_{\text{coopJoe}} = P + P^2 + P^3 + P^4 + \ldots P^{n+1} + \ldots = \sum_{n=1}^{n=\infty} P^n \tag{8.1.1}$$

Subtracting (8.1.1) from (8.1) gives $(1 - P)\ \text{EPO}_{\text{coopJoe}} = 1$ and therefore $\text{EPO}_{\text{coopJoe}} = \dfrac{1}{1-P}$.

7  The sums of the infinite series in (8.3) and (8.4) are found in the same way as the sum of the infinite series in (8.1) (*see* previous note).

8  See note 1 for the intuition here. As an example consider €100 invested today at a rate of interest, r, of 10 per cent (r = 0.1). In a year's time this amount will be worth €110 (€100 multiplied by (1+ 0.1)). So €100 in a year's time must be worth less than €100 today. To see this consider the value of €110 received next year. If the interest rate is 10 per cent the present value (the value today) of €110 in a year's time is only €110/(1 – 0.1) = €100 as €100 invested today at a an interest rate of 10 per cent will be worth €110 in a year's time. More generally the present value of a sum of money, X, received in a year's time is $X/(1 + r)$ where r is the rate of interest and the present value of X received in n year's time is $X/(1 + r)^n$.

9  As $(1 + r) > 1$, $1/(1 + r) < 1$ and therefore $X/(1 + r)$ must be less than X. And for any positive value of n $X/(1 + r)^{n+1} < X/(1 + r)^n$.

10 In experiments tit-for-tat has been shown to be particularly successful in generating the cooperative outcome in repeated prisoners' dilemmas possibly because of its relative simplicity (*see* Rapaport, 1974). However, from a theoretical perspective tit-for-tat can only sustain cooperation in a perfect Nash equilibrium if $b + c \leq 2a$ otherwise the players might prefer to alternate between {cooperate, defect} and {defect, cooperate} as the game progresses.

11 The stick is the punishment and the carrot is the reward which follows punishment if a deviant player reverts to cooperation (*see* Abreu, 1986 or for a summary Lyons and Varoufakis, 1989). If P or F is not high enough for grim strategies to enforce cooperation in the indefinitely or infinitely repeated prisoners' dilemma then an alternative 'stick and carrot' strategy that punishes defection (the stick) for a shorter duration (the carrot) may be able to generate the cooperative outcome.

12 If you are satisfied with the knowledge that Kreps et al. (1982) confirm the intuition that uncertainty for one of the players about the other's strategy for the game resolves the paradox of backward induction, you may wish to skip the analysis in Section 8.3.1 at least on your first reading of this chapter.

13 For simplicity zero discounting is assumed.

14 If Row is rational and Column knows then $M_{c2}$ = defect.

15 The equilibrium will be Bayesian since it will need to incorporate the players' beliefs modelled by P. Since the players' equilibrium strategies for the whole game will need to specify moves in response to actions by the other player that might never happen the equilibrium will also need to be perfect (*see* Chapter 7, Section 7.2).

16 It seems a little odd but by cooperating a rational Row is trying to signal that he is in fact irrational.

17 Even Kreps et al. (1982: 247) admit this would be difficult.

18 As in Chapter 7, Section 7.2, I am going to delineate the entrant as female and the monopolist as male.

19 *See* Note 8 in Chapter 7 and the answer to Problem 1 in that chapter: e is the entrant's pay-off from entry followed by concession divided by her pay-off from entry followed by concession minus her pay-off from entry followed by a fight: $e/(e - (e - 1)) = e$.

20 If you are satisfied with the knowledge that Kreps et al. (1982) confirm the intuition that uncertainty about the pay-offs of the chain store resolves the chain store paradox then you may wish to skip Section 8.4.1.

21 See expression (7.10) in Chapter 7 and the discussion that precedes it. In expression (7.10) $w_s$ is the probability that the weak monopolist sends the signal, $P_{rob}(SIG \mid M_w)$. Here the signal is fighting in the previous round and the weak monopolist or chain store is assumed to fight with probability $X_n$.

22 The weak monopolist will randomise between fighting and conceding to raise $P_n$ if $P_n < P_n^*$. As concession is potentially very expensive the weak monopolist will randomise with just enough probability of concession so that $P_n = P_n^*$ and no more.

23 Remember that if there is entry in the last localised market when $n = 1$, the weak chain store will concede as there is no incentive to fight to deter entry in any subsequent repetitions, as there are none. This implies that $X_1 = 0$ or $(1 - X_1) = 1$.

24 $(1 - Y_1)$ is the probability of entry in the last round and $Y_1 m + (1 - Y_1)0$ is the weak chain store's expected pay-off in the last repetition of the game if he fights in the penultimate repetition (remember that in the last repetition of the game, the weak chain store always concedes, he has no incentive to do anything else).

25 The weak chain store fights entry if $P_n \geq e^{n-1} = P_{n-1}^*$ because the chain store does not need to raise $P_{n-1}$ by randomising in the nth repetition. Remember that randomising is risky because there is a positive probability of concession and if the chain store concedes just once there will be entry in all the subsequent local markets; the weak chain store only randomises to raise $P_{n-1}$ which he doesn't need to do if $P_n$ is already greater than or equal to $P_{n-1}^*$.

26 Remember that $P_1^*$ equals the entrant's pay-off e divided by $(e - (e - 1))$ from expression (8.22) and this equals e.

27 The role of learning in strategic games more generally has been investigated extensively in experiments with repeated games (*see* Camerer, 2003: Chapter 6 for a summary and Garcia-Gallego, 1998 for an example in relation to oligopoly markets).

28 *See*, for example, Bachus and Driffill (1985) for an application.

29 *See*, for example, Carmichael (1992).

30 $(\frac{5}{6})^2 \approx 0.694 > 0.5$, $(\frac{5}{6})^3 \approx 0.579 > 0.5$ but $(\frac{5}{6})^4 \approx 0.482 < 0.5$.

31 Staying out with probability $Y_n = \frac{1}{4}$ because from above $Y_n = \frac{1}{m}$ and m = 4 in Table 8.3.

# BARGAINING AND NEGOTIATION

## Concepts and techniques

- The Nash bargaining solution
- The Nash product
- Binding contracts
- Threat outcomes
- Bilateral monopoly
- Ultimatum games
- Alternating offers.

After working through this chapter you will be able to:

- Analyse cooperative and non-cooperative bargaining games
- Explain the difference between a cooperative game and a non-cooperative game
- Define the Nash bargaining solution
- Characterise the Nash bargaining solution in cooperative bargaining games
- Model a bargaining game as a non-cooperative sequential-move game
- Determine the subgame perfect Nash equilibrium of a non-cooperative bargaining game.

## Introduction

In this chapter you are going to see how game theory can be used to analyse interactions that involve negotiation or bargaining. The essential feature of a bargaining situation is that two or more people are competing for shares in a divisible resource. However, there is a conflict of interest as each contestant wants a larger share for himself and a larger share than the other contestants would wish to grant him. Nevertheless, all the contestants would prefer to share the resource than allow the negotiations to breakdown. This implies that there is scope for a mutually beneficial outcome in the event of agreement. That is, there are possible gains from trade.

In this chapter we are going to look at two different models of bargaining. In Sections 9.1 to 9.3 cooperative bargaining games are analysed. Non-cooperative games are analysed in Sections 9.4 and 9.5. Bargaining games have been the subject of a considerable amount of experimental work. The main results of this work are outlined in Section 9.6.

## 9.1 Cooperative and non-cooperative bargaining theory

In Chapter 1 cooperative games were defined as games in which agreements are binding or enforceable, for example by law. When agreements are binding players can negotiate outcomes that are mutually beneficial. In non-cooperative games agreements are not binding and players may have an incentive to deviate from a collusive agreement if they perceive deviation to be to their advantage. Therefore the outcome of a game in which binding agreements are possible is likely to be different from the outcome of the same game when they are not. The distinction between cooperative and non-cooperative games is clear in prisoners' dilemma games like the one in Matrix 9.1.

**Matrix 9.1** Prisoners' dilemma

|  |  | Prisoner 2 | |
|---|---|---|---|
|  |  | **deny** | **confess** |
| **Prisoner 1** | **deny** | −1, −1 | −3, 0 |
|  | **confess** | 0, −3 | −2, −2 |

If the prisoner's dilemma in Matrix 9.1 is a non-cooperative, single-stage game then as you saw in Chapter 3 the dominant strategy of both players is to confess. This is not a Pareto efficient outcome since both players could improve their pay-off if they agreed to deny. But in a non-cooperative game neither player can rely on the other to keep to an agreement to deny as it is in their individual interests to confess. On the other hand, if the players could make the agreement to deny binding they would both benefit.[1] This shows how binding agreements can change the predicted outcome of a game. If a game is cooperative these kinds of agreements are possible.

More generally if players can make binding agreements they have an incentive to agree on outcomes that they won't regret. They will regret signing up to a particular agreement if they believe that they could have negotiated a pay-off improving alternative. If no pay-off improving alternative is negotiable then the outcome is optimal from the player's perspective. If the negotiated outcome is optimal for all the players then it is a Pareto efficient outcome.[2] In the prisoners' dilemma in Matrix 9.1 {deny, deny} is a Pareto efficient outcome since neither player could improve their pay-off without making the other worse off. In cooperative bargaining theory the players are assumed to be able to agree on Pareto efficient outcomes. When bargaining is not cooperative, agreements are not binding and the determination of the bargaining outcome through a haggling process of offer, counter-offer and concession is critical. In non-cooperative bargaining games this process is modelled explicitly as part of a sequential-move game in which the players take turns making offers.

## 9.2 Bargaining problem

Bargaining is likely to be a feature of any transaction where the object of the trade is unique in some sense but its desirability is limited. Uniqueness gives players a degree of monopoly or bargaining power and this is what makes a breakdown in negotiations so costly. If a contestant had no monopoly power then, in the event of breakdown, the other contestants would simply go elsewhere. Monopoly power allows players to influence the terms of trade, it elevates them to the status of price makers rather than price takers. If both sides of a trading relationship have monopoly power then they need to negotiate the terms of the trade. In a simple sales transaction between a buyer and a seller, the buyer prefers a lower price and the seller a higher price; if neither is a price taker they will haggle over price. The lower the negotiated price the greater the buyer's share of the gains from the trade and the lower the seller's. People also bargain over 'who gets what' when they are splitting a divisible resource such as a sum of money, a territory, a cake or a pie and any positive fraction is preferred by both but each wants the greater share. Bargaining over 'who does what' is also common, for example when family members negotiate over the allocation of household chores to determine who does the washing up or walks the dog. And it is not only people that bargain. Maynard Smith (1982: 151–61) describes the process of egg-trading by the black hamlet, a coral reef fish, and the shell trading of hermit crabs, to illustrate this point.

An example of bargaining in the human world is the annual round of wage negotiations conducted between employers and their workers in labour markets characterised by bilateral monopoly. In a bilateral monopoly, both the employer and the workers have monopoly power and neither is a price or in this case a wage taker. The workers will have monopoly power if they are represented by a single union. In this case the union is a monopoly seller of their labour. An employer has monopoly power when it is the only employer or the main employer in a labour market. An employer in this situation is called a monopsonist. Some large firms in isolated towns are effectively monopsonists because they employ a high percentage of the town's population. Alternatively, if a number of firms that are the only employers of a particular kind of skilled worker collude, by forming an employers' organisation, then this would put them in a monopsony position. The clubs in some national sports leagues operate in this way. For instance, if the clubs in the English Football League agree to introduce a salary cap or some other restriction on wages, then the footballers concerned, unless they are good enough to play elsewhere, have no choice but to accept the wage control.[3]

In their negotiations over the wage the employer and the union in a bilateral monopoly are effectively bargaining over a share in the firm's profits. The firm prefers a lower wage and the union a higher wage. The higher the wage, the higher the union's share of the firm's profits. The agreed wage will be the outcome of negotiations between them and any agreement will depend on their relative bargaining power. However, all we can really be sure of at the outset of bargaining is the upper and lower limits of the bargaining zone or zone of indeterminacy. Bargaining theory attempts to predict the likely outcome within this zone.

To illustrate the bargaining problem we can look in more detail at the particular example of a single firm bargaining with a single union representing all the firm's employees. We will examine the situation first from the firm's perspective and then the union's (for a more detailed discussion see, for example, Sapsford and Tzannatos, 1993: Chapter 11). The situation from the firms' perspective is illustrated in Figure 9.1.

The labour demand curve reflects the incremental or marginal contribution of labour to the firm's income, its revenue. The labour demand curve is downward sloping in line with the theory of diminishing marginal returns to variable factors. This implies that the marginal contribution to output of labour falls as more labour is hired. As the firm is a monopsonist it faces an upward sloping labour supply curve; to attract more labour it has to pay a higher wage to all its workers. The labour supply curve determines the average cost of labour. Because average cost is rising the incremental or marginal cost of labour must be higher than average cost[4] and therefore the marginal cost curve lies

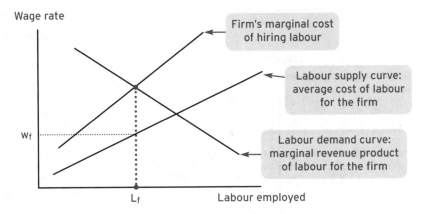

**Figure 9.1** The monopsonist firm's profit-maximising choice

above the labour supply curve. The firm maximises profits by hiring labour up to the point where the marginal cost of hiring labour is equal to the marginal revenue it earns.[5] This condition is satisfied when the firm employs $L_f$ labour. To employ $L_f$ labour it will need to pay at least $w_f$.

The situation from the union's perspective is illustrated in Figure 9.2. The union wants to maximise its gains from the negotiations as well. The union's gains are measured in terms of its economic rent. This is the difference between its members' total wage income and their total willingness to supply labour. The latter is determined by their individual preferences over work and leisure and is reflected by the area under the labour supply curve.[6] The labour demand curve determines the union's average return or revenue and since this is downward sloping the union's marginal revenue curve lies below the labour demand curve. The union's economic rent is maximised when the union's marginal costs of supplying labour are equal to its marginal revenue. This condition is satisfied when $L_u$ of labour is hired and paid a wage of $w_u$.

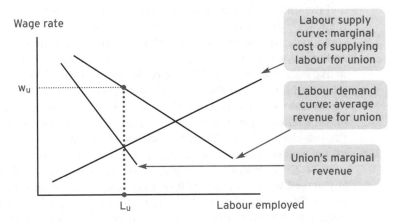

**Figure 9.2** The union's perspective

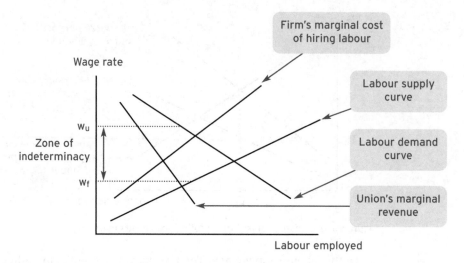

**Figure 9.3** The zone of indeterminacy

Since both the firm and union have monopoly power neither of their preferred outcomes are guaranteed and there is a zone of indeterminacy between $w_u$ and $w_f$ as illustrated in Figure 9.3.

The upper limit of the bargaining zone is determined by $w_u$ and the lower limit is determined by $w_f$. $w_u$ (the wage that maximises the union's monopoly rent) is a possible starting wage demand for the union and $w_f$ (the wage that maximises monopsony profit) is a possible initial wage offer for the firm.

However, the bargaining zone may be narrower than the zone of indeterminacy indicated in Figure 9.3. The union will be unlikely to agree to any wage less than that its members could earn if they left the firm and secured employment elsewhere, if necessary by moving home or changing career. This wage, $w^o$, reflects the union's best alternative wage option, the wage that would be earned by the union's members if no agreement was made between the firm and the union. The firm will also be unlikely to agree to any wage higher than the wage, $w^{\Pi min}$, that leaves the firm with the minimal level of profits that it could make by closing down or sacking all the workers and hiring new ones. $w^o$ and $w^{\Pi min}$ are the threat outcomes of the union and the firm, their best alternative outcomes or their fallback positions, in the event of no agreement. The pay-off of a player at their threat outcome determines the credibility of their threat not to accept the other's offer and to hold out for more. The better a player's fallback position the more credible their threat of resorting to it and the less they will be willing to concede to avoid it. It seems unlikely that a player would agree to something that leaves them worse off than their outcome in the event of no agreement. We can therefore be fairly confident that any agreed wage outcome will lie between $w_u$ and $w_f$ and that it will also be higher than or equal to $w^o$ but less than or equal to $w^{\Pi min}$. Where the precise outcome will lie between these extremes and how much labour will be employed will depend on a process of negotiation between the union and the firm. Bargaining theory attempts to predict the likely outcome of that process in this particular situation and others like it.

> - Threat outcome: **the fallback position of a player in a bargaining game. A player's pay-off at their threat outcome is their best alternative pay-off in the event of no agreement.**

## 9.3 Cooperative bargaining theory

In cooperative game theory agreements are binding by definition. Wage bargaining between an employer and a labour union is an example of cooperative bargaining since the outcome of the game is a legally binding contract if they can agree. It is a threat outcome if they do not, where as noted above a player's threat outcome or threat utility is their best alternative outcome in the event of no agreement. In cooperative games players have an incentive to make agreements that are worth making and that they won't regret. As stated by Friedman (1986: 6) it is therefore 'natural to focus attention on what players ought, in some sense, to agree on'. Two restrictions on the bargaining outcome follow from such common-sense observations:

1 Individual rationality: players won't agree to anything less than they could get by not reaching an agreement.

2 Group rationality: players should agree on something they cannot jointly improve on.

Individual rationality indicates that the players won't agree to any outcome that gives them a lower pay-off than their pay-off if there is no agreement. Group rationality implies that the negotiated outcome should be Pareto efficient. In geometric terms these restrictions mean that the outcome of bargaining must lie on the contract curve or pay-off possibility frontier (sometimes known as the utility increments frontier).

Figure 9.4 illustrates some of these features in relation to the wage bargaining problem outlined in Section 9.2. The firm's utility, $U_f(w)$, for alternative wage outcomes, w, is measured along the horizontal axis and the union's utility, $U_u(w)$, is measured along the vertical axis. The higher the wage outcome the greater the union's share of the firm's profits and the higher the union's utility but the lower the firm's utility. The curve labelled CC' is the pay-off possibility frontier. Along the pay-off possibility frontier, CC', all the firm's profits are shared between the firm and the union. As the union's share of profits is a negative function of the firm's share the pay-off possibility frontier maps the maximum possible value of $U_u(w)$ as a function of $U_f(w)$. That is, movements down and along CC′ (e.g. from $t_f$ to $t_u$) imply a lower wage outcome as the firm's utility is rising and the union's falling. At C all the firm's profits accrue to the union and at C′ they accrue to the firm. Outcomes that lie below CC′ leave some profits unclaimed. Such outcomes do not satisfy group rationality since at least one player could do better without making the other player worse off[7] by securing a wage outcome along CC′. Wage outcomes above CC′ are not available – the firm's profits are not high enough.

$T_f$ and $T_u$ represent the threat outcomes of the firm and the union – their respective utilities in the event of no agreement. The point T is generally referred to as the threat point. You saw in the previous section that $T_u$ is determined by the union's best alternative wage offer which I called $w^o$. If the firm makes some minimal level of profits, $\Pi^{min}$, in the event of no agreement, then the firm's utility at $T_f$ will be the same as its utility if it agrees to a wage that leaves it with $\Pi^{min}$ ($w^{\Pi min}$ in the discussion above). Individual rationality additionally implies that the union will not accept any share of profits than gives the union less utility than $T_u$. Similarly, the firm won't accept any share of profits lower than that implied by $T_f$. Together, group rationality and individual rationality imply that the wage outcome should lie between $t_f$ and $t_u$ along CC′.

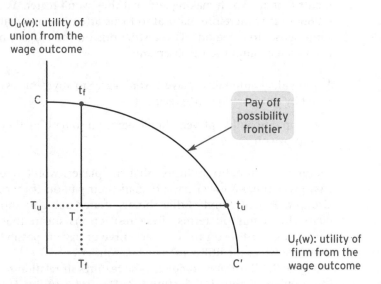

**Figure 9.4** The pay-off possibility frontier

To narrow the range of possible outcomes further Nash (1950) proposed three additional axioms in addition to that of Pareto efficiency that he thought represented reasonable restrictions on possible agreements. These additional axioms were:[8]

1 Anonymity or symmetry: the solution should not depend on the labelling of the players – who is labelled f and who is labelled u in Figure 9.4. This axiom implies that when the players' utility functions and their threat utilities are the same they receive equal shares. That is, any asymmetries in the final pay-off should only be attributable to differences in their utility functions or their threat outcomes. The outcome should be independent of interpersonal comparisons of utilities.

2 Transformation invariance or invariance to equivalent utility representations: the solution shouldn't change if either player's utility function is altered in a linear way. This means that the solution is independent of the units in which utility is measured. For example, if the bargain is over money and one player's utility for money doubles this shouldn't change the monetary outcome but whatever the player gets he will simply value it twice as much.

3 Independence of irrelevant alternatives: if the number or range of possible outcomes is restricted but this doesn't effect the threat point and the previous solution is still available, the outcome shouldn't change.

With these restrictions imposed Nash showed that there is a unique solution to the bargaining problem known as the Nash bargaining solution.[9] The Nash bargaining solution is the outcome which maximises the product of the players' gains from any agreement. This product is known as the Nash product.

---

### Nash bargaining

- The Nash product: **the product of the players' gains from agreement.**

- The Nash bargaining solution: **the outcome of bargaining that maximises the product of the players' gains from agreement.**

---

In Figure 9.5 the point N represents a wage that gives the firm's employees $w_N$. The union's utility from $w_N$ is $U_u(w_N)$ and the firm's utility is $U_f(w_N)$. The union's gain from a wage agreement $w_N$ is the utility increment measured by the vertical distance $U_u(w_N) - T_u$ (XT in the diagram). The firm's gain from the agreement at N is the utility increment represented by the horizontal distance $U_f(w_N) - T_f$ (TY in the diagram). Multiplying these two utility increments together gives $(U_u(w_N) - T_u)(U_f(w_N) - T_f)$. This is the Nash product indicated by the point N and corresponding to the wage agreement $w_N$, that is:

$$\text{Nash product at N: } (U_u(w_N) - T_u)(U_f(w_N) - T_f) \tag{9.1}$$

Can you see that the Nash product $(U_u(w_N) - T_u)(U_f(w_N) - T_f)$ is also represented geometrically by the area of the shaded rectangle XTYN? For any feasible wage

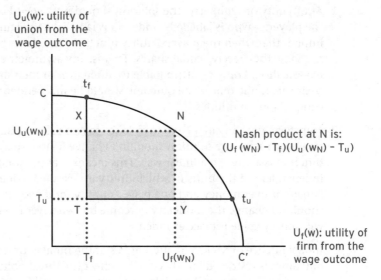

**Figure 9.5** The Nash product at N

agreement, w', represented by a point along the pay-off possibility curve, a similar rectangle can be drawn that has height $(U_u(w') - T_u)$ and length $(U_f(w') - T_f)$. For any given wage agreement, the larger the corresponding rectangle, the larger will be the Nash product. In other words, the wage that maximises the Nash product is the wage agreement that produces the largest rectangle in the area $t_fTt_u$ (below CC'). Since I have drawn Figure 9.5 so that rectangle XTYN is (approximately) the largest rectangle that can be drawn in $t_fTt_u$, $w_N$ is the wage that maximises the Nash product. That is, $w_N$ is the Nash bargaining solution, where $w_N$ is defined by the condition that:[10]

$$(U_u(w_N) - T_u)(U_f(w_N) - T_f) > (U_u(w') - T_u)(U_f(w') - T_f) \tag{9.2}$$

where w' is any other feasible wage outcome.

To generalise this result, assume that there are two players, A and B, who are bargaining over a prize, X. A's share of X is denoted by $s_A$ and B's by $s_B$. The Nash bargaining solution is given by the shares $s_A{}^*$ and $s_B{}^*$ that maximise the utility increments or Nash product $(U_A(s_A) - T_A)$ multiplied by $(U_B(s_B) - T_B)$, that is:

The Nash bargaining solution maximises: $(U_A(s_A) - T_A)(U_B(s_B) - T_B)$ \qquad (9.3)

where $U_A(s_A)$ is the utility of player A from the share $s_A$ and $U_B(s_B)$ is the utility of player B from the share $s_B$. $T_A$ and $T_B$ are the utilities of the players at the threat point. The shares $s_A{}^*$ and $s_B{}^*$ also need to satisfy the condition that $s_A{}^* + s_B{}^* = X$ so that $U_A(s_A{}^*)$ and $U_B(s_B{}^*)$ lie on the players' pay-off possibility frontier.

Dropping the axiom of symmetry generates the asymmetric or generalised Nash bargaining solution. In the wage bargaining illustration the generalised

Nash bargaining solution would be the wage outcome, $w^{**}$, that maximised the weighted utility increments product $(U_u(w) - T_u)^\alpha (U_f(w) - T_f)^\beta$. $\alpha$ and $\beta$ are measures of the relative bargaining power of the union and the firm and it is usually assumed that $\alpha + \beta = 1$. $\alpha$ and $\beta$ will reflect the relative impatience of the players to come to an agreement and this will depend on the costs they incur while the negotiations are ongoing. For example, if the workers threaten to take industrial action while the wage is being negotiated then the union's disagreement costs would be reflected by the reduced earnings of its members and the firm's by its lost revenue.[11] In a more general context $\alpha$ and $\beta$ could be measured by the rate at which the players' discount future pay-offs since more impatient players will discount future pay-offs away more quickly.

In the next section we are going to look at three examples of cooperative bargaining. The first is an example of decision making in households. The second example is a simple bargaining problem that captures the essence of many bargaining scenarios. The third example is a formal extension of the wage bargaining problem examined in Section 9.2.

## 9.3.1 Bargaining in households

In multi-person households there are gains to be made from cooperation but there is also likely to be disagreement on how those gains are distributed. For example, all household members clearly benefit if their home is clean but they are likely to disagree on who does the bulk of the cleaning. More generally household members need to decide on how to allocate their time between paid work and unpaid work in the home. There is a large literature on how these kinds of decisions are made originating with Becker (1965). While Becker's original arguments hinged on the idea of comparative advantage and specialisation, more recent work has modelled decision making in the household as the outcome of a bargaining process (*see* Himmelweit, 2001 for a summary).

In two-person bargaining models of household decision making the household members are usually assumed to be a man and a women and bargaining is over the division of resources within a marriage. Two possibilities have been considered with respect to the threat outcomes of the players. In the divorce threat model the threat point is determined by the pay-offs of the man and woman in the event of a complete breakdown of the marriage. In the separate spheres model the threat point is determined by the utilities of the man and woman when they decide on their allocations of time independently in their own self-interest (the non-cooperative outcome).

Figure 9.6 illustrates the household decision-making problem for a 'typical' married couple. HH' is the pay-off possibility frontier and represents the set of all possible utility combinations for the man and woman. The woman's utility is maximised at H and the man's at H'. H could for instance represent a situation in which the woman does no paid work and the couple pay for home help out of the earned income of the man who works a ten-hour day every day.

H' on the other hand could represent the situation where the woman is a virtual house slave and has no free time for leisure activities. The threat point is initially defined by $T_{w1}$ and $T_{m1}$ at $T_1$. The threat outcomes could represent their utilities either outside the marriage (after divorce) or within the marriage (the non-cooperative outcome). When the threat outcomes are $T_{m1}$ and $T_{w1}$ the Nash bargaining solution lies between $t_{m1}$ and $t_{w1}$ approximately at M. More precisely, it is determined by the allocations of time, between paid and unpaid work, that maximise the Nash product $(U_w - T_{w1})(U_m - T_{m1})$.

Figure 9.6 shows how the Nash bargaining solution can change if the threat outcomes of the players change. In the divorce threat model the threat outcomes could change if there was a change in the law that gave the woman a stronger claim on her husband's income in the event of divorce. In the separate spheres model the woman might improve her threat utility by acquiring more human capital since this would increase her income in the non-cooperative outcome. The man's utility at his threat outcome would worsen if he became more financially dependent on his wife. This might happen if he was demoted at work or made redundant.

If the woman's threat utility rose to $T_{w2}$ and the man's fell to $T_{m2}$ the new threat point would be $T_2$. The Nash solution now lies between $t_{m2}$ and $t_{w2}$, approximately at W. More precisely the solution is determined by the allocations of time that maximise $(U_w - T_{w2})(U_m - T_{m2})$. This is a better outcome for the woman but the man is worse off. Notice that any outcome between $t_{m2}$ and $t_{w2}$, not just W, is preferred by the woman to any outcome between $t_{m1}$ and $t_{w1}$. The opposite is true for the man. Only the threat utilities have changed so the improvement in the woman's position at W relative to M can only be attributable to the improvement in her threat outcome and the worsening of the man's. That is, the Nash bargaining solution is more advantageous for the

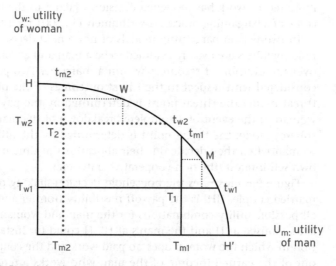

**Figure 9.6** Bargaining in households

women if her fallback position improves and that of the man worsens. This is a general result. It leads to the theoretical prediction that players can only be advantaged by a relative improvement in their threat outcome. However, an improvement in a player's threat outcome won't necessarily improve her pay-off from the Nash bargaining solution. This will depend on the amount by which her threat utility improves and what if anything happens to the other player's threat outcome.

## 9.3.2 Splitting a pie

 In splitting a pie there are two players, Jessie and Rosie, who are trying to divide a pie between them. Each would like a bigger share. Jessie's share is $s_j$ and Rosie's share is $s_r$. They derive the same utility from the pie which means that their utility functions are identical. Jessie's utility function is $U(s_j) = Ks_j$ and Rosie's is $U(s_r) = Ks_r$ where K is a constant. If they cannot agree on how to divide the pie their mother will take it away from them and give it to their pet dog. Therefore their utility in the event of no agreement is zero which implies that at the threat point $T_j$ and $T_r$ are both zero.

The Nash bargaining solution of splitting a pie is that $s_j^* = s_r^* = \frac{1}{2}$. In this case the solution follows straightforwardly from the Pareto efficiency and symmetry axioms. Pareto efficiency implies that $s_j + s_r = 1$. The symmetry axiom implies that each player should receive an identical share if their valuations are equal which Jessie's and Rosie's are since their utility functions are identical.[12]

If the assumption of identical utility functions is dropped then as Jessie becomes more risk averse[13] relative to Rosie, Jessie's pay-off, $s_j^*$, falls relative to $s_r^*$ (*see* Osborne and Rubinstein, 1990: 18 or Binmore, 1991: 193–5). The generalised Nash bargaining solution of splitting a pie maximises $(U(s_j))^\alpha (U(s_r))^\beta$ subject to $s_j + s_r = 1$. With identical utility functions this solves for $s_j^* = \frac{\alpha}{\alpha + \beta}$ and $s_r^* = \frac{\beta}{\alpha + \beta}$. Since both $s_j^*$ and $s_r^*$ depend on $\alpha$ and $\beta$ the solution depends on Jessie and Rosie's relative bargaining power. Jessie's share will be higher, and Rosie's lower, the higher Jessie's bargaining power represented by $\alpha$ relative to Rosie's bargaining power represented by $\beta$. If $\alpha = \beta$ their bargaining power is the same and $s_j^* = s_r^* = \frac{1}{2}$ as you have already seen when $\alpha = \beta = 1$.

These are general results that can be extended to the case where the threat utilities take a positive value. In splitting a pie if $T_j$ and $T_r$ are both positive then the generalised Nash bargaining solution with identical utility functions is that $s_j^* = T_j + \frac{\alpha}{\alpha + \beta} (1 - T_j - T_r)$ and $s_r^* = T_r + \frac{\beta}{\alpha + \beta} (1 - T_j - T_r)$. Now $s_j^*$ and $s_r^*$ depend on the value of Jessie's and Rosie's threat outcomes as well as $\alpha$ and $\beta$ (*see* Montet and Serra, 2003: Section 5.2 or Booth, 1996: 150–1).

Taking these results together, Nash bargaining theory predicts that the outcome of cooperative bargaining games will depend on the relative bargaining power of the players, their attitudes to risk and their threat outcomes. These predictions seem relatively uncontroversial and they can be tested. For instance, Carmichael and Thomas (1993) have examined the extent to which the transfer fees of footballers in the English football leagues are determined by the relative bargaining power of buying and selling clubs. Their evidence is largely supportive of Nash bargaining theory as is more recent work on transfers in association football by Gerrard and Dobson (2000). The related experimental evidence is discussed in Section 9.4.

## 9.3.3 Nash wage bargaining

The literature on wage bargaining between employers and labour unions is extensive. The example in this section is illustrative of the axiomatic or Nash approach to wage bargaining (for a more detailed discussion see Booth, 1996: Chapter 5). In this model bargaining is over the wage only but the union's utility is assumed to depend on the number of union members employed by the firm as well as their wages. The union's utility function is given by:

*The union's utility function*: $U_u(w) = Lw + (M - L)w^o$

where M is the number of union members, L is the number of union members employed by the firm, w is the negotiated wage and $w^o$ is the wage that union members are paid if they are not employed by the firm (their outside wage option). Note that this utility function implies that the union is risk neutral and $T_u$, the union's threat utility, is given by $Mw^o$. With this utility function $U_u(w) - T_u$ is given by:

$$U_u(w) - T_u = Lw + (M - L)w^o - Mw^o = Lw - Lw^o = L(w - w^o) \qquad (9.4)$$

The firm's utility function is given by:

*The firm's utility function*: $U_f(w) = TP_L - Lw$

where $TP_L$ is the total product of labour,[14] the total contribution of labour to output, and Lw is the wage bill. With this utility function the firm, like the union, is risk neutral and the firm's utility is equal to its profits if labour is the firm's only input and product price equals 1. In this case if the wage is equal to the average product of labour, $\frac{TP_L}{L}$, the firm profits are zero. The firm can make zero profits in the event of no agreement so a wage equal to the average product of labour is the absolute maximum that it will agree to. Since the firm's threat utility, $T_f$, is zero the firm's gain from any agreement is:

$$U_f(w) - T_f = TP_L - Lw \qquad (9.5)$$

The Nash product is $L(w - w^o)(TP_L - Lw)$ and the Nash bargaining solution, the wage that maximises the Nash product, is found by differentiating the Nash product with respect to w. This procedure[15] solves for $w^*$ where:

$$\text{Nash bargaining solution} = w^* = \frac{w^o + \dfrac{TP_L}{L}}{2} \qquad (9.6)$$

$\frac{TP_L}{L}$ is the average product of labour and therefore $w^*$ is equal to the average of the outside wage option and the average product of labour. As $w^o$ is the minimum acceptable offer for the union and $\frac{TP_L}{L}$ is the maximum payable by the firm, with risk-neutral utility functions the predicted wage, the wage that solves the Nash bargaining problem, shares the potential gains from trade equally.

## 9.4 Non-cooperative, strategic bargaining with alternating offers

In strategic bargaining theory the bargaining process is modelled as a dynamic game in which the players take turns making proposals and counter-proposals. The process of offer and counter-offer comes to an end when one party makes an offer that is accepted by the other. Since the players move sequentially the appropriate solution concept is that of a subgame perfect Nash equilibrium. As you saw in Chapter 4 a defining characteristic of subgame perfect equilibrium strategies was that any implied threats are credible. In bargaining models the players' strategies are the shares that they propose. A counter-proposal represents a threat to hold out for a better offer from the other player. In a subgame perfect Nash equilibrium, any counter-offer of this kind needs to be credible.

If there is a limit to the number of offers and counter-offers that can be made the game is finite. Finite bargaining games can be resolved using backward induction to work back from the last offer made. An extreme example of a finite bargaining game is an ultimatum game. In ultimatum games one player makes an initial offer, the other either accepts or refuses. If the second player refuses the first player's offer both players receive a pay-off of zero.

In bargaining games there will usually be some bargaining or negotiating costs for the players. These give the players an extra incentive to come to an agreement. Bargaining costs may be direct or indirect. If bargaining costs are direct a cost per bargaining period has to be paid that is independent of a player's actual pay-off from the bargaining game. For example, players may face a fixed penalty every time one of them rejects an offer from the other. Bargaining with fixed costs is analysed in Section 9.4.3. If bargaining costs are indirect the value of the object of bargaining, the prize, shrinks or decays. The rate at which the prize decays can be proportionate to the value of the prize. If decay is proportionate the value of the prize shrinks but never to nothing so the game has no predetermined end. Costs are incurred this way if time has a value and players have varying degrees of impatience. This will then be reflected by the rate at which they discount their future pay-offs. With discounting, the value of the prize shrinks towards nothing but always retains a positive value, albeit one that might become very small. Bargaining games where costs are proportional to the value of the prize are analysed in Section 9.4.2.

If the rate of decay is not proportionate then the value of the object of bargaining shrinks or decays by some fixed amount rather than some fraction with each new offer. This type of bargaining cost makes bargaining a finite game as there will always be a point where the maximum pay-off from the bargain, the value of what's left of the prize, is zero. If the prize is worth nothing there is no point in continuing so the game will end. You can think about an ultimatum game in these terms. In an ultimatum game the players' bargaining costs are so high that after one round of offer and counter-offer the object of bargaining is worth nothing. Games in which costs are not proportional to the value of the prize are analysed in the next section.

## 9.4.1  Bargaining games with non-proportional decay

The ultimatum game illustrated in Figure 9.7 is a strategic version of the pie splitting game you saw in Section 9.3.2. Jessie and Rosie are still trying to divide the  pie between them but now Jessie has the first move. The diagram shows the extensive form of this ultimatum game. At the start of the game, at $t = 0$, Jessie makes an initial offer of a piece of the pie, $p_r$, to Rosie, keeping the rest of the pie, $p_j$, for herself. After Jessie has made her offer, Rosie decides whether to accept or reject Jessie's offer at the end of the first bargaining period at $t = 1$. If Rosie rejects Jessie's offer both players receive a pay-off of zero as their mother will give the pie to the dog. To keep things simple let's assume that the value of the whole pie to either player is 1 and therefore $p_j + p_r = 1$.

We can use backward induction to find the equilibrium of this game. At Rosie's decision node at $R_1$ she can either accept or reject Jessie's offer. If she rejects the offer her pay-off is zero and if she accepts it her pay-off is $p_r$. As long as $p_r$ is greater than zero Rosie's best response to Jessie's offer is to accept it.

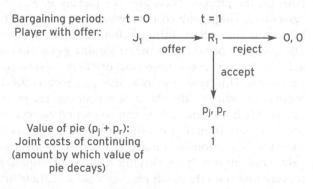

**Figure 9.7**  Ultimatum version of splitting a pie

Knowing this Jessie should offer Rosie the smallest piece of the pie that she can cut. Rosie will accept Jessie's minimal offer as she can do no better and only do worse by rejecting it. The subgame perfect equilibrium of the game is therefore for Jessie to offer $(p_j, p_r)$, where $p_r$ is the smallest fraction of the pie that can be cut, and for Rosie to accept.

The ultimatum game is a very unusual bargaining game as there is no chance for the player who moves second, Rosie in this case, to make a counter-offer. Nevertheless, the methodology used to analyse the ultimatum game can be extended to analyse more complex bargaining games like the game illustrated in Figure 9.8. Figure 9.8 looks a bit like a centipede game (*see* Chapter 4) and these games do have some features in common. For instance, the players in both games move in turn and at each decision-node a player decides whether the game should continue or end. In a bargaining game the game ends if one player accepts the other's offer. This is shown by the arrow pointing *down* from a player's decision-node. The bargaining game continues if a player rejects the other's offer and makes her own counter-offer. This is indicated by the arrows pointing *across* from the players' decision-nodes. However, in bargaining games the determination of the players' pay-offs is part of the game and their joint pay-off shrinks as negotiations continue. In contrast, the pay-offs in centipede games are predetermined and they go up and down as the game continues.

In the bargaining game in Figure 9.8 the two players are Az and Baz who are labelled A and B in the diagram. Az and Baz are hunters playing a stag hunt game like the one analysed in Chapter 5. Az and Baz have chosen to cooperate and have caught and killed a stag together. The stag has an initial worth of 10 units of their common currency. However, Az and Baz are from different villages and need to agree on a way to divide the stag so that each can take a share home. They negotiate in a very formal way, as is their custom, with Az making the first offer (he comes from the more powerful community) and Baz responding. An additional problem for Az and Baz is that while they are negotiating, vultures and other scavengers are feasting on the dead animal at an irregular rate. If Az and Baz do not come to an agreement within five rounds of offer and counter-offer then by $t = 6$ the scavengers will have eaten everything. Not a pleasant picture I admit, especially if you are a vegetarian, but it does capture the idea of a decaying prize.

In the game in Figure 9.8 Az makes an initial offer to Baz of a share in the stag worth $s_{b1}$ keeping a share worth $s_{a1}$ for himself, where $s_{a1} + s_{b1} = 10$. If Baz accepts the game ends. Baz receives $s_{b1}$ and Az receives $s_{a1}$. This is shown by the pay-offs written at the end of the arrow pointing down from Baz's first decision-node at $t = 1$. If Baz rejects Az's offer he makes a counter-offer to Az of a share worth $s_{a2}$ keeping $s_{b2}$ for himself but because the vultures are eating the stag $s_{a2} + s_{b2}$ is only worth 9. Az either accepts or rejects Baz's offer at the end of the second bargaining period at $t = 2$. If Az rejects the offer he makes a counter-offer which Baz can either accept or reject at $t = 3$. This process of offer and counter-offer can continue indefinitely but if at $t = 5$ Baz doesn't accept Az's offer then the most he can expect by continuing is zero, since by $t = 6$ the vultures will have eaten the lot. This is shown by the zero pay-offs at the end of

| Bargaining period: | t = 0 | t = 1 | t = 2 | t = 3 | t = 4 | t = 5 | t = 6 |
|---|---|---|---|---|---|---|---|
| Player with offer: | A→ | B→ | A→ | B→ | A→ | B→ | (0, 0) |

$(S_{a1}, S_{b1})$ $(S_{a2}, S_{b2})$ ............................ $(S_{a5}, S_{b5})$

| | | | | | |
|---|---|---|---|---|---|
| Value of stag = $(S_a + S_b)$: | 10 | 9 | 7 | 6 | 2 |
| Joint costs of continuing (amount prize decays) | 1 | 2 | 1 | 4 | 2 |
| Credible offers and counter-offers (pay-offs) | (4, 6) | (3, 6) | (3, 4) | (2, 4) | (2, 0) |

**Figure 9.8** Az and Baz's bargaining game

the arrow pointing across from Baz's decision-node at t = 5.

Az knows that the most Baz can expect by rejecting Az's offer at t = 4 is zero and so at t = 4 Az can offer Baz zero (or some minuscule amount marginally greater than zero) keeping what's left of the stag, which is worth 2, for himself. Baz should accept this offer by Az – there is no point in holding out for more, but equally there is no reason for him to accept anything less. Therefore Az knows that at t = 4 the most he can get by rejecting Baz's offer made at t = 3 is 2. Baz also knows this so at t = 3 Baz can offer Az 2 keeping 4 for himself and Az might as well accept. At t = 3 both players know that the most Baz can get by rejecting Az's offer is 4 so Az will offer Baz 4 at t = 2 keeping 3 for himself. But at t = 2 the most Az can get by rejecting Baz's offer is 3 so Baz will offer Az 3 at t = 1 keeping 6 for himself. At t = 1 the most Baz can get by rejecting Az's offer is 6 so Az will offer Baz 6 in the first negotiating period at t = 0 keeping 4 for himself. This sequence of credible offers and counter-offers is shown in the last row of Figure 9.8.

The backward induction logic outlined in the previous paragraph implies that if Az offers Baz 6 at t = 0 Baz can do no better if he rejects Az's offer and makes a credible counter-offer. He should therefore accept Az's offer. This means that if the players are rational they will agree to a split of 4 to Az and 6 to Baz right at the start of the game. This is the subgame perfect Nash equilibrium of the game.

Take a closer look at the players' predicted pay-offs from this game. Az's share is just the sum of the joint costs of continuing at t = 1, t = 3 and t = 5 where Baz has the decision to accept or reject. Baz's share is the sum of the joint costs of continuing at t = 2 and t = 4 where it is Az's turn to accept or reject Baz's offer.

This result is a general one in bargaining games where the prize decays non-proportionally. To see this take a look at the more abstract bargaining game in Figure 9.9 where the players are Ali and Bill who are again labelled A and B in the diagram. Ali and Bill are bargaining over a prize worth M. M decays by an amount $m_i$ after the ith rejection ($m_1$ after the first rejection, $m_2$ after the

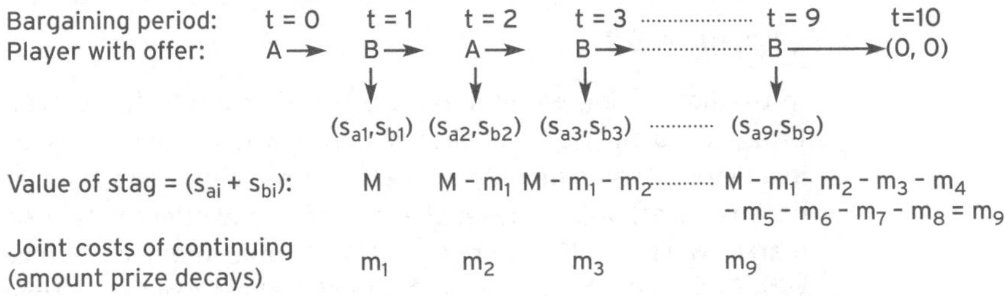

Bargaining period:  $t = 0$  $t = 1$  $t = 2$  $t = 3$ ................ $t = 9$  $t = 10$
Player with offer:  A→  B→  A→  B→ .................... B────▶(0, 0)

$$(s_{a1}, s_{b1}) \quad (s_{a2}, s_{b2}) \quad (s_{a3}, s_{b3}) \quad ........... \quad (s_{a9}, s_{b9})$$

Value of stag = $(s_{ai} + s_{bi})$: $\quad$ M $\quad$ M - m$_1$ $\quad$ M - m$_1$ - m$_2$ ........ M - m$_1$ - m$_2$ - m$_3$ - m$_4$
$$- m_5 - m_6 - m_7 - m_8 = m_9$$

Joint costs of continuing
(amount prize decays) $\quad$ m$_1$ $\quad$ m$_2$ $\quad$ m$_3$ $\quad\quad$ m$_9$

**Figure 9.9** Ali and Bill's generalised bargaining game with non-proportional decay

second rejection and so on). This implies, for example, that after the second rejection the prize is only worth $M - m_1 - m_2$ and after the third rejection it is only worth $M - m_1 - m_2 - m_3$ as shown in Figure 9.9. You can imagine the vultures in the Az and Baz game eating Ali and Bill's prize if this helps but here they eat $m_i$ in each bargaining round i and by $t = 10$ they have eaten everything.

Ali makes the first offer at $t = 0$. She offers Bill a share in M of $s_{b1}$ keeping $s_{a1}$ for herself where $s_{b1} + s_{a1} = M$. At $t = 1$ Bill either accepts or rejects Ali's offer. If Bill accepts the game ends. If Bill rejects Ali's initial offer the game continues with a counter-offer by Bill. It is then Ali's turn to either accept or reject Bill's counter-offer. If the game reaches the ninth bargaining round at $t = 9$ then if Bill rejects Ali's offer what's left of the prize decays by a further $m_9$ and is worth nothing. This implies that at $t = 9$ what's left of the prize, $M - m_1 - m_2 - m_3 - m_4 - m_5 - m_6 - m_7 - m_8$ must only be worth $m_9$. Similarly at $t = 8$ what's left of the prize is worth $m_8 + m_9$, at $t = 7$ the prize is worth $m_7 + m_8 + m_9$ and so on. At $t = 1$ what's left of the prize is worth $m_1 + m_2 + m_3 + m_4 + m_5 + m_6 + m_7 + m_8 + m_9 = M$.

At $t = 9$ Bill has a choice whether to accept or reject the offer made by Ali at $t = 8$ but he has nothing to gain by rejecting. $t = 9$ is therefore equivalent to $t = 5$ in Az and Baz's game. The same backward induction logic implies that at $t = 8$ Ali can offer Bill virtually nothing keeping $m_9$ (or marginally less than $m_9$) for herself and if Bill is rational he will accept. At $t = 7$ Bill can offer Ali $m_9$ keeping $m_8$ for himself and Ali, who can do no better by rejecting, should accept. Working back to the start of game Ali will offer Bill $m_2 + m_4 + m_6 + m_8$, keeping $M - (m_2 + m_4 + m_6 + m_8) = m_1 + m_3 + m_5 + m_7 + m_9$ for herself and Bill will accept. This line of reasoning shows that the subgame perfect equilibrium of the game is for Ali to offer Bill $s_{b1} = m_2 + m_4 + m_6 + m_8$ at the start of the game and for Bill to accept. In this equilibrium Ali's pay-off is $s_{a1} = m_1 + m_3 + m_5 + m_7 + m_9$.

## Exercise 9.1

In the bargaining game illustrated in Figure 9.10 the players are two firms, Alpha and Beta (labelled A and B), who are bargaining over shares in a market that is initially worth 10 units (where 1 unit is equivalent to a billions euros). Alpha makes the first offer and offers Beta a share of the market worth $s_{b1}$. If Beta rejects Alpha's offer the negotiations continue with Beta making an offer to Alpha of a share worth $s_{a2}$. Unfortunately for Alpha and Beta their market is vulnerable to competition and while they are negotiating the value of their joint share shrinks at a constant rate of c units per bargaining period where c = 1. At this constant rate of decay the market is only worth $10 - (t - 1)c = 10 - (t - 1)$ to Alpha and Beta at time t . At t = 10 the market will be worth nothing if Alpha rejects Beta's offer. What is the subgame perfect equilibrium of this non-cooperative bargaining game?

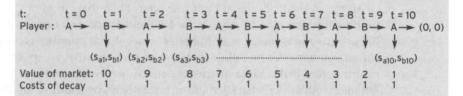

**Figure 9.10** Bargaining between Alpha and Beta with a constant rate of decay

## 9.4.2  Bargaining games with proportional decay

In some bargaining games players may value a prize more if they receive it sooner rather than later. In these games the value of future pay-offs from bargaining needs to be discounted.[16] Discounting in bargaining games means that after two bargaining periods, at t = 2, a prize of M is only worth dM where d is the player's discount factor. After three bargaining periods the prize will only be worth $d^2M$ and after four bargaining periods at t = 4 it will only be worth $d^3M$. Generalising, after t bargaining periods the prize will only be worth $d^{t-1}M$. The discount factor equals $\frac{1}{1+r}$ where r is the player's discount rate, their rate of return on any investments. Since r > 0 d is a fraction and the value of the prize to the player decays proportionately as the game progresses.

In the game illustrated in Figure 9.11 the players are Alf and Bert, labelled A and B as before. Alf and Bert are two thieves who have recently stolen €M million from a bank. They are currently bargaining over their shares in M. Alf is the gang leader and he makes the first offer, a share $s_{b1}$, to Bert hoping to keep a share $s_{a1}$ for himself. While they are negotiating the money is left buried in a safe place. Alf and Bert both prefer to have the money sooner rather than later;

while it is buried they cannot make good their escapes and the money isn't earning any interest in their secret Swiss bank accounts. Alf and Bert's preference for money now implies that the value of M decays as the negotiations continue. For Alf, M in bargaining period t is only worth $d_a^{t-1}$ M where $d_a$ is Alf's discount factor. For example, at t = 3 M is only worth $d_a^2$ M to Alf (as shown in Figure 9.11). For Bert, M at time t is only worth $d_b^{t-1}$ M where $d_b$ is Bert's discount factor. If $d_a > d_b$ then Bert is more impatient, or more desperate, for the money than Alf and the opposite will be true if the inequality were reversed. Intuitively, we should expect Bert's pay-off from bargaining to be higher the less impatient he is relative to Alf and this intuition is formalised below.

We cannot find the equilibrium of this game by working back from the bargaining round in which M is worth nothing because although the value of M falls continuously it remains positive. However, Rubinstein (1982) has shown that when the value of Alf and Bert's money decays in this way there is a unique perfect equilibrium in which the money is divided so that Alf's share of M is $\frac{1-d_b}{1-d_a d_b}$ and Bert's share of M is $\frac{d_b - d_a d_b}{1-d_a d_b}$. If $d_a = d_b = d$ this implies shares of $\frac{1}{1+d}$ and $\frac{d}{1+d}$ respectively.

The simplest way to show this[17] is to initially assume that $d_a = d_b = d$ and that M = 1. Discounting implies that if in bargaining period t the most Alf can possibly obtain by rejecting Bert's offer[18] is X, then at time t Alf should accept any offer by Bert that gives him at least dX. This is so because the value of X to Alf in bargaining round t + 1 is $d^t X$ and the value of dX at time t is $d^{t-1}dX = d^t X$. Thus dX is a credible offer by Bert in bargaining round t and a threat by Alf to hold out for more is not credible. To see this more clearly consider the following example. Suppose that the most Alf can possibly obtain if the game continues beyond t = 4 is 0.5 (half of M) then an offer by Bert at t = 3 of 0.4 will be accepted by Alf at t = 4 if $d^3 0.4 \geq d^4 0.5$ or $0.4 \geq d0.5$. At this point in the game, any threat by Alf to hold out for more than d0.5 would not be credible (and therefore could not be part of a subgame perfect Nash equilibrium).

With this in mind if X is the maximum that Alf can obtain in any equilibrium of the subgame starting at t = 2, where Alf makes the offer, then Alf should offer Bert 1 – X, keeping X for himself. The discounted value of X to Alf at t = 2 is dX so Alf cannot credibly hold out for more than this when Bert makes his offer at t = 1. This means Bert can credibly offer Alf dX keeping 1 – dX for

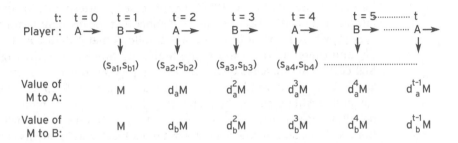

| t: | t = 0 | t = 1 | t = 2 | t = 3 | t = 4 | t = 5 ·············· t |
|---|---|---|---|---|---|---|
| Player : | A→ | B→ | A→ | B→ | A→ | B→ ·········· A→ |
| | | ↓ | ↓ | ↓ | ↓ | ↓ ↓ ↓ |
| | | $(s_{a1}, s_{b1})$ | $(s_{a2}, s_{b2})$ | $(s_{a3}, s_{b3})$ | $(s_{a4}, s_{b4})$ | ····························· |
| Value of M to A: | M | $d_a M$ | $d_a^2 M$ | $d_a^3 M$ | $d_a^4 M$ | $d_a^{t-1} M$ |
| Value of M to B: | M | $d_b M$ | $d_b^2 M$ | $d_b^3 M$ | $d_b^4 M$ | $d_b^{t-1} M$ |

**Figure 9.11** Proportional decay of Alf and Bert's money

himself. At t = 0 Alf has to offer Bert at least $d(1 - dX$ but can keep $1 - (d - d^2X)$ for himself.[19]

But the game at t = 0 is the same as the game at t = 2. In each case the two players look down the same infinite path of offers and counter-offers. Hence the maximum amounts Alf can get in each subgame (the one starting at t = 2 and the one starting at t = 0) must be the same. This implies that:

$$X = 1 - (d - d^2X) \tag{9.7}$$

(9.7) solves for:

$$X = \frac{1-d}{1-d^2} = \frac{1-d}{(1-d)(1+d)} = \frac{1}{1+d} \tag{9.8}$$

$\frac{1}{1+d}$ is also the minimum that Alf can get. To see this change the argument in the preceding paragraph around so that X is the minimum that Alf can get. Working through the argument again leads to the same result. Therefore $X = \frac{1}{1+d}$ defines the unique outcome of the game implying that Alf receives $\frac{1}{1+d}$ and Bert receives $1 - \frac{1}{1+d} = \frac{d}{1+d}$.

If $d_a$ and $d_b$ are not the same then following the same logic the value of X at t = 3 discounted to t = 2 is $d_a X$. At t =1 Bert can credibly offer Alf $d_a X$ keeping $1 - d_a X$ for himself. At t = 0 Alf has to offer Bert at least $d_b(1 - d_a X)$ but can keep the remainder for herself. This leads to $X = 1 - d_b(1 - d_a X)$ or $X = \frac{1-d_b}{1-d_a d_b}$. The equilibrium outcome is that Alf receives $\frac{1-d_b}{1-d_a d_b}$ and Bert receives $1 - \frac{1-d}{1-d_a d_b}$ $= \frac{d_b - d_a d_b}{1-d_a d_b}$.

Notice that the higher $d_b$, Bert's discount factor, the higher Bert's pay-off from bargaining and the lower Alf's. A player with a higher discount factor, d, values future pay-offs more and is therefore less impatient than a player with a lower discount factor. A more patient player therefore has more bargaining power. As a consequence their pay-off from non-cooperative bargaining will be higher.

Interestingly, when the interval between offer and counter-offer is sufficiently small, this solution to the non-cooperative bargaining game approximates the generalised Nash bargaining solution with bargaining powers[20] $\alpha = \frac{1}{r_a}$ and $\beta = \frac{1}{r_b}$ (see, for example, Binmore, 1992: 203–12 or Binmore, Rubinstein and Wolinsky, 1986). In this case $r_a$ corresponds to Alf's discount rate and $r_b$ to Bert's discount rate. Remember that the discount factor of a player, d, is $\frac{1}{1+r}$ where r is their discount rate. It follows that Alf's discount factor, $d_a$, is $\frac{1}{1+r_a}$ and therefore the lower $r_a$ the higher $d_a$. Since $\alpha = \frac{1}{r_a}$, the higher $d_a$ the higher $\alpha$. Similarly Bert's discount factor is $\frac{1}{1+r_b}$ and the lower $r_b$, the higher $d_b$ and $\beta$. You saw in Section 9.3.2 that a player's pay-off from asymmetric Nash bargaining will be higher the higher their bargaining power modelled by either $\alpha$ or $\beta$. Consequently, when $\alpha = \frac{1}{r_a}$ and $\beta = \frac{1}{r_b}$ a player's pay-off will be higher from Nash bargaining the higher their discount factor, as in Rubinstein's model.

However, the two models only converge when the time delay between bargaining periods is very small. But as noted by Binmore (1992: 206–7) 'This limiting case is the case of greatest interest because, in the real world, nothing constrains a negotiator to keep to a strict timetable, and given that a player has just refused an offer, the optimal thing to do next is to make a counter offer as soon as possible.' The coincidence arises since as the time delay shrinks, the first-mover advantage in the non-cooperative model disappears. With no first-mover advantage the outcome in either model depends only on the players' relative bargaining power which is reflected by their discount factors. This is an important result. It suggests, as noted by Binmore ( 1992: 208) 'that the intuitions embodied in the Nash axioms ... are sound'.

### Exercise 9.2

In Alf and Bert's bargaining game what is the outcome predicted by non-cooperative bargaining theory if M = 1 and $d_a = d_b = 0.9$?

## 9.4.3 Bargaining games with direct negotiating costs

If costs are incurred directly then the bargainers incur some fixed but not necessarily the same cost in every negotiating period. When costs are fixed in this way the actual value of the prize does not decay as such but the value, net of costs, of a given share of the prize does decay, as a player's costs mount up. For example, if the whole prize is worth €100 to a player but his bargaining costs are €10 per bargaining period then after five bargaining rounds a half share in the prize would be worth nothing although a three-quarters share giving him €75 would still be worth having. Whether such a split would be acceptable to the other player would depend on her bargaining costs. If her bargaining costs were only €1 per bargaining period then €25 would still represent a positive pay-off to her, as would €50.

This example shows that when bargaining costs are fixed, whether a player's pay-off from a given division of the prize has a positive value depends not only on the number of bargaining rounds that have gone before but also on the particular division that is being proposed. There is therefore no unique end game where the players' pay-offs simultaneously take a zero value. Instead a zero valued pay-off could result much earlier for one player depending on the proposed division and the player's bargaining costs. Rubinstein (1982) shows that in these circumstances the equilibrium pay-offs depend on the order of moves and whose costs are higher. Specifically, players are at an advantage if their bargaining costs are lower that those of the other player and it also helps to be the player who moves first. We are going to examine the bargaining game illustrated in Figure 9.12 to see why this is the case.

| t: | t = 0 | t = 1 | t = 2 | t = 3 | t = 4 | t = 5 | t = 6 ········ t = 10 | t = 11 |
|---|---|---|---|---|---|---|---|---|
| Player : | A→ | B→ | A→ | B→ | A→ | B→ | A→ ········ A→ | B→ |
| | ↓ | ↓ | ↓ | ↓ | ↓ | ↓ | ↓ | ↓ |
| Net value of A's share: | $\alpha T$ | $\alpha T - c_a$ | $\alpha T - 2c_a$ | $\alpha T - 3c_a$ | $\alpha T - 4c_a$ | $\alpha T - 5c_a$ | $\alpha T - 9c_a$ | $\alpha T - 10c_a$ |
| Net value of B's share: | $\beta T$ | $\beta T - c_\beta$ | $\beta T - 2c_\beta$ | $\beta T - 3c_\beta$ | $\beta T - 4c_\beta$ | $\beta T - 5c_\beta$ | $\beta T - 9c_\beta$ | $\beta T - 10c_\beta$ |
| Total cost to A | 0 | $c_a$ | $2c_a$ | $3c_a$ | $4c_a$ | $5c_a$ | $9c_a$ | $10c_a$ |
| Total cost to B | 0 | $c_b$ | $2c_b$ | $3c_b$ | $4c_b$ | $5c_b$ | $9c_b$ | $10c_b$ |

**Figure 9.12** Bargaining has direct costs for Ajax and Barca

In the bargaining game in Figure 9.12 the players, Presidents Ajax and Barca, are the leaders of two neighbouring states who are negotiating over a disputed territory. The territory in question has been colonised by Ajax's compatriots but is geographically under Barca's jurisdiction. For simplicity I shall call the disputed territory T. Ajax and Barca take it in turns to make offers but Ajax, as the more powerful leader of the two, makes the initial offer. While the negotiations proceed, their electorates perceive them to be weak and they lose votes at a constant rate. The more vulnerable their electoral positions the more votes they lose.

Every time Barca rejects an offer by Ajax or Ajax rejects an offer from Barca, Barca loses votes that represent a cost to him of $c_b$. Therefore, if Barca refuses Ajax's initial offer the net value of the whole territory to Barca is at most $T - c_b$. If Ajax then rejects Barca's offer the whole territory is worth at most $T - 2c_b$ (as shown in Figure 9.12). With every round of rejection and counter-offer the territory they are disputing has less net value for Barca. As the negotiations proceed, the net value of the territory will fall more quickly the higher $c_b$ which depends on Barca's electoral position. The less secure he is the more votes he will lose and the higher $c_b$.

Similarly, every time Ajax rejects an offer made by Barca and makes a counter-offer, or Barca rejects Ajax's offer, Ajax incurs a fixed cost $c_a$. The outcome of the negotiations for Ajax is a share, $\alpha$, of the territory. Barca's negotiated share is $\beta$ and $\alpha + \beta = 1$. Barca's direct costs imply that if Barca accepted an offer of $\beta T$ at $t = 4$ it would only be worth $\beta T - 4c_b$ to him and in general $\beta T$ at $t$ is only worth $\beta T - t_b$. Similarly for Ajax, $\alpha T$ offered at $t$ is only worth $\alpha T - tc_a$.

Rubinstein (1982) shows that $\alpha$ and $\beta$ will depend on who moves first, Ajax in this case, and whether $c_a > c_b$, $c_a = c_b$ or $c_a < c_b$. Before looking at some specific cases, it is helpful to clarify what constitutes a non-credible threat in this game and what constitutes a credible offer. A threat to hold out for more won't be credible if a player can do no better by rejecting the other's offer. Equivalently, a credible offer is one that the other player can't reject. Only credible threats and offers can be part of a subgame perfect Nash equilibrium. To formalise this a little let's assume that Barca offers Ajax a share of the territory, T, equal to $s_{at}$ at t. Then Ajax should accept Barca's offer if the most she can hope to get by continuing is worth less than $s_{at}$. Holding out for more in these circumstances would not be a credible threat and $s_{at}$ would constitute a credible offer by B.

An example should make this clearer. Consider a situation where $T = 1$, $s_{at} = 0.45$, $c_a = 0.1$ and the most Ajax can hope to receive by rejecting $s_{at}$ is 0.5. If Ajax rejects Barca's offer and receives 0.5 in the next round this would be worth $0.5 - (t + 1)0.1 = 0.4 - 0.1t$ to her. If, on the other hand Ajax accepts Barca's offer of 0.45 at t this is worth $0.45 - 0.1t > 0.4 - 0.1t$ implying that 0.45 at t is worth more to Ajax than 0.5 is worth at $t + 1$. Therefore, holding out for more is not a credible threat for her while 0.45 is a credible offer by Barca.

In fact any offer, $s_{at}$, at t by Barca worth more than $0.5 - (t + 1)0.1$ will be accepted by Ajax. Since $s_{at}$ at t is worth $s_{at} - 0.1t$ Ajax will accept $s_{at}$ as long as $s_{at} > 0.5 - (t + 1)0.1 + 0.1t = 0.5 - 0.1 = 0.4$. More generally if the maximum Ajax can hope to get by rejecting Barca's offer at t is Z which will be worth at most $Z - (t + 1)c_a$ then she should accept any offer, $s_{at}$, by Barca where $s_{at} - tc_a > Z - (t + 1)c_a$ or $s_{at} > Z - c_a$.

With the idea of a non credible threat and a corresponding credible offer in mind we are going to consider three possible scenarios for Ajax and Barca: (i) $c_a > c_b$, (ii) $c_a < c_b$ and (iii) $c_a = c_b$.

## (i) Ajax's bargaining costs are higher: $c_a > c_b$

The subgame perfect equilibrium is that Ajax offers Barca $T - c_b$ at $t = 0$, keeping $c_b$ for herself and Barca accepts.

To show that this is an equilibrium keep in mind that Ajax's fixed costs are higher than Barca's and therefore Barca has a cost advantage but Ajax moves first. Now, consider what happens if Barca offers 0 to Ajax at $t = 1$ then T is the most Barca can possibly get by rejecting Ajax's offer at $t = 0$. Knowing this Ajax can offer $T - c_b$ to Barca at $t = 0$ (keeping $c_b$ for herself) and Barca will accept as T at $t = 2$ is only worth $T - c_b$ to Barca. Because Ajax moves first she can ensure $c_b$ for herself even though she has higher bargaining costs. Thus $(c_b, T - c_b)$ is an equilibrium outcome if Ajax believes that because she is at a disadvantage she will do worse by making a lower offer to Barca at $t = 0$.

You may not be entirely convinced by this argument. However, it can be extended to show in a more precise way that $(c_b, T - c_b)$ is an equilibrium outcome. Because $c_a > c_b$ there will be some bargaining round where even if Barca offers the whole prize to Ajax it is worth less than $c_a$ to her but more than $c_a$ to him. To be more precise, think about a specific negotiating round at time t where if Barca were to offer the whole territory to Ajax it would only be worth x to her[21] where $x < c_a$. In these circumstances, the most Ajax can get by rejecting Barca's offer (whatever it is) is less than x and this is less than nothing as $x - c_a$ is less than zero. Ajax should therefore accept any offer by Barca greater than or equal to x. Barca can work this out and so will only offer Ajax x keeping $T - x$ for himself.

Since $T - x$ is now the most Barca can expect by rejecting Ajax's offer at $t - 1$, Ajax can offer Barca $T - x - c_b$. To Barca this is worth $T - x - c_b - (t - 1)c_b = T - x - tc_b$

which is the value of his pay-off if he rejects Ajax's offer.[22] Barca can do no better by rejecting so he should accept and Ajax will keep $x + c_b$. $x + c_b$ is worth $x + c_b -$ $(t-1)c_a$ to her and this is more than she would get by continuing.[23] In round $t - 2$ Barca should offer Ajax $x + c_b - c_a$. Ajax will accept as $x + c_b - c_a$ is worth $x + c_b - c_a -$ $(t-2)c_a = x + c_b - (t-1)c_a$ so she can do no better by rejecting. As a result Barca will keep $T - x - c_b + c_a$ and this is worth $T - x - c_b + c_a -(t-2)c_b = T - x + c_a - (t-1)c_b$ to him which is more than he would get by continuing.

This mental exercise can be continued back to $t = 0$. In each round either Ajax or Barca can make an offer which the other cannot credibly reject and which gives them the other's gain from not continuing into the next round. So, for example, in round $t - 3$ Ajax will offer Barca $T - x + c_a - 2c_b$ keeping $x - c_a +$ $2c_b$ for herself. In round $t - 4$ Barca will offer Ajax $x - 2c_a + 2c_b$ keeping $T - x +$ $2c_a - 2c_b$ for himself. Table 9.1 shows the full sequence of offers up to $t - 6$ where Barca offers Ajax $x + 3(c_b - c_a)$ keeping $T - x + 3(c_b - c_a)$ for himself.

**Table 9.1** The sequence of offers working back from time t to time t-6

| time | t − 6 | t − 5 | t − 4 | t − 3 | t − 2 | t − 1 | t |
|---|---|---|---|---|---|---|---|
| Player with offer: | Barca | Ajax | Barca | Ajax | Barca | Ajax | Barca |
| **If offer accepted** | | | | | | | |
| Ajax gets | $x-3c_a+3c_b$ | $x-2c_a+3c_b$ | $x-2c_a+2c_b$ | $x-c_a+2c_b$ | $x-c_a+c_b$ | $x+c_b$ | $x$ |
| Barca gets | $T-x+3c_a-3c_b$ | $T-x+2c_a-3c_b$ | $T-x+2c_a-2c_b$ | $T-x+c_a-2c_b$ | $T-x+c_a-c_b$ | $T-x-c_b$ | $T-x$ |
| Net value of offer to Ajax | $x+3c_b-(t-3)c_a$ | $x+3c_b-(t-3)c_a$ | $x+2c_b-(t-2)c_a$ | $x+2c_b-(t-2)c_a$ | $x+c_b-(t-1)c_a$ | $x+c_b-(t-1)c_a$ | $x-tc_a$ |
| Net value of offer to Barca | $T-x+3c_a-(t-3)c_b$ | $T-x+2c_a-(t-2)c_b$ | $T-x+2c_a-(t-2)c_b$ | $T-x+c_a-(t-1)c_b$ | $T-x+c_a-(t-1)c_b$ | $T-x-tc_b$ | $T-x-tc_b$ |

Look carefully at the sequence of credible offers in Table 9.1. Can you see how these offers can be generalised? At any time $t - n$, where Barca makes the offer and therefore n is an even number, Barca will offer Ajax $x + (n/2)(c_b - c_a)$ keeping $T - x + (n/2)(c_a - c_b)$. Since $c_a > c_b$, $(n/2)(c_a - c_b)$ represents an advantage for Barca which only increases as the game gets closer and closer to the first round. For sufficiently large T (relative to $c_a$ and $c_b$) Barca's advantage will rise so that at some point Barca secures the whole prize. For example at $t - n^*$ if x is less than $(n^*/2)(c_a - c_b)$ then Barca's share of $T - x + (n^*/2)(c_a - c_b)$ is greater than T and Ajax gets nothing.

Looking forward from the start of the game Ajax and Barca will be able to see that if the game gets as far as $t - n^*$ Ajax will get nothing. Barca will take advantage of this and whatever Ajax offers Barca at $t = 0$, Barca will offer Ajax 0 at $t = 1$, keeping T for himself and Ajax might as well concede. So the only feasible strategy for Ajax at $t = 0$ is to offer Barca $T - c_b$ because if Barca rejects this offer and keeps T for himself at $t = 1$ it will only be worth $T - c_b$ so he might as well accept $T - c_b$ at $t = 0$. $T - c_b$ is therefore a credible offer by Ajax and $(c_b, T - c_b)$ is an equilibrium outcome.

It may help you to understand the logic underlying the derivation of this equilibrium outcome if we look at a numerical example of Ajax and Barca's bargaining game with $c_a > c_b$. Let's assume that T, $c_a$ and $c_b$ are all quantifiable in terms of millions of votes and that the territory is initially worth 10 to both Ajax and Barca. While the negotiations continue Ajax incurs a cost of 2.75 per bargaining period, that is $c_a = 2.75$ while $c_b$ is only 0.25. Ajax is clearly in a weaker position than Barca in this version of the game which is illustrated in Figure 9.13.

At $t = 3$ even if Barca offers Ajax the whole territory it is only worth 1.75 to her. If she rejects Barca's offer at $t = 3$ the most she can get will be worth less than nothing as $1.75 < 2.75$. Barca should offer her at most 1.75 keeping 8.25 for himself. At $t = 2$ Ajax should offer Barca $8.25 - 0.25 = 8$ keeping 2 for herself. At $t = 1$ Barca will offer Ajax $2 - 2.75 = -0.75$ and Ajax can do no better by rejecting. She should therefore offer Barca 9.75 at $t = 0$ and Barca will accept as 10 at $t = 2$ is only worth 9.75. You could also use the expression we derived earlier that at $t = 1$ Barca should offer $x + (n/2)(c_b - c_a)$ where in this case $x = 1.75$, $t = 3$ and $n = 2$ (the backward induction started at $t = 3$). Substituting for $c_b$ and $c_a$ implies that at $t = 1$ Barca should offer $1.75 + 0.25 - 2.75 = -0.75$ as before. In this version of the game, although Ajax moves first, her advantage is all but wiped out since her bargaining costs are higher than Barca's. Her weaker electoral position means she cannot afford to prolong the negotiations and her pay-off reflects this.

| t: | t = 0 | t = 1 | t = 2 | t = 3 | t = 4 | t = 5 | t = 6 | t = 7 | t = 8 | t = 9 | t = 10 | t = 11 |
|---|---|---|---|---|---|---|---|---|---|---|---|---|
| Player : | A→ | B→ | A→ | B→ | A→ | B→ | A→ | B→ | A→ | B→ | A→ | B→ |
| | ↓ | ↓ | ↓ | ↓ | ↓ | ↓ | ↓ | ↓ | ↓ | ↓ | ↓ | ↓ |
| Value of T: | | 10 | 10 | 10 | 10 | 10 | 10 | 10 | 10 | 10 | 10 | 10 |
| $\Sigma c_a$ | | 0 | 2.75 | 5.5 | 8.25 | 11 | 13.75 | 16.5 | 19.25 | 22 | 24.75 | 27.5 |
| $\Sigma c_b$ | | 0 | 0.25 | 0.5 | 0.75 | 1 | 1.25 | 1.5 | 1.75 | 2 | 2.25 | 2.5 |

**Figure 9.13** Ajax's costs are greater than Barca's

## (ii) Ajax's bargaining costs are lower: $c_a < c_b$

The subgame perfect equilibrium is that Ajax offers Barca nothing at $t = 0$, keeping the whole territory for herself and Barca accepts.

Now Ajax has the cost advantage and moves first so she takes everything. Intuitively Barca has more to lose than Ajax by delaying and delay doesn't change the situation except by diminishing both players' pay-offs. Therefore Ajax secures the whole territory without incurring any bargaining costs. If you want to check this you can work though the logical process we used before. You will find that $(n/2)(c_b - c_a)$ which is greater than zero as $c_b > c_a$, now represents Ajax's advantage. Ajax's advantage becomes larger with n and at some point Barca's pay-off of $T - x + (n/2)(c_a - c_b)$ will be negative, implying that Barca offers Ajax the whole territory. As Ajax moves first she might as well secure the whole territory at $t = 0$ without incurring any bargaining costs. Since, in this version of the game, Ajax has lower bargaining costs and a first-mover advantage she controls the situation. Barca has nothing to gain by prolonging the negotiations and should give up his claims on the territory without weakening his electoral position still further.

### (iii) Ajax's bargaining costs are the same as Barca's: $c_a = c_b = c$

There is no unique subgame perfect Nash equilibrium but Ajax can ensure at least c.

When $c_a = c_b$ the players' fixed costs mount up at the same rate for both players. Neither has a cost advantage but Ajax moves first so she can ensure at least c. However, there is no unique subgame perfect Nash equilibrium. Working through the logical process we used before shows that if Barca offers x to Ajax at t then Ajax can ask for $x + c$ at $t - 1$ as before. But at $t - 2$ Barca's credible offer is x once again and as x is arbitrary there is no unique solution. Rubinstein (1982: 107) also shows that when the players costs are the same they won't necessarily come to an agreement instantly at $t = 1$. Agreement may be delayed until $t = 2$ when Ajax accepts Barca's first counter-offer.

We can look at a numerical example to show that Ajax can ensure at least c. Let's assume that $T = 10$ as in the previous example but now $c_a = c_b = 1$. This version of Ajax and Barca's game is illustrated in Figure 9.14.

Consider what happens if the negotiations reach $t = 10$ where if Ajax rejects Barca's offer she gets nothing. There is therefore little point in Ajax rejecting Barca's offer so Barca can make a derisory offer to Ajax at $t = 9$. That offer is the most Ajax can expect by rejecting Barca's offer at $t = 8$. Let's denote Barca's offer at $t = 9$ as y then at $t = 8$ Ajax will offer $10 - y - c_b = 10 - y - 1$ (keeping $y + 1$ for herself) and as Barca can do no better by continuing he will accept. Working back to $t = 1$ Barca will offer Ajax $y + (\frac{1}{2})(c_b - c_a) = y + (\frac{1}{2})(1 - 1) = y$. So we are none the wiser as y can take almost any value depending on which negotiating period we

| t: | t = 0 | t = 1 | t = 2 | t = 3 | t = 4 | t = 5 | t = 6 | t = 7 | t = 8 | t = 9 | t = 10 | t = 11 |
|---|---|---|---|---|---|---|---|---|---|---|---|---|
| Player : | A→ | B→ | A→ | B→ | A→ | B→ | A→ | B→ | A→ | B→ | A→ | B |
|  | ↓ | ↓ | ↓ | ↓ | ↓ | ↓ | ↓ | ↓ | ↓ | ↓ | ↓ | ↓ |
| Value of T: |  | 10 | 10 | 10 | 10 | 10 | 10 | 10 | 10 | 10 | 10 | 10 |
| $\Sigma c_a$ |  | 0 | 1 | 2 | 3 | 4 | 5 | 6 | 7 | 8 | 9 | 10 |
| $\Sigma c_b$ |  | 0 | 1 | 2 | 3 | 4 | 5 | 6 | 7 | 8 | 9 | 10 |

**Figure 9.14** Ajax's costs are the same as Barca's

start the backward induction from hence there is no unique equilibrium. Nevertheless, we can be sure that Ajax secures at least c because if she offers Barca $T - c_b$ at $t = 0$ Barca will accept as he can secure at most $T - c_b$ by rejecting Ajax's offer. Consequently, when Ajax and Barca have equal bargaining costs, the indeterminacy we saw in Section 9.2 is not resolved and almost any outcome is theoretically possible.

## 9.5 Experimental evidence

There have been many experiments on bargaining and these are surveyed in detail in Roth (1995a and b) and Camerer (2003: Chapter 4). Experimental tests of cooperative bargaining theory have tended to focus on the prediction that the outcome of bargaining will depend only on the preferences of the bargainers and their attitudes to risk. The earliest experiments were not generally supportive of the theory but these experiments did not control for the expected utility functions of the bargainers (e.g. Rapoport, Frenkel and Perner, 1977). They assumed risk neutrality and therefore the results of this work are difficult to judge. Roth and Malouf (1979) controlled for the bargainers' utility by using binary lottery games (like the ones you saw in Chapter 5). In their experiments each subject, i, could win either a large prize, $Z_i$, or a smaller prize, $x_i$. Players bargained over the distribution of lottery tickets to determine who would have the highest probability of winning the larger prize. Players were allocated a certain time to come to agreement. If no agreement was reached each received $x_i$. Nash's theory predicts that the outcome of bargaining should be independent of the size of the prizes or whether the bargainers know the monetary value of one another's prizes.[24] Roth and Malouf tested these predictions by changing the values of the prizes and the amount of information available to the players. They found that when the prizes were equal and the players knew or the prizes were unequal but the players didn't know, observed agreements clustered very tightly around the outcome associated with an equal probability of winning the large prize. This outcome is consistent with the Nash model.

However, when the prizes were unequal and the players knew, disagreements were more likely and the agreements that were made fell between two focal points:[25] the equal probability of winning agreement and the outcome that gave both bargainers the same expected value. The mean agreement fell about halfway between these two focal points implying that the bargainer with the lower prize tended to receive a higher share of tickets. These results were largely confirmed by Roth, Malouf and Murnigham (1981) and Roth and Murnigham (1982). They suggest that the outcome of bargaining depends critically on what each player knows about the prizes of the other. This is not implied by Nash bargaining theory and Roth (1995a: 44) argues that these results support an alternative hypothesis, 'that there is a "social" aspect to the focal point phenomenon that depends on something like the players' shared perceptions of the credibility of any bargaining position'.

In further experiments Murnigham, Roth and Schoumaker (1988) tested whether risk averse players were disadvantaged in bargaining as is predicted by the theory. They found a weak effect of risk aversion but this was sometimes overpowered by the focal point affect of the equal probability agreement. These experiments (like many others) can be criticised on the grounds that any risk aversion effects were drowned out because not enough money was at stake. Nevertheless the experiments provide some support for some of the theoretical predictions about the effects of risk aversion. Significantly, the experimental results also suggest that changes in information may be far more important in bargaining games than is predicted by the theoretical models. The incidence of disagreement was also found to be non-negligible. Deadline effects, whereby a high proportion of agreements were reached in the final seconds before the deadline, were also found.

The experimental evidence related to strategic models of bargaining is more recent. As you have seen these theories predict that players who are more patient, because they have lower bargaining costs or a higher discount factor, will be able to negotiate more favourable outcomes. In addition there is a predicted first-mover advantage. Initial experiments focused on one-period ultimatum games. In the experiments conducted by Guth, Schmittberger and Schwarz (1982) player 1 was asked to propose a division, between himself and player 2, of a fixed sum of k deutsche marks. Player 2 could then either accept or reject Player 1's offer. If the offer was rejected both players received nothing. The equilibrium offer by Player 1, as you saw in Rosie and Jessie's ultimatum game, is virtually nothing to Player 2 and Player 2 should accept. However, the mean observed offer by Player 1 to Player 2 was a little over 30 per cent of k. About a fifth of offers were also rejected. Guth et al. concluded that social aspects incorporating ideas of fairness influenced the subjects' behaviour.

The first structured experiment with multi-period alternating offers was conducted by Binmore, Shaked and Sutton (1985). In their experiment an initial prize of 100 British pence shrank to 25 pence after the first rejection and then to nothing if the second player's counter-offer was also rejected. The subgame perfect equilibrium offer in the first period is a 75 to 25 pence split in favour of Player 1, the player with the offer. If Player 1's offer is rejected then the game effectively becomes an ultimatum game with Player 2 holding the offer. In these circumstances the theoretical prediction is that Player 2 should offer Player 1 virtually nothing.

Binmore et al. found that the most commonly observed opening offer was a 50:50 split. If this was not accepted the counter-offer by the second player shifted towards the predicted 25 pence demand. Binmore et al. argue that the shift towards the theoretical prediction by the second player is indicative of learning behaviour. However, their results have not been replicated in similar experiments (e.g. Ochs and Roth, 1989, and Bolton, 1991). More generally in experiments of this kind opening offers have been found to lie between an equal split and the equilibrium prediction. Some rejections are also followed by disadvantageous counter-offers. The evidence in support of the strategic theory is therefore somewhat mixed. In a response to this evidence, Binmore, McCarthy, Ponti, Samuelson and Shaked (2002) explore why and how subjects fail to play the subgame perfect equilibrium in alternating offers bargaining games. They find evidence of social preferences as in previous experiments and they also find systematic violations of subgame consistency.

## Summary

In this chapter you have seen how Nash bargaining theory can be used to resolve cooperative bargaining games where agreements are binding. You have also seen how non-cooperative bargaining games can be modelled as strategic games. In strategic bargaining games the process of offer and counter-offer is modelled as a sequence of moves and the theoretical solution is found using backward induction.

The Nash bargaining solution can be criticised because its approach is axiomatic: it starts with a list of properties that the solution is required to satisfy. This approach ignores the whole process of offer and counter-offer that characterises bargaining and, perhaps more seriously, the possibility of breakdown. The model may therefore be more relevant to bargaining with arbitration. For example, in some labour–management negotiations in the UK the Advisory, Conciliation and Arbitration Service, ACAS,[26] is called in to settle a dispute and in negotiations over compensation that reach a court of law a judge adjudicates. However, many bargaining problems are not resolved through third-party arbitration and in these cases strategic or non-cooperative bargaining theory is potentially a more useful way of modelling the bargaining process.

The axioms underlying the Nash bargaining solution, especially those of symmetry and independence, have also been criticised. Removing these axioms completely changes the bargaining solution. For instance, if the axiom of symmetry is dropped, the predicted outcome is the generalised Nash bargaining solution. Removing the independence axiom leads to the Kalai-Smorodinsky solution (Kalai and Smorodinsky, 1975).[27] Symmetric Nash bargaining theory additionally predicts that the bargaining outcome is dependent only on the players' utility functions and their threat outcomes. This prediction is not consistent with the related experimental evidence. However, the generalised Nash model overcomes this criticism to some extent by incorporating the effect of relative bargaining power.

In spite of the criticisms levelled at Nash bargaining theory, the model also has a number of advantages. First, as it does not specify a particular bargaining process the approach can be used to analyse a diverse range of examples. The model is also relatively simple and transparent. Lastly, the solution it defines is unique.

In non-cooperative bargaining the sequence of offers and counter-offers is modelled as a sequential-move game. The players are assumed to incur costs which give them an incentive to come to an agreement sooner rather than later. The costs may be direct or indirect and, if the latter, proportional or not. The predicted outcome is a subgame perfect Nash equilibrium and, as you have seen, although the sequence of offers and counter-offers is explicitly modelled, the theoretical prediction is that in most cases the game ends after the first offer is accepted. This result appears to assume away the bargaining process in much the same way as the cooperative theory. Consequently, breakdowns in the negotiation process are not considered. Yet, as noted by Roth (1995: 253), there is considerable evidence from experiments 'that a non-negligible frequency of disagreement is a characteristic of bargaining in virtually all kinds of environments'. This points to a descriptive weakness of the theory that is resolved to some extent by allowing for asymmetric information. Rubinstein (1985) shows that when the players are unsure about each other's bargaining costs, agreement can be delayed. This can be rational behaviour if by delaying agreement players are able to acquire or convey information.

Whether there is asymmetric information or not, the solution to the alternating offers model assumes that both players are able to apply backward induction logic. This assumption has been criticised since backward induction can sometimes require quite complex computations in relation to events that never actually take place.[28] However, there is some experimental evidence to suggest that, with guidance, subjects can learn how to use backward induction even if they don't do it instinctively.[29] Lastly, as noted in Section 9.4.2, under certain assumptions the outcome predicted by non-cooperative theory converges to the asymmetric Nash bargaining solution. This result suggests, as Nash himself claimed, that the axiomatic and strategic approaches are complementary in that 'each helps to justify and clarify the other' (Nash, 1953: 129).

## Answers to exercises

### 9.1

At $t = 10$ the market is worth nothing if Alpha rejects Beta's offer. So Alpha will accept any offer by Beta made at $t = 9$ even it is only marginally greater than zero. Thus Beta will offer (0, 1), that is 0 to Alpha and 1 for himself (or $(0 + e, 1 - e)$ where $e$ is minuscule) since $1 = 10 - 9c = c$ is all that is left of the market. At $t = 8$ Alpha will offer $(1, 1) = (0 + c, c))$ and as Beta can do no better by continuing Beta will accept. The process of offering the other only as much as he or she could get by continuing while keeping the gain from agreeing now for his or herself will continue back to $t = 0$. At $t = 0$ Alpha will offer $(5, 5) = (5c, 5c)$ and Beta will accept. Figure 9.10.1 shows the equilibrium sequence of offer and counter offer.

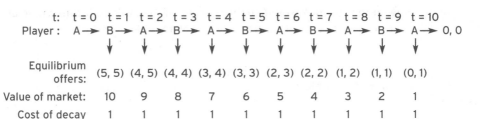

| t: | t = 0 | t = 1 | t = 2 | t = 3 | t = 4 | t = 5 | t = 6 | t = 7 | t = 8 | t = 9 | t = 10 |
|---|---|---|---|---|---|---|---|---|---|---|---|
| Player : | A → | B → | A → | B → | A → | B → | A → | B → | A → | B → | A → 0, 0 |
| Equilibrium offers: | (5, 5) | (4, 5) | (4, 4) | (3, 4) | (3, 3) | (2, 3) | (2, 2) | (1, 2) | (1, 1) | (0, 1) | |
| Value of market: | 10 | 9 | 8 | 7 | 6 | 5 | 4 | 3 | 2 | 1 | |
| Cost of decay | 1 | 1 | 1 | 1 | 1 | 1 | 1 | 1 | 1 | 1 | |

**Figure 9.10.1** Bargaining with a constant rate of decay

### 9.2

In Alf and Bert's bargaining game what is the outcome predicted by non-cooperative bargaining theory if $M = 1$ and $d_a = d_b = 0.9$?

The theoretical prediction is that Alf's share will be $\frac{1}{1+d} = 1/1.9 \approx 0.53$. Bert's share is $d/(1 + d) = 0.9/1.9 \approx 0.47$.

## Problems

1  In Alf and Bert's bargaining game represented in Figure 9.11 what is the outcome predicted by non-cooperative bargaining theory if $M = 1$ and $d_a = d_b = 0.5$?

2  In Alf and Bert's bargaining game, what is the outcome predicted by non-cooperative bargaining theory if $M = 1$ and $d_a = 0.5$ and $d_b = 0.2$? Compare your answer to the answer you obtained in Exercise 9.2 and your answer to Problem 1.

## Questions for discussion

1  What predictions follow from Nash's bargaining theory? Do you think these predictions are reasonable?

2  How well do you think non-cooperative bargaining theory captures the salient features of real-life bargaining problems?

3  In the bargaining game played between presidents Ajax and Barca analysed in Section 9.4, Ajax and Barca were both assumed to be politically vulnerable to some extent. This was modelled by assuming that each incurred constant costs per bargaining period, representing votes lost. The outcome of the negotiations between them was shown to depend on who moved first and whose costs were higher. How do think the game should be modelled and

what to you think would be the outcome if Ajax was politically vulnerable but Barca was the authoritarian leader of an undemocratic state?

## Answers to problems

1  The theoretical prediction is that Alf's share will be $1/1.5 \approx 0.67$. Bert's share is $0.5/1.5 \approx 0.33$. Alf's share is larger than in Exercise 9.2 because the discount factor is lower implying that both players are more impatient. Alf, the player with the first move, benefits.

2  Now $d_a > d_b$ indicating that Bert is more impatient than Alf. Alf's predicted pay-off is $(1 - 0.2)/(1 - 0.2(0.5)) \approx 0.8/0.9 \approx 0.89$. Bert's predicted pay-off is $(0.2 - 0.1)/0.9 \approx 0.1$. Now Alf's pay-off is much larger. He benefits because Bert is relatively more impatient and Alf still has the first move.

## Notes

1  The players could make the agreement binding by paying a third party to punish confession (as discussed at the end of Section 3.1 in Chapter 3, and *see* Problem 2 of that chapter), or they might be tied into a tight social network where confession was unacceptable.

2  Sometimes Pareto efficient outcomes are said to be Pareto optimal. However, a Pareto efficient (or optimal) outcome needn't be optimal in the sense that it is necessarily preferred by both players. After all, {confess, deny} is preferred by Prisoner 1 to {deny, deny} and {deny, confess} is preferred by Prisoner 2. {confess, deny} and {deny, confess} are also Pareto efficient. This is so because in either case one of the players can only improve his position by worsening the position of the other. In the {confess, deny} outcome, for instance, Prisoner 2 can only improve his pay-off by confessing which makes Prisoner 1 worse off. If Prisoner 1 denies this improves Prisoner 2's pay-off but Prisoner 1 is again worse off. Considerations of this kind weaken the attraction of Pareto efficiency as a measure of the desirability of an outcome. To see this, think about a distribution in a population where one person owns all the wealth and everyone else has nothing. Such an allocation would be Pareto efficient as the rest of the population could only be made better off by worsening the position of the only wealthy person.

3  Before free agency was established in association football the individual football clubs in the UK (and much of the rest of Europe) were in effect monopsonist employers, as players were tied by the retain and transfer system to their clubs (*see*, for example, Dobson and Goddard, 2001, or Thomas, 2004). In professional team sports in the USA players were tied to their clubs in the same way by reserve rules.

4  When it employs more labour the firm has to pay higher wages to all its workers not just those additionally employed.

5  If marginal revenue is greater than marginal cost then the firm can raise profits by hiring more labour as revenue is increasing relative to costs. If marginal cost is greater than marginal revenue then the firm can increase profits by hiring less labour.

6  The union can only secure more employment at the expense of a lower wage for all its members, those previously as well as additionally employed.

7  For example, at the wage agreement represented by point T the union could raise its utility by moving to the wage agreement represented by $t_f$ and the firm would be no worse off.

8  *See* Osborne and Rubinstein (1990), Binmore (1992) or Elster (1989) for a more detailed discussion of Nash's axioms.

9  *See*, for example, Osborne and Rubinstein (1990) or Binmore (1992) for precise derivations of the Nash bargaining solution.

10  The Nash bargaining solution is found by setting the players' utilities equal to zero at the threat point T (making T the origin) and drawing a straight line frontier that is a tangent to the non-linear, concave frontier $t_f t_u$ and is bisected at the point of contact. The mid-point of the linear frontier will be the point at which the utility increments product corresponding to both the linear and non-linear frontiers is maximised. This point on $t_f t_u$ determines the Nash bargaining solution or more specifically the symmetric Nash bargaining solution.

11  The generalised Nash bargaining solution was originally proposed by Harsanyi and Selten (1972) to take into account some of the uncertainties for the players in bargaining scenarios characterised by asymmetric information. *See* Binmore (1992: Chapter 5) for a more detailed discussion of the generalised Nash bargaining solution.

12  Mathematically the solution is derived by maximising the Nash product $U_j(s_j)U_r(s_r) = Ks_jKs_r$ with respect to $s_j$ and $s_r$ subject to the constraint that $s_j + s_r = 1$. Substituting from the constraint the Nash product (the objective function) becomes $Ks_jK(1 - s_j)$ or $K^2(s_j - (s_j)^2)$ . Differentiating with respect to $s_j$ leads to the first order condition that $K^2(1 - 2s_j) = 0$ which solves for $s_j = \frac{1}{2}$.

13  To see this you could assume that Jessie's utility function was $U(s_j) = s^{\frac{1}{2}}$ and $U(s_r) = s_r$. If you do this and follow the procedure in the previous note you will obtain $s_j^* = \frac{1}{3} < \frac{1}{2}$ and $s_r^* = \frac{2}{3}$.

14  $TP_L$ will depend on how much labour is employed. As a simplification it is assumed that L maximises $TP_L - (M - L)W°$. This is consistent with the Pareto efficiency assumption.

15  The first order condition is that $-2L^2w + L^2w° + TP_L L = 0$, dividing through by $2L^2$ solves for $w^*$.

16  As you saw in Chapter 8 (Section 8.2).

17  *See* Elster (1989: 67–74) for a very readable account of this procedure. Alternatively, Montet and Serra (2003: 214–16) give a more formal proof.

18  It might help to imagine that there are a number of possible equilibrium outcomes but X is the highest pay-off to Alf in any of them.

19  Alternatively the value to Alf of X at t = 3 (discounted to t = 0) is $d^2X$ so Alf cannot credibly hold out for more than this at t = 1 where Bert makes the offer. The total value of the prize at t = 1 is d so Bert can credibly offer Alf $d^2X$ keeping $d - d^2X$ for himself. At t = 0 A has to offer Bert at least $d - d^2X$ but can keep $1 - (d - d^2X)$ for himself.

20  Or, equivalently: $\alpha = r_b/(r_a + r_b)$ and $\beta = r_a/(r_a + r_b)$. *See* Montet and Serra (2003: 241).

21  That is, $T - tc_a = x$

22  $T - x$ offered at time t is worth $T - x - tc_b$ to Barca.

23  She gets x by continuing but this is only worth $x - tc_a$ which is less than $x + c_b - (t - 1)c_a$.

24 These predictions follow from the axioms of invariance and anonymity.

25 Psychologically prominent divisions that are recognised by both players.

26 *See* www.acas.org.uk.

27 For a discussion *see*, for example, Elster (1989: Chapter 2).

28 *See*, for example, Kreps (1993: Chapter 5) or Elster (1991: 3–7) for a discussion of the possible limitations of the backward induction method.

29 *See* Johnson, Camerer, Sen and Rymon (2002).

# BIBLIOGRAPHY

Abreu, D. (1986) 'Extremal equilibria of oligopolistic supergames', *Journal of economic theory*, 39, pp. 191–225.

Allais, M. (1953) 'Le comportement de l'homme rationnel devant le risqué: Critique des postulats et axioms de l'ecole Americaine', *Econometrica*, 21, pp. 503–46.

Axelrod, R. (1980a) 'Effective choice in the iterated prisoners' dilemma', *Journal of Conflict Resolution*, 24, pp. 3–25.

Axelrod, R. (1980b) 'More effective choice in the prisoners' dilemma', *Journal of Conflict Resolution*, 24, pp. 379–403

Axelrod, R. (1984) *The Evolution of Cooperation.* NY: Basic Books.

Bachus, D. and Driffill, J., (1985) 'Rational expectations and policy credibility following a change in regime', *Journal of Economic Studies*, LII, pp. 211–21.

Bain, J. S. (1956) *Barriers to New Competition.* Cambridge, Mass: Harvard University Press.

Bain, J. S. (1968) *Industrial Organisation* (2nd edn.) NY: John Wiley.

Basu, K. (2003) 'Globilisation and the politics of international finance: The Stiglitz verdict', *Journal of Economic Literature*, XLI: 3, pp. 885–903.

Battalio, R. C., Kagel, J. H. and MacDonald, D. N. (1985) 'Animals' choices over uncertain outcomes: Some initial experimental evidence', *Journal of Risk and Uncertainty,* 3, pp. 25–50.

Beard, T. R. and Beil, T. (1994) 'Do people rely on the self–interested maximization of others? An experimental test', *Management Science*, 40, pp. 252–62.

Becker, G. S. (1965) 'A theory of the allocation of time', *Economic Journal,* 75, 299, pp. 493–517.

Bierman, H. S. and Fernandez, L. (1998) *Game Theory with Economic Applications.* Reading, Mass: Addison-Wesley.

Binmore, K. (ed.) (1990) *Essays on the Foundations of Game Theory.* Oxford: Basic Blackwell.

Binmore, K. (1992) *Fun and Games: A text on game theory*. Lexington, Mass: D.C. Heath.

Binmore, K., Rubinstein, A. and Wolinsky, A. (1986) 'The Nash bargaining solution in economic modelling', *RAND Journal of Economics*, 117, pp. 176–88.

Binmore, K., Shaked, A. and Sutton, J. (1985). 'Testing non-cooperative bargaining theory: A preliminary study', *American Economic Review*, 75, pp. 1178–80.

Binmore, K., McCarthy, J., Ponti, G., Samuelson, L. and Shaked, A. (2002) 'A backward induction experiment', *Journal of Economic Theory*, 104, pp. 48–88.

Biswas, T. (1997) *Decision-Making Under Uncertainty*. Basingstoke: Macmillan.

Bloomfield, R. (1994) 'Learning a mixed strategy equilibrium in the laboratory', *Journal of Economic Behaviour and Organization*, 25, pp. 411–36.

Bolton, G. (1991) 'A comparative model of bargaining: Theory and evidence'. *American Economic Review*, 81, pp. 1096–36.

Booth A. L. (1996) *The Economics of the Trade Union*. Cambridge: Cambridge University Press.

Camerer, C. (1995) 'Individual decision making', Chapter 8 in Hagel, J. H. and Roth, A. E. (eds) *The Handbook of Experimental Economics*. Princeton, NJ: Princeton University Press.

Camerer, C. F. (2003) *Behavioural Game Theory: Experiments in strategic interaction*. Princeton, NJ: Princeton University Press.

Camerer, C. F. and Thaler, R. H. (2003) 'In honor of Matthew Rabin: Winner of the John Bates Clark Medal', *Journal of Economic Perspectives*, 17: 3, pp. 157–76.

Camerer, C. F. and Weigelt, K. (1988) 'Experimental tests of a sequential equilibrium reputation model', *Econometrica*, 56, pp. 1–36.

Carmichael, F. (1992) 'Multinationals and strikes: Theory and evidence', *Scottish Journal of Political Economy*, 39, February, pp. 52–68.

Carmichael, F. (2002) 'Catch-22 in a signalling game', *Journal of Institutional and Theoretical Economics*, 158: 33, pp. 375–92.

Carmichael F. and Thomas D. A. (1993) 'Bargaining in the transfer market', *Applied Economics*, 25, pp. 1467–76.

Cho, I. K. and Kreps, D. M. (1987), 'Signaling games and stable equilibria', *Quarterly Journal of Economics*, CII: 2, pp. 179–221.

Cooper, D., Garvin, S. and Kagel, J. (1989) 'Signalling and adaptive learning in an entry limit pricing game', *RAND Journal of Economics*, 28, pp. 662–83.

Cooper, R., DeJong, D., Forsyth, R. and Ross, T. (1989) 'Communication in coordination games', Working Paper Series 89–16, College of Business Administration, University of Iowa.

Cooper, R., DeJong, D., Forsyth, R. and Ross, T. (1990) 'Selection criteria in coordination games: Some experimental results', *American Economic Review*, 80, pp. 218–33.

Dawson, G. (2001) 'Measuring welfare: are people better off?' Chapter 4 in Himmelweit, S., Simonetti, R. and Trigg, A. (eds) *Microeconomics: Neoclassical and Institutionalist Perspectives on Economic Behaviour*. Milton Keynes: Open University/Thomson Learning.

Dixit, A. (1980) 'Recent developments in oligopoly theory', *American Economic Review, Papers and Proceedings,* 72, pp. 12–17.

Dixit, A. (1981) 'The role of investment in entry deterrence', *Economic Journal,* 90, pp. 95–106.

Dixit, A. and Skeath, S. (1999) *Games of Strategy*. NY: Norton.

Dobson, S. and Goddard, J. (2001) *The Economics of Football*. Cambridge: Cambridge University Press.

Elster, J. (1989) *The Cement of Society*. Cambridge: Cambridge University Press.

Field, B. C. and Field, M. K. (2002) *Environmental Economics: An introduction*. NY: McGraw-Hill.

Flood, M. (1952) 'Some experimental games', Santa Monica, CA, RAND RM–798, RAND Corporation.

Frank, R. H. (2003) *Microeconomics and Behaviour*. NY: McGraw-Hill.

Friedman, J.W. (1971) 'A non-cooperative equilibrium supergame', *Review of Economic Studies,* 38, pp.1–12.

Friedman, J. W. (1986) *Game Theory with Applications to Economics*, NY: Oxford University Press.

Fudenberg, D. and Tirole, J. (1991) *Game Theory*. Cambridge, MA: MIT Press.

Garcia-Gallego, A. (1998) 'Oligopoly experimentation of learning with simulated markets', *Journal of Economic Behaviour and Organization',* 35, pp. 333–55.

Gates, S. and Humes, B. D. (1997) *Games, Information and Politics: Arguing game theoretic models to political science*. Michigan: University of Michigan.

Gerrard, B. and Dobson, S. (2000) 'Testing for monopoly rents in the market for playing talent: evidence from English professional football', *Journal of Economic Studies,* 27: 3, pp. 142–64.

Gibbons, R. (1992) A *Primer in Game Theory*. Hemel Hemstead: Harvester Wheatsheaf.

Gibbons, R. (1997) 'An introduction to applicable game theory', *Journal of Economic Perspectives,* 11: 1, Winter, pp. 127–49.

Glicksberg, I. L. (1952) 'A further generalisation of the Kakutani fixed point theorem with application to NE points', *Proceedings of the National Academy of Sciences,* 38, pp. 87–100.

Greene, W. H. (1993) *Econometric Analysis*. NY: Macmillan.

Guth, W., Schmittberger, R. and Schwarz, B. (1982) 'An experimental analysis of ultimatum bargaining', *Journal of Economic Behaviour and Organization,* 3, pp. 367–88.

Hanley, N., Shogren, J. F., and White, B. (2001) *Introduction to Environmental Economics*. Oxford: Oxford University Press.

Hardin, G. (1968) 'Tragedy of the commons', *Science,* 161, 13 December, pp. 1243–8.

Hargreaves Heap, S. P. (1989) *Rationality in Economics*. Oxford: Blackwell.

Hargreaves Heap, S. P. and Varoufakis, Y. (1997) *Game Theory: A critical introduction*. London: Routledge.

Harsanyi, J. (1973) 'Games with incomplete information played by Bayesian players', *International Journal of Game Theory*, 2, pp. 1–23.

Harsanyi, J. and Selten, R. (1972) 'A generalised Nash solution for two-person bargaining games with incomplete information', *Management Science*, 18, pp. 80–106.

Haywood, O. (1954) 'Military decisions and game theory', *Journal of the Operations Research Society of America*, November, pp. 365–85.

Himmelweit, S. (2001) 'Decision making in households', Chapter 6 in Himmelweit, S., Simonetti, R. and Trigg, A. (eds) *Microeconomics: Neoclassical and Institutionalist Perspectives on Economic Behaviour*. Milton Keynes: Open University/Thomson Learning

Himmelweit, S., Simonetti, R. and Trigg, A. (eds) (2001) *Microeconomics: Neoclassical and Institutionalist Perspecitives on Economic Behaviou*r. Milton Keynes: The Open University/Thomson Learning.

Horstmann, I. and Markusen, J. (1987) 'Strategic investments and the development of multinationals', *International Review*, 28, pp. 109–21.

Hsu Shih-Hsun, Huang Chen-Ying and Tang Cheng-Tao (2003) 'Equilibrium or simple rule at Wimbledon? An empirical study', *Department of Economics Seminar Paper*, National Taiwan University, September.

Hutton, W. (1996) *The State We're In*. London: Vintage.

Johnson, E. J., Camerer, C., Sen, S. and Rymon, T. (2002) 'Detecting failures of backward induction: Monitoring information search in sequential bargaining', *Journal of Economic Theory*, 104, pp. 16–47.

Jung, Yun Joo, Kagel, J. H. and Levin, D. (1994) 'On the existence of predatory pricing: An experimental study of reptutation and entry deterrence in the chain–store game', *RAND Journal of Economics*, 25, pp. 72–93.

Kagel, J. H. (1987) 'Economics according to the rats (and pigeons too)', in Roth, E. (ed.) *Laboratory Experimentation in Economics: Six Points of View*. Cambridge: Cambridge University Press.

Kahneman, D. (2003) 'Maps of bounded rationality: Psychology for behavioural economists', *American Economic Journal*, 93: 5, pp. 1449–75.

Kahneman, D. and Tversky, A. (1979) 'Prospect Theory: An analysis of decision under risk', *Econometrica*, 47: 2, pp. 263–91.

Kalai, E. and Smorodinsky, M. (1975) 'Other solutions to Nash's bargaining problem', *Econometrica*, 43, pp. 513–18.

Katz, M. L. and Rosen, H. S. (1998) *Microeconomics*. Boston: Irwin/McGraw-Hill.

Kaufman, H. and Becker, G. M. (1961) 'The empirical determination of game-theoretical strategies', *Journal of Experimental Psychology*, 61, pp. 462–68.

Kemp, J. (1988) 'Money can't buy me love', paradoxes and expected utility theory: a clarification, *Scottish Journal of Political Economy*, 35, 2, May, pp. 149–61.

Knickerbocker, F. T. (1973) *Oligopolistic Reaction and the Multinational Enterprise*. Boston: Division of Research, Graduate School of Business Administration, Harvard University.

Kreps, D. M. (1990) *A Course in Microeconomic Theory*. Princeton, NJ: Princeton University Press.

Kreps, D. M. (1993) *Game Theory and Economic Modelling*. Oxford: Clarendon Press.

Kreps, D. M. and Wilson, R. (1982) 'Reputation and imperfect information', *Journal of Economic Theory*, 27, pp. 253–79.

Kreps, D. M., Milgrom, P., Roberts, J. and Wilson, R. (1982) 'Rational cooperation in the finitely repeated prisoners' dilemma', *Journal of Economic Theory*, 27, pp. 245–52.

Ledyard, J. O. (1995) 'Public goods: A survey of experimental research', Chapter 2 in Roth, A.E. (ed.) *The Handbook of Experimental Economics*. Princetown, NJ: Princetown University Press.

Lichentenstein, S. and Slovic, P. (1971) 'Reversals of preferences between bids and choices in gambling decisions', *Journal of Experimental Psychology*, 89, pp. 46–55.

Lindman, H. R. (1971) 'Inconsistent preferences among gambles', *Journal of Experimental Psychology*, 89, pp. 390–7.

Loomes, G. and Sugden, R. (1983) 'A rationale for preference reversal', *American Economic Review*, 73, pp. 428–32.

Loomes, G. and Sugden, R. (1986) 'Disappointment and dynamic consistency in choice under uncertainty', *Review of Economic Studies*, 53: 2, pp. 271–82.

Lyons, B. and Varoufakis, Y. (1989) 'Game theory, oligopoly and bargaining', in Hey, J.D. (ed.) *Current Issues in Microeconomics*. Basingstoke: Macmillan.

Machina, M. J. (1982) 'Expected utility theory without the independence axiom', *Econometrica*, 50, pp. 277–323.

Machina, M. J. (1987) 'Problems solved and unsolved', *Journal of Economic Perspectives*, 1, pp. 121–54.

Machina, M. J. (1989) 'Choice under uncertainty: Problems solved and unsolved', in Hey J.D. (ed.) *Current Issues in Microeconomics*. Basingstoke: Macmillan.

Malcolm, D. and Lieberman, B. (1965) 'The behaviour of responsive individuals playing a two-person zero-sum game requiring the use of mixed strategies', *Psychonomic Science*, 2, pp. 373–4.

Martin, S. (2001) 'Competition policy', Chapter 6 in Artis, M. and Nixon, F. (eds) *The Economics of the European Union*. Oxford: Oxford University Press.

Mason, C. F., Phillips, O. R. and Redington, D. B. (1991) 'The role of gender in a non-cooperative game', *Journal of Economic Behaviour and Organisation*, 15, pp. 215–35.

Maynard Smith, J. (1982) *Evolution and the Theory of Games*. Cambridge: Cambridge University Press.

McKelvey, R. D. and Palfrey T. R. (1992) 'An experimental study of the centipede game', *Econometrica*, 60, pp. 803–36.

McNeil, B. J., Pauker, S. G. and Tversky, A. (1988) 'On the framing of medical decisions', in Bell, D. E., Raiffa, H. and Tversky, A. (eds) *Decision Making: Descriptive, Normative, and Prescriptive Interactions*. Cambridge: Cambridge University Press.

Mirowski, P. (2002) *Machine Dreams: Economics becomes a cyborg science*. Cambridge: Cambridge University Press.

Montet, C. and Serra, D. (2003) *Game Theory and Economics*. Basingstoke: Palgrave Macmillan.

Murnigham, J. K., Roth, A. E. and Schoumaker, F. (1988) 'Risk aversion in bargaining: an experimental study', *Journal of Risk and Uncertainty*, 1, pp. 101–24.

Myerson, R. (1991) *Game Theory: An analysis of conflict*. Cambridge, MA: Cambridge University Press.

Nash, J. F. (1950) 'The bargaining problem', *Econometrica*, 18, pp. 155–62.

Nash, J. F. (1953) 'Two-person cooperative games', *Econometrica*, 21, pp. 128–40.

Ochs, J. (1995) 'Coordination problems', Chapter 3 in Hagel, J.H. and Roth, A. E. (eds) *The Handbook of Experimental Economics*. Princeton, NJ: Princeton University Press.

Ochs, J. and Roth, A. E. (1989) 'An experimental study of sequential bargaining', *American Economic Review*, 79, pp. 355–84.

O'Neill, B. (1987) 'Nonmetric test of the minimax theory of two-person zero-sum games', *Proceedings of the National Academy of Sciences*, USA, 84, pp. 2106–9.

Osborne, M. J. and Rubinstein, A. (1990) *Bargaining and Markets*. San Diego, CA: Academic Press.

Palacios-Huerta, I. (2003) 'Professionals play minimax', *Review of Economic Studies*, 70: 2, April, pp. 395–415.

Pindyck, R. S. and Rubinfeld, D.L. (2001) *Microeconomics*. NJ: Prentice–Hall.

Rabin, M. (1993) 'Incorporating fairness into game theory and economics', *American Economic Review*, 83, pp. 1281–94.

Rapoport, A. (1974) 'Prisoner's dilemma – recollections and observations', in Rapoport, A. (ed) *Game Theory as a Theory of Conflict Resolution*. Dordrecht, Holland: D. Reidel.

Rapoport, A., Frenkel, O. and Perner, J. (1977) 'Experiments with cooperative 2 x 2 games', *Theory and Decision*, 8, pp. 67–92.

Rasmusen, E. (2001) *Games and Information: An introduction to game theory*. Malden, MS: Blackwell.

Ridley, M. (1996) *The Origins of Virtue*. NY: Penguin.

Rosenthal, R. W. (1981) 'Games of perfect information, predatory pricing and the chain-store paradox', *Journal of Economic Theory*, 25, pp. 92–100.

Roth, A. E. (1995a) 'Introduction to experimental economics', Chapter 1 in Hagel, J. H. and Roth, A. E. (eds) *The Handbook of Experimental Economics*. Princeton, NJ: Princeton University Press

Roth, A. E. (1995b) Bargaining experiments', Chapter 4 in Hagel, J. H. and Roth, A. E. (eds) *The Handbook of Experimental Economics*. Princeton, NJ: Princeton University Press.

Roth, A. E. and Malouf, M. W. K. (1979) 'Game-theoretic models and the role of information in bargaining', *Psychological Review*, pp. 574–94.

Roth, A. E. and Murnigham, J. K. (1978) 'Equilibrium behaviour and repeated play of the prisoners' dilemma', *Journal of Mathematical Psychology*, 17, pp. 189–98.

Roth, A. E. and Murnigham, J. K. (1982) 'The role of information in bargaining: An experimental study', *Econometrica*, 50, pp. 639–47.

Roth, A. E., Malouf, M. W. K. and Murnigham, J. K. (1981) 'Sociological versus strategic factors in bargaining', *Journal of Economic Behaviour and Organization*, 2, pp. 153–77.

Rubinstein, A. (1982) 'Perfect equilibrium in a bargaining model', *Econometrica*, 50: 1, pp. 97–109.

Rubinstein, A. (1985) 'A bargaining model with incomplete time preferences', *Econometrica*, 53:5, pp. 1151–72.

Sabater-Grande, G. and Georgantzis, N. (2002) 'Accounting for risk aversion in repeated prisoners' dilemma games: An experimental test', *Journal of Economic Behaviour and Organization,* 48, pp. 37–50.

Sapsford, D. and Tzannatos, Z. (1993) *The Economics of the Labour Market.* London: Macmillan.

Schelling, T. (1960) *The Strategy of Conflict.* Oxford: Oxford University Press.

Selten, R. (1978) 'The chain store paradox', *Theory and Decision*, 9, pp. 127–59.

Selten, R. and Stoecker, R. (1986) 'End behaviour in sequences of finite prisoner's dilemma supergames: A learning theory approach', *Journal of Economic Behaviour and Organization*, 7, pp. 47–70

Simon, H. (1982) *Models of Bounded rationality*, 2 vols. Cambridge, MA MIT Press.

Slovic, P. and Tversky, A. (1974) 'Who accepts Savage's Axiom?' *Behavioural Science*, 19, pp. 368–73.

Smith, A. (1987) 'Strategic investment, multinational corporations and trade', *European Economic Review*, 31, pp. 89–96.

Spence, M. (1973) 'Job market signalling', *Quarterly Journal of Economics*, 87, pp. 355–74.

Spence, M. (1974) *Market Signalling.* Cambridge, MA: Harvard University Press.

Spence, M. (1977) 'Entry, capacity, investment and oligopolistic pricing', *Bell Journal of Economics,* 8, pp. 534–44.

Starmer, C. (2000) 'Developments in non–expected utility theory', *Journal of Economic Literature*, 38: 2, pp. 332–82.

Starmer, C. and Sugden, R. (1989) 'Violations of the independence axiom in common ratio problems: An experimental test of some competing hypotheses', *Annals Operational Res*, 19, pp. 79–102.

Sylos-Labini, P. (1962) *Oligopoly and Technical Progress.* Cambridge, MA: Harvard University Press.

Thomas, D. A. (2004) 'The retain and transfer system', Mimeo, University of Aberystwyth, Department of Business and Management, and (forthcoming) as *The Player Transfer System in Soccer*, in Szymanski, S., Andreff, W. and Borland J. (eds) *Readings on the Economics of Sports,* Edward Elgar.

Tucker, A. W. (1950) 'A two-person dilemma', Mimeo, Stanford University. Published under the heading 'On jargon: The prisoners' dilemma', *UMAP Journal*, 1 (1980), pp. 101.

Tversky, A. and Kahneman, D. (1981) 'The framing of decisions and the psychology of choice', *Science*, 211, pp. 453–8.

Tversky, A. and Thaler, R. H. (1990) 'Preference reversals', *Journal of Economic Perspectives*, 4, pp. 201–11.

Van Huyck, J., Battalio, R. and Beil, R. (1990) 'Tacit coordination games, strategic uncertainty, and coordination failure', *American Economic Review*, 80, pp. 234–48.

Van Kooten, G. C. and Bulte, E. H. (2000) *The Economics of Nature: Managing biological assets*. Malden, MA: Blackwell.

Venables, A. (2003) 'International trade and production', Chapter 14 in Dawson, G., Athreye, S., Himmelweit, S. and Sawyer, M. (eds) *Economics and Economic Change*. Glasgow: Open University.

Vickers, J. (1985) 'Strategic competition among the few – some recent developments in the economics of industry', *Oxford Review of Economic Policy*, 1: 3, pp. 39–60.

Von Neuman, J. and Morgenstern, O. (1944) *Theory of Games and Economic Behaviour*. NY: Wiley (reprint 1964).

Walker, M. and Wooders, J. (2001) 'Minimax play at Wimbledon', *American Economic Review*, 91, pp. 1521–38.

Watson, S. R. and Bude, D. M. (1987) *Decision Synthesis*. Cambridge: Cambridge University Press.

## Web sites

Battle of the Bismarck Sea: www.combinedfleet.com/bismksea.htm, 6 April 2004.

The Competition Commission: www.competition-commission.org.uk, 12 April 2004.

Office of Fair Trading: www.oft.gov.uk, 12 April 2004.

Tony Martin: www.tonymartinsupportgroup.org, 4 April 2004.

Australian Bureau of Agriculture and Resource Economics: www .abare.gov.au/research/fisheries, 12 April 2004.

The European Union and the European Commission: www.europa.eu.org/comm/archives, 3 April 2004.

## Newspaper references

Guardian (2001) 'The big tuna', Kathy Marks, 20 April.

Guardian (2003) 'Fear of trade war after US steel tariffs ruled illegal', Andrew Osborne and David Gow, 11 November.

# INDEX